Erik Olin Wright was born in Berkeley, California, in 1947 while his father was in medical school on the G.I. Bill. He grew up in Lawrence, Kansas, where both of his parents were professors of psychology at the University of Kansas. Aside from a year spent in Australia in 1960, he remained in Kansas until 1964 when he entered Harvard University. After graduating with a B.A. degree in social studies in 1968, he spent two years studying history at Oxford University, working especially with Christopher Hill. Upon returning to the United States in 1970, he spent one year in a Unitarian Theological Seminar in Berkeley, during which time he worked at San Quentin Prison as a student chaplin. On the basis of material gathered while working in the prison, he wrote *The Politics of Punishment: a critical analysis of prisons in America* (New York: Harper Colophon Books, 1973). In 1971 he entered graduate school in sociology at the University of California where he stayed until completing his doctoral dissertation on *Class Structure and Income Inequality* in the spring of 1976. Author of *Class, Crisis and the State* (New Left Books, 1980), he is currently Professor of Sociology at the University of Wisconsin, Madison.

Erik Olin Wright

Verso

Classes

Verso is the imprint of **New Left Books**

British Library
Cataloguing in Publication Data

Wright, Erik Olin
  Classes.
  1. Social classes
  I. Title
  305.5   HT609

First published 1985
© Erik Olin Wright

Verso Editions
15 Greek Street London W1V 5LF

Typeset in Times Roman by
Spire Print Services Ltd,
Salisbury, Wiltshire

Printed in Great Britain by
The Thetford Press Ltd,
Thetford, Norfolk

ISBN 0-86091-104-7
    0-86091-812-2 pbk

Contents

To the life of M. Erik Wright, my father.

Preface

'You must learn to write in such a way that it will be as easy as possible for your critics to know why they disagree with you.'

Beatrice A. Wright
(circa 1960)

I began work on this book nearly five years ago, fully anticipating that I would finish it within a year or so. In the course of these years several important things have occurred in my life which have had a major impact on the content and schedule of the project.

To begin with, I have had a significant change in what sociologists call my 'reference group', the circle of people whose opinions and evaluations are in the back of my mind as I type away on my word processor. My earlier work on class structure, the state, income inequality and related topics was all basically written or at least launched while I was a graduate student at the University of California in the first part of the 1970s. Up until about 1980 most of my published material was either initially formulated in my student years or developed as a direct spin-off of that period.

My reference group while a graduate student was a circle of Marxist scholars affiliated with the journal *Kapitalistate* and a loose organization called the 'Union of Marxist Social Scientists'. Most of these people were students, most had been radicalized during the heyday of the civil rights and anti-war movements of the 1960s, and most were committed to some variety of Marxist approach to social theory. While many of us considered ourselves to be rather unorthodox in various ways, the basic categories of Marxist analysis, from the labour theory of value to the theory of the capitalist state, were more or less taken for granted as points of departure. There was a great deal of fervour and excitement and we all felt that we had a firm grip on the truth.

As it is commonplace to say, times have changed. Many of the students who engaged in the revitalization of American Marxism in the 1970s have subsequently been employed in professional and academic posts, and a good number of the academics have by now received tenure. The feeling of assurance that we had answers to every question has generally been tempered by a more cautious and nuanced stance. In many cases, in fact, Marxism has become the object of considerable criticism on the academic left, and many radical scholars are identifying with what some have labelled 'post-Marxism'.

On a personal level, I became an Assistant Professor and then a tenured faculty member at the University of Wisconsin. And I have also become more aware of the problems in Marxist theory and the need for a more rigorous and reflective approach. But I have not, I hope, shifted my basic commitment to the project of Marxist theory and to the fundamental insights contained within it.

To sustain that commitment I helped to establish a graduate training programme in the Wisconsin Sociology Department, the Class Analysis and Historical Change Program. That programme, in turn, has become a crucial element in my new reference group. Unlike my student circle in Berkeley, the Class Analysis programme in Madison is ideologically much more diverse and certainly less wedded to a traditional Marxist perspective. As a teacher in the programme, therefore, I have had to defend actively the core theses of Marxism and make them compelling to a sympathetic yet unconvinced audience. In the course of doing so, particularly in the context of arguing with energetic students in a year-long course on the Theory and Methodology of Marxist Social Science which I regularly teach, I have questioned, clarified and reformulated many of the basic ideas that I had earlier taken for granted.

My role as a professor constitutes only one aspect of this change in reference group. Perhaps even more important for the specific intellectual direction which my work is now taking, I have become very involved with a group of leftist scholars of varying degrees of sympathy to Marxism who meet once a year to discuss one another's work. This group includes G. A. Cohen, John Roemer, Jon Elster, Philippe van Parijs, Robert van der Veen, Robert Brenner, Adam Przeworski and Hillel Steiner. The central intellectual thread of the group is what they term 'Analytical Marxism', by which is meant the systematic interrogation and clarification of basic concepts and their reconstruction into a more coherent theoretical structure. The discussions within this group and the exposure it has given me to a range of new ideas and perspectives have had a considerable impact on my thinking and on my work.

If these reference groups define the positive forces I have encountered in the formulation of new ideas, other aspects of my current situation constitute negative pressures. In the transition from graduate student to tenured professor I have also become integrated into a nexus of rewards that is very alluring. My research on class has led to a series of large research grants which pay parts of my salary and allow me to take time off from teaching to write. As my reputation has grown, I have had numerous opportunities for travel and lecturing in various places around the world. And I have been handsomely rewarded by my Sociology Department and the University of Wisconsin. As a Marxist materialist and class analyst, I cannot suppose that all of this has no effect on me and that by an act of will I can immunize myself from the seductions of the safe and comfortable life of an affluent academic in a liberal-democratic advanced capitalist society.

The privileges bestowed by elite universities have, with good reason, made many radicals suspicious of 'academic Marxists'. Such suspicion may be particularly acute in the United States, where the absence of a cohesive, mass socialist movement, let alone a revolutionary working-class political party, has made it difficult for many academic Marxists to be systematically linked to socialist struggles on a day-to-day basis. Certainly in my own case, I have not been a political activist in recent years. While my work has been informed by social and political events, it has not been forged in direct engagement with popular struggle.

I do not know the ways in which the ideas elaborated in this book have been shaped by these institutional and political realities and choices. I do not even really know whether or not, in the present historical circumstances, the work has benefited or suffered from the particular conditions under which it was produced. The time, travel and intellectual stimulation that my present position gives me may expand the space for critical thought more than the privileges I enjoy erode it. What I do know is that I have been aware of these issues and I have tried to maintain the kind of self-reflective stance that might minimize the negative effects of these material conditions on my work.

Aside from these various professional considerations, my life has undergone one other massive change since I first began work on this book: the birth of my two daughters, Jennifer and Rebecca, now aged five and four. I do not know if my theoretical sensibilities have been altered by the wonderful transformation these two little persons have brought to my life, but I am certain that the book would have been finished a couple of years earlier if I had not embraced the joys of liberated fatherhood.

In the course of writing this book I have received considerable feedback on specific chapters and arguments from a large number of people. I am particularly grateful to Andrew Levine, who attempted, with some success, to delay the completion of the manuscript by giving me too many difficult comments. Michael Burawoy was very important in helping me to clarify the initial agenda of the book during the exciting year he spent in Madison. The arguments in the book have also benefited decisively from a series of comments and discussions I have had with John Roemer. Robert Manchin, a Hungarian sociologist who spent a year at the University of Wisconsin, contributed greatly to working through the ideas embodied in chapter three. I am also grateful for written comments from Adam Przeworski, Göran Therborn, Perry Anderson, Daniel Bertaux, Ron Aminzade, Richard Lachmann, Philippe van Parijs, Robert van der Veen, Trond Petersen and Sheldon Stryker, and for stimulating discussions of the issues raised in the book with Ivan Szelenyi, Jon Elster, G. A. Cohen, Göran Ahrne and the many students in my courses and seminars who have pressed me continually on these problems. Various technical issues in the empirical chapters were clarified by Charles Halaby, Robert Hauser, Rob Mare and Tom Colbjornson. I would like to thank the research team that worked on the class structure project—especially Kathleen Cairns, Cynthia Costello, David Hachen, Bill Martin and Joey Sprague—for the enormous contribution they have made to the empirical investigations in the book. To my wife, Marcia Kahn Wright, I owe a special debt of gratitude for not letting me get too obsessed with my work and helping me to keep things in perspective. Finally, I would like to acknowledge the financial support for the research and writing that has gone into this project from the National Science Foundation, The German Marshall Fund of the United States and the Wisconsin Alumni Research Foundation.

While this book was being written, four people whom I loved have died. My grandmother, Sonia Posner, whose love of learning and life-long commitment to revolutionary ideals deeply shaped my life, died in the spring of 1980. Luca Peronne, whose comradeship and brilliance helped me begin my first attempts at class analysis, died later that year. My father, M. Erik Wright, whose nurturance and vitality and curiosity will always be with me, died in 1981. And Gene Havens, a *compañero* and colleague who showed me how to be an academic and a serious Marxist, died just before the book was finished in the summer of 1984. To the memory of these four I dedicate this book.

Erik Olin Wright
Madison, Wisconsin
November 1984

1

Posing the Problem

The Agenda of Class Analysis

The Legacy of Marx

As has frequently been remarked and bemoaned, Marx never systematically defined and elaborated the concept of class, in spite of the centrality of that concept in his work. To the perpetual frustration of people who seek in the texts of Marx authoritative answers to theoretical problems, in the one place where he promises such an elaboration—the final chapter of *Capital* Volume 3, entitled 'Classes'—the text stops after only a page. Just before the end of this incomplete text Marx wrote, 'The first question to be answered is this: What constitutes a class?'. Two short paragraphs later comes Engels's sad comment, 'Here the manuscript breaks off'.

While Marx never systematically answered this question, his work is filled with class analysis. With some exceptions, most of this work revolves around two problems: the elaboration of *abstract structural maps* of class relations, and the analysis of *concrete conjunctural maps* of classes-as-actors. The first of these kinds of analyses concerns the way in which the social organization of production determines a structure of 'empty places' in class relations, places filled by people. This structural analysis of classes is found particularly in Marx's most celebrated theoretical works, especially in *Capital* where he decodes the structure and dynamics of the capitalist mode of production. The second kind of analysis, on the other hand, is not concerned with class structure as such, but with the ways in which the people within class structures become organized into collectivities engaged in struggle. This analysis of class formation is found most notably in Marx's political and historical writing, where Marx is trying to understand the interplay of collectively organized social forces in explaining specific historical transformations.

The images that emerge from these two sorts of accounts are quite different. From the abstract structural account of classes comes the characteristically polarized map of class relations which runs through most of Marx's analysis of the capitalist mode of production in *Capital* and much of his more abstract discussion of epochal trajectories of historical development: masters and slaves, lords and serfs, bourgeoisie and proletariat. While non-polarized positions are occasionaly referred to in these abstract discussions of class relations, they are never given a rigorous theoretical status and are generally treated as having strictly peripheral importance.

In contrast to this simple, polarized, abstract map of class relations, Marx's conjunctural political analyses are characterized by a complex picture of classes, fractions, factions, social categories, strata and other actors on the political stage. In the *Eighteenth Brumaire of Louis Bonaparte,* for example, he refers to at least the following actors in social conflicts: bourgeoisie, proletariat, large landowners, artistocracy of finance, peasants, petty bourgeoisie, the middle class, the lumpen-proletariat, industrial bourgeoisie, high dignitaries. No attempt is made by Marx to present a sustained theoretical analysis of these various categories and of the conceptual status of all of the distinctions being employed. His preoccupation in this text is with understanding the relationship between the struggles among these actors and the state. In particular, he tries to explain the patterns of victories and defeats in these struggles, the effects of those victories and defeats on changes in the state, and the effects of changing regimes on the pattern of alliances and struggles among these actors. He is not concerned with elaborating a rigorous map of the concrete social structure inhabited by the protagonists in the drama. This is characteristic of Marx's political-conjunctural writings. While he gives us a list of descriptive categories corresponding to the actual actors in the conflicts, he does not provide a set of precise concepts for decoding rigorously the structural basis of most of those categories.

What we have then, in Marx's own work, is a polarized abstract concept of the 'empty places' generated by class relations and a descriptively complex map of concrete actors within class struggles, with no systematic linkage between the two. Marx of course felt that the historical tendency of capitalism was towards increasing concrete polarization. 'Society as a whole,' he wrote with

Engels in the *Communist Manifesto*, 'is more and more splitting up into two great hostile camps, into two great classes directly facing each other: bourgeoisie and proletariat.' Lest one think that this thesis of a tendency to polarization was simply a polemical flourish in a political pamphlet, an identical position is staked out in the ill-fated last chapter of *Capital* Volume 3.:

> In England, modern society is indisputably most highly and classically developed in economic structure. Nevertheless, even here the stratification of classes does not appear in its pure form. Middle and intermediate strata even here obliterate lines of demarcation everywhere (although incomparably less in rural districts than in the cities). However, this is immaterial for our analysis. We have seen that the continual tendency and law of development of the capitalist mode of production is more and more to divorce the means of production from labour, and more and more to concentrate the scattered means of production into large groups, thereby transforming labour into wage-labour and the means of production into capital.[1]

Throughout his work he refers to the petty bourgeoisie (self-employed who employ little or no wage-labour) as a 'transitional' class and emphasizes the dissolution of the peasantry. While there are a few passages where he acknowledges the growth of vaguely defined 'middle strata', the basic thrust of his work is to stress the increasingly polarized character of the concrete class relations of capitalist societies.[2] Given such an assumption, then, the conceptual gap between the abstract and polarized categories used to analyse class structures and the concrete descriptive categories used to analyse social actors in specific historical conjunctures would tend to be reduced over time. The real movement of capitalist development would thus produce an effective correspondence between the abstract and concrete categories of class analysis.

The Agenda of Contemporary Marxist Class Analysis

The historical record of the past hundred years has convinced many Marxists that this image of a pervasive tendency towards radical polarization of class relations within capitalist societies is incorrect. To be sure, there has been a steady decline in the proportion of the population owning their own means of production—the self-employed—in advanced capitalist countries, at least until the recent past.[3] But among wage-earners, the growth of professional and technical occupations and the expansion of managerial hierarchies in large corporations and the state have at least

TABLE 1.1

Theoretical Objects and Levels of Abstraction in Marxist Class Analysis

Level of Abstraction	*Theoretical Object of Analysis*	
	CLASS STRUCTURE	CLASS FORMATION
MODE OF PRODUCTION	Polarized Class relations	Epochal struggle between classes
SOCIAL FORMATION	Co-existence of classes based in different modes of production and different stages of development of a given mode	Class alliances
CONJUNCTURE	Institutional variability in class relations in given jobs	Concrete class organizations: parties, shop floor organization unions

created the appearance of a considerable erosion of a simple polarized structure.

Given that it is no longer generally accepted that the class structure within capitalism is increasingly polarized, it has become more difficult to side-step the theoretical problem of the gap between the abstract polarized concept of class relations and the complex concrete patterns of class formation and class struggle. It is no longer assumed that history will gradually eliminate the conceptual problem. Resolving this problem has been one of the central concerns of the resurgence of Marxist class analysis in the past twenty years.

To understand the theoretical agenda of this new body of Marxist work on class it will be helpful to distinguish formally two dimensions of class analysis that have been implicit in our discussion so far: first, whether the analysis focuses primarily on class structure or on class formation, and second, the level of abstraction at which classes are analysed. This yields the six possible foci of class analysis illustrated in Table 1.1.

The distinction between *class structure* and *class formation* is a basic, if often implicit, distinction in class analysis. Class structure refers to the structure of social relations into which individuals (or, in some cases, families) enter which determine their class interests. We will have a great deal to say about how these relations should be defined in subsequent chapters. The point to emphasize here is that class structure defines a set of empty places or positions filled by individuals or families. This implies that with respect to class structures we can talk about 'vacant' positions (positions which are not currently filled by actual people), about an 'absolute surplus population' (an excess of people with respect to the places within the class structure), and 'incumbents' of class positions (people actually located within a given class structure). While this does not imply that class structure exists independently of people, it does mean that it exists independently of the specific people who occupy specific positions.[4]

Class formation, on the other hand, refers to the formation of organized collectivities within that class structure on the basis of the interests shaped by that class structure. Class formation is a variable. A given type of class structure may be characterized by a range of possible types of class formation, varying in the extent and form of collective organization of classes. Class-based collectivities may be organized, disorganized or reorganized within a given class structure without there necessarily being any fundamental transformations of the class structure itself.[5] If class structure is defined by social relations *between* classes, class formation is defined by social relations *within* classes, social relations which forge collectivities engaged in struggle.

The distinctions among levels of abstraction of class analysis is a somewhat more complex issue. Three levels of abstraction typically characterize Marxist discourse on class: mode of production, social formation and conjuncture.

The highest level of abstraction is mode of production. Classes are here analysed in terms of pure types of social relations of production, each embodying a distinctive mechanism of exploitation. When Marx talks above of the 'pure form' of classes in capitalist society he is referring to the analysis of classes at this highest level of abstraction.

In many discussions of the 'mode of production' level of abstraction it is assumed that no *variability* within a mode of production is admissable at this level of abstraction: all capitalisms are equivalent when discussing the mode of production. This, I think, is a mistake. Without shifting levels of abstraction, it is still entirely possible to define different forms of a given mode of production. Indeed it has been one of the central themes of Marxist theories of the capitalist mode of production that this mode of production itself has an intrinsic logic of development. This logic of development means that the capitalist mode of production itself has an intrinsic tendency to pass through different 'stages', each with a distinctive form of capitalist social relations (primitive accumulation, competitive capitalism, monopoly capitalism, etc.). Like all tendencies, of course, this tendency may be blocked by various mechanisms, and the investigation of the actual processes which may facilitate or impede this trajectory of forms does require moving the analysis to a lower level of abstraction. But the analysis of the developmental logic of capitalist relations as such must be theorized at the level of abstraction of the mode of production itself.[6]

The term 'social formation' has come to derive its meaning from the analysis of societies as specific combinations of distinct modes of production or types of relations of production.[7] The analysis of the presence of pre-capitalist classes within capitalist society, and more rarely, the analysis of post-capitalist classes within capitalist society, are examples of analysing class structure at the level of abstraction of social formation. The analysis of the specific ways in which different forms of capitalist relations are combined within a given society is also a problem of the social formation level of abstraction. For example, analysing the specific combination of competitive, small-scale capitalist production with large, concentrated and centralized capitalist production in a given society would be a social formation analysis. The problem of alliances between classes and fractions of classes is the principal object of the analysis of class formation at this level of abstraction.

Conjunctural analysis involves the investigation of societies in terms of the concrete institutional details and contingent historical factors that enter the story.[8] The analysis of specific forms of labour-market segmentation within the working class, or the legal practices which define the powers of managers over workers, or the credit relations that link petty bourgeois to bankers, would all be instances of conjunctural analyses of class structures. The analysis of unionization, party formation, class-based social movements, etc., would be the analysis of class formation at this most concrete level.

The conjunctural level of analysis is also the level of abstraction at which the most sustained analyses of the relationship between class and non-class relations and practices usually occur (e.g. class and race or class and gender). This is not to say that in principal such issues cannot be addressed at higher levels of abstraction, but the conceptual apparatus for such more abstract investigation is rather underdeveloped and when attempts are made they tend to be reductionist. For example, when the gender–class relationship is explored at the level of mode of production, most marxist analyses effectively end up reducing male domination to class domination. Typically this reduction occurs in some sort of functionalist manner: the existence and form of patriarchy is explained by the essential functions it fulfils in reproducing the basic class relations of capitalism.

In these terms, many debates can be interpreted as disagreements over the appropriate level of abstraction for addressing certain problems. If gender and class have completely contingent relations between them—that is, the causal interconnections between them occur simply because they affect the same people but not because they presuppose each other in any way—then their relationship can only really be analysed at the conjunctural level. If, on the other hand, there are structural properties of these two relations which are intrinsically related, then a mode of production analysis may become possible. To take another example, some theorists, such as Nicos Poulantzas, have argued that the relationship between the form of the state and social classes can be analysed at the level of abstraction of mode of production and this leads him to try to construct a general concept of 'the capitalist state'. Other theorists, such as Theda Skocpol, argue that the state cannot legitimately be theorized at this level of abstraction and insist on a strictly historical (i.e. conjunctural) investigation of the relationship between states and classes.[9]

An analogy may help to clarify the distinctions being made between these levels of abstraction. In the scientific study of the chemistry of a lake, the highest level of abstraction involves specifying the particular way that the basic elements that go into making water, hydrogen and oxygen, combine to make water, H_2O. The study of the different forms of water—ice, liquid water, evaporation, etc.—would all be at this most abstract level. The middle level of abstraction corresponding to social formation analysis involves investigating the ways in which this compound, H_2O, interacts with other compounds in lakes. Finally, the conjunctural level involves investigating the myriad of contingent factors—nitrogen washed down from farms, chemical waste dumping from factories, etc.—which concretely distinguish a given lake chemically from all other lakes in time and space.

In terms of Table 1.1 the bulk of Marx's analyses of classes is concentrated in the upper left hand cell and the lower two right hand cells. Of course, Marx had something to say somewhere about every cell in the table, but he never provided a systematic theoretical exposition of the lower two levels of abstraction of class structure. Nor, as already stated, did he ever provide a sustained theory of the causal linkage between class structure and class formation, of the process through which positions within class structures analysed at different levels of abstraction become formed into organized collectivities.

Much of the recent development of Marxist theory and research on classes can be viewed as attempts at bridging the gap between the abstract analysis of class structure and the analysis of class formation. This new class analysis has had two principal thrusts: first, filling in the undertheorized cells in the structural side of the typology; and second, much more systematically analysing the problem of the translation of this structure of relations into the formation of collective actors.

In the work that has focused on the problem of class structure in advanced capitalist societies, the pre-eminent preoccupation has been with the 'embarrassment of the middle classes'. The evidence of the existence and expansion of the 'new middle class' has been at the heart of most critiques of Marxist class theory, and Marxists have found it necessary to respond to those critiques in one way or another. However, the concern with the middle class, or, equivalently, with specifying the conceptual line of demarcation between the working-class and non-working-class wage earners, is not simply a defensive response to bourgeois attacks. Resolving this conceptual problem is also seen as essential if the classical concerns of Marxism—understanding the development of the contradictions of capitalism and the conditions for the revolutionary transformation of capitalist society—are to be analysed in a rigorous way.

The parallel problem for the structural analysis of classes in third-world capitalist societies is the 'embarrassment of the peasantry', which at least according to many earlier Marxist analyses was thought to be a class in rapid decline. The introduction of the concept of 'articulation of modes of production', which attempts to give specificity to the relationship between peasants workers and capitalists, and the elaboration of the world-systems approach to the study of third world societies were both important strategies for rethinking the class structures of these societies.[10]

As we will see in the next chapter, the result of these attempts to solve the problem of the middle classes and the peasantry has been a range of alternative conceptualizations of class structure at the middle levels of abstraction. In the course of building these new concepts, the more abstract mode of production analysis has itself been subjected to scrutiny, and various elements in that analysis have been challenged and altered by different theorists. The full ramifications of these various conceptual innovations are still working themselves out.

The second general thrust of recent work attempting to bridge the gap between the abstract analysis of class structures and the analysis of class formation has focused on the process of class formation. The starting point of most of these analyses has been a firm rejection of the view that particular kinds of class formation can be deduced directly from the class structure. In its place is the general view that the process of class formation is decisively shaped by a variety of institutional mechanisms that are themselves 'relatively autonomous' from the class structure and which determine the ways in which class structures are translated into collective actors with specific ideologies and strategies. Some of this research has focused primarily on the political mediations of the process, showing how the process of class formation is shaped by the forms of the state, the strategies of parties and other political factors.[11] Other research has dealt primarily with the role of the labour-process and the organization of work in structuring the process of class formation.[12] Nearly all of this research has been concerned with showing the complex and contingent character of the relationship between class structure and class formation.

Neither of these kinds of contributions—contributions to the conceptual map of empty places in the class structure and contributions to the theory of the formation of collective actors from those empty places—is entirely new in the Marxist tradition. Theoretical discussions of the middle class can be found in scattered places and certainly by the time when Karl Kautsky wrote about the middle classes around the turn of the century, it was recognized as a significant problem.[13] And the classical Marxist theory of the state and parties, particularly as elaborated by Lenin, is pre-eminently concerned with the political mediations in the formation of class actors, particularly the revolutionary working class.

But while the themes in this recent work are rooted in classical Marxism, the new Marxist class analysis is distinctive in two respects: first, much of this work has attempted a level of self-conscious conceptual precision that was only rarely encountered in earlier Marxist discussions of these problems. Secondly, it has systematically tried to develop concepts and theories at the 'middle level' of abstraction, less abstract than the exploration of modes of production but more abstract than the concrete investigation of the concrete situation. Increasing attention is being paid to the theoretical dimensions of variability in 'actually existing capitalisms'. While the more abstract debates of course continue, there is an emerging recognition that it is not enough to have good abstract concepts of the capitalist state, of bourgeois ideology, of the capitalist labour-process and of the capitalist class structure; we also need a repertoire of concepts capable of specifying the variabilities in each of these at more concrete levels of analysis.

This book will attempt to make a contribution to these debates on class structure. Part One will revolve largely around conceptual issues. Since these debates on class centre on the production and transformation of concepts, chapter two will begin with a brief methodological discussion of the problem of concept formation and then continue by exploring in considerable detail the development of one particular conceptual solution to the problem of the 'middle class', the concept of 'contradictory locations within class relations'. The chapter will end with an inventory of internal inconsistencies and theoretical problems with this conceptualization. Chapter three will then offer a new general strategy for analysing class structure which avoids the problems posed by the concept of 'contradictory locations'. The essential argument is that the concept of contradictory locations, like much neo-marxist class analysis, has effectively displaced the concept of 'exploitation' from the core of the concept of class structure, replacing it with the concept of 'domination'. The strategy proposed in this chapter attempts to specify the concept of exploitation in such a way that it can be reinstated as the central basis for defining class structures in general, and solving the conceptual problem of the 'middle classes' in particular. Chapter four will then explore the theoretical implications of this new approach for a wide range of problems of interest to radical scholars: the theory of history, the problem of class formation and class alliances, the problem of legitimation, the relationship between class and gender, and a number of other issues.

Part two of the book will deploy this new conceptualization of class structure in a series of empirical investigations. Too often conceptual debates are carried out strictly in terms of the internal logic and consistency of a conceptual apparatus with at best anecdotal reference to empirical research. Chapters five to seven, therefore, will systematically explore a range of empirical problems using quantitative operationalizations of the abstract concepts elaborated in chapter three. Chapter five will attempt a systematic empirical comparison of the merits of the definition of the working class based on the framework elaborated in chapter three with two other definitions, one based on the criterion of productive labour and one on the criterion of manual labour. Chapter six will use the new conceptualization to compare the United States and Sweden on a variety of issues involving class structure: the distribution of the labour-force into class locations, the relationship between this distribution and a variety of other structural properties of the society (economic sectors, state employment, firm size, etc.), the relationship between class and sex, the class structures of families, the effects of class on income, and a number of other problems. Finally, in chapter seven we will examine empirically the complex problem of the relationship between class structure and class consciousness.

Marx asked on the final page of *Capital* Volume 3, 'What constitutes a class?' This is the basic question this book hopes to answer. The answer which will be developed in the course of the analysis will undoubtedly not be the one which Marx would have given if he had finished his chapter. Not only have there been a hundred years of theoretical discussion of the problem of class since Marx's death, there have also been a hundred years of history, and if Marxist theory is at all scientific one would expect conceptual advances to have occurred in such a period. Nevertheless, the answer which I will propose will try to be faithful both to the theoretical agenda forged in Marx's work and the political goals that agenda was meant to promote.

Notes

1. Karl Marx, *Capital* vol. 3, London 1974, p. 885.
2. The very few passages within which Marx acknowledges the tendencies of certain types of 'middle classes' to expand are located in relatively unfamiliar texts and are largely unconnected to his more abstract theoretical discussions of class. For example, in *Theories of Surplus Value* Marx writes: 'What he [Ricardo] forgets to emphasize is the constant increase of the middle classes, who stand in the middle between the workers on one side and the capitalists and landed proprietors on the other, who are for the most part supported directly out of revenue, who rest as a

burden on the labouring foundation and who increase the social security and power of the upper ten thousand.' Quoted in Martin Nicolaus, 'Proletariat and Middle Class in Marx', *Studies on the Left*, no. 7, 1967, p. 247.

3. The data seem to indicate that in many capitalist countries self-employment began expanding in the early 1970s. In the United States, the lowest level of self-employment was reached in about 1972 at a level of about nine per cent of the labour force (according to official US Government figures). Since then self-employment has increased steadily every year, at least until 1984.

4. The problem of properly describing the relationship between flesh-and-blood human individuals and social relations has been the object of protracted and often obscure debates in sociology. It is often argued that since social relations would not exist if all the human individuals within those relations ceased to exist, it therefore makes no sense to distinguish the structure from the individuals within the structure. The formulation I have adopted does not give social relations an existence independent of people as such, but does give them an existence independent of particular persons. Stated differently: you can change all of the actual individuals in a factory in the course of a generation and yet the class structure of the factory could remain the same.

5. Understanding the variability of class formation in terms of the organization, disorganization and reorganization of class-based collectivities is derived from the work of Adam Przeworski. See in particular, 'From Proletariat into Class: The Process of Class Struggle from Karl Kautsky's *The Class Struggle* to Recent Debates', *Politics & Society*, vol. 7, no. 4, 1977.

6. It is because Marxist theory treats the developmental stages of capitalism as in some sense intrinsic to the logic of the capitalist mode of production that these stages can be analysed at the level of abstraction of the mode of production. This is similar to saying that the physiological stages of development of a human being can be analysed at the same level of abstraction as the general structural properties of the human being, since these stages are themselves a specific kind of general structural property (i.e. intrinsic to the structure of the organism). Specifying the properties which distinguish a child from an adult is not 'less abstract' than discussing the properties which are identical in both.

7. As I will use the term, 'social formation' refers to a level of abstraction, whereas 'society' refers to a 'unit of analysis'. Society is contrasted with groups, organizations and individuals; social formation is contrasted to mode of production and concrete conjuncture.

8. This does not imply that a conjunctural analysis has to be a 'snap-shot' situated statically in time and space. The point is that a conjunctural analysis includes the operations of contingent details and historically specific processes that are untheorized at the level of social formation and mode of production.

9. See Nicos Poulantzas, *Political Power and Social Classes*, NLB, London 1973; Theda Skocpol, *States and Social Revolutions*, New York 1979, and 'Bringing the State Back In: False Leads and Promising Starts in Current Theories and Research' in Peter Evans, Theda Skocpol and Dietrich Rueschemeyer, eds, *Bringing the State Back In*, New York 1985.

10. See Harold Wolpe, ed, *The Articulation of Modes of Production*, London 1980.

11. The most innovative and important work on the political mediations of the process of class formation has been done, in my view, by Adam Przeworski. See in particular, 'From Proletariat into Class', op.cit; 'Social Democracy as an Historical Phenomenon', *New Left Review*, 122, 1980; 'Material Interests, Class Compromise

and the Transition to Socialism', *Politics & Society*, vol. 10, no. 2, 1980; 'The Material Bases of Consent: Economics and Politics in a Hegemonic System', in Maurice Zeitlin, ed., *Political Power and Social Theory*, vol. 1, Greenwich Connecticut 1979. Other examples of important work on the political mediations of the process of class formation include, Göran Therborn, 'The Prospects of Labor and the Transformation of Advanced Capitalism', *New Left Review*, 145, 1984; David Abraham, *The Collapse of the Weimar Republic*, Princeton 1981; Ron Aminzade, *Class, Politics and Early Industrial Capitalism*, Binghampton 1981.

12. See especially Michael Burawoy, *Manufacturing Consent*, Chicago, 1979 and *The Politics of Production*, Verso, London 1985; Richard Edwards, *Contested Terrain*, New York, 1979; David Noble, 'Social Choice in Machine Design', *Politics & Society*, Vol. 8, nos. 3–4, 1978.

13. See Przeworski, 'From Proletariat into Class . . .' for a discussion of Kautsky's view on the problem of middle strata.

Part One

Conceptual Issues

2

The Biography of a Concept

Contradictory Class Locations

In this chapter we will examine in some detail the process by which a particular concept for solving the problem of the middle classes in capitalism was produced, the concept of 'contradictory locations within class relations'. This will not be a literal chronological account of the development of that concept, but rather a kind of logical reconstruction of the process. The actual history of the concept was not quite so neat, and the implications of specific innovations were often not fully realized until sometime later. The story, then, is an attempt at revealing the underlying logic of the development of the concept. The emphasis will be on the theoretical structure of the process and the theoretical dimensions of the adjudication of contending class concepts.

Before we embark on this enterprise it will be helpful to discuss briefly certain methodological issues involved in the process of concept formation. A great deal of substantive debate in the Marxist tradition is couched in an idiom of debates over the methodological and philosophical principles which underlie social analysis. Frequently this has the effect of altogether displacing concern with substantive theoretical issues by a preoccupation with epistemological problems. I wish to avoid such a displacement in this book. Nevertheless, I think that it is necessary to lay out as clearly as possible the logic of concept formation that I will be using in the analysis. The purpose of this discussion will not be to explore in any depth the epistemological problem of the status of concepts or the alternative approaches to the problem of concept formation that various theorists have advocated, but rather, simply to make accessible the rationale for the approach that will be followed in the rest of this book.[1]

The Logic of Concept Formation

Concepts are produced. The categories that are used in social theories, whether they be the relatively simple descriptive categories employed in making observations, or the very complex and abstract concepts used in the construction of 'grand theory', are all produced by human beings. And this is true regardless of one's epistemological prejudices and methodological predilections, whether one regards concepts as cognitive mappings of real mechanisms in the world or as strictly arbitrary conventions in the imagination of the theorist. They are never simply given by the real world as such but are always produced through some sort of intellectual process of concept formation.

The production of concepts that figure in scientific theories takes place under a variety of constraints. By 'constraint' I mean that in any given situation there is only a limited range of possible concepts that can be produced; while concepts are produced by the human imagination, they are not produced in a completely free and unstructured manner which makes anything possible. To be more specific, the production of scientific concepts operates methodologically under both theoretical and empirical constraints.[2] First, concepts have theoretical presuppositions. In some instances these presuppositions function as explicit, systematic theoretical requirements imposed on the production of a new concept; in other instances, the theoretical presuppositions act more as unconscious cognitive filters implicitly shaping what is thinkable and unthinkable by the theorist. In either case, such theoretical presuppositions determine, if only vaguely and implicitly, the range of possible concepts that can be produced.

Scientific concepts, no matter how embedded in an elaborated theoretical framework, are never constrained exclusively by theoretical presuppositions. They also face what can be called 'empirically mediated real-world constraints', or simply 'empirical constraints' for short. This cumbersome expression— 'empirically mediated real-world constaint'—is meant to convey two things: first, that the constraint in question comes from real mechanisms in the world, not simply from the conceptual framework of the theory; and second, that this real-world constraint operates through data gathered using the concepts of the theory. The constraint is thus empirically mediated, rather than directly imposed by the 'world as it really is'.[3] Concepts must not only conform to the conceptual rules and assumptions specified in the theoretical framework, they must also be used in explanations of various sorts. The fact that a concept is consistent with its theoretical framework does not, in and of itself, establish that it will be capable of an effective role in explanations of any empirical problem using that theoretical framework.

Concepts differ within and across theories in the relative strength of these two constraints on their formation. *Within* a given theory, concepts which are meant to be used directly in empirical observations are in general much more constrained empirically than concepts which figure in the most abstract propositions of the theory. Indeed, the empirical constraints in the most abstract theoretical formulations may become so attenuated that the concepts appear to be strictly logical constructions. On the other hand, in general, the theoretical constraints will tend to become relatively attenuated in the production of concrete concepts. Because of the contingencies that enter theories as you move from the most abstract to the most concrete levels of analysis, there tends to be a fair amount of slippage between the theoretical stipulations of the abstract theory and the specification of concrete concepts used in research.

The variability in the strength of theoretical and empirical constraints *across* theories is equally striking. Some theoretical frameworks take their conceptual presuppositions almost directly from the 'commonsense' categories of everyday discourse. The theoretical requirements for the production of concepts are unelaborated, not subjected to conscious scrutiny and, often, inconsistently applied. The empirical requirements of concepts, however, may be quite rigorously and ruthlessly applied. On the basis of empirical 'findings' concepts may be adopted or their boundaries redrawn or they may even be abandoned altogether. In other theoretical frameworks, the theoretical requirements imposed on the production of concepts are systematic and elaborate, and applied with self-conscious consistency. A powerful critique of a given concept is to show that it is inconsistent with some of these theoretical requirements and that it is therefore not a 'legitimate' concept. Empirical constraints will also operate, but they may do so in a much more diffuse and roundabout way.

It is an achievement of a scientific theory for such theoretical constraints to operate systematically and consciously on the production of new concepts. However, if the imposition of such systematic theoretical constraints runs ahead of the explanatory success of the theory, then the theory runs the risk of 'theoreticism', that is, of effectively immunizing the theory from the operation of empirical constraints required by the explanatory tasks of the theory. On the other hand, if a theory is organized in such a way that it blocks the development of such self-conscious theoretical constraints, then it is guilty of what is sometimes called 'empiricism'.[4] If the methodological sins of theoreticism or empiricism are carried to extremes, then the very status of the resulting concepts as 'scientific' may be jeopardized.[5]

When the production of concepts takes place within an established conceptual framework, then in general the process of concept formation is simultaneously a process of *adjudication* between rival concepts. The assessment of the adequacy of a given concept is not simply a question of examining its own consistency with the theoretical requirements of the framework and with the empirical observations of research using that framework. While the presence of theoretical and empirical inconsistencies with a given concept may provide the motivation to seek an alternative, in and of themselves they are generally not a sufficient basis for rejecting a concept. The reason for this is that in the absence of a better, rival concept, it is not possible to know whether the culprit in these inconsistencies is the concept itself, or problems in the various constraints being used to evaluate the concept. Empirical anomalies with respect to a given concept, for example, may reflect observational problems or the presence of causes absent from the theory rather than a problem with the concept in question. And theoretical inconsistencies may reflect problems in certain elements in the abstract theoretical requirements imposed by the general theory, rather than a failure of the specific concept in question. Unless there is a rival concept which fares better with respect to both the theoretical and empirical constraints on concept formation, therefore, it is often difficult to draw definitive conclusions about the adequacy of a given concept.

By 'rival concepts' I mean, in general, rival *definitions* of the same theoretical object. Examples would include rival definitions of the working class, capitalism or the state, within a Marxist theoretical framework or rival definitions of bureaucracy, social closure or rationalization within a Weberian theoretical framework. In each case there is an agreed-upon theoretical object, but its appropriate definition is a matter of contention.[6] Disputes over theoretical objects themselves—that is, over what are the important theoretical objects to explain and what theoretical objects should figure in the explanations—generally involve problems of theory adjudication, not simply concept adjudication.[7]

Conceptual adjudication is a double process. It compares rival concepts in terms of their respective consistency both with the abstract conceptual requirements of the general theory in which they figure and with the empirical observations generated using the theory. For example, in the case of the concept of the working class in Marxist theory, this implies assessing the consistency of alternative definitions of the working class with a number of abstract elements in the concept of class (e.g. classes must be defined in relational terms where exploitation is intrinsic to the relation) and the consistency of the alternatives with a variety of empirical observations (e.g. the patterns of class formation and the distribution of class consciousness).

Such double adjudication is often a difficult and contentious project. In terms of the theoretical adjudication, it is rare that social scientific theories are so well integrated and internally coherent that it is clear precisely which requirements apply to a given concept. And even where there is some consensus on this point, it is often the case that rival concepts may each fare better with respect to different conceptual requirements. In terms of the empirical adjudication, the empirical expectations tied to given concepts are not often so precise that a given 'finding' decisively discriminates between contending concepts. And of course, as is often the case, the verdicts of the theoretical and the empirical adjudication may contradict each other. It is because of these difficulties and ambiguities that disputes over concepts can be so durable.

When a process of concept formation and adjudication is launched there is no guarantee, of course, that a satisfactory concept *can* be produced within the constraints it faces. One of the main impulses for the much more arduous task of theory reconstruction is precisely the repeated failure in efforts at concept formation within a given theory, to produce concepts which simultaneously satisfy theoretical and empirical constraints. What we mean by 'dogmatism' is the refusal of a theorist to call into question elements of the general theory in light of such repeated failures (or, equivalently, to deal with such failures by denying their existence).[8] 'Eclecticism', on the other hand, is the refusal to worry about theoretical coherence. Old concepts are modified and new concepts are adopted from various theoretical frameworks in an ad hoc manner without regard to their compatibility or their integration into a general framework. What is needed is a balance between theoretical commitment to maintain and strengthen the coherence of given general theoretical frameworks with theoretical openness to allow for concept transformation and theory reconstruction.

In the actual development of scientific theories, the process is never as tidy as methodological prescriptions suggest. Inevitably there are periods of work which tend towards theoreticism or empiricism in the formation of concepts, dogmatism and eclecticism in the elaboration of theories. The point of these methodological injunctions, therefore, is not so much the hope of producing a 'pure' path of theoretical development, but to provide tools for criticizing and correcting the inevitable deviations that occur.

Steps in the Analysis of the Formation of the Concept of Contradictory Locations

On the basis of the general logic of concept formation outlined above, our analysis of the development of the concept 'contradictory locations within class relations' will proceed in the following steps:

(1) *The Empirical Setting.* This will involve indicating the empirical problems which did not seem adequately mapped by the prevailing specification of the concept of class structure within Marxist theory and which first stimulated the effort at concept transformation.

(2) *Theoretical Constraints.* If the concept that attempts to resolve the problems specified under the empirical setting is to be incorporated within Marxist theory, it is important to specify the critical elements of the general theory of class and class structure that act as parameters to the process of concept formation. It must be emphasized that it is not a foregone conclusion that this process of concept formation will be successful. It is always possible that the constraints imposed by the general theory of class preclude the formation of adequate concepts of specific classes that are needed to deal with the empirical problems set out initially. If this proves to be the case, then the attempt at forming such concepts may ultimately lead to a process of transformation of the more general theoretical framework. The presupposition of such an effort, however, is that a rigorous account of the theoretical constraints has been elaborated. This will be the objective of this part of the discussion.

(3) *Alternative Solutions*. When there are striking empirical limitations with the prevailing conceptual maps of a theory, a variety of alternative new concepts will generally be proposed. The process of concept formation is usually at the same time a process of concept adjudication and there are often a number of contending alternatives. To understand the specificity of the new concept I proposed, it is important to understand the nature of the available alternatives.

(4) *Building a New Concept*. Conceptual innovations do not usually spring full-blown into the heads of theorists, but are built up through a series of partial modifications and reformulations. While it would be too tedious to describe all the steps of this process for the concept of contradictory locations within class relations, I will reconstruct the principal stages of the concept's formation and transformation.

(5) *Unresolved Issues*. The concept of contradictory locations generated a new set of problems. There remained unresolved issues, tensions with various aspects of the general theory of class, internal weaknesses within the concept, and empirical anomalies. Ultimately these problems became substantial enough to provoke a new process of concept formation which fundamentally transformed the concept of contradictory locations within class relations itself. This new framework will be explored in the next chapter.

The Empirical Setting

I did not initially engage the problem of the 'middle class' as a general conceptual difficulty in Marxist theory. Rather, my first encounter with the issue occurred in the context of the practical problems of conducting a statistical study of income determination within a Marxist framework. Empirical research on stratification has been at the very core of American sociology, and as a graduate student I thought that it would be a good idea to bring the general Marxist critique of sociology to bear on this body of research. In particular, I wanted to do more than simply present theoretical arguments for the superficiality of 'status attainment' research; I wanted to develop an empirical critique of it as well. To do this I began a series of empirical studies, at first with the collaboration of

Luca Perrone, which investigated the relationship between class and income inequality.[9]

This is not the place to discuss the substance, the strategy or conclusions of this research. The important point here is that to launch this kind of empirical study we immediately faced the problem of how to categorize people with respect to class. From a practical point of view this was a problem of taxonomy: how to pigeon-hole cases so that a statistical study of the relationship between class and income could proceed. But of course the taxonomic problem was really a conceptual one. How should we deal with the numerous cases of people who did not really seem to be either bourgeois or proletarian?

These diverse positions are colloquially referred to as the 'middle class', but this designation hardly solves the conceptual difficulties. The problem of concept-formation which we faced, therefore, was how to generate a class concept for concrete analysis which adequately maps these locations while at the same time preserving the general assumptions and framework of Marxist class analysis. How can we, in other words, transform the ideological category 'middle class' into a scientific concept?

Once we began to explore the issues it became clear that the problem of the middle class impinged on a wide range of empirical problems within Marxism. Even in contexts where the 'middle class' was not itself an object of investigation, the conceptual problem was often present, since to define the working class is, at least in part, to specify the conceptual line of demarcation with the 'middle class'. What began as a problem of how to conduct a statistical investigation, soon escalated into a general theoretical problem of how to conceptualize class relations in capitalist society.

As we will see, a number of solutions to this problem have been proposed by Marxists, including the claim that it is not a problem at all and that the simple polarization concept is correct for concrete as well as abstract analyses of capitalism. But before we can examine these alternatives, it is necessary to specify the general theoretical constraints that the requisite concepts must respect.

Theoretical Constraints

One of the pivotal problems in any process of systematic concept formation is knowing what the theoretical constraints on the process are. In the case of the concept of class, there is hardly a consensus among Marxists as to what constitutes the general Marxist theory of class relations, and depending upon how the constraints within that general theory are characterized, the range of possible solutions to the transformation of a specific concept of class will be different. A great deal potentially hinges, therefore, on precisely how those constraints are specified.

The specification of the characteristics of the general concept of class which I will propose cannot be taken either as an authoritative reading of the texts of classical Marxism or as an account of some implicit majority position among Marxists. While I do feel that the theoretical conditions elaborated below are consistent with Marx's general usage and the underlying logic of many contemporary Marxist discussions, I will make no attempt to validate this claim. At a minimum, these characteristics are central elements within Marxist debates on the concept of class, even if they are not exhaustive or uncontentious.

The task at hand, then, is to specify the constraints imposed by the *abstract* theory of classes in Marxism on the process of producing more *concrete* concepts, in this case a concrete concept capable of dealing with 'middle classes' in contemporary capitalism. Two general types of constraints are especially important: (1) constraints imposed by the *explanatory role* of the concept of class within the Marxist theory of society and history; and (2) constraints imposed by the *structural properties* of the abstract concept of class which enable it to fulfil this explanatory role in the general theory.

THE EXPLANATORY AGENDA

The concept of class figures as an explanatory principle, in one way or another, in virtually all substantive problems addressed within Marxist theory. Two clusters of explanatory claims for the concept of class, however, are the most important: one revolving around the inter-connections among class structure, class formation, class consciousness and class struggle, and a second revolving around the relationship between class and the epochal transformation of societies. Let us look at each of these in turn.

CONCEPTUAL CONSTRAINT 1: Class structure imposes limits on class formation, class consciousness and class struggle. This statement implies neither that these four sub-concepts within the general concept of class are definable independently of each other nor that they only have 'external' or 'contingent' inter-relationships. It simply means that classes have a structural existence which is irreducible to the kinds of collective organizations which develop historically (class formations), the class ideologies held by individuals and organizations (class consciousness) or the forms of conflict engaged in by individuals as class members or by class organizations (class struggle), and that such class structures impose basic constraints on these other elements in the concept of class.

This is not an uncontentious issue. E. P. Thompson, for example, has argued that the structural existence of classes is largely irrelevant outside the lived experiences of actors. While he does not go so far as to reject the concept of class structure altogether, he certainly marginalizes it within his elaboration of class.[10] Most Marxists, however, implicitly or explicitly incorporate such distinctions within their class analysis. In general, when they do so, class structure is viewed in one way or another as the 'basic' determinant of the other three elements, at least in the sense of setting the limits of possible variation of class formation, class consciousness and class struggle.

The rationale behind this kind of claim revolves around the concept of class 'interests' and class 'capacities'. The argument is basically as follows. Whatever else the concept of 'interests' might mean, it surely includes the access to resources necessary to accomplish various kinds of goals or objectives. People certainly have an 'objective interest' in increasing their capacity to act. The argument that the class structure imposes the basic limits on class formation, class consciousness and class struggle is essentially a claim that it constitutes the basic mechanism for distributing access to resources in a society, and thus distributing capacities to act. Class consciousness, in these terms, is above all, the conscious understanding of these mechanisms: the realization by subordinate classes that it is necessary to transform the class structure if there are to be any basic changes in their capacities to act, and the realization by dominant classes that the reproduction of their power depends upon the reproduction of the class structure. Class formation, on the other hand, is the process by which individual capacities are organizationally linked together in order to generate a collective capacity to act, a capacity which can potentially be directed at the class structure itself. Given that the class structure defines the access of these individuals to the pivotal resources that have the potential to be mobilized collectively, it imposes the basic limits on the possibilities for the formation of such collectively organized capacities.

Two points must be added to this characterization of the explanatory role of class structure to avoid misunderstanding. First, the claim that class structure limits class consciousness and class formation is not equivalent to the claim that it alone determines them. Other mechanisms (race, ethnicity, gender, legal institutions, etc.) operate within the limits established by the class structure, and it could well be the case that the *politically* significant explanations for variation in class formation or consciousness are embedded in these non-class mechanisms rather than in the class structure itself. There is no reason to insist, for example, that the most important determinant of variations *across* capitalist countries in the process of class formation and consciousness lies in variations in their class structures (although this could be the case); it is entirely possible that variations in institutional, racial, ethnic or other kinds of mechanisms may be more significant. What is argued, however, is that these non-class mechanisms operate within limits imposed by the class structure itself.

Second, the above characterization does not provide an account of precisely how class structure imposes these limits. In the case of the class consciousness argument, this would require an analysis of cognitive structures and social psychology, basically an analysis of the psychological process by which people come to understand the social determination of their capacities and options. My assumption is that however these psychological mechanisms operate, the real social mechanisms operating in the world which shape the objective capacities available to people impose the basic limits on how people will view those capacities. In the case of class formation, the full elaboration of the effects of class structure would require an analysis of the organizational dynamics by which individual capacities to act, as determined by class location, become mobilized into collective forms of class practice.[11] Again, the assumption is that whatever this process is, it is limited by the form of class relations which distributes the basic access to the resources in question.

The interconnections among these four constituent elements in the concept of class can be formalized within what I have elsewhere called a 'model of determination'.[12] Such a model specifies the particular forms of determination between elements. In the present context, three of these are particularly important: *limitation* in which one element imposes limits of possible variation on

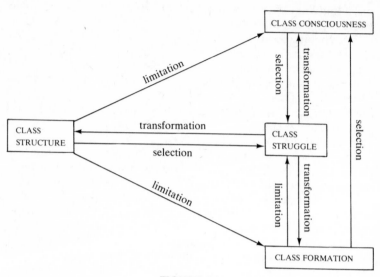

FIGURE 2.1
Model of Determination Linking Class Structure, Class Formation,
Class Consciousness and Class Struggle

another; *selection*, in which one element imposes narrower limits of variation on another element within a range of already established broader limits; and *transformation* in which a practice by social actors (individuals and organizations of various sorts) transforms a given element within the constraints of limitations and selections.

Using these terms, one possible specification of the relationship between class structure, class formation, class consciousness and class struggle is illustrated in Figure 2.1. Class struggle provides the basic transformative principle within this model of determination. Consciousness, class formation and class structures are all objects of class struggle and are transformed in the course of class struggles. Such transformations, however, are constrained structurally. In the most direct way, class struggles are limited by the forms of class organization (class formations), which are themselves limited by the existing class structure.

While the details of this model of determination may be contested, I think that the central thrust of the model generally conforms to the logic of the Marxist theory of class. This means that any attempt at forming a new concept for mapping the concrete class structure of capitalist societies must be able to fit into this model (or a closely related one). The new concept must be capable of designating a basic structural determinant of class formation, class consciousness and class struggle. As we shall see, one of the bases for my critique of some of the proposed new concepts for dealing with the 'middle class' (eg. Poulantzas's concept of productive/unproductive labour) is that they cannot function effectively within such models.

CONCEPTUAL CONSTRAINT 2: Class structures constitute the essential qualitative lines of social demarcation in the historical trajectories of social change. Not only should class structures be viewed as setting the basic limits of possibility on class formation, class consciousness and class struggle, but they also constitute the most fundamental social determinant of limits of possibility for other aspects of social structure. Class structures constitute the central organizing principles of societies in the sense of shaping the range of possible variations of the state, ethnic relations, gender relations, etc., and thus historical epochs can best be identified by their predominant class structures.

Several points of clarification on this theoretical claim are needed. First, the thesis as formulated is agnostic on the issue of 'technological determinism'. Many Marxists would add the additional claim that the range of possible class structures is fundamentally limited by the level of development of the forces of production. This is at the heart of the classical argument of the 'dialectic' of forces and relations of production. But even within the classical argument, the crucial historical line of social demarcation remains class relations.[13]

Secondly, although in classical historical materialism this thesis typically takes the form of a functionalist account of the relationship of 'superstructures' to 'bases', such class functionalism is unnecessary. The functional argument not only says that class relations impose limits of possibility on other social relations, but that the specific form of those relations are explained by their functional relation to classes. Thus, for example, the form of the state is often explained by the functions it fulfils for the reproduction of class relations. The primacy of class, however, can be maintained without such explanations. It is sufficient to argue that the class structure constitutes the central mechanism by which various sorts of resources are appropriated and distributed, therefore determining the underlying capacities to act of various social actors. Class structures are the central determinant of social power. Consequently, they may determine what kinds of social changes are possible, even if they do not functionally determine the specific form of every institution of the society.[14] Of course, as a result of such power (capacities to act) institutional arrangements may tend to become 'functional' for the reproduction of class relations, but that is a consequence of struggles rooted in such class relations; it is not spontaneously or automatically caused by the class structures themselves.[15]

Third, I am not arguing that class structures define a unique path of social development. Rather, the claim is that class structures constitute the lines of demarcation in trajectories of social change. There is no teleological implication that there is a 'final destination' towards which all social change inexorably moves. There may be multiple futures to a given society, forks in the road leading in different directions.[16] The argument here is simply that along such a road, the critical junctures are specified by changes in the class structures.

Finally, to say that class defines the pivotal lines of demarcation is not to say that all other social relations are uniquely determined by class relations. While class relations may establish limits on possible variations, within those limits quite autonomous mechanisms may be operating. And in specific cases it is even possible that the most crucial forms of variation in a given relation are all contained within a given set of class limits. A case can be made, for example, that in advanced capitalism, the destruction of institutionalized forms of male domination falls within the limits of possibility determined by the class structure. The persistence of such domination and the specific forms that it takes, therefore, cannot be explained by class relations as such, but rather are to be explained by mechanisms directly rooted in gender relations.[17]

The claim that class structures define the qualitative lines of demarcation in trajectories of social change is, typically, combined with a closely related proposition—namely, that class struggles are the central mechanism for moving from one class structure to another. If the map of history is defined by class structures the motor of history is class struggle.

There are three basic ways in which class struggle has been defined: by the nature of the *agents* in conflicts, by the *objectives* of conflict, by the *effects* of conflict. Agency definitions of class conflict insist that for a given conflict to count as 'class struggle', the actors involved must be class actors (either individuals in given classes or organizations representing given classes) and the lines of opposition in the conflict must be class lines. Thus, for example, conflict between religious groups, even if they produce class-pertinent effects would not normally count as a 'class struggle', unless the opposing religious groups were also classes (or at least plausible 'representatives' of classes). Objectives definitions, on the other hand, argue that to count as class struggles the balance of power or distribution of resources between classes must be a conscious objective of the struggle. It is not enough that the protagonists be collective organizations representing classes; they must be consciously contesting over class issues. Finally, effects definitions argue that any conflict, regardless of objectives or actors, which has systematic effects on class relations should count as a 'class struggle'.

The first of these definitions seems to me to be the most fruitful theoretically. With effects definitions the proposition that class struggle explains trajectories of historical change comes perilously close to being a tautology: if trajectories are defined by changes in class structures, and class struggles are defined as struggles which have effects on class structures, then it is almost a trivial conclusion that class struggles explain trajectories of historical change.[18] Objectives definitions of class struggle, on the other hand, have the danger of reducing class struggles to the relatively rare historical instances in which highly class conscious actors engage in struggle. Whereas effects definitions include too much in the concept of class struggle, thus reducing its substantive meaning, objectives definitions tend to restrict the concept too much, thus reducing its plausibility as an explanation of historical trajectories of change.

The definition of class struggle in terms of the class nature of the protagonists in conflicts, therefore, seems to be the most satisfactory. This means, on the one hand, that various kinds of non-class struggles may have class effects without thereby being considered class struggles, and, on the other, that class struggles are not restricted to cases where the actors are self-consciously struggling over questions of class power. The thesis that class struggle is the 'motor' of history, then, means that it is conflict between actors defined by their location within class structures which explains the qualitative transformations that demarcate epochal trajectories of social change.

As a trans-historical generalization, this proposition has come under a great deal of criticism, both by non-Marxists and Marxists. Still, I think that it is fair to say that the thesis that class struggle constitutes the basic mechanism for movement between forms of society remains a broadly held view among Marxists, and, in spite of uncertainties, it is generally thought to be one of the hallmarks of the Marxist concept of class. I will therefore continue to treat it is a theoretical constraint on the process of formation of specific class concepts within Marxist theory.

STRUCTURAL PROPERTIES OF THE CONCEPT OF CLASS

As an abstract concept, the Marxist concept of class is built around four basic structural properties: classes are *relational;* those relations are *antagonistic*; those antagonisms are rooted in *exploitation*; and exploitation is based on the social relations of *production*. Each of these properties can be considered additional conceptual constraints imposed on the process of concept formation of concrete class concepts.

CONCEPTUAL CONSTRAINT 3. The concept of class is a relational concept. To say that class is a relational concept is to say that classes are always defined within social relations, in particular in relation to other classes. Just as the positions 'parent' and 'child' have meaning only within the social relationship which binds them together—unlike 'old' and 'young', which can be defined strictly in terms of individual attributes of age—classes are definable only in terms of their relations to other classes.[19] The names of classes, therefore, are derived from the relations within which they are located: lords and serfs within feudal class relations; bourgeoisie and proletarians within capitalist class relations. Such relational concepts of class are to be contrasted with purely *gradational* concepts of class.[20] In gradational notions of class, classes differ by the quantitative degree of some attribute (income, status, education, etc.) and not by their location within a determinate relation. Thus the names of classes within gradational approaches have a strictly quantitative character: upper class, upper middle class, middle class, lower middle class, lower class, and so on. Of course, relationally defined classes also have gradational properties—capitalists are rich, workers are poor— but it is not these distributional properties as such which define them as classes.

Marxists are committed to relational notions of class for three basic reasons. First of all, if class structures are meant to explain class formation and class struggle, then relational notions are clearly preferable to gradational ones. It takes opposing groups to have social conflicts, and such opposition implies that the groups are in some kind of social relation to each other. The premiss of relational definitions of the underlying class structure is that a relational specification of the positions which become formed into contending groups has more explanatory power for such formations than a non-relational specification. 'Upper' and 'lower' classes have no necessary relation to each other and therefore this gradational distinction does not, of itself, give any explantory leverage for understanding the generation of real social conflicts. Now it may happen in a particular society that the positions designated as 'upper class' in a gradational approach in fact do have some sort of determinate social relation to the positions designated 'lower class', and thus a structural basis for the formation of opposing groups in conflict between upper and lower classes would exist. But in such a case it is still the social relation which defines the line of cleavage, not the sheer fact of the gradational distinction.

Second, only a relational concept of class is capable of satisfying the second constraint specified above. Of course, one could construct typologies of societies within a gradational framework: in some societies there is a big middle class, in others the class structure looks like a pyramid, in others it might look like an hour glass. For some purposes, such distribution-based typologies might be of considerable interest. But they cannot plausibly form the basis for lines of demarcation in historical trajectories of social change and thus serve as the basis for a theory of history.[21]

The third reason for adopting relational definitions of class structures is that Marxists generally contend that such class relations are capable of explaining the essential features of gradational inequalities (distributional inequalities). Income inequality, which is usually the core axis of gradational definitions of class, is fundamentally explained, Marxists argue, by the structure of certain social relations, in particular by the social relations of production. Defining classes in terms of social relations, therefore, identifies the concept with a more fundamental structure of social determination than distributional outcomes.

CONCEPTUAL CONSTRAINT 4: The social relations which define classes are intrinsically antagonistic rather than symmetrical.
'Antagonistic' means that the relations which define classes intrin-

sically generate opposing interests, in the sense that the realization of the interests of one class necessarily implies the struggle against the realization of the interests of another class. This does not imply that a 'compromise' between antagonistic interests is never possible, but simply that such compromises must entail realizing some interests *against* the interests of another class. What is impossible is not compromise, but harmony.

CONCEPTUAL CONSTRAINT 5: The objective basis of these antagonistic interests is exploitation. While Marx (and certainly many Marxists) sometimes describe class relations in terms of domination or oppression, the most basic determinant of class antagonism is exploitation. Exploitation must be distinguished from simple inequality. To say that feudal lords exploit serfs is to say more than they are rich and serfs are poor; it is to make the claim that there is a causal relationship between the affluence of the lord and the poverty of the serf. The lord is rich because lords are able, by virtue of their class relation to serfs, to appropriate a surplus produced by the serfs.[22] Because of this causal link between the wellbeing of one class and the deprivation of another, the antagonism between classes defined by these relations has an 'objective' character.

This is not the place to discuss the knotty philosophical problems with the concept of 'objective interests'. Marx certainly regarded class interests as having an objective status, and the issue here is what it is about those relations that might justify such a claim. The assumption is that people always have an objective interest in their material welfare, where this is defined as the combination of how much they consume and how hard they have to work to get that consumption. There is therefore no assumption that people universally have an objective interest in *increasing* their consumption, but they do have an interest in reducing the toil necessary to obtain whatever level of consumption they desire. An exploitative relation necessarily implies either that some people must toil more so that others can toil less, or that they must consume less at a given level of toil so that others can consume more, or both. In either case people universally have an objective interest in not being exploited materially, since in the absence of exploitation they would toil less and/or consume more.[23] It is because the interests structured by exploitation are objective that we can describe the antagonisms between classes as intrinsic rather than contingent.

CONCEPTUAL CONSTRAINT 6: The fundamental basis of exploitation is to be found in the social relations of production. While all Marxists see exploitation as rooted in the social organization of production, there is no agreement among them as to how the 'social relations of production' should be defined, or about what aspects of those relations are most essential for defining classes. Much of the recent Marxist debate over the concept of class can be interpreted as a debate over how classes should be specified within the general notion of production relations. Poulantzas, for example, has emphasized the importance of the political and ideological dimensions of production relations in the definition of classes; Roemer has argued that classes should be defined strictly in terms of the property relations aspects of production relations; I have argued that classes are defined by various relations of control within the process of production. In all of these cases, however, class is defined as a production-centred relational concept.

These six constraints imposed by the general Marxist theory of class constitute the conceptual framework within which the attempt at transforming the ideological concept 'middle class' into a theoretical concept will occur. This attempt may fail, in which case the more complex problem of rethinking or transforming some of these basic presuppositions may be necessary. But to begin with, I will take these elements as fixed and use them to try to produce the needed concept.

Alternative Solutions

The gap between the simple class map of capitalism consisting solely of a bourgeoisie and a proletariat and the concrete empirical observations of actual capitalist societies has been apparent to Marxists for a long time. As a result, considerable attention has been paid in recent years to the problem of theorizing the class character of the 'middle class'. The motivation for these analyses has generally been a realization that a conceptual clarification of the 'middle class' was needed in order properly to specify the working class. Such a clarification involves two essential tasks: first, establishing the conceptual criteria by which the working class is distinguished from non-working class wage earners, and second, establishing the conceptual status of those wage-earner locations that are excluded from the working class on these criteria.

Four alternative types of solutions to the problem dominated most discussions at the time I began work on the concept of class: (1) The gap between the polarized concept and reality is only apparent. Capitalist societies really are polarized. (2) Non-proletarian, non-bourgeois positions constitute part of the petty bourgeoisie, generally referred to as the 'new' petty bourgeoisie (and sometimes less rigorously as the 'new middle class'). (3) Non-proletarian, non-bourgeois locations constitute a historically new class sometimes referred to as the 'professional-managerial class' and sometimes simply as the 'new class'.[24] (4) Non-proletarian, non-bourgeois positions should be referred to simply as 'middle strata', social positions that are not really 'in' any class. Since I have discussed these alternatives thoroughly elsewhere, I will not provide an extended exegesis here.[25] What I will try to do is to explain briefly the central logic of each position and indicate some of the problems with respect to the constraints in the general concept of class.

SIMPLE POLARIZATION

The simplest response to the emergence of social positions in capitalist societies which appear to fall neither into the working class nor the capitalist class is to argue that this is simply 'appearance'; that the 'essence' is that nearly all of these new positions are really part of the working class. At most, professional and managerial wage-earners constitute a privileged stratum of the proletariat, but their existence or expansion does not require any modification of the basic class map of capitalism.[26]

The rationale behind this claim is that managers and professional employees, like all other workers, do not own their means of production and must therefore sell their labour power in order to live. This, it is argued, is sufficient to demonstrate that they are capitalistically exploited, and that in turn is sufficient to define them as workers. Except for top executives in corporations who actually become part owners through stock options and the like, all wage-earners are therefore part of the working class.

A simple wage-labour criterion for the working class does conform to some of the theoretical criteria laid out above. It is consistent with a general historical typology of class structures distinguishing capitalism from pre-capitalist societies (constraint 2), it is a relational concept (constraint 3), the relations do have an antagonistic character to them (constraint 4), nearly all wage-earners probably suffer some exploitation (constraint 5) and the basis for the exploitation under question is defined within the social organization of production, although perhaps in a fairly impoverished way (constraint 6). Where this view of the 'middle class' fails dismally is in satisfying the first theoretical constraint. It is hard to see how a definition of the working class as all wage-earners could provide a satisfactory structural basis for explaining class formation, class consciousness and class struggle. It is certainly not the case that 'all things being equal' top managers are generally more likely to side with industrial workers than with the bourgeoisie in class struggles. Indeed, it is difficult to imagine any conceivable circumstances when this would be the case. Drawing the boundary criteria for the working class at wage-earners, therefore, does not create a category which is in any meaningful sense homogeneous with respect to its effects.

The alternatives to simple polarization concepts of class structures usually begin by arguing that the social relations of production cannot be satisfactorily characterized exclusively in terms of the buying and selling of labour power. While the wage-labour exchange is important, various other dimensions of production relations bear on the determination of class relations. Sometimes the political aspect of those relations are emphasized (domination), sometimes the ideological, sometimes both. In any case, once production relations are understood in this way, new solutions to the problem of the 'middle class' are opened up.

THE NEW PETTY BOURGEOISIE

The first systematic solution proposed by Marxists in the recent debates over the conceptual problem at hand is to classify the 'middle class' as part of the petty bourgeoisie. Sometimes the rationale for this placement is that such positions involve 'ownership' of skills or 'human capital', and this places them in a social relation with capital akin to that of the traditional petty bourgeoisie (owners of individual physical means of production). A more common rationale for this solution revolves around the category 'unproductive labour', i.e. wage-labour which does not produce surplus-value (eg. clerks in banks). Such wage-earners, it is argued, in a sense 'live off' the surplus-value produced by productive workers and thus occupy a different position from workers within the relations of exploitation. Some theorists, most notably Nicos Poulantzas, add various political and ideological criteria to this analysis of unproductive labour, arguing that supervisory labour and 'mental' labor, even when they are productive, are outside of the working class.[27] Yet such non-working-class wage-earners are clearly not part of the bourgeoisie because they do not own or even really control the means of production. Poulantzas insists that these positions should be placed in the petty bourgeoisie for two reasons: first, because their ideological predispositions are essentially like those of the petty bourgeoisie (individualism, hostility to the working class, etc.) and secondly, because, like the traditional petty bourgeoisie, the new petty bourgeoisie is caught between the proletariat and the bourgeoisie in class conflicts.

The concept of the 'new petty bourgeoisie' suffers from some of the same problems as the simple polarization stance. It is very hard to see how the diverse categories of unproductive and/or supervisory and mental wage-earners (secretaries, professionals, managers, unproductive manual workers in the state, salespersons, etc.) are in any sense homogeneous with respect to the problem of class formation, class consciousness and class struggle. It is therefore difficult to understand why they should be seen as members of a common class. In many cases unproductive wage-earners have interests which are indistinguishable from industrial workers, or which are at least much closer to the interests of industrial workers than they are to other 'members' of the 'new petty bourgeoisie'.

Furthermore, even if we were to grant that unproductive employees were outside of the working class, their ascription to the petty bourgeoisie violates the sixth criterion of the general concept of class. By no stretch of the concept of social relations of production, can an unproductive employee in a bank and a self-employed baker be seen as occupying the same position within the social relations of production. The concept of the new petty bourgeoisie is therefore unsatisfactory because it both employs a criterion for a class boundary which does not easily conform to the requirements of the first constraint, and because the positions defined by this criterion share none of the salient relational properties of the petty bourgeoisie, thus violating the sixth constraint.

THE NEW CLASS

Dissatisfaction with both the simple polarization and new petty bourgeoisie solutions to the problem of the 'middle class' has led some Marxists to suggest that these various non-proletarian, non-bourgeois positions constitute a new class in its own right. This new class has been defined in various different ways. Gouldner defines it primarily in terms of its control of 'cultural capital'; Szelenyi and Konrad emphasize the 'teleological' function of intellectuals as the key to their potential class power; Barbara and John Ehrenreich argue that the new class—the 'professional–managerial class' in their analysis—is defined by common positions within the social relations of *reproduction* of capitalist class relations. The various advocates of this view also differ in the extent to which they view this new class as essentially an emergent tendency within capitalism (Szelenyi), a rival to the bourgeoisie itself for class dominance (Gouldner), or simply a new kind of subordinate class within capitalism (Ehrenreichs). All of these views have one critical feature in common: they solve the problem of the 'middle class' by redefining such positions in terms of their relationship to cultural production in one way or another.

This solution to the problem of producing a theoretical outline of the category 'middle class' avoids some of the problems of the other solutions. At least some of the categories included in the 'new class' clearly do have the potential to form organizations for collective action, distinct from both the bourgeoisie and the working class. And a good case can be made that 'new class' positions generate distinctive forms of consciousness. The concept therefore does not seem necessarily at odds with the first criterion of the general concept of class. Furthermore, Gouldner and Szelenyi make the case that the 'new class' is in some way implicated in the distinction between capitalism and 'actually existing socialism'. The concept may therefore conform to the second criterion of the abstract theory of class.

What is much less evident is whether or not the concept is consistent with the fifth and sixth criteria. It is not usually clear how the diverse categories of 'intellectuals' subsumed under the 'new class' rubric share common interests based on exploitation or occupy a common position within the social relations of production. Some of them occupy managerial positions within capitalist firms, directly dominating workers and perhaps even participating in the control of investments. Others are employees in the state and may exercise no control whatsoever over other employees (eg. teachers, nurses). Others may be technical employees within capitalist firms, outside the managerial hierarchy and working on specific problems assigned to them by their superiors. While such diverse positions may have some cultural features in common by virtue of education or expertise, it is difficult to see them as occupying a common position within production relations, sharing common exploitation interests, and thus constituting a single class by the criteria laid out in the general concept of class.[28]

MIDDLE STRATA

The final alternative solution is undoubtedly the most popular. Rather than transform any of the specific class concepts, positions which do not seem to fit into the bourgeois–proletarian dichotomy are simply labelled 'middle strata'. This kind of formulation is encountered frequently in Marxist historiography and in some sociological works as well. At times this solution represents either an agnostic position on where such positions belong in the class structure or a retreat from theoretical precision. But in some cases this formulation is itself a theoretical stance: some positions in the social structure, it is argued, simply do not fall into any class locations at all. Calling them 'middle strata' reflects the peculiarities of their social location: they are middle *strata* rather than middle *classes* because they are outside of the basic class relation; they are *middle* strata, rather than some other kind of social category, because in the class struggle they are forced to take sides with either the bourgeoisie or the proletariat. They are in a sense 'caught in the middle'.

As an interim solution to a conceptual weakness, the use of the term 'middle strata' is undoubtedly preferable to some of the problematic solutions we have already discussed. Yet, it is itself misleading in certain important ways. Above all, the view that the categories identified as 'middle strata' are generally 'outside' of the basic classes of capitalist society is not satisfactory. Many of these positions are directly involved in production, they are directly structured by the relations of domination and exploitation within the production system. Even if the positions do not constitute classes as such, they do have a class character and this is lost by the designation 'strata'.

Building a New Concept

None of the available alternatives, therefore, seemed adequate. In one way or another they were inconsistent with at least some of the theoretical constraints of the general theory of class. I therefore attempted yet another strategy for transforming the 'middle class' into a coherent class concept.

The starting point for the formation of a new concept for mapping the 'middle class' was the observation that all of the other alternatives implicitly share a common thesis, namely, that every position within a class structure falls within one and only one class. It was assumed that there is an isomorphic relationship between the categories of the class structure and the actual locations filled by individuals. Rarely is this assumption made explicit, but it does operate in each of the cases we have examined. In the first solution, all positions are either in the working class, the capitalist class or the traditional petty bourgeoisie; in the second solution, the only change is that the petty bourgeoisie has two segments, old and new; in the third alternative every position not in the traditional classes of capitalism falls into a 'new class'; and in the final alternative, positions which are not part of the traditional classes are treated as non-class positions—middle strata.

If we drop this assumption, an entirely new kind of solution to the problem of conceptually mapping the 'middle class' becomes possible. Instead of regarding all positions as located uniquely within particular classes and thus as having a coherent class character in their own right, we should see some positions as possibly having a multiple class character; they may be in more than one class simultaneously. The class nature of such positions is a derivative one, based as it is on the fundamental classes to which they are attached. Such positions are what I have termed 'contradictory locations within class relations'.[29]

A brief note on terminology is needed, since this expression may be confusing. As a number of critics have pointed out, the basic class relation of capitalism is itself 'contradictory'. Workers in their relationship to capitalists, therefore, should be considered the most 'contradictory location'. In the original exposition of the concept I stated that the full expression should be something like: 'contradictory locations within contradictory class relations', but that the simpler expression 'contradictory locations' would be used for convenience. But why should positions which are simultaneously bourgeois and proletarian be viewed as 'contradictory' in any sense? The rationale is that the basic class relation of capitalism generates objectively contradictory *interests* for workers and capitalists, interests which are intrinsically (rather than just contingently) opposed to each other. Contradictory locations are contradictory precisely in the sense that they partake of both sides of these inherently contradictory interests. The characterization of such positions as 'contradictory' therefore does not deny the basic contradiction of capitalist class relations; it is derived from that basic contradiction.

The actual process by which this new concept was formed began as a problem of formally operationalizing class locations within the statistical study of income inequality discussed earlier. We had two pieces of data in that initial project which we used to operationalize classes: (1) whether the individual was self-employed; and (2) whether the individual supervised the labour of others. With two criteria, each of which had two values, we immediately had a little four-fold table.

TABLE 2.1
Initial Typology of Class Structure in the Development of the Concept of Contradictory Class Locations

		SELF–EMPLOYED	
		Yes	No
SUPERVISE THE LABOUR OF OTHERS	Yes	Capitalists	Managers
	No	Petty Bourgeois	Workers

The diagonal cells in the table (upper-left and lower-right) posed no problem: self-employed people who supervised others were capitalists (typically quite small); employees without subordinates were workers. And self-employed without subordinates also fell nicely into a conventional Marxian category: the petty bourgeoisie. But what about the non-self-employed with subordinates? In the first presentations of the research we referred to such managerial positions as having an 'ambiguous' class character, neither fish nor fowl. In a seminar discussion of the conceptual framework, the suggestion was made that this was not quite precise: such positions were really *both* fish and fowl, and therefore they should be seen as internally contradictory rather than ambiguous.[30]

That shift in labels—from ambiguous locations to contradictory locations—was the crucial step in the development of the new concept. 'Ambiguity' suggests that the problem is taxonomic: some people don't fit the slots properly; 'contradictoriness', on the other hand, suggests that the slots themselves have a complex character that can be identified as internally contradictory and given a positive theoretical status.

In the earliest formulations of contradictory locations, the only such location discussed was that of managers, a location characterized as simultaneously bourgeois and proletarian. Managers were considered bourgeois in that they had the capacity to tell workers what to do, to punish them for doing their jobs improperly and in various other ways being directly involved in central decisions concerning the process of production; they were proletarian, on the other hand, because they were themselves told what to do and could be fired by their employers and because they were excluded from basic control over the flow of resources into production itself (i.e. they were non-owners of capital assets). In their relation to workers as positions of domination they were in the bourgeoisie; in their relation to capitalists as positions of subordination, they were in the working class.

Two features of this initial construction seemed unsatisfactory. First, the specification of 'managers' as a contradictory location seemed too undifferentiated. Within this category were simple line supervisors and top executives, positions which involved vastly different kinds of control not just 'degrees' of control. Some further elaboration seemed necessary in order to have a more nuanced class map of the contradictory locations of managers. Secondly, there were positions which did not meet the criterion of supervising/controlling the labour of others which did not correspond to an intuitive idea of the working class. A wide range of technical and professional jobs, both in the capitalist firms and the state, are usually viewed as 'middle class' but do not involve supervision.

In this context I re-read a number of theoretical works by followers of Althusser which deal with problems of class analysis, particularly Balibar's essay 'The Basic Concepts of Historical Materialism' and Poulantzas's books, *Political Power and Social Classes* and *Classes in Contemporary Capitalism.*[31] Although not designed to be used in quite this way, Balibar's discussion of the distinction between 'ownership' and 'possession' of the means of production proved particularly helpful in furthering the elaboration of the concept of contradictory locations. Balibar used this distinction as a way of specifying the core differences between different modes of production, but in the context of my attempts at refining contradictory locations, the distinction suggested a way of differentiating categories within the general managerial contradictory location. In my use of Balibar's distinction, I defined 'ownership' as real control over investments (the flow of financial resources into and out of production); 'possession', on the other hand, referred to control over the actual operation of the means of production. Such control, I argued, could itself be broken down into two dimensions: control over the physical means of production as such, and control over labour within production (authority or supervision).

Capitalists could now be defined as positions of control over investments, the physical means of production and labour; workers were positions excluded from all three kinds of control. Various kinds of managers could then be specified, depending upon the specific combinations of these three criteria.

On further reflection, however, this extension of the initial criteria still did not go far enough. Clearly, with respect to each of the 'resources' in the three dimensions of control—money, physical means of production, labour—it was not true that a position either did or did not involve control. Because different positions were structured into a complex hierarchy of domination relations, they also involved different 'amounts' of control. Some supervisors could only issue warnings to subordinates; others could fire subordinates; and still others could control the authority hierarchy as such, not just their immediate subordinates. Some managers made decisions only on the day-to-day operation of production processes; others were involved in basic decisions on the kinds of technology to use. To map the texture of the contradictory location between capital and labour properly, some account of such 'levels' of control was needed.[32]

This led to the much more complex formalization of the class criteria that appeared in the theoretical essay that publicly introduced the concept 'contradictory locations'.[33] There were three criteria or dimensions of class relations—relations of control over money capital, physical capital and labour—and several 'levels' of control within each of these relations—full, partial, minimal and none. Workers and capitalists were defined by perfect polarization along all three of these dimensions; managers ranged from having full or partial control over some, but not all, of the dimensions (top executives) to having no control over money capital and physical capital and only partial or minimal control over labour (foremen and line supervisors).

This elaboration of the formal criteria for contradictory locations also provided the initial solution to the second general problem with the first formulation—namely, the specification of the class character of non-managerial technical and professional jobs. Whereas managers were characterized as simultaneously bourgeois and proletarian, such technical/professional positions were generally characterized as simultaneously petty-bourgeois and proletarian: they were proletarian in that they were separated from the means of production, had to sell their labour power for a wage and were controlled by capital within production; but they were petty-bourgeois because, I argued, they had real control over their own immediate labour process within production.

How should such real control over the immediate labour process be formally specified? In the early formulations I moved back and forth between three different specifications: (1) Control over one's immediate labour process should be considered a minimal level of control over *labour*, the third dimension of class relations (i.e. control over one's own labour); (2) It should be considered a minimal level of control over one's own *physical means of production* (i.e. control over how one does one's job); (3) It should be considered a minimal level of control over *investments* (i.e. control over what one produces, not just how one produces).[34] None of these seemed entirely satisfactory, but I finally settled for seeing effective control over one's labour process as control over what one produces and how one produces it, but exclusion from control over what other people produce and how they produce it. This seemed to characterize the situation of research scientists, some designers, teachers and a variety of other technical and professional positions. For want of a better name, such positions were referred to as 'semi-autonomous class locations'.

One final contradictory location remained to be specified, the one which combined bourgeois and petty-bourgeois classes. This location I identified with small employers: positions within which the owner of the means of production was simultaneously a self-employed direct producer (and thus in the petty bourgeoisie) and an employer of wage-labour (and thus in the capitalist class).

The result of these elaborations was the 'class map' illustrated in figure 2.2. While I subsequently made various modifications in this picture—adding a position called 'non-managerial technocrats' between managers and semi-autonomous employees and adding 'franchise operators' between small employers and managers—this diagram remained the basic representation of the reformulated concept of class structure which I proposed.[35]

This was as far as the development of the concept of contradictory

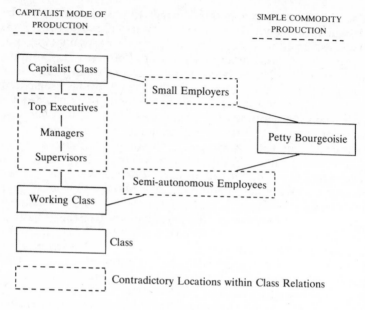

CAPITALIST MODE OF
PRODUCTION

SIMPLE COMMODITY
PRODUCTION

Capitalist Class

Small Employers

Top Executives
|
Managers
|
Supervisors

Petty Bourgeoisie

Semi-autonomous Employees

Working Class

Class

Contradictory Locations within Class Relations

FIGURE 2.2
Basic Class Map of Capitalist Society

locations had gone by 1979. At that time I embarked on a large empirical project on class structure, class experience and class consciousness. The heart of the research involved developing a survey questionnaire which opertionalized the class criteria in my proposed class map of advanced capitalist societies together with a wide range of other variables (measuring alternative concepts of class, class consciousness, class biographies, gender attitudes, and other things). This questionnaire was then given to random samples of the working population of a number of advanced capitalist societies.[36] At the end of all of my previously published empirical work I had always bemoaned the fact that the data used in my statistical investigations had been gathered by bourgeois sociologists and economists, using non-Marxist categories. While this provided me with a convenient excuse for problems in my own analyses, I felt that it would be useful to generate a substantial body of statistical data explicitly gathered within a Marxist framework.

Once I began the task of trying to formulate specific questions to operationalize my proposed class concepts, it became very clear that in certain important ways they remained vague or incomplete. In particular, the 'semi-autonomous employee' location was impossible to operationalize in a rigorous manner. This practical difficulty stimulated a rethinking of the logic of this category.

The rethinking of the category 'semi-autonomous employees' coincided with my initial work on a paper on post-capitalist societies, eventually published as 'Capitalism's Futures'.[37] At the heart of the analysis of that paper was a discussion of what I termed the 'inter-penetration' of modes of production, i.e. forms of production relations which combine aspects from distinct modes of production in a systematic way. This concept was important for rigorously specifying the tendencies towards post-capitalist societies generated within capitalism itself.

The concept of interpenetration of distinct relations of production also had a bearing on the persistent problem of properly defining semi-autonomous employees. In all of the earlier work I had specified a set of criteria for class relations and then defined particular class locations and contradictory locations by their values on this *common* set of criteria. But if certain classes are defined by *different* types of production relations (modes of production), then different criteria are clearly needed. Feudal serfs, for example, could not be defined by values based on capitalist criteria. A criterion specifying relations of personal bondage would be needed, a criterion which is absent from the specification of any class in the capitalist mode of production.

In other words, the global concept of 'contradictory locations within class relations' needed to be formally differentiated into two distinct sub-concepts: contradictory locations within a mode of production, and contradictory locations between modes of production.[38] In the former case, contradictory locations can be specified within a single set of criteria; in the latter, the contradictory character of the location requires two distinct sets of criteria, each rooted in different production relations.

This re-conceptualization meant that to define properly the category of semi-autonomous employees we had to specify the appropriate criteria for the petty bourgeoisie, i.e. for the class determined within simple commodity production. The necessary clarification to accomplish this task came out of my debate with John Roemer over the role of domination in the concept of classes.[39] As a result of that debate I was convinced that the central defining criterion for the social relations of production, which in

TABLE 2.2
Developed typology of Class Structure

	Capitalist Mode of Production				Simple Commodity Production	
	Domination		Appropriation		Domination	Appropriation
	Dominant	Subordinate	exploiter	exploited	self-direction within the labour process	individual self-appropriation of surplus
Bourgeoisie	+	−	+	−		
Top managers	+	+	+	+		
Lower managers and supervisors	+	+	−	+		
Workers	−	+	−	+		
Semi-autonomous Employees	−	+	−	+	+	−
Petty Bourgeoisie					+	+
Small Employers	+	−	+	−	+	+

+ = criterion present
− = criterion absent

Bourgeoisie: Basic Class Location
Top managers: Contradictory Locations within Class Relations

turn provides the basis for defining classes was the unity of appropriation relations and domination relations.[40] This led to a simplification of my original criteria for capitalist class relations from three to two. I now felt that control over the operation of the physical means of production and direct control over work should be treated as two alternative mechanisms of domination of workers, rather than two dimensions of class relations with equivalent conceptual status to control over investments. Classes, and accordingly contradictory locations, are therefore to be defined by their position within particular types of appropriation and domination relations.

In these terms, the problem became one of specifying appropriation and domination relations within simple commodity production. I took the appropriation relations to be unproblematic, defined by individual appropriation of the product of one's own labour (i.e. self-employment).[41] Domination relations within simple commodity production were, in a parallel manner, defined as self-control, (i.e. the individual self-direction within the labour process). Such 'self-direction' in operational terms was the ability to put one's own ideas into practice within work, or in traditional Marxian language, the 'unity of conception and execution'.[42]

This meant that semi-autonomous employees were now defined as positions which did not involve self-appropriation of the product of labour (i.e. they were capitalistically exploited) but did involve self-direction within work (i.e. they were not capitalistically dominated in that they retained an effective unity of conception and execution). It was still a difficult task to operationalize this criterion but the concept had more precision than earlier versions had.

These modifications lead to the final version of the class typology of contradictory locations represented in Table 2.2. This is a long way from the initial, simple four-fold table which began the story of contradictory locations. And, as we shall see, there were sufficient remaining problems with the conceptual framework that eventually I became convinced that it in turn needed to be superseded.

Problems With the Conceptualization

The concept of contradictory locations within class relations was, I believe, an advance over the alternative ways of dealing with the problem of the 'middle class' in advanced capitalist societies. Both in terms of the explanatory agenda for the concept of class and in terms of the abstract structural properties of the concept, it fared better than its rivals. Yet, from the start there were problems. Some of these were apparent quite early; others became clear only in the course of the development and use of the concept, particularly in the context of my empirical investigations. Four of these problems were particularly significant: the claim that contradictory locations are contradictory; the status of 'autonomy' as a criterion for class; the relevance of the concept of contradictory locations for post-capitalist societies; the marginalization of the concept of exploitation in the concept of class.

(1) The Contradictoriness of Contradictory Locations. From the first publication using the concept of contradictory locations, the use of the term 'contradiction' has been criticized.[43] In the case of managers a plausible story can be told. If we accept the characterization of managerial positions as combining relational properties of proletarian and bourgeois class locations, and if we accept the general Marxist thesis that the objective interests of workers and capitalists are intrinsically antagonistic, then at a minimum it makes sense to describe the interests of managers as internally inconsistent. Because of the systematic character of this inconsistency, it would not be unreasonable to characterize it as contradictory as well.

But why in the world should semi-autonomous employees be viewed as having internally inconsistent interests? To say that semi-autonomous employees have contradictory (rather than simply heterogeneous) interests is to imply that the proletarian pole of their class location generates interests that contradict those generated by the petty-bourgeois pole of their location. Presumably this petty-bourgeois pole defines interests in the preservation of autonomy within the labour process. By virtue of what does autonomy within the labour process define objective interests that contradict working-class interests? The only answer I could provide was to say that workers had interests in the *collective* control over the labour process—collective autonomy if you will—which was opposed to the individualized autonomy of semi-autonomous employees. This, however, was unsatisfactory since collective control over the labour process is not necessarily opposed to significant spheres of individual control over one's own work.

A similar problem exists for the small-employer contradictory location, the location which combines petty-bourgeois and capitalist classes. While it may be that small employers have specific immediate interests opposed to large capitalists when those large capitalists compete with them, it is not obvious that they have any fundamental interests that are necessarily opposed.[44] They may face various kinds of dilemmas in competing successfully in a world of large corporations, but this does not obviously imply that they have internally contradictory basic interests.

What I have called 'contradictory locations within class relations', therefore, may be 'dual', or 'heterogeneous' locations, but except in the case of managers and supervisors, they are not obviously 'contradictory' locations. The term could therefore be retained for what I called contradictory locations *within* modes of production, but seems less appropriate for contradictory locations between modes of production.

(2) *Autonomy as a Class Criterion.* A second problem with the elaboration of contradictory locations centres on the category 'semi-autonomous employees'. Three issues seem especially troubling: the claim that autonomy is a 'petty-bourgeois' property of class relations; the relatively unstable or underdetermined character of autonomy in certain work settings; and empirical anomalies in the use of the concept.

Even if we accept provisionally the idea that autonomy is an aspect of class relations, does it make sense to treat autonomy as having a 'petty-bourgeois' class character? There are both structural and historical objections to this characterization.

Structurally, the characterization of autonomy as 'petty bourgeois' rests largely on what may be a rather romantic image of the petty bourgeoisie as independent direct producers characterized by a 'unity of conception and execution'.[45] The contrast between independent producers (self-employed artisans, craftspersons, shop-keepers, farmers, etc.) with such autonomy and proletarian wage-labourers without such autonomy may simply be incorrect. On the one hand, for a variety of reasons, self-employed petty-bourgeois producers may have little choice over how they produce or, in some circumstances, even over what they produce. Their options are constrained by markets, by credit institutions, by long-term contracts with capitalist enterprises, and so on. On the other hand, it is easy to exaggerate the extent to which workers in modern capitalist firms are indeed fully separated from 'conception', since in many factory settings the actual operation of production continues to depend heavily on a wide range of accumulated knowledge on the shop floor, knowledge which must constantly be applied in non-routinized ways.[46] Such autonomy, therefore, may not have a distinctively 'petty bourgeois' character at all. The only thing which defines the petty bourgeois is ownership of certain kinds of *assets*—land, tools, a few machines, perhaps in some cases 'skills' or credentials—and self-employment, but not work autonomy.[47]

The characterization of work autonomy as petty-bourgeois is also very problematic when looked at historically. The semi-autonomous employee category contains two quite distinct sorts of positions: highly autonomous craft wage-earners, and professional-technical wage-earners. The former could plausibly be considered combinations of petty-bourgeois and proletarian classes, since the independent artisan is an historical antecedent to the modern craft worker. It makes less sense to see a research scientist, a university professor, an industrial engineer or a social welfare counsellor as having a petty-bourgeois character combining elements from the capitalist mode of production and simple commodity production. The kinds of autonomy that occur within contemporary bureaucratically organized institutions cannot be treated as remnants of 'simple commodity production', but this is what is implied by treating semi-autonomous class locations as combinations of proletarian and petty-bourgeois classes.

A second problem with semi-autonomy as a class criterion is what could be called its structural underdetermination. Whether or not a given job is 'semi-autonomous' could easily be a consequence of rather contingent characteristics of the work setting. For example, a research technician could move from a job where the scientist in charge assumed that technicians were incompetent and thus gave them no responsibilities, to a laboratory in which the scientist was lazy and left a great deal of discretion and decision-making up to the technicians. In the second job the technician would probably be classified as semi-autonomous; in the former as proletarianized. Should such a shift in jobs be viewed as a change in the *class* character of the technician-position? Is the former position purely working class while the latter, semi-petty bourgeois? The concept of class is meant to designate fairly stable and structurally determinate properties of locations within the social relations of production. At a minimum, the seemingly contingent character of autonomy in certain jobs is a weakness in the claim that autonomy is a class criterion.[48]

A final problem with autonomy as a class criterion revolves

round a number of empirical anomalies that have emerged in the course of the empirical research involving the concept. For example, if autonomy is defined in terms of control over what one produces and how one produces it, then many janitors in schools who also perform a variety of 'handyman' tasks will end up being more autonomous than airline pilots. Now, one could regard this as a deep discovery about the nature of the class location of pilots, in spite of its apparently counter-intuitive character. It is more plausible that it indicates the problematic status of the claim that autonomy should be viewed as a basic criterion for class.

3) *Classes in Post-capitalist Societies.* Classical Marxism was absolutely unequivocal about the historical prognosis for capitalism: socialism—and ultimately communism—was the future of capitalist societies. The bearer of that necessary future was the working class. The polarized class structure between the bourgeoisie and the proletariat within capitalism thus paralleled the polarized historical alternatives *between* capitalism and socialism.

The actual historical experience of the twentieth century has called into question, although not unambiguously refuted, this historical vision, and it is thus necessary at least to entertain the possibility of post-capitalist class structures. The difficulty is that with few exceptions, the conceptual frameworks adopted by Marxists for analysing classes in capitalist societies do not contain adequate criteria for systematically understanding post-capitalist classes. Whereas in the analysis of feudal societies, the classes of capitalism appear as emergent classes, there is very little theoretical work which either systematically conceptualizes post-capitalist classes or shows how they emerge within capitalist societies.[49] The result is a tendency for discussions of postcapitalist class structures—the class structures of 'actually existing socialisms'—to have a very ad hoc character to them.

The concept of contradictory locations within class relations as I had developed it was particularly vulnerable to this criticism. All of the class categories in my analysis were either situated firmly within capitalist relations (bourgeoisie, managers, workers) or in contradictory locations involving relations that were basically pre-capitalist (semi-autonomous employees, the petty bourgeoisie and small employers). What was perhaps even worse, the formal operational criteria used in much of the empirical analysis of classes could be applied to either capitalist or 'actually existing socialist

societies' almost without modification.[50] There were no ele
ments within this analysis of class relations which could give an
real specificity to the class structures of post-capitalist societies c
point the direction for the analysis of the emergence of post
capitalist classes within capitalism. Now, it could be argued tha
this empirical insensitivity of the operational criteria for classes t
the differences between West and East reflects the basic similarit
of their real class structures, and thus is a strength rather than
weakness. However, since I do not in fact believe that state
socialist societies are 'really' capitalist, this insensitivity remains
significant problem.

(4) *The Shift from Exploitation to Domination.* Throughout th
development of the concept of contradictory class locations
insisted that this was a reformulation of a distinctively Marxis
class concept. As part of the rhetoric of such an enterprise,
affirmed the relationship between class and exploitation.

Nevertheless, in practice the concept of contradictory location
within class relations rested almost exclusively on relations c
domination rather than exploitation. Reference to exploitatio
functioned more as a background concept to the discussion c
classes than as a constitutive element of the analysis of class struc
tures. Managers, for example, were basically defined as a cor
tradictory location because they were simultaneously dominato
and dominated. Relations of domination were also decisiv
in defining the class character of 'semi-autonomous em
ployees'—locations which, I argued, were simultaneously petty
bourgeois and proletarian by virtue of their self-direction withi
the labour process—since 'autonomy' defines a condition wit
respect to domination. This same tendency to substitute domina
tion for exploitation at the core of the concept of class is found i
most other neo-Marxist conceptualizations of class structure.

For some people, of course, marginalizing the concept of exploi
tation is a virtue, not a sin. My own view, however, is that this is
serious weakness for two reasons. First, the shift to a dominatior
centred concept of class weakens the link between the analysis c
class locations and the analysis of objective interests. The concep
of 'domination' does not, in and of itself, imply that the actors hav
any specific interests. Parents dominate small children, but th
does not imply that parents and children have intrinsicall
opposed interests. What would make those interests antagonistic
if the relation of parents to children were also exploitative. Explo

ation intrinsically implies a set of opposing material interests. Second, domination-centred concepts of class tend to slide into the 'multiple oppressions' approach to understanding society. Societies, in this view, are characterized by a plurality of oppressions each of which are rooted in a different form of domination—sexual, racial, national, economic, etc.—none having any explanatory priority over any other. Class, then, becomes just one of many oppressions, with no particular centrality to social and historical analysis.[51] Again, this displacement of class from the centre stage may be viewed as an achievement rather than a problem. However, if one wants to retain the traditional centrality Marxism has accorded to the concept of class, then the domination-centred concept of class does pose real problems.

Of these four conceptual problems—the contradictoriness of contradictory locations, the status of autonomy, the absence of an analysis of postcapitalist societies and the displacement of exploitation by domination in the concept of class—the fourth one seems to me to be the most fundamental. In one way or another, each of the other issues is tied up with marginalization of exploitation.

Given a recognition of this situation, there are two main theoretical alternatives that could be pursued. One possibility is to celebrate the shift to a domination-centred concept and use this new class concept as the basis for analysing both capitalist and post-capitalist society. This would lead class analysis firmly in the direction of Dahrendorf's analysis of classes as positions within authority relations.[52] A second alternative is to attempt to restore exploitation to the centre of class analysis in such a way that it can both accommodate the empirical complexities of the 'middle class' within capitalism and the historical reality of post-capitalist class structures. I will persue this second course of action in the next chapter.

Notes

1. The analysis below will not discuss the practical task of producing and transforming concepts, only the logic of engaging in this task. For a brief discussion of a range of practical strategies that can be used in the process of concept formation, see appendix I at the end of this book.
2. All scientific activity also takes place, of course, under social constraints (institutional constraints from the scientific establishment, economic constraints on the freedom of theorists, etc.). While these may be of tremendous importance for

explaining why certain concepts emerge when they do, my concern here is with the methodological issues in the formation of concepts, not the sociological problems of the production of knowledge.

3. The fact that real-world constraints operate through concepts has sometimes led people to treat the constraint imposed by empirical investigation as identical to the constraint imposed by the general theoretical framework, since both operate, in a sense, 'in thought'. This, I think, is a mistake. Even though there is not a one-to-one relationship between the way the world 'really is' and the data of an empirical investigation (since that data is gathered through pre-given concepts), the data is constrained by real mechanisms in the world. If the world were different, the data would be different, just as the data would be different if the concepts were different. This implies that the empirical constraint on concept formation—the constraint imposed by the fact that concepts must directly or indirectly figure in explanations of empirical phenomena—can be viewed as a mediated constraint of the real world itself.

4. As I am using the term, empiricism is not simply the absence of such self-conscious theoretical constraints, but a methodological stance that proscribes the elaboration of such constraints. In the development of most theories there are sub-areas that do not operate under highly systematized, explicit theoretical constraints, where the investigations are undertheorized and largely descriptive. This is only a problem, as opposed to a stage of development, if the procedures adopted within the theory prevent the further development of the theoretical structure.

5. It should be noted that there is no absolute virtue in scientific concepts over other sorts of concepts—aesthetic concepts, moral concepts, theological concepts etc. Theoreticism and empiricism, defined in the above manner, are sins only with respect to the objective of producing concepts for scientific purposes, i.e. concepts which can figure in explanations of the real world.

6. The disputes in question are therefore not simply terminological debates over how to use *words*. One could decide, for example, that the word 'bureaucracy' was to be used to describe any complex organization. The problem of concept adjudication would then concern the appropriate criteria for defining a 'complex organization', the theoretical object to which the word 'bureaucracy' was to be applied. Alternatively, following Weber's usage, the term bureaucracy could be reserved for a particular kind of complex organization, one organized strictly along principles of formal rationality. The debate would then be over the appropriate criteria for specifying the properties of such an organization.

7. Depending upon the levels of abstraction involved and the scope of theoretical objects being brought into question, such theory adjudication can take place within a single general theory (as in the perennial theoretical debates within Marxism) or between general theories.

8. Dogmatism is sometimes confused with a systematic application of theoretical requirements. Faithfulness to a theoretical structure in the formation of concepts, however, only becomes dogmatic when the theoretical structure is viewed as inviolable.

9. The initial paper from this research was written in 1973 and published in 1977. Erik Olin Wright and Luca Peronne, 'Marxist Class Categories and Income Inequality', *American Sociological Review*, vol. 42, no. 1, February 1977. The research eventually culminated in my dissertation and was published as *Class structure and Income Determination*, New York 1979.

10. See especially the introduction to E. P. Thompson, *The Making of the English Working Class*, Harmondsworth 1968. For a careful critique of Thompson's

rejection of the structural definition of classes, see G. A. Cohen, *Karl Marx's Theory of History: A Defence,* Oxford 1978, pp. 73–77.

11. For an extremely interesting discussion of this problem, see Claus Offe and Helmut Wiesenthal, 'Two Logics of Collective Action', in Maurice Zeitlin, ed, *Political Power and Social Theory,* vol. 1, Greenwich, Conneticut 1980.

12. See *Class, Crisis and the State*, pp. 15–29, 102–108, for a discussion of such models of determination.

13. For a defence of the technological determinist version of this constraint, see G. A. Cohen, *Karl Marx's Theory of History.* For a critique of Cohen's position relevant to the present discussion, see Andrew Levine and Erik Olin Wright, 'Rationality and Class Struggle', *New Left Review*, 123, 1980, pp. 47–68.

14. See Erik Olin Wright, 'Gidden's Critique of Marxism', *New Left Review*, 139, 1983, for an elaboration of this argument.

15. In recent years there has been a productive debate among Marxists over this functional form of class reductionism. This debate has been particularly sparked by the discussions around G. A. Cohen's *Karl Marx's Theory of History*, although earlier discussions of 'structuralist' Marxism of the Althusserian school raised many of the same issues of functionalism and functional explanation. For an interesting set of exchanges over these issues, see Jon Elster, 'Marxism, Functionalism and Game Theory', and G. A. Cohen, 'Reply to Elster', *Theory and Society*, vol. 11, no. 3, July 1982. For a useful non-Marxist assessment of Marxian functionalism, see Anthony Giddens, *A Contemporary Critique of Historical Materialism*, Berkeley California 1982.

16. For a more systematic defence of this thesis, see Erik Olin Wright, 'Capitalism's Futures', *Socialist Review*, no. 18, March–April 1983.

17. Such a claim, however, may still maintain that it is transformations of class relations—the development of advanced forms of capitalist production accompanied by emerging elements of state production—that explains why it is that the elimination of institutionalized forms of male domination has become historically possible (if indeed it has).

18. I say 'almost' trivial, because it is not necessarily the case that any kind of struggle 'explains' trajectories; trajectories of change could be explained by processes other than struggle: cultural diffusion, technical change which does not play itself out through conflict, etc. Still, effect-definitions of class struggle make the theoretical content of the proposition much less substantial than agency or objectives definitions.

19. At first glance it might seem that the use of the term 'class' to describe the petty bourgeoisie (self-employed commodity producers who employ no wage labor) is an exception to this. Even in this case, however, the concept is still basically relational, for the petty bourgeoisie is a class only in so far as petty-bourgeois producers engage in systematic exchange relations with other classes. If *all* producers were in fact petty bourgeois (a situation that has never occurred historically) then they would cease to be a 'class' in the proper sense of the term.

20. The contrast between relational and gradational notions of class was made forcefully in slightly different terms by Stanislaus Ossowski in *Class Structure in the Social Consciousness*, London 1963. For an extended discussion of this distinction which bears directly on the present analysis, see Erik Olin Wright, *Class Structure and Income Determination,* chapter 1.

21. It is noteworthy in this regard that theorists who adopt gradational notions of class structure tend to treat class in an extremely ahistorical manner. All societies have 'upper' and 'lower' classes, and gradational accounts of class tend to treat

these terms as having the same meaning regardless of historically specific features of the society. Thus, for example, Seymour Martin Lipset, in *Political Man*, Garden City, N.J. 1963, p. 311, argues that the relationship between 'status or class position' and party loyalty in the United States has been essentially the same since the late 18th century: in all cases the upper classes tended to support the more conservative party while the lower classes the more 'liberal'. This of course ignores the vast transformation of what kinds of actors were in the 'lower' classes and how this affected the content of what was 'liberal': the proletarianized worker of 1980 and the small farmer of 1800 are in qualitatively different relational classes, and this has systematic consequences for the content of the politics of the two periods and the forms of political conflict, even though both were 'lower' class.

22. See chapter 3 below for a more elaborate discussion of this conceptualization of exploitation. It should be noted that at the time of the development of the concept of contradictory class locations I accepted a much more classic conceptualization of exploitation based directly on the labour theory of value. That is, I saw exploitation as a relationship in which one class appropriated the surplus labour of another, which in capitalism meant appropriating surplus value. While I now prefer the more general characterization of exploitation offered here, the basic arguments in this chapter do not depend upon which characterization of exploitation is adopted.

23. This formulation obviously side-steps a number of difficult issues, in particular the definitions of material well-being and toil. While in the end there may be an irreducibly subjective element in defining the specific content of each of these, nevertheless I believe that there is sufficient continuity of meaning of these terms across contexts that it is reasonable to treat exploitation and the interests structured by exploitation as having an objective status.

24. The expression 'professional-managerial class' (or PMC) was introduced in an influencial article in the American Left by Barbara and John Ehrenreich, 'The Professional-Managerial Class', *Radical America*, vol. 11, no. 2, 1971. This article along with a series of critical responses has been reprinted in a book edited by Pat Walker, *Between Capital and Labor*, Boston 1979. The expression 'new class' has a longer pedigree, but most recently has been associated with the writings of Alvin Gouldner and Ivan Szelenyi. See Alvin Gouldner, *The Future of Intellectuals and the Rise of the New Class*, New York 1979, and George Konrad and Ivan Szelenyi Intellectuals on the Road to Class Power, New York 1979; Ivan Szelenyi and Robert Manchin, 'Social Policy and State Socialism', in G. Esping-Anderson, L. Rainwater and M. Rein, eds., *Stagnation and Renewal in Social Policy*, White Plains 1985.

25. See Erik Olin Wright, 'Varieties of Marxist Conceptions of Class Structure, *Politics & Society*, vol. 9, no. 3, 1980.

26. Examples of this position include Carles Loren, *Classes in the United States* Davis, California 1977; Francesca Freedman, 'The Internal Structure of the Proletariat: a Marxist Analysis', *Socialist Revolution*, no. 26, 1975; and James F Becker, 'Class Structure and Conflict in the Managerial Phase', *Science & Society* vol. 37, nos. 3 and 4, 1973 and 1974.

27. See especially *Classes in Contemporary Capitalism*, London 1975. For a detailed exposition and critique of Poulantzas's work on classes, see *Class, Crisi and the State*, chapter two.

28. This may mean that we should abandon these two criteria and allow social relations of reproduction or cultural production to become the basis for specifying certain classes. This would certainly constitute a major reconstruction of the Marx

ist concept of class, but perhaps it is a necessary reconstruction. In any event, none of the theorists who have advanced the concept of the 'new class' have attempted such a general reconstruction. It should be noted here that the new reformulation of the problem of class elaborated in chapter three below is much more friendly to 'new class' approaches than my original concept of contradictory class locations.

29. G. Carchedi, in his book, *The Economic Identification of Social Classes*, London 1977, developed a similar conceptualization, although he preferred to label such positions 'new middle class' and he treated their class determination as 'ambiguous' rather than calling it 'contradictory'. Nevertheless, the heart of his argument was that such positions were simultaneously bourgeois and proletarian in so far as they fulfilled both the functions of capital and the functions of labour. For a discussion of the differences between Carchedi's conceptualization and my own, see my essay, 'Varieties of Marxist Conceptions of Class Structure', pp. 355–365.

30. The actual suggestion for the shift in label came from the anthropologist Brigit O'Laughlin who then taught at Stanford University. Although it was tossed out in the discussion in the usual off-handed way that comments are made in academic seminars, it immediately sparked off a rapid clarification of the conceptual problem with which I was grappling. I doubt very much if O'Laughlin remembers her comment or is aware of the ramifications which it stimulated, but I remain grateful to her for it.

31. See Etienne Balibar, 'The Basic Concepts of Historical Materialism', in Louis Althusser and Etienne Balibar, *Reading Capital*, London 1970; Nicos Poulantzas, *Political Power and Social Classes*, London 1973 and *Classes in Contemporary Capitalism*, London 1975.

32. The term 'levels' in this context seemed to suggest an emergent gradational notion of class. The argument, however, was that the positions were defined by their location within a complex hierarchy of social relations. As a result of such relations, a given position involved certain capacities for decision-making and control over others. The degree of control was therefore posed as an indicator of a location within a complex pattern of relations.

33. 'Class Boundaries in Advanced Capitalist Societies', *New Left Review*, 98, 1976.

34. In the essay published in *New Left Review* in 1976, I adopted the second formulation; in the revised version appearing in *Class, Crisis and the State* I opted for both the second and the third. The formulation in terms of minimal control over labour was entertained, but never appeared in print.

35. The formal typology which provided the criteria for this class map appears as Tables 2.7, 2.8 and 2.9 in *Class, Crisis and the State*.

36. As of 1984, surveys have been completed in the United States, Finland, Sweden, Norway, Canada, New Zealand and Great Britain, and a regional survey has been completed in South Australia. Future surveys will be conducted in West Germany, Denmark and Australia, and possibly in Japan. The United States data are available from the Inter-University Consortium for Political and Social Research University of Michigan, Ann Arbor. The comparative data will be available from ICPSR in 1986.

37. The first version of 'Capitalism's Futures' was written during the summer of 1979 and presented at a conference at the University of Toronto in December of that year. The revised version of the paper was published in *Socialist Review*, 68, 1983.

38. Two brief terminological points: first, strictly speaking the second type of location is not 'between' modes of production, but combines elements from distinct

modes of production. The spatial metaphor is potentially misleading here, as it is in general in discussions of classes. Second, I am using the expression 'mode of production' non-rigorously here to describe any distinct form of production relations, not simply those forms which can become dominant within a social formation. Most Marxist theorists do not refer to simple commodity production—the production relations within which the petty bourgeoisie is determined—as a 'mode' of production, but simply a 'form' of production. For present purposes this nuance is not important.

39. See John Roemer, *A General Theory of Exploitation and Class*, Cambridge, Massachusetts 1982, and the special issue of the journal *Politics & Society*, vol. 11, no. 3, which deals with Roemer's work.

40. 'Appropriation relations' is a more general term than 'exploitation relations' and refers to the relations within which the social surplus is appropriated. When the surplus is appropriated by one class from another, appropriation relations become exploitation relations.

41. Since self-employed individuals often have part of the product of their labour appropriated by capital through credit relations and other forms of exchange relations, self-employment is obviously insufficient to define self-appropriation.

42. This formulation also owed a great deal to Harry Braverman's *Labor and Monopoly Capital*, New York 1974. Braverman's characterization of traditional artisanal, craft labor as embodying a unity of conception and execution comes very close to saying that such wage-earners are incompletely proletarianized, and thus in a contradictory class location combining petty-bourgeois (independent, self-employed artisanal labor) and proletarian elements.

43. See Stewart, et al., *Social Stratification and Occupations*, London 1980; J. M. Holmwood and A. Stewart, 'The Role of Contradiction in Modern Theories of Social Stratification', *Sociology*, no. 17, May 1983; Anthony Giddens, postscript to *The Class structure of the Advanced Societies*, second edition, New York 1979, p. 304.

44. The distinction between immediate and fundamental interests is between interests defined within a given set of 'rules of the game' (immediate interests) and interests over the basic rules themselves (fundamental interests). For a fuller discussion of this distinction, see *Class, Crisis and the State*, pp. 88–91.

45. This image is clearly indebted to the work of Harry Braverman on the degradation of labour. Even though Braverman's work has come under increasing attack in recent years for minimizing class struggle, for seeing degradation as too monolithic a process, for romanticizing traditional artisanal labour, and so on, I feel that his essential intuition remains sound, namely that proletarianization is a process both of dispossession of ownership of the means of production and of loss of real control over the means of production.

46. See David Noble, 'Social Choice in Machine Design', *Politics and Society*, vol. 8, no. 3–4, 1978, for an interesting discussion of how workers retain substantial involvement over 'conception' even under conditions of high automation.

47. If one wanted to maintain the characterization of autonomy as petty bourgeois, the above observations could be interpreted as suggesting that there are two, not one, kind of contradictory location combining proletarian and petty-bourgeois classes: semi-autonomous employees (petty-bourgeois autonomy within capitalist production) and semi-proletarianized self-employed (proletarian subordination within petty-bourgeois production). In the former case, the position occupies a proletarian location within appropriation relations but a petty bourgeois location within domination relations; in the latter, the position occupies a petty-

burgeois location within appropriation relations and a proletarian location within domination relations.

48. One possible line of defence against this criticism would be to argue that the unit of analysis is not the specific job actually held by a given individual, but rather the general properties of a given occupational category. In the technician example above it could be argued that the technician *occupation* is characterized structurally by its potential for individual autonomy, but that the actual level of autonomy empirically manifested in a given technician *job* depends upon relatively contingent processes, such as the personality of the research director of the laboratory, the particular training or interests of the particular technician, etc. By this reasoning technician positions might generally be considered semi-autonomous even if a particular laboratory technician is uninterested in acting autonomously or is unable to do so because of his or her personal relations to superiors. Such an approach to the problem of autonomy, however, poses a host of additional problems, particularly the problem of how to draw meaningfully the boundaries between occupations and how to define 'potential' autonomy.

49. The exception to this are certain analyses of the 'new class'—such as Alvin Gouldner's *The Future of Intellectuals* and Ivan Szelenyi and William Martin's *New Class Theories and Beyond* (unpublished manuscript), 1985—which do suggest at least some elements of how classes within capitalism can be analysed in a way which allows for post-capitalist class structures.

50. The realization that the operational criteria for classes in my analysis of the United States could be applied to state socialist societies with very little modification came in the course of a comparative investigation of the United States and Hungary with the Hungarian sociologist, Robert Manchin. Manchin was the first person to point out to me the unfavorable implications of this for my conceptualization of the class structure of capitalist society.

51. This multiple-oppressions view of society within which class has no necessary centrality is characteristic of what is sometimes called 'post-Marxist' radical theory. Some of the leading proponents include Michael Albert and Robin Hahnel, *Marxism and Socialist Theory*, Boston 1981; Jean Cohen, *Class and Civil Society*, Amherst Massachusetts 1982; Stanley Aaronowitz, *The Crisis of Historical Materialism*, New York 1981.

52. See Ralph Dahrendorf, *Class and Class Conflict in Industrial Society*, Stanford 1959.

3

A General Framework for the Analysis of Class[1]

The previous chapter told the story of the development of the concept of contradictory locations within class relations. The account ended with a discussion of a number of important weaknesses within that concept and a general diagnosis of the source of the problem—the shift from exploitation to domination as the basis for class relations.

It is one thing to identify the weaknesses, inconsistencies and gaps in a particular array of concepts; it is quite another to reconstruct the concept to overcome these weaknesses. My dissatisfactions with the concept of contradictory locations accumulated for a long time before I saw any viable strategy for transforming it in a constructive way. It was only after an extended engagement with the work of John Roemer, particularly his work on the concept of exploitation, that I began to see a coherent solution to these problems.[2] While Roemer himself has not been particularly concerned with problems of empirical investigation or the elaboration of concrete maps of class structures, his work does nevertheless provide a rich foundation for such endeavours. As I will attempt to show, with suitable modification and extension, his analytical strategy can provide a much more consistent basis for the concept of contradictory class locations.

Roemer's Account of Class and Exploitation

THE CONCEPT OF EXPLOITATION

We observe inequalities in the distribution of incomes, the real consumption bundles available to individuals, families and groups.

The concept of exploitation is a particular way of analysing such inequalities. To describe an inequality as reflecting exploitation is to make the claim that there exists a particular kind of causal relationship between the incomes of different actors. More concretely, in Roemer's analysis the rich are said to exploit the poor when it can be established that the welfare of the rich causally depends upon the deprivations of the poor—the rich are rich *because* the poor are poor, they are rich at the expense of others.[3]

Note that this need not be the case for all inequalities. Suppose that two subsistence farmers each have land of the same quality, but one is lazy and works minimally on the land while the other is industrious. In this case there is no causal relationship between the affluence of the one and the poverty of the other. The rich farmer would not become worse off if the lazy farmer started working harder. To count as exploitation it must be demonstrated that one person's welfare is obtained at the expense of the other.

The traditional Marxist concept of exploitation is clearly a special case of this general concept. In Marxian exploitation one class appropriates the surplus labour performed by another class through various mechanisms. The income of the exploiting class comes from the labour performed by the exploited class. There is thus a straightforward causal link between the poverty of the exploited and the affluence of the exploiter. The former benefits at the expense of the latter.

Roemer has attempted to elaborate this view of exploitation using two strategies. The first of these involves studying in great detail the flows of 'surplus labour' from one category of actors to another in the course of various exchange relations; the second involves a kind of game theory approach to specifying different forms of exploitation. Let us briefly examine each of these in turn.

The Labour Transfer Approach. The analysis of labour transfers is an extension of the traditional Marxist view of exploitation, although Roemer self-consciously does not rely on the labour theory of value in order to explore such labour transfers.[4] The main target of his analysis is the view commonly held by Marxists that a necessary condition for the exploitation of labour in a market economy is the institution of wage labour. Roemer demonstrates two basic propositions: first, that exploitation (labour transfers) can occur in a situation in which all producers own their own means of production, but differ in the amount of physical assets which they own; and second, that there is complete symmetry in the structure of exploitation in a system in which capital hires wage labourers and in one in which workers rent capital.

Roemer demonstrates that exploitation can occur in an economy in which every producer owns his or her own means of production and in which there is no market in labour power and no borrowing (i.e. no credit market). The only things that are traded are products. In such an economy if different producers own different amounts of productive assets such that different producers have to work different numbers of hours to produce the exchange-equivalent of their own subsistence, then free trade among these producers will lead to exploitation of the asset-poor by the asset-rich. It is not simply that some producers work less than others for the same subsistence, but that the workers who work less are able to do so *because* the less-endowed producers have to work more. The critical proof in this example is that if the asset-poor person simply stopped producing—died—and the asset-rich person took over the asset-poor person's assets, then the asset-rich producer would have to work longer hours than before to maintain the same level of subsistence.[5] There is thus not merely an inequality among the producers in this economy, but exploitation as well.

In the analysis of exploitation in credit and labour markets, Roemer compares the class structures and patterns of exploitation on two imaginary islands, 'labour-market island' and 'credit market island'. On both islands some people own no means of production and other people own varying amounts of the means of production. The distribution of these assets is identical on the two islands. And on both islands people have the same motivations: they all seek to minimize the amount of labour-time they must expend to achieve a common level of subsistence. The two islands differ in only one respect: on the labour-market island people are allowed to sell their labour power, whereas on the credit-market island people are prohibited from selling their labour power but are allowed to borrow, at some interest rate, the means of production.

Roemer demonstrates two main theses using these models. First, he shows that on each island there is a strict correspondence between class location, exploitation status and the quantity of assets owned by individuals. This is what he terms the 'class-exploitation correspondence principle'. Table 3.1 illustrates this correspondence for 'labour-market island'. The logic of the table is as follows: each individual decides whether to hire labour power,

TABLE 3.1[a]
Assets Ownership, Exploitation and Class in Capitalism

Class	Hires labour power	Sells labour power	Works for self	Exploitation	Amount of assets
1. Capitalists	Yes	No	No	Exploiter	A great deal
2. Small Employer	Yes	No	Yes	Exploiter	Moderate
3. Petty Bourgeois	No	No	Yes	Ambiguous	Close to per capita share
4. Semi-proletarian	No	Yes	Yes	Exploited	Little
5. Proletarians	No	Yes	No	Exploited	None

[a]Adapted from John Roemer, *A General Theory of Exploitation and Class*, chapter 2.

to sell labour power or to work with the means of production he or she owns. Each individual makes this decision in order to minimize the amount of labour expended for a given amount of consumption. As a result of these decisions two things happen: first, people emerge as members of one of five classes, where classes are defined by distinctive locations within the social relations of production; and second, some people perform labour which is appropriated by others, some people appropriate the labour of others, and still others are neither exploiters nor exploited. The substantive result is that an exact correspondence exists between the two outcomes of the choices made by the actors.[6]

The second basic thesis Roemer derives from the analysis of these models is that their respective class structures are completely isomorphic: every individual on one island would have exactly the same exploitation status and class location on the other island.[7]

On the basis of these two propositions, Roemer argues that market-based exploitation and the class relations associated with it can be formally derived simply from inequalities in the distribution of property rights in the means of production. While historically these may typically emerge through the operation of a labour market, this is only one possible institutional form for such exploitation; it is not the necessary condition for the exploitation to occur.

The Game Theory Approach. The labour-transfer approach to studying exploitation and class is a powerful and compelling one under certain simplifying assumptions. It runs into difficulty, Roemer demonstrates, when some of these assumptions are relaxed. In particular, labour transfers become difficult to define coherently when the labour inputs into production are heterogeneous (i.e. of different degrees of productivity). Because of these complications, Roemer introduced a second strategy for exploring exploitation, a strategy rooted in 'game theory'. This approach, as we shall see, has a further advantage in that it allows for a particularly elegant way of characterizing the different mechanisms of exploitation in different types of class structures.

The basic idea of this approach is to compare different systems of exploitation by treating the organization of production as a 'game'. The actors in this game have various kinds of productive assets (i.e. resources such as skills and capital) which they bring into production and which they use to generate incomes on the basis of a specific set of rules. The essential strategy adopted for the analysis of exploitation is to ask if particular coalitions of players would be better off if they withdrew from this game under certain specified procedures in order to play a different one. The alternative games differ in the ways the assets are allocated. Different types of exploitation are defined by the particular withdrawal rules that would make certain agents better off and other agents worse off.

More formally, Roemer argues that a coalition of actors S can be said to be exploited, and another coalition S′ (the complement of S) can be said to be exploiting, if the following conditions hold:

'(1). There is an alternative, which we may conceive of as hypothetically feasible, in which S would be better off than in its present situation.

(2). Under this alternative, the complement to S, the coalition . . . S′, would be worse off than at present'[8]

Condition (1) is necessary, because it only makes sense to talk about exploitation if the exploited would be better off in the absence of exploitation (i.e. in the alternative game); Condition (2) is necessary, because in Roemer's words, 'it must be the case that the exploited coalition is exploited by other people, not by nature or technology'.[9]

By themselves, however, these two criteria are insufficient to define exploitation properly. In the absence of a third criterion of some sort, they create certain kinds of nonsensical exploitation verdicts. For example, on the basis of these two criteria alone one would have to describe as 'exploitative' a situation in which two islands existed, and there was no interaction between them, but where one of them had a great deal of capital and the other had little. If the citizens of the poor island withdrew from the 'game' with their per capita share of the total capital of the two islands, they would be better off and the citizens of the rich island worse off. But it hardly makes sense to describe the rich island as exploiting the poor island in such a case. Or, to take another example, when subsidies are given to the handicapped by the able-bodied, the two criteria cited above would suggest that the handicapped are exploiting the able-bodied. Again, this runs counter to the explanatory purpose of the concept.

Roemer has thus proposed a variety of possible supplementary criteria which are designed to rule out such cases. The most general of these is to add the criterion that 'S′ is in a relationship of dominance to S', where 'domination' in this context should be understood as implying that 'S′ prevents S from withdrawing to the alternative game'. The handicapped do not dominate the able-bodied and the rich island does not dominate the poor island in the above examples and thus these would no longer be considered examples of exploitation.[10] In his analysis of exploitation, Roemer basically treats this criterion as a kind of background condition, and focuses entirely on the operation of the first two in the elaboration of his formal mathematical models.

The purpose of these formal criteria is to provide a way of diagnosing economic inequalities in terms of exploitation and adjudicating disputes between people over whether or not exploitation exists in a given situation. When people disagree about whether or not a given category of actors is exploited, we can examine whether they differ over the choice of the appropriate alternative game used to 'test' for exploitation, or whether they disagree in their evaluations of the verdict of a similar test.

Roemer uses this strategy to define four kinds of exploitation: feudal exploitation, capitalist exploitation, what he refers to as socialist exploitation, and something he calls 'status' exploitation. Let us begin with capitalist exploitation. Workers own no physical assets (means of production) and sell their labour power to capitalists for a wage. Are workers exploited under capitalism? The answer to this question in the game-theoretic formulation requires proposing as an alternative to the capitalist game a game in which the two conditions specified above hold. What is this alternative? It is a game within which each worker receives his or her *per capita share of society's total productive assets*. What Roemer demonstrates is that if the coalition of all wage-earners were to leave the game of capitalism with their per capita share of society's assets, then they would be better off than if they stayed in capitalism, and capitalists would be worse off. The 'withdrawal rule' in this case—leaving the game with per capita shares of physical assets—then becomes the formal 'test' of whether or not a particular social system involves capitalistic exploitation.

In contrast, the withdrawal rule which specifies feudal exploitation involves leaving the game with one's *personal assets* (rather than one's *per capita* share of total assets). This is equivalent to a situation where the feudal serf is freed from all obligations based on personal bondage. Peasants would be better off in such circumstances and feudal lords would be worse off. By this specification of feudal exploitation, workers in capitalism are *not* feudally exploited; they would be worse off, not better off, if they withdrew from the game of capitalism with only their personal assets. As Roemer argues, the claim by neo-classical theorists that wage-earners in capitalism are not exploited is generally equivalent to the claim that they are not *feudally* exploited, i.e. that they are not subjected to surplus extraction based on relations of personal bondage which would have the effect of giving them a wage permanently below the value of their marginal product.[11] In these terms, the dispute between Marxists and neoclassical economists over the existence of exploitation in capitalism is a dispute over which withdrawal rule to use as a test.

The concept of socialist exploitation is less systematically worked out in Roemer's analysis. The withdrawal rule in this case is leaving the game with one's *per capita share of inalienable assets* (roughly equivalent to talents or skills). A coalition will be said to be socialistically exploited if it would improve its position by leaving with its *per capita* skills while its complement would be worse off under such circumstances. This implies that people with high levels of skills in the existing game receive high income not simply because they have a high level of skill, but because of the skill differentials among actors. The highly skilled would become worse off if the unskilled obtained skills; they thus have an interest in maintaining skill differentials, and this is what underpins the claim that their income reflects exploitation.

If a skilled person's income reflected no more than the amount of time it takes to obtain the skill, then there would be no skill-based exploitation. The higher incomes would simply be reimbursement for real costs incurred. The argument behind skill exploitation is that people with scarce skills receive incomes above the costs of producing those skills, a 'rent' component to their income; it is this element that constitutes exploitation.

Although Marx referred neither to the inequalities in income in a socialist society as the result of 'exploitation', nor to the relation between the skilled and unskilled as a *class* relation, Roemer's account nevertheless corresponds well to Marx's analysis of inequality in socialism as laid out in his *Critique of the Gotha Programme*. In that document Marx emphasized that skill-based inequalities would persist in socialism and that distribution would be on the basis of 'from each according to his abilities, to each according to his work'. While there is some ambiguity in what the phrase 'according to his work' means, it is consistent with the notion that skill-based exploitation would exist in a socialist society. Only in communism would distribution be on the basis of need, which in effect implies that skills would cease to be a form of private-property assets.[12]

The final form of exploitation discussed by Roemer is what he has termed 'status' exploitation.[13] The exploitation exercised by bureaucrats is the prototypical example. 'If these positions', Roemer writes,

> required special skills, then one might be justified in calling the differential remuneration to these positions an aspect of socialist [skill-based] exploitation. . . . [However] there is some extra remuneration to holders of those positions which accrues solely by virtue of the position and not by virtue of the skill necessary to carry out the tasks associated with it. These special payments to positions give rise to *status exploitation*. A coalition will be status-exploited if it could improve the lot of its members by withdrawing with its own assets but exempting itself from the dues to status, and if the complementary coalition fared worse.[14]

Status exploitation is much less systematically theorized in Roemer's analysis than any of the other forms he explores. Its theoretical function is to provide a way of understanding the bureaucratically-based exploitation in 'actually existing socialist societies', but it does so in a way that does not fit comfortably into the rest of the analysis. As we will see shortly, transforming the concept of 'status' exploitation will be necessary in order to deploy Roemer's approach for the analysis of concrete class structures.

CLASS AND EXPLOITATION

The central message of both of Roemer's strategies for analysing exploitation is that the material basis of exploitation lies in inequalities in the distribution of productive assets, usually referred to as property relations. The asset–exploitation nexus depends in each case upon the capacity of asset-holders to deprive others of equal access to that asset, whether it be alienable or inalienable. On the one hand, inequalities of assets are sufficient to account for transfers of surplus labour; on the other hand, different forms of asset inequality specify different systems of exploitation. Classes are then defined as positions within the social relations of production derived from the property relations which determine the patterns of exploitation.

These conclusions have led Roemer to challenge directly the tendency of Marxists like myself to define class relations primarily in terms of relations of domination *within* production. Of course, exploiting classes dominate exploited classes in the sense of preventing the exploited classes from taking the exploiting class's productive assets (if they are alienable) or redistributing property rights in those assets (if they are inalienable). As we noted above, Roemer has to introduce some notion of dominance even to be able fully to specify exploitation in the game-theory approach. However, domination, in this context, enters the analysis in a way which, clearly, is conceptually subordinate to exploitation. Most importantly for the thrust of much neo-Marxist class structure analysis, domination *within* the production process or within the labour process does not enter into the definition of class relations as such.[15]

In previous work I have criticized Roemer's position on this issue.[16] I argued that class relations intrinsically involved domination *at the point of production*, not simply in the repressive protection of the property relations as such. I now think that Roemer is correct on this point. While the fact that capitalists supervise workers within production is unquestionably an important feature of most historic forms of capitalist production and may play an important role in explaining the forms of class organization and class conflict within production, the *basis* of the capital-labour relation should be identified with the relations of effective control (i.e. real economic ownership) over productive assets as such.

One of the reasons why I resisted Roemer's conceptualization of classes in terms of property relations is that it seemed to blur the difference between Marxist definitions of class and Weberian definitions. Weberian definitions, as I construed them, were 'market-based' definitions of class, whereas Marxist definitions were 'production based'. The reputed advantage of the latter was that production was more 'fundamental' than exchange, and therefore production-based class concepts had more explanatory power than market-based ones.

What now seems clear to me is that definitions of classes in terms of property relations should not be identified with strictly market-based definitions. Property relations accounts of classes do not define classes by income shares, by the results of market transactions, but by the productive assets which classes control, which lead them to adopt certain strategies within exchange relations, and which in turn determine the outcomes of those market transactions. As we shall see in chapter four, there remain significant differences between the Weberian use of market criteria for defining classes and the Marxist use of property relations, but the distinction is not captured by the simple contrast between 'exchange' and 'production'.

Towards a General Framework of Class Analysis

The heart of Roemer's analysis is the link between the distribution of property rights in productive assets of various sorts on the one hand, and exploitation and class on the other. Different mechanisms of exploitation are defined with respect to different kinds of assets and different class systems are defined by the social relations of production that are built upon property rights in those assets. These insights will provide the basis for elaborating a comprehensive framework for analysing class structures in general and for reconceptualizing the problem of the middle classes in particular.

Before examining this general framework, however, it is necessary to modify and extend Roemer's analysis in several respects: first, it will be helpful to introduce a distinction between economic exploitation and economic oppression; second, we need to recast Roemer's account of feudal exploitation in terms of a distinctive type of productive asset; and third, we need to replace Roemer's concept of status exploitation with a new concept, which I shall label 'organization exploitation'.

ECONOMIC EXPLOITATION AND ECONOMIC OPPRESSION

One of the criticisms that is often raised about Roemer's methodological device of using 'withdrawal rules' from a 'game' to define different forms of exploitation is that it abandons the Marxist identification of exploitation with transfers of labour from one category of actors to another. While Roemer's procedure allows us to assess inequalities that are the result of causal interconnections between actors, it lacks the additional force of the view that the inequalities in question are produced by real transfers from one actor to another.

Roemer himself has come to reject completely all labour-transfer views of exploitation on the ground that situations can occur in which labour transfers occur from the rich to the poor, situations in which we would not want to say that the poor were exploiting the rich.[17] For example, imagine a society with rich and poor peasants in which everyone has the following preferences for the performance of labour relative to the consumption of leisure: the wealthier one is, the less one values leisure relative to labour. Now, suppose that a given rich peasant has performed all necessary work on his or her land and would prefer to rent some more from a poor peasant than to remain idle. Given these preference structures, the poor peasant might prefer to receive the rent and have a great deal of leisure than work the land him/herself. In this situation, the only transfers of labour are from the rich peasant to the poor peasant (in the form of rent). Does it make sense to say that the poor peasant is 'exploiting' the rich peasant in such a situation? Now, one might want to call this a fanciful example, but it does show that simple flows of labour or the products of labour are insufficient to define what we mean by 'exploitation'.

I think that it is possible to restore the central thrust of the traditional Marxist concept of exploitation by making a distinction between what can be called 'economic oppression' and exploitation. I would argue, that in and of itself, the withdrawal rule procedure simply defines a situation of economic oppression. In the example above, the poor peasant is economically oppressed by the rich peasant through the property rights in land. Exploitation, on the other hand, implies more than just economic oppression; it includes both economic oppression and the appropriation of the fruits of the labour of one class by another (which is equivalent to a transfer of the surplus from one class to another).[18] The poor peasants would not exploit the rich peasants in the example, since they do not economically oppress them.

With this usage of terms, we can identify a fairly wide range of inequalities that we might want to condemn on the basis of economic oppression, but which are not examples of exploitation. The poverty of the permanently disabled or of the unemployed, for example, would in general be cases of economic oppression, but not of exploitation. They would surely be better off under the counterfactual conditions of the withdrawal rules, but the fruits of their labour are not appropriated by any class (since they are not producing anything). The same can be said of the children of workers: they may be economically oppressed by capital, but they are not exploited by capital.[19]

Now, it might be argued that the concept of economic oppression would be sufficient to provide the basis for a class concept, since it does define a set of objective material interests. What, then, is added by the distinction between economic oppressions that involve appropriation of the fruits of labour and those that do not? The critical addition is the idea that in the case of exploitation, the welfare of exploiting class *depends upon the work* of the exploited class. In a case of simple economic oppression, the oppressing class only has interests in protecting its own property rights; in the case of exploitation it also has interests in the productive activity and effort of the exploited. In the case of economic oppression, the oppressors' material interests would not be hurt if all of the oppressed simply disappeared or died.[20] In the case of exploitation, on the other hand, the exploiting class needs the exploited class. Exploiters would be hurt if the exploited all disappeared.[21] Exploitation, therefore, binds the exploiter and exploited together in a way that economic oppression need not. It is this peculiar combination of antagonism of material interests and inter-dependency which gives exploitation its distinctive character and which makes class struggle such a potentially explosive social force.

This notion of exploitation has a relatively straightforward intuitive meaning for feudal exploitation, where feudal lords directly appropriate a surplus produced by serfs, and for capitalist exploitation, where capitalists appropriate the total product out of which they pay the workers a wage. It is much less obvious that what Roemer calls 'socialist exploitation', exploitation rooted in skills, should be viewed as exploitation in this sense. Let us look at skill-based exploitation more closely to see why it should be considered an instance of exploitation defined in the above way.

To appropriate the fruits of someone else's labour is equivalent to saying that a person consumes more than they produce. If the income of a person with skill assets is identical to their 'marginal product', as neo-classical economists like to argue, how can we say that they are consuming 'more' than their own contribution?

Through what mechanism are they appropriating the fruits of any-one else's labour?

The answer to this question is easiest when skill-asset exploita-tion is based on *credentials* which have the effect of restricting the supply of skills.[22] Let us compare two situations, one in which a mechanism for granting credentials is in operation which restricts the supply of a given skill and one in which credentials are absent. When credentials are operating, employers will bid up the wages of the owners of the credential above the costs of producing the skills. (In the absence of the credential-awarding process, addi-tional labourers would acquire the skills if wages were above the costs of producing the skills, thus ultimately driving the wages down to those costs). The result of this is that the *price* of the commodities produced with those skills will be higher than they would be in the absence of the credentials. In effect, we can say that while the possessor of a credential is being paid a wage equal to the *price* of his or her marginal product, this price is above the 'value' of the marginal product (or, equivalently, the price of the marginal pro-duct in the absence of credentials).[23] That difference is the exploitative transfer appropriated by the possessor of a credential. For this reason, possessors of credentials have interests in main-taining skill differentials as such, in maintaining the restrictions on the acquisition of credentials.

Credentials, of course, are not the only way the price of skilled labour power may exceed its costs of production; natural talents are a second mechanism. Talents can be viewed as affecting the efficiency with which skills can be acquired. A talented person is someone who can acquire a given skill at less cost (in time, effort and other resources) than an untalented person. In extreme cases, this may mean that the cost to the untalented becomes infinite (i.e. it is impossible to acquire the skill in question). Should talents themselves be viewed as a basis for exploitation in the sense we have been discussing it? In the case where an individual has an extremely rare talent which enables him or her to acquire some correspondingly rare skill, does it make sense to say that the price of the 'marginal product' of that person is greater than its value, as we did in the case of credentials?

While I cannot give a rigorous defence of this position, I think that it is appropriate to regard the extra income that accrues to people with talents (i.e. people who acquire skills through the deployment of their talents) as a kind of 'rent', quite parallel to the rent obtained by the owner of particularly fertile land. This added income comes from the *differentials* in talents—or fertility of land— as such, not simply from the actual productivity that the possession of the skill produced with that talent confers. If this reasoning is correct, then talents, like credentials, should simply be treated as a specific kind of mechanism for creating a stable scarcity of a given skill, which in turn is the basis for an exploitative appropriation.

It is, of course, an empirical question whether inequalities of underlying talents or inequalities generated by institutionalized credentials are more important in creating the skill assets that are the basis of skill exploitation. While I will generally emphasize credentials because of their relatively clear status as a 'property right', this is not meant to imply that talents themselves are necessarily less important.

To recapitulate the argument of this section: throughout the rest of this book exploitation will be defined as an economically oppressive appropriation of the fruits of the labour of one class by another. Not all appropriations are economically oppressive and not all forms of economic oppression involve such appropriation. It is the combination of economic oppression with appropriation that makes exploitation such a powerful basis for objective antagonisms of material interests.

RECASTING THE CONCEPT OF FEUDAL EXPLOITATION

In Roemer's own formulation, only two kinds of assets are considered formally: physical assets (in his terminology alienable assets) and skill assets (inalienable assets). In his exposition, the distinction between exploitation in feudalism and capitalism revolves around the nature of the withdrawal rules with respect to physical assets, rather than the nature of the assets themselves. Roemer defines feudal exploitation in terms of withdrawing with one's individual physical assets in contrast to capitalism where exploitation is defined in terms of withdrawing with one's per capita share of total assets.

The feudal case, however, can be characterized in a somewhat different way. Labour power is a productive asset.[24] In capitalist societies everyone owns one unit of this asset, namely themselves. In feudalism, on the other hand, ownership rights over labour power are unequally distributed: feudal lords have more than one unit, serfs have less than one unit. This is what 'personal bondage' means economically: feudal lords partially own the labour power of their vassals. To be sure, it is not typical of feudalism for serfs to own no labour power—they are not generally slaves divested of all ownership rights in their own labour power—but they do not have complete effective control over their own persons as productive actors.[25]

The empirical manifestation of this unequal distribution of ownership rights over labour power in classical feudalism is the coercive extraction of labour dues from serfs. When corvee labour is commuted to rents in kind and eventually to money rents, the feudal character of the exploitation relation is reflected in the legal prohibitions on the movement of peasants off the land. The 'flight' of a peasant to the city is, in effect, a form of theft: the peasant is stealing part of the labour power owned by the lord.[26] The withdrawal rule which defines feudal exploitation can then be specified as leaving the feudal game with one's per capita share of society's assets in labour power, namely one unit. Feudal exploitation is thus exploitation (economic oppression in which there are transfers of labour or its fruits from the oppressed to the oppressor) which results from inequalities in the distribution of assets in labour power.[27]

Reformulating feudal exploitation in this manner makes the game-theoretic specification of different exploitations in Roemer's analysis symmetrical: feudal exploitation is based on inequalities generated by ownership of labour power assets; capitalist exploitation, on inequalities generated by ownership of alienable assets; socialist exploitation, on inequalities generated by ownership of inalienable assets. Corresponding to each of these exploitation-generating inequalities of assets, there is a specific class relation: lords and serfs in feudalism, bourgeoisie and proletariat in capitalism, experts and workers in socialism.

ORGANIZATION ASSET EXPLOITATION

The anti-capitalist revolution in Russia resulted in the virtual elimination of private property in the means of production: individuals cannot own means of production to a significant extent, they cannot inherit them or dispose of them on a market, etc. And yet it seems unsatisfactory to characterize societies like the Soviet Union simply in terms of skill-based exploitation. Experts do not appear to be the 'ruling class' in those societies, and the dynamic of the societies does not seem to revolve around skill inequalities as such. How, then, should exploitation be understood in 'actually existing socialism'?

As already noted, Roemer has attempted to deal with this problem by introducing what he termed 'status exploitation'. This is not, I believe, a very satisfactory solution. In particular, there are two problems with this concept. First, the category 'status exploitation' is outside the logic of the rest of Roemer's analysis of exploitation. In each of the other cases, exploitation is rooted in the relation of people or coalitions to the forces of production. Each of the other forms of exploitation is 'materialist' not just in the sense that the concept is meant to explain material distribution, but because it is based in this relation to the material conditions of production. 'Status' exploitation has no necessary relationship to production at all. Second, it is hard rigorously to distinguish status exploitation from feudal exploitation. The 'lord' receives remuneration strictly because of incumbency in a 'position', not because of skills or ownership of capital.[28] Yet, it hardly seems reasonable to consider the logics of exploitation and class in the contemporary Soviet Union and in 14th-century feudal Europe as being essentially the same.

The problems with the concept of status exploitation can potentially be solved by analysing exploitation based on a fourth element in the inventory of productive assets, an asset which can be referred to as 'organization'. As both Adam Smith and Marx noted, the technical division of labour among producers was itself a source of productivity. The way the process of production is organized is a productive resource distinct from the expenditure of labour power, the use of means of production or the skills of the producer. Of course there is an inter-relationship between organization and these other assets, just as there is an interdependence between means of production and skills. But organization—the conditions of coordinated cooperation among producers in a complex division of labour—is a productive resource in its own right.

How is this asset distributed in different kinds of societies? In contemporary capitalism, organization assets are generally controlled by managers and capitalists: managers control the organization assets within specific firms under constraints imposed by the ownership of the capital assets by capitalists. Entrepreneurial capitalists directly own both kinds of assets (and probably skill assets as well); pure rentier capitalists (coupon-clippers) only own capital assets. Because of the anarchy of the capitalist market, no set of actors controls the technical division of labour across firms.

In statist societies (or, perhaps, 'state socialist' societies), organization assets assume a much greater importance.[29] Control of the technical division of labour—the coordination of productive activities within and across labour processes—becomes a societal task organized at the centre. Control over organization assets is no longer simply the task of firm-level managers, but extends into the central organs of planning within the state. When it is said that exploitation in such societies is based on bureaucratic power what is meant is that the control over organization assets defines the material basis for class relations and exploitation.

This notion of organization assets bears a close relation to the problem of authority and hierarchy. The asset is organization. The activity of using that asset is co-ordinated decision-making over a complex technical division of labour. When that asset is distributed unequally, so that some positions have effective control over much more of the asset than others, then the social relation with respect to that asset takes the form of hierarchical authority. Authority, however, is not the asset as such; organization is the asset which is controlled through a hierarchy of authority.

The claim that the effective control over organization assets is a basis of exploitation is equivalent to saying (a) that non-managers would be better off and managers/bureaucrats worse off if non-managers were to withdraw with their per capita share of organization assets (or, equivalently, if organizational control were democratized); and (b) that by virtue of effectively controlling organization assets managers/bureaucrats control part or all of the socially produced surplus.[30]

Two objections to the characterization of 'organization' as an exploitation-generating asset need to be addressed: first, that this asset is not 'owned' and thus cannot constitute the basis of a property relation; and second, that as an exploitation-mechanism it is effectively indistinguishable from the means of production itself.

'Ownership' has come to have two kinds of meanings in contemporary Marxist discussions of class: ownership as a property right and effective economic control. In the first usage, to 'own' something fully implies that one can sell it, dispose of it or give it away; in the second usage, to 'own' something is to exercise the real control over its use. A good case can be made that managers and bureaucrats do have effective economic control over the use of organization assets. Even though capitalists retain the right to fire managers, in practice in the modern corporation the actual exercise of control over organization assets is in the hands of managers.

However, does it make sense to talk about 'ownership' of organization assets as a property right? Clearly, managers cannot actually sell the organization assets they control, either in capitalist firms or state enterprises, and this may imply that it really makes no sense to talk about their 'owning' the asset. Nevertheless, while managers individually cannot sell organization assets, there is one sense in which they have a kind of property right in such assets, namely in their collective control over the transfer of rights to use the asset. While capitalists may formally retain the right to hire, fire and promote managers, in practical terms it is management itself which effectively has the capacity to transfer rights to control organization assets from one person to another, and this could be considered one crucial aspect of having a property right in the asset itself. Still, in spite of the fact that managerial control of the allocation of people to positions with organizational assets has this property-like character, it does seem an abuse of the term 'ownership' to say that managers personally own the assets as a result of such control. As a result, in our analysis of organization assets I will generally talk about the ways in which these assets are 'effectively controlled' rather than 'owned'. This does not undermine the claim that the effective control over these assets is a basis for exploitation, but it does reduce the strict symmetry in the analysis of the different kinds of assets associated with different kinds of exploitations.

The second objection to the treatment of organization assets as an asset on a par with labour power, means of production and skills is that it is ultimately indistinguishable from the means of production itself. State planners in a 'statist' society control the flow of investments throughout the society, and if they 'own' or 'control' anything, therefore, they own the means of production, not just 'organization assets'. What sense does it make, therefore, to distinguish the organization aspect of their positions?

Let me try to clarify the issue by examining the case of state planners. In *all* exploitation relations, whether based on ownership of labour power, skills, means of production or organization assets, what exploitation generates is effective claims on the social surplus. This in turn gives exploiters at least some effective control over investments, at least in so far as they have the ability to dispose of that surplus for investment purposes. Skill exploiters in capitalism, for example, can invest the surplus they appropriate through credentials.

The issue at hand in the present context, however, is not what exploiters *do* with the surplus they control, but rather on what *basis* they gain control over that surplus. And in that respect, there is a sharp difference between capitalist and statist societies: in capitalism, when skill or organization-asset exploiters invest the surplus which they obtain on the basis of their skills or organization assets, they will, in the future, begin to obtain a flow of surplus from these investments themselves. They can, in other words, *capitalize* their skill and organization exploitation. In a statist system of production, this is precisely what is not possible. Except in very limited ways, managers, bureaucrats and state planners cannot convert the surpluses they control into future exploitation except in so far as their use of the surplus enhances their organizational position (i.e. their control over organization assets). They cannot capitalize their present exploitation. The contrast between capitalism and statism is parallel in this respect to the contrast between feudalism and capitalism: in capitalism, capitalists are prohibited from feudalizing their surplus. In early capitalism, of course, this was a serious issue, as capitalist profits were frequently diverted from capitalist investment into the purchase of feudal titles and estates. Just as bourgeois revolutions block the feudalization of capitalist exploitation, so anti-capitalist revolutions block the capitalization of organization and skill exploitation.

A GENERAL TYPOLOGY OF CLASS AND EXPLOITATION

If we add organization assets to the list in Roemer's analysis, we generate the more complex typology presented in Table 3.2 below. Let us briefly look at each row of this table and examine its logic. Feudalism is a class system based on unequal distribution of ownership rights in labour power. Feudal lords may also have more means of production than serfs, more organizational assets and more productive skills (although this is unlikely) and thus they may be exploiters with respect to these assets as well. What defines the society as 'feudal', however, is the primacy of the distinctively feudal mechanisms of exploitation, and which, accordingly, means that feudal class relations will be the primary structural basis of class struggle.

The bourgeois revolutions radically redistributed productive assets in people: everyone, at least in principle, owns one unit—themselves. This is at the heart of what is meant by 'bourgeois freedoms', and it is the sense in which capitalism can be regarded as a historically progressive force. But capitalism raises the second type of exploitation, exploitation based on property relations in means of production, to an unprecedented level.[31]

TABLE 3.2
Assets, Exploitation and Classes

Type of class structure	*Principal asset that is unequally distributed*	*Mechanism of exploitation*	*Classes*
Feudalism	Labour power	Coercive extraction of surplus labour	Lords and serfs
Capitalism	Means of production	Market exchanges of labour power and commodities	Capitalists and workers
Statism	Organization	Planned appropriation and distribution of surplus based on hierarchy	Managers/ bureaucrats and non-management
Socialism	Skills	Negotiated redistribution of surplus from workers to experts	Experts and workers

The typical institutional form of capitalist class relations is capitalists having full ownership rights in the means of production and workers none. However, other possibilities have existed historically. Workers in cottage industry in early capitalism owned some of their means of production, but did not have sufficient assets to actually produce commodities without the assistance of capitalists. Such workers were still being capitalistically exploited even though there was no formal labour market with wages, etc. In all capitalist exploitation, the mediating mechanism is market exchanges. Unlike in feudalism, surplus is not directly appropriated from workers in the form of coerced labour or dues. Rather, it is appropriated through market exchanges: workers are paid a wage which covers the costs of production of their labour power; capitalists receive an income from the sale of the commodities produced by workers. The difference in these quantities constitutes the exploitative surplus appropriated by capitalists.[32]

Anti-capitalist revolutions attempt to eliminate the distinctively capitalist form of exploitation, exploitation based on private ownership of the means of production. The nationalization of the principal means of production is, in effect, a radical equalization of ownership of capital: everyone owns one citizen-share. What anti-capitalist revolutions do not necessarily eliminate, and may indeed considerably strengthen and deepen, are inequalities of effective control over organization assets. Whereas in capitalism the control over organization assets does not extend beyond the firm, in statist societies the coordinated integration of the division of labour extends to the whole society through institutions of central state planning. The mechanism by which this generates exploitative transfers of surplus involves the centrally planned bureaucratic appropriation and distribution of the surplus along hierarchical principles. The corresponding class relation is therefore between managers/bureaucrats—people who control organization assets—and non-managers.

The historical task of the revolutionary transformation of statist societies revolves around the equalization of effective economic control over organization assets. What precisely does such equalization mean? It would be utopian to imagine that in any society with a complex division of labour all productive actors would share equally in the actual *use* of organization assets. This would be equivalent to imagining that the equalization of ownership of means of production implied that all such actors would actually use an identical amount of physical capital. Equalization of control over organization assets means essentially the democratization of bureaucratic apparatuses.[33] This need not imply a thoroughgoing direct democracy, where all decisions of any consequence are directly made in democratic assemblies. There will still be delegated responsibilities, and there certainly can be representative forms of democratic control. But it does mean that the basic parameters of planning and co-ordination of social production are made through democratic mechanisms and that the holding of delegated positions of organizational responsibility does not give the delegates any personal claims on the social surplus.

Lenin's original vision of 'soviet' democracy, in which officials would be paid no more than average workers and would be subject to immediate recall, and in which the basic contours of social planning would be debated and decided through democratic participation, embodied such principles of radical equalization of organization assets. Once in power, as we know, the Bolsheviks were either unable or unwilling seriously to attempt the elimination of organization exploitation. Upon that failure, a new class structure emerged and was consolidated.[34]

The equalization of organization assets and the eradication of class relations rooted in organization exploitation would not in and of itself eliminate exploitation based on skills/credentials. Such exploitation would remain a central feature of socialism.

In this conceptualization of socialism, a socialist society is essentially a kind of non-bureaucratic technocracy. Experts control their own skills or knowledge within production, and by virtue of such control are able to appropriate some of the surplus from production. However, because of the democratization of organization assets, the actual making of planning decisions would not be under the direct control of experts but would be made through some kind of democratic procedure (this is in effect what democratization of organization-assets means: equalizing control over the planning and co-ordination of social production). This implies that the actual class power of a socialist technocratic-exploiting class will be much weaker than the class power of exploiting classes in previous class sytems. Their ownership rights extend to only a limited part of the social surplus.

This much more limited basis of *domination* implied by skill-based exploitation is consistent with the classical claim in Marxism that the working class—the direct producers—are the 'ruling' class in socialism.[35] The democratization of organization assets necessarily means that workers effectively control social planning. Another way of describing socialism, then, is that it is a society within which the ruling class and the exploiting classes are distinct.

Indeed, one might even want to make a stronger claim, namely that 'experts' in socialism are not really a proper class at all. Unlike in the cases of capital assets, labour power assets and organization assets, it is not at all clear that one can derive any relational properties from the ownership of skill assets as such.[36] To be sure, if skill assets are a criterion for recruitment into positions within organizational hierarchies, then individuals with skills or credentials may be in a particular relation to people without such credentials, but this is because of the link between skill and organization assets, not because of skill assets themselves. The most one can say here is that experts and non-experts exist in a kind of diffuse relation of dependence of the latter on the former. This is a considerably weaker sense of 'social relation' than is the case for the other three types of class relations.

It seems therefore that, while skills or credentials may be a basis for exploitation, this asset is not really the basis of a class relation, at least not in the same sense as labour power, capital and organization assets. In these terms socialism (in contrast to statism) could be viewed as a society with exploitation but without fully constituted classes.[37] Such a characterization of socialism is also consistent with the spirit, if not the letter, of Marx's claim that socialism is the 'lower stage' of communism, since classes are already in a partial state of dissolution in a society with only skill-based exploitation.

'Communism' itself would be understood as a society within which skill-based exploitation had itself 'withered away', i.e., in which ownership rights in skills had been equalized. This does not mean, it must be stressed, that all individuals would actually *possess* the same skills as each other in communism. It is ownership rights in the skills that are equalized. This is quite parallel to what it means to equalize ownership over physical assets: different workers may continue to work in factories with different capital intensities, productivities, amounts of physical assets. Equalization does not mean that everyone physically uses the same means of production, but simply that there are no longer any ownership rights that are differentially distributed with respect to those means of production. No one receives a higher income (or controls a larger part of the social surplus) by virtue of using more physical assets. Similarly the equalization of ownership rights in skills implies that differential incomes and control over the social surplus cease to be linked to differential skills.[38]

THE MIDDLE CLASSES AND CONTRADICTORY LOCATIONS

The point of elaborating the rather complex inventory of forms of exploitation and corresponding class relations in Table 3.2 was not primarily to be able to give more precision to the abstract mode of production concepts (feudalism, capitalism, statism, etc.), but rather to provide the conceptual tools for analysing the class structures of contemporary capitalism at a more concrete level of analysis. In particular, as was stressed in chapter two, this means providing a more coherent and compelling way of theorizing the class character of the 'middle classes'.

Two different kinds of non-polarized class locations can be defined in the logic of this framework:

(1) There are class locations that are neither exploiters nor exploited, i.e. people who have precisely the per capita level of the relevant asset. A petty-bourgeois, self-employed producer with average capital stock, for example, would be neither exploiter nor

exploited within capitalist relations.[39] These kinds of positions are what can be called the 'traditional' or 'old' middle class of a particular kind of class system.

(2) Since concrete societies are rarely, if ever, characterized by a single mode of production, the actual class structures of given societies will be characterized by complex patterns of intersecting exploitation relations. There will therefore tend to be some positions which are exploiting along one dimension of exploitation relations, while on another are exploited. Highly skilled wage-earners (e.g. professionals) in capitalism are a good example: they are capitalistically exploited because they lack assets in capital and yet are skill-exploiters. Such positions are what are typically referred to as the 'new middle class' of a given class system.

Table 3.3 presents a schematic typology of such complex class locations for capitalism. The typology is divided into two segments: one for owners of the means of production and one for non-owners. Within the wage-earner section of the typology, locations are distinguished by the two subordinate relations of exploitation characteristic of capitalist society—organization assets and skill/credential assets. It is thus possible to distinguish within this framework a whole terrain of class-locations in capitalist *society* that are distinct from the polarized classes of the capitalist *mode of production*: expert managers, non-managerial experts, non-expert managers, etc.

What is the relationship between this heterogeneous exploitation definition of the middle class and my previous conceptualization of such positions as contradictory locations within class relations? There is still a sense in which such positions could be characterized as 'contradictory locations', for they will typically hold contradictory interests with respect to the primary forms of class struggle in capitalist society, the struggle between labour and capital. On the one hand, they are like workers in being excluded from ownership of the means of production;[40] on the other, they have interests opposed to workers because of their effective control of organization and skill assets. Within the struggles of capitalism, therefore, these 'new' middle classes do constitute contradictory locations, or more precisely, contradictory locations within exploitation relations.

This conceptualization of the middle classes also suggests that the principle forms of contradictory locations will vary historically

TABLE 3.3
Typology of Class Locations in Capitalist Society

Assets in the means of production

	Owners of means of production	Non-owners [wage labourers]			Organization assets
Owns sufficient capital to hire workers and not work	1 Bourgeoisie	4 Expert Managers	7 Semi Credentialled Managers	10 Uncredentialled Managers	+
Owns sufficient capital to hire workers but must work	2 Small Employers	5 Expert Supervisors	8 Semi Credentialled Supervisors	11 Uncredentialled Supervisors	>0
Owns sufficient capital to work for self but not to hire workers	3 Petty Bourgeoisie	6 Experts non-managers	9 Semi Credentialled Workers	12 Proletarians	−
		+	>0	−	

Skill/credential assets

depending upon the particular combinations of exploitation relations in a given society. The historical pattern of principal contradictory locations is presented in Table 3.4. In feudalism, the critical contradictory location is constituted by the bourgeoisie, the rising class of the successor mode of production.[41] Within capitalism, the central contradictory location within exploitation relations is constituted by managers and state bureaucrats. They embody a principle of class organization which is quite distinct from capitalism and which potentially poses an alternative to capitalist relations. This is particularly true for state managers who, unlike corporate managers, are less likely to have their careers tightly integrated with the interests of the capitalist class. Finally, in statist societies, the 'intellegentsia' broadly defined constitutes the pivotal contradictory location.[42]

TABLE 3.4
Basic Classes and contradictory locations in successive modes of production

Mode of production	Basic classes	Principal contradictory location
Feudalism	Lords and serfs	Bourgeoisie
Capitalism	Bourgeoisie and proletariat	Managers/bureaucrats
State bureaucratic socialism	Bureaucrats and workers	Intellegentsia/experts

One of the consequences of this reconceptualization of the middle class is that it is no longer axiomatic that the proletariat is the unique, or perhaps even universally the central, rival to the capitalist class for class power in capitalist society. That classical Marxist assumption depended upon the thesis that there were no other classes within capitalism that could be viewed as the 'bearers' of a historical alternative to capitalism. Socialism (as the transition to communism) was the only possible future to capitalism. What Table 3.4 suggests is that there are other class forces within capitalism that have the potential to pose an alternative to capitalism.

Alvin Gouldner and others have argued that the beneficiaries of social revolutions in history have not been the oppressed classes of the prior mode of production, but 'third classes'. Most notably, it was not the peasantry who became the ruling class with the demise of feudalism, but the bourgeoisie, a class that was located outside the principal exploitation relation of feudalism. A similar argument could be extended to manager-bureaucrats with respect to capitalism and experts with respect to state bureacuratic socialism in each case these constitute potential rivals to the existing ruling class.

In the case of capitalism, it might seem rather far-fetched to claim that managers and state bureaucrats constitute potential challengers to the class power of the bourgeoisie. At least in the advanced capitalist countries, corporate managers are so closely integrated into the logic of private capital accumulation that it seems quite implausible that they would ever oppose capitalism in favour of some sort of statist organization of production. As critics of the 'managerial revolution' thesis have often argued, whatever special interests or motives corporate managers have, the realization of those interests is contingent upon the profitability of their firms and they will therefore adopt strategies consistent with the interests of capital. And even for state managers, who arguably have a power base that is at least partially independent of capital it still seems very unlikely that they would ever become consistently anti-capitalist because of the multiple ways in which the interests of the state are subordinated to and co-ordinated with the interests of capital. Since in a capitalist society state revenue depend upon privately generated profits (because the state itself does not organize production), the state is systematically constrained to act in a way that supports the profitability of capital and thus capitalist exploitation. Regardless of their personal preferences, therefore, state managers cannot afford to act in anti-capitalist ways.[43] It therefore seems completely unrealistic to treat managers and bureaucrats as even potential class rivals to the bourgeoisie.

Behind each of these claims about the effective integration of managers and bureaucrats into the capitalist social order is the assumption that capitalism is successful as a system of exploitation and accumulation. So long as firms, in general, are able to make profits, they are able to integrate their managers into a logic of capital accumulation; and so long as capitalism reproduces a revenue base for the state, state managers will have their interests tied to the interests of capital. But what happens to these interests and strategies if capitalism permanently stagnates? If profits can no longer be assured in the long-run? If the career prospects for large numbers of managers became very insecure and precarious?

Would statist appeals for greater direct state involvement in controlling investments and flows of capital become more attractive to corporate management? Would statist options be seen as more realistic for state managers? I do not want to suggest that statist solutions that undermine the power of the capitalist class would automatically be pursued by managers and bureaucrats under such economic conditions. There would also have to be a range of political and ideological conditions to make such strategies viable, and there is no necessary reason why such political and ideological conditions would be forthcoming even in situations of chronic stagnation.[44] The important point in the present context is not that there be any inevitability to the emergence of such conditions, but that one can imagine historical conditions under which managers and bureaucrats even in the advanced capitalist countries (let alone third world countries) would find anti-capitalist, statist solutions attractive.

The historical typology of contradictory locations in Table 3.4 does not imply that there is any inevitability to the sequence feudalism-capitalism-statism-socialism-communism. There is nothing which implies that state bureaucrats are destined to be the future ruling class of present-day capitalisms. But it does suggest that the process of class formation and class struggle is considerably more complex and indeterminate than the traditional Marxist story has allowed.[45]

This way of understanding contradictory class locations has several advantages over my previous conceptualization:

(1) Certain of the specific conceptual problems of the earlier analysis of contradictory locations within class relations disappear: the problem of autonomy, the anomolous situations where positions like pilots are considered more proletarianized than many unskilled workers, etc.

(2) Treating contradictory locations in terms of relations of exploitation generalizes the concept across modes of production. The concept now has a specific theoretical status in all class systems, and has furthermore a much more focused historical thrust as represented in Table 3.4.

(3) This way of conceptualizing 'middle-class' locations makes the problem of their class interests much clearer than before. Their location within class relations is defined by the nature of their material optimizing strategies given the specific kinds of assets they own/control. Their specific class location helps to specify their

interests both within the existing capitalist society and with respect to various kinds of alternative games (societies) to which they might want to withdraw. In the previous conceptualization it was problematic to specify precisely the material interests of certain contradictory locations. In particular, there was no consistent reason for treating the material interests of 'semi-autonomous employees' as necessarily distinct from those of workers.

(4) This exploitation-based strategy helps to clarify the problems of class alliances in a much more systematic way than the previous approach. In the case of contradictory locations it was never clear how to assess the tendencies for contradictory locations to ally themselves with workers or non-workers. I made claims that such alliance tendencies were politically and ideologically determined, but I was not able to put more content into such notions. In contrast, as we shall see in chapter four, the exploitation-based concept of contradictory locations helps to provide a much clearer material basis for analysing the problem of alliances.

Once Again, Unresolved Problems

The process of concept formation is a continual process of concept transformation. New solutions pose new problems, and the efforts at resolving those problems in turn generate new solutions. Thus, the conceptual apparatus elaborated in this chapter has generated a new set of difficulties. Ultimately, of course, these difficulties may prove 'fatal' to the proposed concept; at a minimum they call for further clarifications and refinements.

Four such problems seem particularly pressing: (1) the status of 'organization' in organization assets; (2) the relationship between skill exploitation and classes; (3) causal interactions among forms of exploitation; (4) non-asset-based mechanisms of exploitation. While I will suggest possible strategies for dealing with these issues, I regard them as genuine problems for which I do not have entirely satisfactory solutions.

THE STATUS OF 'ORGANIZATION' IN ORGANIZATION ASSETS

Even if one accepts the claim that managers and bureaucrats are exploiters, one might still be rather sceptical of the argument that the basis of their exploitation is the control—let alone the 'ownership'—of organization assets. Two alternatives should be considered: first, that these are really just a specialized type of skill asset—managerial ability; and second, that this is just a special case of a more general problem that might be termed 'positional' exploitation.

It is certainly plausible that whatever claims managers are able to make on the surplus is a function of the specialized skills they possess. These may be quite firm-specific, acquired through experience as managers with the organization itself; nevertheless, it could be argued that skills are the basis of managerial exploitation, not the organization assets which they control.

It is difficult to know how one would refute this argument empirically. My claim is that the responsibility attached to a position by virtue of its control over organization assets gives the incumbent of such a position a claim on the surplus that is distinct from any claims rooted in skills/credentials, but since firm-specific skills will co-vary with such control/responsibility, it is hard to establish this in an unambiguous way. There is some evidence, however, which at least is consistent with the view that organization assets are not just proxies for skill or experience. If exploitation linked to managerial positions were entirely the result of skill and experience, then it would be expected that the income differences between managers and non-managers would disappear if we statistically controlled for these two variables. This is simply not the case: managerial incomes remain substantially higher than non-managerial incomes even after adjustment for education, age, years of experience on the job and occupational status.[46] Such results, of course, do not resolve the issue definitively, since it is always possible that the remaining income differences between managers and non-managers could be the result of unmeasured differences in skills. Nevertheless, they do provide some support for the analysis of organization assets proposed in this chapter.

A more serious problem revolves around the possibility that it is not the organization assets as such which are the basis for exploitation, but a more general property of these positions, the property of their 'strategic' importance within organization. 'Strategic jobs' can be defined by the intersection of two dimensions: first, the extent to which the tasks in a job are well-defined and can easily be monitored continuously; and second, the extent to which variability in the conscientiousness and responsibility with which individuals carry out those tasks can affect the overall productivity of the organization. Managerial positions, in these terms, are one instance, but by no means the only instance, of jobs which are difficult to monitor but are highly sensitive to differences in conscientiousness.

Strategic jobs pose a serious social-control problem to employers. The absence of easy, ongoing monitorability makes it difficult to rely on repressive sanctions as a strategy of social control, but the potential impact on productivity of job performance makes such social control necessary. The solution to this problem is a heavy reliance on positive rewards, particularly positive rewards built into career trajectories, as a way of eliciting the necessary responsible, conscientious behaviour. The exploitation transfers commanded by managers, therefore, should be viewed as a 'loyalty dividend'. While control over organization assets may be the most important example of such jobs, they are nevertheless a special case of a more general problem. The exploitation in such jobs, therefore, should be characterized as 'positional exploitation', rather than organization exploitation.

There are attractive features of this alternative. It pre-empts the problem of managerial, firm-specific skills by saying that it is unimportant whether the privileges managers enjoy are rooted in skills or organization assets so long as the positions pose the social control dilemmas that require loyalty dividends. In terms of skills themselves, this social control view makes it possible to distinguish skill-based exploitation that works through mechanisms involved in restricting the supply of particular kinds of skilled labour power, and skill-based exploitation that revolves around the organization of work itself. Finally, this alternative makes it possible to define certain positions which may involve neither organization assests nor skill assets and yet occupy strategic jobs requiring 'loyalty dividends'.

One might ask: why should we retain the concept of organization assets in the face of these apparent advantages of the strategic-job conception? The central reason is because of the way control over organization assets constitutes the basis for a particular structure of social relations—the relations between managers and workers. The objective of the analysis is not simply to identify possible mechanisms of exploitation, but to elaborate the exploitation–class nexus. We cannot derive any clear class relations from the analysis of strategic jobs as such: the incumbents in such jobs have no intrinsic social relation to incumbents in non-strategic jobs. It is therefore difficult to identify such positions as having a distinctive class character, in spite of the fact that they may consti-

te the basis for a form of exploitation. Thus, while effective
ontrol over organization assets remains only one possible basis
or incumbency in strategic jobs, it is this specific kind of strategic
ob that is simultaneously the basis for a class relation.

SKILLS AND CLASSES

he issues raised by the analysis of strategic jobs relate to the more
eneral problem of the relationship between skill and class. This
sue has already been alluded to in the discussion of experts in a
ocialist society. While the ownership of skill assets may be the
asis of exploitation mediated by market exchanges and internal
abour-markets, it is much less clear that it is the basis of a class
elation, except insofar as skills or talents enable one to gain access
o other kinds of assets. Experts may have distinct interests from
on-experts, but they are not clearly constituted as a class in rela-
on to non-experts.

In spite of this, I have continued to retain skill assets in the
nalysis of class structures. In particular, skill/credential assets
lay an important role in the analysis of the problem of middle
lasses in capitalism. This link to the concept of class, has not,
owever, been theorized satisfactorily.

One possible strategy for dealing with this situation may be to
eat skill exploitation as the basis of internal divisions within clas-
es. Indeed, this may be the proper way rigorously to define class
ractions', to use a classical Marxist term. Class fractions could be
efined as positions which share common locations within class
elations but occupy different locations with respect to exploita-
on. I will not puruse the problem of exploitation-based strata
ithin classes, but this may be the most appropriate way of dealing
ith these kinds of complexities in a coherent manner.

INTERACTIONS AMONG FORMS OF EXPLOITATION[47]

ven if we grant that the ownership of organization and skill assets
onstitutes the basis for mechanisms of exploitation, there is still
n important potential problem in linking these mechanisms to
lass structures. Let us suppose that there are significant and sys-
ematic interactions between mechanisms of exploitation. For
xample, it could be the case that the ability of a 'controller' of
rganization assets to make claims on the social surplus is greater
n a society with capitalist exploitation than in a society without

capitalist exploitation. Capitalist exploitation could enhance th
exploitation-capacity of organization (or skill) assets. Under such
situation, even though an individual manager or expert may ow
no capital assets at all, they would be worse off if those assets wer
equally distributed. In effect, then, even though managers are no
in the capitalist class in relational terms, they effectively partake i
capitalist exploitation and accordingly share basic class interest
with capitalists by virtue of the way capitalism enhances thei
organization exploitation.

Throughout this chapter I have assumed that the differen
mechanisms of exploitation had strictly additive effects. Th
efficacy of any one mechanism of exploitation was independent o
any of the others. Empirically, this is not a very plausible assump
tion.

If we drop the assumption that forms of exploitation do not rein
force each other, then the relationship between the map of class
locations defined with respect to assets and objective class inter
ests becomes much more problematic. This does not necessarily
destroy the usefulness of the basic strategy of analysis proposed i
this chapter, but it does add considerably to the complexity of the
analysis of the inter-relationship between assets, exploitation and
classes. While some of the implications of this added complexity
will be addressed in the discussion of class alliances in the nex
chapter, I will generally continue to adopt the simplifying assump
tion that forms of exploitation are independent of each other.

NON-ASSET BASES OF EXPLOITATION

Throughout the analyses of this chapter I have self-consciously
limited the discussion to exploitation rooted in control or ownership of productive forces, i.e. the various kinds of inputs used in
production. But there may be other mechanisms through which
individuals or groups may be able to appropriate part of the social
surplus. Control over the means of salvation may give Churches an
ability to exploit believers. Control over military violence may
give the state an ability to appropriate part of the surplus whether
or not it is also involved in controlling aspects of the forces of
production. Male domination within the family may enable men to
appropriate surplus labour in the form of domestic services from
their wives. Racial domination may enable whites as such, regardless of economic class, to exploit blacks.

The issue then becomes: why should property relations be

rivileged in the analysis of classes? Why should the analysis evolve around ownership/control of the productive forces and the xploitation and class relations that are built on that ownership? Vhy not talk about religious classes, or military classes, or sex lasses, or race classes?

To begin with, it should be noted that if the mechanism which llows priests, officers, men or whites to exploit others is their wnership/control over productive assets, then there is no particu- ar challenge posed to the strategy of analysis proposed in this hapter. While these non-asset social criteria would be important n explaining the social distribution of productive assets, it would emain the case that class and exploitation would remain defined n terms of property relations.

The difficulties arise when various kinds of non-productive ategories have direct, enforceable claims on the surplus, unmedi- ated by their relationship to the system of production. Men, for xample, may appropriate surplus labour from women simply by virtue of being men within the gender relations of the family and lot by virtue of the gender distribution of productive assets. Such ossibilities pose a more serious challenge to the approach I have een pursuing.

There are basically two reasons why I think the concept of class hould be restricted to exploitation rooted in production relations and not extended to encompass all possible social relations within which exploitation occurs. First, the concept of class is meant to figure centrally in epochal theories of social change, theories of the overall trajectory of historical development. In such epochal theories, the development of the productive forces—of technology and other sources of productivity—play a pivotal role.[48] Even if we do not accord the development of the productive forces an auton- omous, trans-historical, dynamic role in a theory of history, nevertheless it can be argued that whatever directionality histori- cal development has is the result of the development of the pro- ductive forces.[49] If we grant this, then the effective control over the productive forces and the exploitation which such control gener- ates has a particularly important strategic significance in the theory of history. Such control—property relations broadly con- ceived—defines the basic terrain of interests with respect to histor- ical development. For this reason, it can be argued, it is appropri- ate to restrict the concept of class to property relations.

Even if we reject the thesis that the productive forces play a pivotal role in the theory of history, there is still a second argument for restricting the concept of class to production relations. exploitation rooted in production relations has a distinct logic from exploitation rooted in other relations, then one would be justifie in treating property-based exploitation and the associated socia relations as a distinct category, that of a 'class'.

What is this 'distinct logic'? Above all, production relations ar a distinctive basis for exploitation because of the way they ar systematically implicated in the basic subsistence of the exploited Property relations not only determine mechanisms by which sur plus is appropriated; they simultaneously determine mechanisms b which the exploited gain access to subsistence, to their means c existence. Other mechanisms of exploitation are essentially *redis* tributive of a social product already produced within a set of prop erty relations; property-based exploitation is directly bound u with the social production of that product in the first place. We ar justified, therefore, in considering production-based exploitation distinct category from non-production exploitations because of th specific type of interdependency it creates between the exploite and the exploiter.

This distinctiveness does not, in and of itself, say anything abou the relative importance of class exploitation over other forms c exploitation. Military exploitation or gender exploitation could b more fundamental for understanding social conflict than clas exploitation (although I do not in fact think that this is the case) The distinctive form of interdependency constituted by productio based exploitation, however, does provide a rationale for restrict ing the usage of the concept of 'class' to that kind of exploitation.

I do not feel that my responses to any of these problems have bee entirely satisfactory. Nevertheless, at some point in any process o concept formation it is necessary to suspend the pre-occupatio with conceptual coherence and logical refinement and forge ahead in order to actually use the concept theoretically and empirically This will be the objective of the rest of this book. In the nex chapter we will explore a range of theoretical issues using the framework elaborated in this chapter. This will be followed b three chapters which use the concept to investigate a variety o empirical problems.

Notes

1. I would like to express my particular thanks to Robbie Manchin for an intense Sunday afternoon's discussion of the problem of class and exploitation which led to development of the core ideas in this chapter. His ideas in that discussion were particularly important for developing the concept of 'organization assets' discussed below.

2. John Roemer is a Marxist economist engaged in a long term project of reconstructing what he calls the 'microfoundations' of Marxist theory. His most important work is entitled *A General Theory of Exploitation and Class*, Cambridge, Massachussets 1982. A debate over this work in which I participated, appears in the journal *Politics & Society,* vol. 11, no. 3, 1982.

3. If the poor are able to force a partial redistribution of income from the rich through political means it might seem that by this definition this could be construed as a situation of the poor exploiting the rich: the poor become less poor at the expense of the rich. It is important, therefore, to examine the total causal context before assessing exploitation relations. In the case in question, *if* the rich obtained their incomes through exploitation, then a redistribution should be viewed as a reduction in exploitation rather than counter-exploitation.

4. While Roemer's work should not be viewed as an example of the 'Sraffian' critique of the labour theory of value, he shares with Sraffian economists like Ian Steedman (*Marx After Sraffa*, London 1977) the thesis that the labour theory of value should be dismissed entirely. It is, in Roemer's view, simply wrong as the basis for any theoretical understanding of exchange and unnecessary for an understanding of capitalist exploitation.

5. The technical form of the argument involves constructing general equilibrium models based on relatively simple maximizing behaviours of the actors. As in all general equilibrium models, these models depend upon the specific assumptions adopted concerning preference structures and production functions. Recently, Roemer has shown that it is possible to construct models in which the outcomes violate the logic of the concept of exploitation. For example, if the preference for leisure over labour *declines* as ownership of assets increase, then it can happen that labour transfers will flow from the rich to the poor under certain institutional arrangements. See Roemer, 'Should Marxists be Interested in Exploitation', University of California, Davis, Department of Economics, working paper no. 221, 1983. For the purposes of the present analysis, I will ignore these complications.

6. The important property of this demonstration is that both class and exploitation are derived from the initial ownership of means of production (property relations). Classes need not be initially defined in terms of exploitation; it is a discovery of the model that class relations are exploitative.

7. The claim that labour-market island and credit-market island are isomorphic is equivalent to the neo-classical economist's claim that it does not matter whether capital hires labour or labour rents capital. Roemer agrees with the neo-classical argument, but adds one crucial observation: in both cases it is capital that exploits labour. In neo-classical economics, of course, the identity of the two situations is described in terms of the identity in income returns rather than exploitation relations.

8. John Roemer, *A General Theory of Exploitation and Class* (GTEC), p. 194.

9. Ibid., p. 195.

10. An alternative criterion is to say 'S' would be worse off if S simply stopped

producing'. This solves the problem for the two island case, since the welfare of the rich island would not be affected by the activities on the poor island, and it conveys the idea that there is a causal relationship between the payoffs to the two coalitions. But it does not handle the handicapped case, since the handicapped would be worse off if the able-bodied stopped producing. Because of this, I will rely more on the domination criterion in this discussion.

11. See Roemer, GTEC, p. 206. In effect, personal bondage prevents market mechanisms from operating in ways which bring wages in line with the value of the marginal product.

12. Roemer introduces what he terms 'needs exploitation' as an additional concept for understanding the transition from socialism to communism. If people have different real needs, then a perfectly equal distribution of income would be situation of 'needs exploitation' in which the more needy are exploited by the less needy, GTEC, pp. 279–283. Since the concept of need exploitation has a distinctively different logic from the other types of exploitation and since it does not correspond to a class relation—the needy are not in a social relation of production to the less needy—I will not discuss it further here.

13. Roemer is an economist and the use of the word 'status' is not meant to evoke the meanings generally attached to this word in sociology.

14. John Roemer, GTEC, p. 243.

15. This is not to imply that domination in the labour process is *institutionally* unimportant, or indeed, that such domination does not in practice intensify capitalist exploitation and reinforce the capital–labour class relation. Roemer's point is simply that it is not the actual criterion for class relations; that criterion is strictly based on property relations as such.

16. See Erik Olin Wright, 'The Status of the Political in the Concept of Class Structure', *Politics & Society*, vol. 11, no. 3, 1982.

17. This position is most forcefully staked out in Roemer's essay, 'Why Should Marxists be Interested in Exploitation?' The illustrative example discussed here comes from this essay.

18. Two technical points: first, I use the expression 'the fruits of labour' rather than 'labour' since the definition is meant to be independent of the tenets of the labour theory of value. (For a specific discussion of the distinction between viewing exploitation as appropriation of the fruits of labour rather than the appropriation of labour values, see G. A. Cohen, 'The Labour Theory of Value and the Concept of Exploitation', in *The Value Controversy*, Steedman *et al.*, London 1981). Second, 'surplus' is notoriously hard to define rigorously once the labour theory of value is abandoned, since its magnitude (i.e. its 'value') can no longer be defined independently of prices. Throughout this discussion, when I refer to transfers of surplus or claims on the surplus I am referring to the surplus *product* which will be appropriated by an exploiting class.

19. Roemer has recognized that there is a difference in capitalism between the exploitation of workers and the exploitation of the unemployed. He has captured this difference by introducing the additional criterion mentioned in footnote 1 above: capitalists would be worse off if workers stopped producing, but not if the unemployed stopped producing. When Roemer introduces this additional criterion he refers to the unemployed as 'unfairly treated' rather than exploited, where unfair treatment is essentially equivalent to what I am here calling 'economic oppression'. While I cannot prove this formally, I believe that the criterion Roemer adopts in this instance is equivalent to what I term 'appropriation of the fruits of labour by the exploited': to say that capitalists would be worse off if workers stopped produc-

ng (or, equivalently, if they left the game of capitalism with their personal assets, which in this case would only be their labour power) is the same as saying that in fact there is a transfer of surplus occurring from workers to capitalists.

20. Indeed, in many practical cases, the oppressor would be better off if the oppressed died, since oppression typically imposes costs on the oppressor in the form of social-control expenses, and sometimes even subsidies to the oppressed (as in the welfare-state provisions of minimum standards of living for the poor). In the example of the rich and poor peasant above, the rent paid to the poor peasant is like a welfare-state payment by the rich peasant: the rich peasant would be better off if he simply killed the poor peasant and took over the poor peasant's land.

21. It follows from this that, except under peculiar circumstances, exploiters would not have material interests in the genocide of the exploited, whereas non-exploiting oppressors might.

22. The awarding of credentials can restrict the supply of skilled power in a variety of ways: there may be straightforward restrictions on the numbers of people admitted to the schools which confer the credentials; cultural criteria (based on what some sociologists like to call 'cultural capital') may be established for admission to schools which effectively restrict the number of admissions even when no formal limit is imposed; the immediate costs of obtaining a credential may be prohibitively high, even though the ultimate returns would more than compensate for them. For the present purposes it does not matter a great deal which precise mechanisms explain the restrictions on the supply of skilled labour power. For a discussion of the importance of credentials in contemporary structures of stratification, see R. Collins, *The Credential Society*, Orlando 1979.

23. The distinction between the value of a commodity and its price is, of course, one of the cornerstones of the labour theory of value. But even if we abandon the labour theory of value because of the various technical problems which it encounters when dealing with heterogeneous labour and other issues, it is still possible to define a kind of value, distinct from empirical prices, which accounts for the kinds of transfers we are talking about. The 'value' of a commodity is the price it would have if there were no barriers to entry for labour or capital. When the price is above this value, then an appropriation takes place.

24. See G. A. Cohen, *Karl Marx's Theory of History*, pp. 409–41, for a discussion of why labour power should be considered part of the forces of production (i.e. a productive asset).

25. Slavery should thus be viewed as a limiting case of feudal exploitation, where the slave has no ownership rights at all in his or her own labour power, while the slave owner has complete ownership rights in slaves. In this formulation the common practice of lumping all pre-capitalist class societies together under a single heading—'precapitalist'—has some justification since, for all of their differences, they rest on a similar logic of surplus extraction.

26. In this logic, once peasants are free to move, free to leave the feudal contract, then feudal rents (and thus feudal exploitation) would be in the process of transformation into a form of capitalist exploitation. That transformation would be complete once land itself became 'capital'—that is, it could be freely bought and sold on a market.

27. In this formulation it might be possible to regard various forms of discrimination—the use of ascriptive criteria such as race, sex, nationality, etc., to bar people from certain occupations, for example—as a form of feudal exploitation. In effect there is not equal ownership of one's own labour power if one lacks the capacity to use it as one pleases equally with other agents. This view of discrimina-

tion corresponds to the view that discrimination is antithetical to 'bourgeois freedoms'.

28. Roemer, GTEC, p. 243, acknowledges the similarity between feudal and status exploitation, but treats this just as an interesting parallel rather than a problem.

29. The term 'statist societies' is somewhat awkward, since 'statism' is politically associated with a generic opposition to the expansion of state interventions rather than more narrowly with the problem of centralized, authoritarian state control over production as such. Other terms, however, have greater drawbacks. The expressions 'state bureaucratic socialism' or simply 'state socialism', for example, contribute to the conflation of socialism with authoritarian state controlled production. With some trepidation, therefore, I will employ the expression 'statism' in this exposition.

30. This 'control of the surplus', it must be noted, is *not* the equivalent of the *actual* personal consumption income of managers and bureaucrats, any more than capitalist profits or feudal rents are the equivalent of the personally consumed income of capitalists and feudal lords. It is historically variable both within and between types of societies what fraction of the surplus effectively controlled by exploiting classes is used for personal consumption and what portion is used for other purposes (feudal military expenditures, capitalist accumulation, organization growth, etc.). The claim that managers or bureaucrats would be 'worse off' under conditions of a redistribution of organization assets refers to the amount of income they effectively control, and which is therefore potentially available for personal appropriation, not simply the amount they actually personally consume.

31. It is because capitalism at one and the same time both largely eliminates one form of exploitation and accentuates another that it is difficult to say whether or not in the transition from feudalism to capitalism overall exploitation increased or decreased.

32. It should be noted that this claim is logically independent of the labour theory of value. There is no assumption that commodities exchange in proportions regulated by the amount of socially necessary labour embodied in them. What is claimed is that the income of capitalists constitutes the monetary value of the surplus produced by workers. That is sufficient for their income to be treated as exploitative. See G. A. Cohen, 'The Labor Theory of Value and the Concept of Exploitation', for a discussion of this treatment of capitalist exploitation and its relation to the labour theory of value.

33. This, it should be noted, is precisely what leftist critics within 'actually existing socialist societies' say is the core problem on the political agenda of radical change in those countries.

34. For a discussion of the problem of the democratization of organizational control in the context of the Russian Revolution and other attempts at workers democracy, see Carmen Sirianni, *Workers Control and Socialist Democracy*, London 1982.

35. Or, to use the expression that is no longer in favour in 'polite' Marxist circles, that socialism is the 'dictatorship of the proletariat'.

36. Stated somewhat differently, a table of correspondences between asset ownership and relational location similar to table 3.1 could be constructed for both labour-power assets and organization assets, but not skill assets. Although the form of the derivations involved would be different from the one for capital assets, in each case it would be possible to 'derive' a set of relational properties directly from the ownership of the assets. In the case of organization assets the derivation would

be of the authority relations that would be attached to positions by virtue of the organizational assets controlled by incumbents of the position; in the case of feudal assets there would be a direct correspondence between ownership of a labour-power asset and personal control over the biological possessor of that asset.

37. In the case of capitalist societies this might imply that skill or credential differences should be regarded as the basis for class segments or fractions among workers and among manager-bureaucrats, rather than a proper dimension of the class structure. I will continue in the rest of this book to treat credential-exploitation as the basis of a class relation, as reflected in table 3.2, but this characterization should be treated cautiously.

38. One can imagine three possible degrees of equalization: (1) equalization of actual possession of an asset; (2) equalization of the control over the acquisition and use of the asset; (3) equalization of the income generated by the asset. Eliminating exploitation requires, at a minimum, the satisfaction of (3) for each asset. It may or may not require (1). In the case of the transition from feudalism to capitalism, for example, actual possession of labour power was basically equalized as well as effective control. In the transition from socialism to communism it seems implausible that actual possession of skills could be equalized, but probably control over the use of socially productive skills could be.

39. Note that *some* petty bourgeois, in this formulation, will actually be exploited by capital (through unequal exchange on the market) because they own such minimal means of production, and some will be capitalistic exploiters because they own a great deal of capital even though they may not hire any wage-earners. Exploitation status, therefore, cannot strictly be equated with self-employment/wage-earner status.

40. This is not to deny that many professionals and managers become significant owners of capital assets through savings out of high incomes. To the extent that this happens, however, their class location begins to shift objectively and they move into a bourgeois location. Here I am talking only about those professional and managerial positions which are not vehicles for entry into the bourgeoisie itself.

41. The old middle class in feudalism, on the other hand, is defined by the freed peasants (yeoman farmers), the peasant who, within a system of unequally distributed assets in labour power own their per capita share of the asset (i.e. they are 'free').

42. Theorists who have attempted to analyse the class structures of 'actually existing socialism' in terms of concept of a 'new class' generally tend to amalgamate state bureaucrats and experts into a single dominant class location, rather than seeing them as essentially vying for class power. Some theorists, such as G. Konrad and I. Szelenyi, *Intellectuals on the Road to Class Power*, and Alvin Gouldner, *The Future of Intellectuals . . .* , do recognize this division, although they do not theorize the problem in precisely the way posed here.

43. For discussions of the ways in which the capitalist state is systematically tied to the interests of the bourgeoisie, see Claus Offe, 'Structural Problems of the Capitalist State: class rule and the political system', in C. von Beyme ed., *German Political Studies*, vol. 1, Russel Sage, 1974; Göran Therborn, *What Does the Ruling Class Do When it Rules?*, London 1978. For a contrasting view which gives the state much greater potential autonomy from capital, see Theda Skocpol, 'Political Response to Capitalist Crisis: neo-Marxist Theories of the State and the Case of the New Deal', *Politics & Society*, vol. 10, no. 2, 1980.

44. While it has become very fashionable on the left to criticize any hint of 'economism' in social theory, I nevertheless believe that the emergence of the kinds

of political and ideological conditions necessary for the development of anti-capitalist postures by managers and state bureaucrats are more likely under conditions of chronic stagnation and decline than under conditions of capitalist expansion and growth.

45. For a fuller discussion of the implications of the arguments presented here for the Marxist theory of history, see chapter four below.

46. For a detailed analysis of the differences between incomes of managers and workers, see Erik Olin Wright, *Class Structure and Income Determination,* especially pp. 134–138. In that study, managers earned on average $7,000 more per year than did workers (1970 data). When the income figures were adjusted for differences between managers and workers in education, age, seniority, occupational status and several other variables, the average manager still earned over $3200 more per year than the average worker.

47. I would like to thank Robert van der Veen for bringing this specific issue to my attention.

48. This is not the place to enter the debates on the theory of history in general, or the role of the productive forces in such a theory in particular. For a discussion of these problems, see Andrew Levine and Erik Olin Wright, 'Rationality and Class Struggle', *New Left Review*, 123, 1980, and Erik Olin Wright, 'Giddens's Critique of Marxism', *New Left Review*, 139, 1983.

49. The argument is basically that technical change creates a kind of 'ratchet' in which movement 'backward' (regressions) become less likely than either stasis or movement 'forward'. Even if the occurrence of technical change is random and sporadic, therefore, it will generate weak tendencies for historical change to have direction.

4

Implications and Elaborations of the General Framework

Chapter three proposed a general strategy for systematically rethinking the concept of class structure in terms of exploitation relations. In my earlier work and in the work of many other Marxists, the concept of class had effectively shifted from an exploitation-centred concept to a domination-centred concept. Although exploitation remained part of the background context for the discussion of class, it did not enter into the elaboration of actual class maps in any systematic way. That shift undermined the coherence and power of the concept of class and should now be replaced by a rigorous, exploitation-centred conceptualization.

The task of this chapter is to explore in greater detail the theoretical implications of the reconceptualization which was summarized schematically in table 3.2. In particular, we will examine the following problems:

(1) The relationship between Marxist and various non-Marxist class theories;
(2) Mode of production and social formation;
(3) The traditional Marxist theory of history: historical materialism;
(4) The problem of legitimation and incentives;
(5) Class structure and the form of the state;
(6) The relation of class structure to class formation;
(7) The problem of class alliances;
(8) Women and class structure.

In each case my comments will be suggestive rather than exhaustive, indicating the basic lines of inquiry that can be followed from this starting point.

Alternative Class Theories

Certain parallels can be drawn between some of the elements in the concept of class structure elaborated here and other sociological concepts of class, particularly those found in the Weberian tradition. For example, the thesis that exploitation is rooted in the monopolization of crucial productive assets is similar to Frank Parkin's characterization of Weber's concept of social closure as 'the process by which social collectivities seek to maximize rewards by restricting access to resources and opportunities to a limited circle of eligibles'.[1] Although Parkin's central concern is with the kinds of attributes which serve as the basis for closure—race, religion, language, etc.—rather than with the nature of the resources (productive assets) over which closure is organized, and although his theoretical agenda aims to displace class analysis from the central stage of sociological theory, it is nevertheless true that both he and I emphasize effective control over resources as the material basis for class relations.

The conceptualization proposed here of the relationship between class and exploitation is also similar in certain respects to Alvin Gouldner's conception of cultural capital and the 'new class'. Gouldner defines the 'new class' as a *cultural* bourgeoisie defined by its control over 'cultural capital', where 'capital' is defined as 'any produced object used to make saleable utilities, thus providing its possessor with *incomes*, or claims to incomes defined as legitimate because of their imputed contribution to economic productivity'. These claims to income, Gouldner argues, are enforced 'by modifying others' access to the capital-object or threatening to do so'.[2]

Perhaps most obviously, there is an important relationship between the arguments I have laid out and the familiar three-class model proposed by Max Weber and further elaborated in the work of Anthony Giddens and others. Giddens writes:

> There are three sorts of market capacity which can be said to be normally of importance [in structuring classes]: ownership of property in the means of production; possession of educational or technical qualification; and possession of manual labour power. In so far as these tend to be tied to closed patterns of inter- and intragenerational mobility, this yields the foundation of a basic three-class system in capitalist society: an 'upper', 'middle', and 'lower' or 'working' class.[3]

Effective control over productive resources is the material basis for class relations, and different classes are defined with respect to different resources.

These similarities between the concept of class structure elaborated in this chapter and the Weberian one call into question the usual way Marxists (including myself) have characterized the distinction between the rival class concepts. The typical characterization is that Weber adopts a definition of classes based on *market* or *exchange* relations, whereas Marx adopts a *production* relations definition.[4] The real difference is more subtle. Both Marx and Weber adopt production-based definitions in that they define classes with respect to the effective ownership of production assets: capital, raw labour power and skills in Weber; capital and labour power (for the analysis of capitalism) in Marx. The difference between them is that Weber views production from the vantage point of the market exchanges in which these assets are traded, whereas Marx views production from the vantage point of the exploitation it generates, and this in turn, as I will argue below, reflects the fundamental difference between a culturalist and a materialist theory of society.

The difference between viewing production from the vantage point of exchange or exploitation has significant implications for the kind of class theory that is built upon this foundation. For Weber, owners of capital, raw labour power and skills all meet in the market and are all part of a single class system or class logic because the exchanges take place within the same institutional context. Marx, on the other hand, regards the distinctively capitalist class structure as only involving the exchange between capital and labour power because it is this exchange which generates the distinctively capitalist form of exploitation. Skill ownership is irrelevant to the specification of *capitalist* class relations. Of course, real-world capitalist societies involve more than just capitalist exploitation, and it would be at this more concrete level of analysis that the problem of skills would enter the analysis. The Marxist critique of Weber's analysis, therefore, is that Weber collapses together two quite distinct levels of abstraction in the analysis of classes: the levels of abstraction of *mode of production* and *social formation*.[5]

Why should this matter? The conflation of these two levels of abstraction underwrites Weber's treatment of classes as limited to market systems, and thus his unwillingness to treat historical development as a trajectory of qualitatively distinct forms of class structure. For Weber, therefore, the social structures of pre-capitalist feudal societies are not based on class antagonisms rooted in a distinctive form of exploitation, but rather on status orders and, although Weber himself did not systematically analyse post-capitalist society, the typical Weberian treatment would insist that these societies as well were not structured by class and exploitation in any fundamental way, but rather by political-bureaucratic relations. Class is a central feature of social structure only in capitalism; other types of societies are structured by other kinds of social relations.

Underlying this apparent shift in explanatory principle from feudalism to capitalism to post-capitalism in the Weberian perspective is a common fundamental principle: namely, that what really explains the logic of a social order and its development is the meaning systems that shape social action. For Weber, the shift from status to market is, above all, a shift in the meaning systems implicated in action. In feudal societies, status orders provide the central principles of collective identity and meaning. The transformation of traditional into modern societies is above all a process of rationalization, in which rational calculation replaces traditional norms as the central orientation to action. Class becomes the central principle of social stratification and collective identity corresponding to this emergent rationalization of systems of meaning.

What this implies is that although the formal *criteria* for classes in capitalist society are closely related in Weberian and Marxist analysis, the logic for the use of those criteria are quite distinct. The framework elaborated in table 3.2 defends the choice of criteria on the grounds that they determine a system of material exploitation and associated class relations; the use of some of those same criteria by Weber is based on their salience for the meaning systems of actors under given historical conditions. In the Marxist framework, the material interests embedded in these processes of exploitation have an objective character regardless of the subjective states of the actors; in the Weberian perspective, it is only because rationalization implies a particular kind of subjective understanding of material interests by actors that one is justified in describing these relations as class relations at all. At the heart of the distinction between Weberian and Marxist concepts of class, therefore, is the contrast between an essentially culturalist theory of society and history and a materialist theory.

Mode of Production and Social Formation

The formal typology of exploitation relations and corresponding class structures in Table 3.2 is essentially a typology of modes of production. Actual societies, as I have argued, can never be characterized as having only one type of exploitation; they are always complex combinations of modes of production. This is what it means to analyse societies as social formations.

'Combination' is obviously a vague word. If we are to give theoretical specificity to the use of these concepts in the analysis of concrete societies, much more precise content must be given to it. This means, above all, specifying the salient ways in which these combinations vary. Three axes of variability seem especially important: 1) the *relative weight* of different types of exploitation in a given society; 2) the extent to which these diverse exploitations are linked through *internal* or *external* relations; 3) for the internal relations, the extent to which the exploitation relations are *overlapping* or *distinct*. A full-fledged map of the class structure of a given society requires attention to all of these. Let us look at each briefly.

RELATIVE WEIGHT

When we say that a *society* is feudal, or capitalist, or statist, or socialist, we are claiming that one specific form of exploitation is *primary* in the society. Primacy is one particular kind of claim about relative weight of different modes of production. But relative weight is not just a question of primacy. It may matter a great deal for the political conflicts in a society what forms of exploitation are secondary, and how important they are relative to the primary form of exploitation. It is even possible that no one relation of exploitation is primary. While Marxists have tended to argue that one mode of production or another must be dominant, this is generally an unargued assertion. Depending upon precisely how these multiple forms of exploitation are linked together, there is no *a priori* reason to exclude the possibility of relatively equal importance for distinct forms of exploitation. What we need, therefore, is some way of identifying the full range of possible mixes of forms of exploitation within a specific society.

There are several options for defining the relative weight of forms of exploitation in a society, none of which is easy to operationalize. First, relative weight can be a claim about destinations of the social surplus. Owners of different exploitation-generating assets appropriate parts of the surplus based on their property rights; relative weight is a description of the relative, aggregate magnitudes of those appropriations. A society is feudal if the largest proportion of the surplus goes to holders of feudal assets.

Second, relative weight can be a claim about the class power of the actors who obtain surplus through different mechanisms. A feudal society is one in which feudal lords—people who appropriate surplus by virtue of their ownership of distinctively feudal assets—are the 'ruling class', even if as a proportion of total surplus, some other class should receive a greater share. The power of a class, after all, is not just a function of the total amount of surplus controlled in the aggregate by its members; it also depends on the ability of those members to translate their individual class capacity, rooted in their individual appropriation of parts of the surplus, into a collective capacity. It could in principle be the case that the total amount of surplus appropriated by owners of skills in the United States is larger than the total amount of surplus appropriated by capital. But since the numbers of people involved are so large, and, in general, the level of their individual exploitation so small, they are much less able to translate this into collective class power.

Third, relative weight could be interpreted in a functionalist manner as is characteristic of certain treatments in the Althusserian tradition. In this strategy, the dominant mode of production is said to 'assign' specific functions or roles to the subordinate modes of production within the gestalt of the 'structured totality' of society. Much of the discussion of the persistence of peasant subsistence production in third-world capitalist societies has this character: the persistence of such smallholder production is explained by virtue of its functional role for capitalism (for example, by lowering the average wages of workers). Claims for the primacy of a mode of production, then, would be established by demonstrating the ways in which subordinate modes of production systematically fulfil functions for the reproduction of the dominant mode.

Finally, the relative weight of different forms of exploitation could be defined by the dynamic effects of different exploitations. A society, in these terms, would be characterized as capitalist if the logic of development of the society were most pervasively structured by the properties of capitalist exploitation. When Marxists claim that the societies of Western Europe are capitalist, even in cases like Sweden with over 40 per cent of the labour force employed by the state or cases like France with large nationalized sectors of production, they are generally arguing that the essential dynamics of these societies remain governed by the logic of capitalist exploitation and accumulation. This does not imply that all subordinate forms of exploitation need be functional for the dominant form, but simply that the overall trajectory of social change in the society is fundamentally limited by the dynamics of the dominant mode of production.

Given the overall explanatory objectives of Marxist theory, dynamic primacy is in many respects the most fundamental sense in which one can talk about the relative weight of different modes of production and their associated forms of exploitation within the gestalt of a social formation. Unfortunately, given the theoretical underdevelopment of our understanding of the dynamics rooted in each of the forms of exploitation other than capitalism, let alone the possibility of distinctive 'laws of motion' forged by distinctive combinations of these forms of exploitation, it is exceedingly difficult to use this way of assessing the relative weight of different forms of exploitation in a nuanced way.

INTERNAL VS EXTERNAL RELATIONS

There are two principal ways that different forms of exploitation can be linked concretely. By an 'external' link I mean that the two forms of exploitation each exist within distinct production processes, but interact with each other. Trade between capitalist societies and largely feudal or statist societies would be historically important instances of this. But external relations between forms of exploitation can exist within a given society as well. The interaction between simple-commodity producers and capitalist firms, or the relation between state productive apparatuses and capitalist firms would be examples.

'Internal' relations, on the other hand, imply the simultaneous operation of different forms of exploitation within a single production process. The role of organization asset exploitation in the modern corporation is a prime example. Sharecropping, under certain historical conditions, could be regarded as an internal combination of feudal and capitalist relations. Such instances can be considered cases of the 'interpenetration' of modes of production, in contrast to the simpler 'articulation' of modes of production that occurs with external relations.[6]

The forms of conflict and patterns of class formation are likely to be quite different under conditions of interpenetration or articulation of exploitation relations. Where different forms of exploitation are articulated, they are more likely to be seen as having distinct logics generating distinct interests for their respective exploiting and exploited classes than where they are interpenetrated. Managers, for example, are more likely to perceive their interests at odds with the interests of the bourgeoisie when they are located within the state than when they are located within capitalist firms.

OVERLAPPING VS DISTINCT RELATIONS

Finally, societies will differ in the way a given set of exploitation relations combines to create actual positions filled by individuals and families. Skill exploitation and organization exploitation, for example, may correspond closely where most people with skills are recruited into positions involving organization exploitation; or they may be quite distinct if there are large numbers of non-managerial technical and professional jobs. One of the important differences between Sweden and the United States, for example, is precisely this: Sweden has a higher proportion of non-managerial experts in its class structure than does the United States, even though the two countries have approximately the same proportions of managers and experts taken separately.

The extent of overlap of exploitation relations determines in part the extent to which the problem of class formation is a problem of class alliances. Where there is little overlap alliances become much more important, because contradictory locations within exploitation relations—the 'middle classes'—are likely to be more important. Where the different mechanisms of exploitation largely coincide with one another, the concrete class structure will have a much more polarized character to it.

Taken together, these three dimensions of variability provide a basis for elaborating a much more nuanced typology of forms of society than is possible by simply identifying a society with a single mode of production. Treating the problem of combinations of modes of production in this way can be considered analogous to the treatment of chemical compounds as combinations of elements, where modes of production are the elements and social formations the compounds. Relative weight refers to the proportions of different elements in a compound; internal/external relations to the distinction between a suspension and a solution; and overlap to the precise patterns of chemical bonding that link the elements together.

In chemistry, of course, not every combination of elements is possible. Some cannot even be forged; others are unstable. Some can only be produced in the laboratory under peculiar conditions; others exist 'naturally' in the world. Similarly, for social formations: not every combination of these three dimensions may be socially possible, and certainly not every combination has occurred historically.

The future theorization of the compounds of elemental forms of exploitation may enable us to resolve a number of theoretical problems that have confronted contemporary Marxism. Let me briefly discuss two examples: the perennial problem of the 'Asiatic mode of production', and the problem of varieties of capitalisms.

The 'Asiatic mode of production' (or oriental despotism) is a concept employed by Marx in an attempt to theorize the specificity of the class structure and social dynamics of the classic civilizations of China, Egypt, and elsewhere.[7] The central idea is that these civilizations combined powerful, centralized state apparatuses engaged in the construction and supervision of large scale irrigation projects (hence the expression 'hydraulic civilization') with largely autarchic peasant communities. The result of this particular combination was that no dynamic social forces capable of producing qualitative transformations could be generated endogenous to the social structure. As a result, these societies were doomed to perpetual stagnation, to a continual, if not necessarily always peaceful, reproduction of their essential class structure.

In terms of the analysis presented here, the 'Asiatic mode of production' could possibly be understood as a particular compound of basic forms of exploitation, combining feudal and organizational exploitation and class relations, perhaps even in relatively equal proportions. The term, therefore, refers to a particular kind of social formation, not mode of production. The predominant characteristic of Western European feudalism was absolute preeminence of feudal exploitation for a long period of time with the gradual rise of capitalist exploitation as a secondary form. Organization exploitation was virtually absent. Because of the large-scale water-works in the hydraulic civilizations, organization exploitation played a much more important role. One might even want to suggest that the centrality of such organization asset exploitatio in these societies, linked to the development of relatively stron centralized states, may help to explain why there were such wea tendencies for proper capitalist relations to emerge endogenousl within these societies, unlike in Western European feudalism.

The analysis of the combinations of forms of exploitation ma also provide a strategy for specifying more rigorously the variabi ity in class structures in different types of capitalism.[8] Capitali societies clearly differ in the ways these different types of exploita tions are combined. The expansion of the large corporation an the state, for example, can be viewed as increases in the role c organization asset exploitation, and may define the distinctive di ference between advanced capitalist societies and competitive cap italism. The co-existence of a dominant highly exploitative capital ist form of exploitation with a sizeable proportion of the populatio having their 'per capita' share of capital assets (i.e. subsistenc peasants) and a significant presence of secondary feudal element may characterize the 'compound' of many third world capitalism The addition of a relatively strong presence of organization asse exploitation in certain of these societies may be the characteristi 'compound' of those post-colonial societies that are sometime described as having an 'overdeveloped state'.

The analysis of modes of production and social formations ha obviously not even begun the serious theoretical decoding of com pounds. Indeed, our knowledge of the elements is still rathe crude. If Marxist class analysis is to develop into a more powerfu and nuanced theory, the investigation of these 'compounds' i essential. It is in terms of them that practical revolutions ar waged, that possibilities for social change are opened up or close off.

The Theory of History

At the heart of classical Marxism is not only a sociology of class but a theory of history. Much of the theoretical motivation for th analysis of classes comes precisely from the role of class structure and class struggles in understanding the overall trajectory of his torical development.

This is not the place to discuss the general theoretical strength and weaknesses of historical materialism.[9] What I would like to d

TABLE 4.1
Typology of class structures, exploitation and historical transitions

| Type of social formation | Exploitation-generating asset inequality | | | | Historic task of revolutionary transformation |
	Labour power	Means of production	Organization	Skills	
Feudalism	+	+	+	+	individual liberty
Capitalism	−	+	+	+	socializing means of prod.
Statism	−	−	+	+	democratization of organizational control
Socialism	−	−	−	+	substantive equality
Communism	−	−	−	−	self-actualization

is explore the implications of the class framework in table 3.2 for the way the overall trajectory of historical development might be characterized.

Table 4.1 presents a typology of class structures, forms of exploitation and historical transitions. The rows in this table are not 'modes of production' but types of societies (at the 'social formation' level of abstraction) which combine in different ways a plurality of exploitation relations. In each successive row in this table, one form of asset inequality has been eliminated, and along with it the associated form of class relations and exploitation.

In what sense can we say that the above set of historical transitions constitutes a meaningful *sequence* of transitions? How can it be argued that this constitutes a trajectory of some sort? The basic argument is that the probability of *successfully* accomplishing these transitions monotonically increases with the level of development of social productivity. It takes a higher level of productivity to successfully socialize the means of production than to equalize ownership in labor power assets; it takes an even higher level successfully to democratize (equalize) control over organization assets, and a still higher level to successfully equalize control over skill assets. The word 'successful' is important: the claim is not that *attempts* at creating bourgeois freedoms, or socializing the means of production, or democratizing organization or socializing skills cannot occur before a certain level of productivity has been obtained, but simply that the probability of such attempts actually accomplishing their objectives depends upon the level of development of the forces of production. For example, the attempt at creating stable, democratic control over organization assets in a situation where workers must work long hours to produce the basic subsistence needs of a society is much less likely to succeed than in a society in which there are high levels of automation, workers have the time to participate in managerial decision making and democratic economic planning, managerial tasks can be rotated in a reasonable manner, and so forth.

It must be stressed that the claim being made here is a probabilistic one, not an 'iron law'. Another way of stating it is to say that in order for a transition in table 4.1 to occur successfully when the level of development of the forces of production is inadequate, there would have to be some other kind of facilitating mechanism which could compensate for the unfavourable material conditions. One such possibility that revolutionary Marxists have often appealed to is ideological commitment. If there exists a sufficiently high level of ideological commitment on the part of the actors attempting such a transformation (or, at least, on the part of some critical set of actors), then they may be motivated to endure the kinds of sacrifices needed to overcome these relatively unfavourable material conditions. However, since it is difficult to sustain ideological fervour over long periods of time, there would be tendencies for revolutionary transformations occurring under these conditions to restore at least some forms of exploitation and domination. The higher the level of initial development of productive forces, the more flexible would be the other conditions for transition to occur. To the extent that the probability of success of a revolutionary transformation will affect the probability of attempting a transformation—since conscious, rational human actors are more likely to attempt projects that they believe are likely to succeed—then the development of the productive forces will also, if only weakly, increase the probabilities of the attempts as well.[18]

The claim that these forms of class relations constitute a sequence—a trajectory of forms—does not imply that it is inevitable that societies will in fact pass through these stages. The trajectory is a sequence of historical *possibilities*, forms of society that become possible once certain pre-conditions are met. The actual transition from one form to another, however, may depend upon a whole range of contingent factors that are exogenous to the theory as so far elaborated. This is one of the central problems with traditional historical materialism. Traditional historical materialism argues, in effect, that whenever a transition from one form of class relations to another becomes historically possible, forms of class struggle will develop that guarantee that such transitions will occur. It is asserted, but not systematically argued, that the capacity for struggle will always be forthcoming when the 'historic task' of struggle is on the horizon. Class interests beget class capacities. While classical historical materialism may provide a compelling account of the possibilities, it does not elaborate a coherent theory of the necessity of the transitions to actualize those possibilities.

The treatment of these forms as a sequence also does not imply that it is impossible for particular societies to skip stages. The argument about the development of the forces of production specifies the minimum conditions necessary for a transition to have reasonable likelihood of success, but it is entirely possible that a given society has developed far beyond that minimum before a transition (revolutionary transformation) is attempted. It is possible, for example, that contemporary advanced capitalist societies are sufficiently developed to be able simultaneously to socialize the means of production and to democratize the control over organization assets. Political stances in the developed capitalist countries that call for the extension of democracy in all spheres of life as the central demand of the transition to socialism are, in effect, calling for the simultaneous redistribution of rights in means of production and organization assets, that is, for skipping statism as a consolidated mode of production.[11]

This way of reconceptualizing historical materialism will undoubtedly be objectionable to many Marxists since it runs against a number of traditional Marxist claims. In particular, three traditional theses are being challenged. First, the view that socialism is the immediate immanent future to capitalism is brought into question. The transition from capitalism to socialism involves equalizing two kinds of exploitation-assets—means of production and organization—and there is no logical necessity for these to occur at the same time. There are thus at least two futures inherent to capitalism—statism and socialism—and therefore the fate of capitalism is much less determinate than is often allowed.[12] Second, the relative openness of capitalism's futures implies that the proletariat can no longer be assumed to be the only bearer of a revolutionary mission within capitalism. Other classes, as we noted in our discussion of the 'middle classes' in chapter three, have the

118

potential to displace the working class from this role. Third, the characterization of socialism as a form of society with its own distinctive form of exploitation runs counter to the traditional Marxist view of socialism as simply the period of transition to communism. Socialism, in traditional Marxist theory, is decisively *not* a mode of production in its own right. To be sure, Marx acknowledged that classes would continue to exist in a socialist society, but these were seen basically as vestiges of capitalism, not as rooted in the internal relations of socialism as such.

It might be asked: does this reconstruction of the stages of historical development undermine the traditional Marxist idea of history as having a *progressive* character to it? I think not. The sequence of stages are marked by successive eliminations of forms of exploitation. In this sense capitalism is progressive relative to feudalism, statism relative to capitalism, socialism relative to statism. Capitalism may no longer be thought of as the last antagonistic form of society in the trajectory of human development, but the progressive character to the trajectory is retained.[13]

Legitimation and Motivation

While exploitation can be based on the direct and continual coercion of exploited producers, class systems will in general be more stable and reproducible to the extent that some sort of consensus over the legitimacy of the class structure is established. Particularly since one of the hallmarks of exploitation is that the welfare of the exploiter depends upon the *effort* of the exploited, it would normally be expected that such effort would be more readily forthcoming to the extent that there was some minimal level of consensus over the legitimacy, or at least the necessity, of the existing class system. Each system of exploitation thus brings with it particular ideologies which attempt to defend the income returns to specific asset inequalities as natural or just. And, in each transition, the previous system's ideology is taken to be fraudulent and subjected to sustained criticism.[14]

Class systems tend to be legitimized by two different sorts of ideologies: one which makes appeals, explicitly or implicitly, to various kinds of *rights* in order to defend privilege and another which appeals to the general *welfare* in order to defend privilege. The formal language of rights probably does not pre-date the seventeenth century, but rights-like legitimations have an ancient pedigree. Ideological defences of feudalism in terms of the divinely ordained status of kings are as much rights defences as the more explicit claims typical of capitalist societies for the 'natural right' of people to the fruits of their property so long as the property was obtained without force or fraud. Here I want to focus on the welfare arguments. The rights defences of privilege may be important under certain historical circumstances, but the durability of class systems over long periods of time depends more pervasively, I believe, on the cogency of the welfare ideologies. Where claims to privilege based on welfare lack any credibility, their defence in terms of rights will tend to erode over time.[15]

By welfare arguments I mean those defences of a system of inequality—in our terms a class system—which claim that the underprivileged would in fact be worse off in the absence of the greater benefits enjoyed by the privileged.[16] In feudalism, it could be argued, serfs would be worse off in the absence of military protection from their lords, and such protection would not be forthcoming without feudal privileges. In capitalism, workers would be worse off without the investments and risk-taking of the bourgeoisie, and those investments would not be forthcoming unless capitalists derived some advantage from their position. In a statist society, non-managers would be worse off in the absence of responsible, loyal execution of planning decisions by bureaucrats, and such performance would not be forthcoming in the absence of bureaucratic privilege. And under socialism, non-experts would be worse off in the absence of the knowledge of experts, and that knowledge would not be acquired or efficiently deployed in the absence of expert privileges. In each case it is argued that the specific form of inequality is necessary for production to efficiently proceed for the general welfare. In effect, the status of these inequalities as exploitative is denied ideologically by virtue of the alleged general welfare which they promote.

These kinds of welfare defences of exploitative relations are not fabricated out of thin air. Each ideology has a material basis which gives it credibility. For example, in capitalism, what would happen if all capitalist profits were taxed (thus eliminating the exploitation transfer from the asset), but capitalists retained control over the use and disposition of the assets themselves? In all probability they would simply begin to consume their assets, i.e. disinvest. Capitalist exploitation is therefore the necessary *incentive* for investment *given the existence of capitalist property relations.* If those property relations are viewed as unchangeable or natural, then such welfare arguments defending income returns to the sheer ownership of property (i.e. capitalist exploitation) become quite compelling. Similar arguments can be constructed for other forms of exploitation as well.

In all of these cases there is in fact an objective, motivational basis for the ideological system which legitimates exploitation. In each case, it is in fact true that in the absence of exploitation, the productive asset in question will either be withdrawn from production or used less productively.[17] But legitimation depends upon the view that either the asset inequality in question or the motivations associated with that inequality are unchangeable, and that as a result, all incentive questions must take these property relations as fixed.

The critical issue then becomes the extent to which these asset inequalities and the motivations associated with them are in fact alterable. Marxists frequently argue that claims of the 'natural' or inevitable character of such inequalities are pure mystifications. While I do believe that property rights in these various productive assets are radically changeable, the belief in their inevitability and unchangeability is not a completely irrational mystification. There are two principal reasons why it may be rational for people to believe that the existing class structure is inevitable, the first having to do with the real costs of attempting to transform that structure, and the second having to do with the real probabilities of a success in that attempt.

The actual historical process by which a given kind of exploitation is eliminated involves tremendous costs since exploiting classes vigorously resist, often violently, attempts at the redistribution of their strategic assets. This means that it may well be the case in practice that the exploited would be worse off if they *attempt* to eliminate a given form of exploitation, even though counterfactually they would be better off in the absence of such exploitation. If these 'transition costs', to use Adam Przeworski's expression, are sufficiently high and prolonged, then it may well be reasonable for actors to treat the existing form of property relations as inevitable for all practical intents and purposes.[18] This may, to some extent, become a self-fulfilling prophecy, since belief in the unacceptability of the costs of changing a class structure will itself raise the costs of attempts at changing the structure. In such cases, given the practical impossibility of transforming the class structure, the legitimizing ideologies do reflect the necessary motivations and incentives for social production to occur.

Quite apart from the transition costs imposed by threatened exploiting classes, it can be the case that attempts at eliminating certain forms of exploitation may have a very low probability of succeeding. It may be, for example, that while it was possible for the Russian Revolution to destroy capitalist property relations, it would have been impossible to eliminate organization exploitation and skill exploitation given the very low level of development of the forces of production. Organization exploitation may have been an example of what Roemer has called 'socially necessary exploitation', under the specific historical conditions of the Russian Revolution. Accordingly, the ideologies which emerged to justify the inequalities generated by that exploitation reflected unavoidable incentive constraints.[19]

Even if the transition costs for eliminating a given asset inequality are not prohibitively high and the historical conditions structurally allow for such an equalization, it remains to be seen how far the motivational correlates of a given kind of inequality can themselves be radically transformed. If they cannot, then significant incentive problems are likely to emerge in the absence of exploitation, and such incentive problems could conceivably result in a decline in general welfare. The prospects of such a long term decline would themselves constitute a basis for legitimating the system of exploitation itself.

Typically, two contrary positions are taken on this issue. Many Marxists argue that the motivations associated with a given system of exploitation are directly caused by the system of exploitation itself. Capitalism engenders the kinds of motivations necessary to make capitalism work.[20] If capitalism were to be destroyed, then it might be possible to make a fundamental change in those motivations. Non-Marxist theorists, particularly neoclassical economists, on the other hand, tend to regard the distinctive motivational patterns of capitalism as basically trans-historical, as fundamental attributes of human nature. In the absence of exploitation (or, what they would characterize as differential income returns to capital, skills and responsibility) productivity would at least stagnate and probably decline.[21]

It is difficult, of course, rigorously to adjudicate between these contending claims. The historical evidence on either side is at best inadequate. While there are isolated instances of production organized along egalitarian principles without pervasive exploitation, there have never been entire complex economies so organized. What can be said is that the historical condition necessary to gain systematic knowledge of this problem is socialism, for only in a socialist society could alternative 'experiments' in incentive structures and various kinds of inequalities be explored in a serious way. The verdict of such experiments could conceivably be that some degree of what we have been calling capitalist exploitation is desirable, but such a verdict could itself only be reached under socialist property relations.

Class Structure and Form of the State

The different logics of class exploitation presented in table 3.2 have certain systematic implications for the nature of the political institutions likely to be associated with those class relations.[22]

In feudalism, given that the exploitative relation is based on differential ownership rights in people, it is likely that the exploiting class will need to have direct access to the means of repression in order to exercise those ownership rights. There will thus tend to be fusion of state institutions with the distinctively feudal property relation.

In capitalism, in contrast, the elimination of ownership rights in people means that the capitalist class no longer needs to exercise direct political control over the labour force. Domination is needed to protect the property relations as such, but not directly to appropriate the surplus. The institutional separation of the state apparatuses from private property thus becomes much more *possible*. Furthermore, the nature of the competition among owners of the means of production will tend to give each capitalist an active interest in having a state apparatus that enforces the rules of the game without being captured directly by any specific capitalist or group of capitalists. The institutional separation of state and property thus becomes not only possible, but *desirable* from the point of view of capitalists.

In statism, as I have argued, the pivotal exploitation-asset is organization. The state, in this context, becomes the central arena for organizing the organizations, for managing the organization assets for the whole society. *If* the organization assets are to remain unequally distributed and hierarchically controlled, then this makes centralized, authoritarian forms of the state extremely likely. Without the impersonality of the capitalist market to mediate the exploitation relations, any real democratization of the state in such a society would be likely to lead inexorably to a democrat ization of the control over organization assets, i.e. to a serious challenge to the class power of organization-asset exploiters.[23]

Finally, in socialism, the state is likely to take the form of some variety of participatory democracy (undoubtedly combined in some way with institutions of representative democracy). The elimination of inequalities of organization assets implies a democratization of decision making over planning and co-ordination of production, and it is difficult to see how that could be sustained on a societal level without pervasive democratization of the state's political apparatuses in ways which would include forms of direct participation.

Class Structure and Class Formation

In classical Marxism, the relationship between class structure and class formation was generally treated as relatively unproblematic. In particular, in the analysis of the working class it was usually assumed that there was a one-to-one relationship between the proletariat as structurally defined and the proletariat as a collective actor engaged in struggle. The transformation of the working class from a class-in-itself (a class determined structurally) into a class-for-itself (a class consciously engaged in collective struggle over its class interests) may not have been understood as a smooth and untroubled process, but it was seen as inevitable.

Most neo-Marxist class theorists have questioned the claim that there is a simple relationship between class structure and class formation. It has been widely argued that there is a much less determinate relationship between the two levels of class analysis. As Adam Przeworski has argued, class struggle is in the first instance a struggle *over* class before it is a struggle *between* classes.[24] It is always problematic whether workers will be formed into a class or into some other sort of collectivity based on religion, ethnicity, region, language, nationality, trade, etc. The class structure may define the terrain of material interests upon which attempts at class formation occur, but it does not uniquely determine the outcomes of those attempts.

The conceptual framework proposed in this book highlights the nature of the relative indeterminacy of the class structure–class formation relationship. If the arguments are sound, then class structure should be viewed as a structure of social relations that generates a matrix of exploitation-based interests. But because many locations within the class structure have complex bundles of such exploitation interests, these interests should be viewed as constituting the material basis for a variety of *potential* class formations. The class structure itself does not generate a unique pattern of class formation; rather it determines the underlying probabilities of different kinds of class formations. Which of these alternatives actually occurs will depend upon a range of factors that are structually contingent to the class structure itself. Class structure thus remains the structural foundation for class formations, but it is only through the specific historical analysis of given societies that it is possible to explain what kind of actual formation is built upon that foundation.

Class Alliances

Once class analysis moves away from a simple polarized view of the class structure, the problem of class alliances looms large in the analysis of class formations. Rarely, if ever, does organized class struggle take the form of a conflict between two homogeneously organized camps. The typical situation is one in which alliances are forged between classes, segments of classes and, above all, between contradictory class locations.

Individuals in contradictory locations within class relations face a choice among three broad strategies in their relationship to class struggle: first, they can try to use their position as exploiters to gain entry as individuals into the dominant exploiting class itself; second, they can attempt to forge an alliance with the dominant exploiting class; third, they can form some kind of alliance with the principal exploited class.

The immediate class aspiration of people in contradictory locations is usually to enter the dominant exploiting class by 'cashing in' the fruits of their exploitation location into the dominant asset. Thus, in feudalism, the rising bourgeoisie frequently used part of the surplus acquired through capitalist exploitation to buy land and feudal titles, i.e. to obtain 'feudal assets'.[25] Similarly, in capitalism, the exploitative transfers personally available to managers and professionals are often used to buy capital, property, stocks etc., in order to obtain the 'unearned' income from capital ownership. Finally, in statism, experts try to use their control over knowledge as a vehicle for entering the bureaucratic apparatus and acquiring control over organization assets.

Dominant exploiting classes generally pursue class alliances with contradictory locations, at least when they are financially capable of doing so. Such a strategy attempts to neutralize the potential threat from contradictory locations by tying their interests directly to those of the dominant exploiting class. When such 'hegemonic strategies' are effective, they help to create a stable basis for all exploiting classes to contain struggles by exploited classes. One of the elements of such a strategy is to make it relatively easy for individuals in contradictory locations to enter the dominant class; a second is reducing the exploitation of contradictory locations by the dominant exploiting class to the point that such positions involve 'net' exploitation. The extremely high salaries paid to upper level managers in large corporations certainly mean that they are net exploiters. This can have the effect of minimizing any possible conflicts of interests between such positions and those of the dominant exploiting class itself.

Such strategies, however, are expensive. They require allowing large segments of contradictory locations access to significant portions of the social surplus. It has been argued by some economists that this corporate hegemonic stragegy may be one of the central causes for the general tendency towards stagnation in advanced capitalist economies, and that this in turn may be undermining the viability of the strategy itself.[26] The erosion of the economic foundations of this alliance may generate the emergence of more anti-capitalist tendencies among experts and even among managers. Particularly in the state sector where the careers of experts and bureaucrats are less directly tied to the welfare of corporate capital it would be expected that more 'statist' views of how the economy should be managed would gain credence.

The potential class alliances of contradictory locations are not simply with the bourgeoisie. There is, under certain historical situations, the potential for alliances with the 'popular' exploited classes—classes which are not also exploiters (i.e. they are not in contradictory locations within exploitation relations). Such subordinate classes, however, generally face a more difficult task than does the bourgeoisie in trying to forge an alliance with contradictory locations, since they generally lack the capacity to offer significant bribes to people in those positions. This does not mean, however, that class alliances between workers and some segments of contradictory locations are impossible. Particularly under conditions where contradictory locations are being subjected to a process of 'degradation'—deskilling, proletarianization, routinization of authority, etc.—it may be quite possible for people in those contradictory locations which are clearly net-exploited to see the balance of their interests as being more in line with the working class than with the capitalist class.

Where class alliances between workers and various categories of managers and experts occur, the critical question for the working class becomes that of defining the political and ideological direction of the alliance. As I have argued, these contradictory locations are the 'bearers' of certain possible futures to capitalism, futures within which the working class would remain an exploited and dominated class. Should workers support such alliances? Is it in their interests to struggle for a society within which they remain exploited, albeit in non-capitalist ways? I do not think that there are general, universal answers to these questions. There are certainly circumstances in which a revolutionary state bureaucratic socialism may be in the real interests of the working class, even though workers remain exploited in such a society. This is the case, I believe, in many third world societies today. In the advanced capitalist countries, on the other hand, radical democratic socialism, involving the simultaneous socialization of capital and democratization of organization assets, is a viable, if long-term, political possibility. The issue is: what are the real historical possibilities facing the working class and other classes in a given society? It is only in terms of such real possibilities that the concrete political problem of class alliances can be resolved.

Women in the Class Structure

So far I have had little to say about forms of oppression other than class. Much of the recent debate in radical theory has revolved precisely around the issue of such oppressions, particularly around the relationship between gender domination and class.[27] I will not attempt here to present a sustained discussion of the general relationship between class structure and gender relations. Rather, I want to focus on a much narrow issues: the direct implications of the asset-exploitation approach to class for understanding the location of women in the class structure. In particular, I will address three issues: first, the problem of the acquisition and distribution of assets between men and women; second, the problem of the class location of women outside of the labour force (especially housewives); and third, the problem of whether or not women as such should be treated as a 'class'.

ACQUISITION AND DISTRIBUTION ASSETS

It has often been noted that the average wage of women wage-earners is much lower than that of men—about 60 per cent of the male wage in the United States and 85 per cent in Sweden. How might we approach these wage differentials within the framework developed in this book? There are three main possibilities, not necessarily mutually exclusive.

First of all, some or all of the wage differentials between men and women could be attributable directly to the distribution of skill and organization assets between men and women. Gender relations constitute one mechanism among many that helps explain the distribution of exploitation assets among people. Throughout our analysis, the focus has been on the consequences of ownership of productive assets; the *acquisition* of productive assets has been largely ignored. In some societies women are systematically excluded from any possibility of owning the key exploitation assets; in others they are not legally prohibited from such ownership, but gender relations impose serious obstacles through inheritance patterns, processes for obtaining credentials, managerial promotion practices, and so on. The result of the operation of such mechanisms is that the class distribution among women will be very different from the distribution among men.[28]

Second, gender itself could be conceived as a special kind of credential' in skill/credential exploitation. Recall the mechanism by which credentialling generates exploitation: credentials reduce the supply of labour in such a way that the wage is kept above the cost of producing the skills. Credentials need not constitute real qualifications for a job; they simply need to restrict the supply of a particular kind of labour power. Sex-segregation of occupations may function in a quite parallel way, by 'overcrowding' women into a few categories of jobs and reducing the competition in certain jobs held by men.

Finally, gender discrimination could be conceptualized as a truncated form of what we have called 'feudal' exploitation. In effect, there is not equal ownership of one's labour power if one lacks the capacity to use it as one pleases equally with other agents. The common observation by both Marxists and liberals that discrimination is a violation of 'bourgeois freedoms' reflects this 'feudal' character of patriarchy (and, similarly, of racism). The fact that both feudalism and patriarchy are often described as paternalistic–personalistic forms of domination reflects this common structure of the relation. This feudal character is truncated, at least in contemporary capitalist societies, because while women may effectively lack full rights in their own labour power by virtue of discrimination, it is no longer the case that these rights are formally vested in men.[29]

HOUSEWIVES AND THE CLASS STRUCTURE

The class location of housewives who are not part of the labour force has always been a vexing problem for Marxist theory. A variety of solutions have been proposed: some theorists have suggested that housewives of workers are in the working class because they are indirectly exploited by capital in that they contribute to the subsistence of their husbands and thus lower the costs faced by capitalists; others have argued that housewives occupy positions within a domestic or subsistence mode of production and are exploited by their husbands within that subsidiary class relation; still others have argued that the concept of class simply does not pertain to anyone outside of the labour-force, and thus housewives are not in any class at all.

The approach to class and exploitation elaborated in this book suggests that to ask this question we must define the pertinent assets effectively controlled by housewives, the counterfactual games in which they would be better or worse off, and the social relations into which they enter by virtue of their ownership of those assets. In these terms I think we can say the following: first, working-class housewives have no organization assets or credential assets, and at most extremely limited assets in means of production (household appliances). Secondly, like workers, they would be better off and capitalists worse off if they withdrew along with their husbands from the capitalist game with their per capita share of capital assets. Their exploitation-interets *with respect to capitalism*, therefore, do not differ from those of their spouses.[30]

But what about the social relations of production? This is of course the difficult issue. Housewives of workers are embedded in two production relations: first, they are in a social relation with their husbands within the subsistence production in the household; and second, since their family receives its income through wages, as members of a family they are in a social relation with capital. Their class location, *and that of their husbands*, therefore, must be assessed in terms of the relationship between these two relations. To the extent that male workers exploit and dominate their wives within household relations of production, they occupy a kind of contradictory class location: they are exploiters within one relation (household relations) and exploited within another (capitalist relations).

I do not think that it is transparently true that husbands universally exploit their wives within domestic production, and the case has certainly not been rigorously established. From a labour-transfer point of view it is not clear that there is a net transfer of surplus labour from housewives to their working husbands.[31] From the game-theoretic perspective it is even less clear that working class men would be worse off and women better off *within given families* if there was a completely egalitarian division of tasks in both the home and the workforce. This would depend upon how the total wages obtained by a family with two workers is allocated within the family and how the total amount of labour performed by the two would change under the counterfactual conditions. It is entirely possible that both spouses would be materially worse off under the counterfactual conditions, given the existence of gender discrimination in the labour market.[32]

My conclusion, then, is this: the housewives of workers are in the working class in their relation to capital and in a variety of possible classes with respect to their husbands. An assessment of the latter depends upon the real relations of control over assets, income and labour time within the family.

ARE WOMEN AS SUCH A CLASS

It is certainly possible, under particular historical conditions, for women as such to constitute a class. Where women are the chattles of their husbands and, simply by virtue of being women, are placed in a specific location within the social relations of production, then they constitute a class.

However, when certain radical feminists make the claim that women are a class, they are not simply claiming that under special historical conditions this may happen. The claim is that this is the universal condition of women in 'patriarchal' societies. If the term 'class' is to be used in the context of the theoretical arguments elaborated here, then this more universal claim cannot be sustained. 'Class' is not equivalent to 'oppression', and so long as different categories of women own different types and amounts of productive assets, and by virtue of that ownership enter into different positions within the social relations of production, then women *qua* women cannot be considered a 'class'. A capitalist woman is a capitalist and exploits workers (and others), both men and women, by virtue of being a capitalist. She may also be oppressed as a women in various ways and this may generate certain common non-class interests with the women she exploits, but it does not place her and her female employees in a common gender 'class'.

The reason, I believe, that radical feminists have sometimes felt a need to amalgamate the concepts of class and oppression and thus to treat women as a class, is because of the historical salience of Marxism within radical social theory. Many Marxists have insisted, at least implicitly, that 'class' was the only important kind of oppression and that class struggle was the only kind of struggle with genuine transformative potential. Under the terms of this particular discourse, the only way to legitimate the struggle for women's liberation was to treat it as a type of class struggle. This assimilation of women's oppression to class, however, has had the effect both of obscuring the specificity of the oppression of women, and of reducing the theoretical coherence of the concept of class. A more constructive strategy is to examine the relationship between class and gender mechanisms of oppression, to try to elaborate a dynamic theory of their interaction and the conditions for the transformation of each of them.

Conclusion

If the arguments in these last two chapters have been persuasive, the particular exploitation-centred class concept which I have elaborated has several significant advantages over alternative approaches to class. First, the exploitation-centred concept provides a much more coherent way of describing the qualitative differences among types of class structures than has been possible with alternative concepts. The abstract criteria for assessing the class relations of a given society are consistent across qualitatively distinct societies, and yet allow for the specificity of any given society's class structures to be investigated. The potential for generating a nuanced and powerful set of concepts to distinguish among social formations is also enhanced by the exploitation-centred concept of class. The concept thus avoids having the ad hoc quality that plagues most other class concepts as they are applied to historically distinct types of societies.

Second, the exploitation-centred concept provides a much more coherent strategy for analysing the class character of the 'middle classes' in contemporary capitalism. The contradictory nature of contradictory locations is much clearer than it was and the relationship between such locations and the polarized classes in a given class structure is specified much more precisely. This is accomplished in a way that remains consistent with the six theoretical constraints on the concept of class elaborated in chapter two.

Third, the exploitation-centred concept provides a much clearer link with the problem of interests than do domination-based concepts. This in turn provides the basis for a more systematic analysis of the relationship between the objective properties of class structures and the problems of class formation, class alliances and class struggle.

Fourth, the new concept is more systematically *materialist* than domination concepts. Classes are derived from the patterns of effective ownership over aspects of the forces of production. The different kinds of exploitation relations which define different kinds of classes are all linked to the qualitative properties of these different aspects of forces of production.

Fifth, the new concept is more *historically* coherent than the alternatives. It is the development of the forces of production which imparts to epochal social change whatever sense of direction exists.[33] Since the class–exploitation nexus is here defined with respect to specific kinds of forces of production, the development of those forces of production is what gives a historical trajectory to systems of class relations. The order given to the forms of society presented in Table 3.2 and Table 4.1, therefore, is not arbitrary, but defines a developmental tendency in class structures.

Finally, the concept of class elaborated in this chapter has a particularly sustained *critical* character. The very definition of exploitation as developed by Roemer contains within itself the notion of alternative forms of society that are immanent within an existing social structure. And the historical character of the analysis of the possible social forms implies that this critical character of the class concept will not have a purely moral or utopian basis. Class, when defined in terms of qualitatively distinct asset based forms of exploitation, both provides a way of describing the nature of class relations in a given society and of the immanent possibilities for transformation posed by those relations.

Concepts are peculiar kinds of hypotheses: hypotheses about the boundary criteria of real mechanisms and their consequences. A such they are provisional in the way that all hypotheses are. To the extent that a particular concept is more coherent than its rivals meshes better with the overall theory of which it is a part and provides greater explanatory leverage in empirical investigations it is to be preferred.

In such terms the apparatus presented here for analysing class structures in capitalist and other societies is conceptually valid This hardly means that it is without problems, some of which ma ultimately lead to its demise. But for the moment it fares well against its rivals.

So far we have only explored the theoretical origins and development of the new conceptualization and its theoretical merits compared to the main alternatives. In the next chapter we will attempt what is probably an even more contentious undertaking: the empirical adjudication of contending definitions.

Notes

1. Frank Parkin, *Marxism and Class Theory: A Bourgeois Critique,* New Yor 1979, p. 44.

2. Alvin Gouldner, *The Future of Intellectuals and the Rise of the New Class* New York 1979, p. 21.

3. Anthony Giddens, *The Class Structure of the Advanced Societies*, New Yor 1973, p. 107.

4. For examples of this way of describing the differences between Weber and Marx, see Erik Olin Wright, *Class Structure and Income Determination*, chapte one; Rosemary Crompton and John Gubbay, *Economy and Class Structure*, New York 1978, chapter two.

5. See chapter one for an elaboration of this distinction.

6. For an elaboration of the distinction between interpenetration and articula tion, see Erik Olin Wright, 'Capitalism's Futures'.

7. Recent discussions have largely discredited the idea that what is called the Asiatic mode of production is indeed a proper 'mode' of production. Nevertheless it is still generally acknowledged that there is a distinctive gestalt in the social structures of these societies which gives their class structures and class conflicts particular character. For critiques of the concept, see in particular, Perry Anderson *Lineages of the Absolutist State*, London 1974, and Barry Hindess and Paul C Hirst, *Pre-Capitalist Modes of Production*, London 1975. For a general collection of essays exploring the problem, see Ann M. Bailey and Josep R. Llobera, *The Asiat Mode of Production: Science and Politics,* London 1981. For an interesting and important discussion of Marx's view on the problem, see Theodor Shanin, *Lat Marx and the Russian Road,* New York 1984.

8. Capitalist sociezies obviously vary in ways other than their class structures and the comments here are not meant to suggest that elaborating the logic of variability in class structures is sufficient to construct a map of the variability of capitalist societies.

9. I have addressed these issues at some length in my essay 'Capitalism's Futures', and in a co-authored paper with Andrew Levine, 'Rationality and Class Struggle'. For the most sustained a vigorous defence of historical materialism, see G. A. Cohen, *Karl Marx's Theory* . . . .

10. It is important to be clear about the sense in which the thesis stated above is a kind of 'primacy of the forces of production' argument. The primacy being claimed is not based on functional explanations as in G. A. Cohen's argument in *Karl Marx's Theory of History*. . . . All that is being claimed is that the level of development of the forces of production determines the likelihood of successful transitions from one class structure to another, but not that there is any necessity of such transition. The directionality of the development of the productive forces therefore imparts a potential directionality to history, but neither a necessary destination nor an inexorable movement.

11. For two interesting, and important, elaborations of the democratic theory of socialism in the context of American society, see Joshua Cohen and Joel Rogers, *On Democracy*, New York 1983, and Sam Bowles, David Gordon and Thomas Weis-kopf, *Beyond the Wasteland*, New York 1984.

12. Of course, it is always possible to label a society with organization-asset exploitation 'socialist' and to retain therefore the formal appearance that socialism directly replaces capitalism, but the logic of this transition no longer has much similarity to the transition posited by Marx since it involves genuine class-based exploitation, and since it implies that there are two qualitatively distinct kinds of socialisms whose differences are of the same theoretical status as the distinction between capitalism and socialism.

13. To say that the trajectory is 'progressive' is not to claim that people are necessarily less oppressed in a simple, monotonic way as we move from one stage to another. Workers in early capitalism may well have been more oppressed and exploited than serfs at certain stages of feudalism, and workers at certain times in the development of statism have been more oppressed than workers in certain capitalist societies. The progressive nature of the trajectory comes from the potentials for emancipation, not from the empirical record of actual oppression of every society.

14. Roemer has an interesting discussion of the issue of legitimating ideologies of feudal and capitalist exploitation. GTEC, p. 205–208.

15. This need not imply that the privileges themselves will erode over time, since exploitation is reproduced by force as much as by ideology.

16. By 'welfare' defences in this context, I do not mean to refer only to what has come to be known as 'welfarism' in philosophical debates, but rather to any defence of a given structure of inequality in terms of its real consequences for the wellbeing of actors. In these terms, I would describe Robert Nozick's *Anarchy, State and Utopia*, New York 1974, as a clear statement of a rights perspective, and John Rawls, *A Theory of Justice*, Cambridge, Massachussets 1971, as an example of the welfare perspective on inequality.

17. As Gouldner argues, 'these claims to income (by owners of various kinds of capital) are enforced normally by withholding, or threatening to withhold the capital object', *Future of Intellectuals*, p. 21.

18. Adam Przeworski, 'Material Interests, Class Compromise and the Transition to Socialism', *Politics & Society,* vol. 10, no. 2, 1981.

19. For Roemer's discussion of 'socially necessary exploitation' see GTEC, p. 248.

20. Göran Therborn forcefully argues this position in his analysis of ideology and the ways human subjectivity is formed through patterns of 'subjection' and qualification'. See Göran Therborn, *The Power of Ideology and the Ideology of*

Power, London 1982. Of course, contradictions may emerge between the motivational requirements of capitalism and the actual motivations of the actors. Such contradictions, or what is sometimes called a 'motivational crisis', may be one of the signals of the likely demise of a class order. The important point here is that motivations are closely tied to the forms of exploitation and are viewed as highly changeable as those class relations change.

21. It should be noted that even if these conservative motivational assumptions were correct, it would not follow that the general welfare would necessarily decline in the absence of exploitation. Productivity could increase if, for example, wasteful production were reduced (eg. by radically reducing military spending, advertising, etc.) and investments were directed more consistently to satisfying human needs. The productivity argument translates into a welfare argument only if it is assumed that an identical bundle of things is produced. In many ways the real force of the appeal of socialism in terms of general welfare is not that it will achieve greater technical efficiency than capitalism, but that it will achieve greater social efficiency.

22. I am using the term 'likely' deliberately in this discussion to avoid any implication of strict 'derivation' of forms of the state from the 'functional requirements' of a form of class relations in the manner of the 'capital logic' approach to the state (see John Holloway and Sol Picciotto, eds, *State and Capital,* Austin, Texas 1978). I do believe that it is reasonable to talk about such functional requirements, and that they imply a set of pressures and chains of consequences that will tend to generate appropriate forms of political institutions. But these are just strong tendencies, not necessities. Since I will not explore the problem of these pressures, mechanisms and chains of consequences here, I will treat the relation as simply one of expected association of forms of the state with forms of class relations.

23. This implies that in a statist society it is still possible to distinguish the political apparatuses of the state from the economic apparatuses. The claim being made is that if the political apparatuses were radically democratized in a society with a dominant statist mode of production, it would be difficult to reproduce centralized authoritarian class relations within the state economic apparatuses. What would happen, it is predicted, would be either a restoration of essentially capitalist relations or a transformation into socialist relations.

24. 'From Proletariat into Class', Kautsky, 7:4.

25. In these terms, Max Weber's famous analysis of the protestant ethic and the spirit of capitalism can be viewed as an explanation of the way a particular ideological form—Calvinism—acted as a mechanism to prevent the feudalization of capitalist exploitation, thus facilitating the growth of capital accumulation. What Calvinism accomplished ideologically, the bourgeois revolutions accomplished politically by legally prohibiting the feudalization of capitalist accumulation.

26. See Bowles, Gordon and Weisskopf, pp. 166–167. The argument is that the growth of managerial costs associated with the growth of the megacorporation is one of the key factors undermining productivity growth in certain capitalist countries.

27. The issue of race and class poses some of the same problems, but has not received the concentrated theoretical attention given to the question of gender and class. While I do believe that the question of race is of great importance, particularly in the political context of the United States, and that it deserves sustained treatment, I have not engaged the debates over race and class sufficiently to discuss the relevance of the class framework proposed here for the problem of race.

28. See chapter six below for an empirical investigation of the class distributions of men and women in the United States and Sweden.

29. In the nineteenth century when men in fact had the legal power to control the labour power of their spouses in various ways, the relation was much more fully feudal in character.

30. Technically, in terms of the discussion in chapter three, all that I have shown is that the housewives of workers are economically oppressed by capital in the same way as their husbands, not that they are exploited by capital. Some Marxists have argued that surplus labour is indirectly appropriated by capital from housewives via the unpaid housework they perform which reduces the monetary costs of reproducing the labour power of their husbands. I do not think that this claim has been adequately demonstrated. In any event, in the present context, I do not think that the distinction between economic oppression and exploitation matters a great deal.

31. The research data indicates that while it is the case that wives who work in the labour force do a 'second shift' at home and therefore work many more hours per week than their husbands, this is not true for non-labour force housewives. They work on average fewer total hours per week than their spouses. See Heidi Hartman, 'The Family as the Locus of Gender, Class and Political Struggle: The Example of Housework', *Signs*, vol. 6, no. 3, 1981, p. 380, fig. 1.

32. For a forceful defence of this point for the historical conditions of the industrial revolution, see Johanna Brenner and Maria Ramas, 'Rethinking Women's Oppression', *New Left Review*, 144, March-April, 1984, pp. 33–71.

33. See my essay, 'Giddens's Critique of Marxism', for a discussion of why the forces of production can plausibly be viewed as giving history a directionality.

Part Two

Empirical Investigations

5

Empirically Adjudicating Contending Class Definitions

In this chapter we will attempt to adjudicate empirically between contending definitions within the Marxist theory of class. As I argued in chapter two, the problem of the 'middle class' has been at the centre of the contemporary rethinking of Marxist concepts of class structure. The empirical investigation in this chapter will therefore focus on the debates over the line of demarcation between the working class and 'middle-class' wage earners.[1] More specifically, I will propose a strategy for the empirical assessment of the relative merits of the approach to specifying the working class elaborated in chapter three and two important alternatives: the simple identification of the working class with manual wage-labor; and the more complex conceptualization of the working class proposed by Poulantzas. These are not, of course, the only existing alternatives. Many Marxist sociologists adopt a fairly loose definition of the working class that includes all non-supervisory manual labourers plus 'proletarianized' white collar workers (clerical workers especially). Such a definition comes extremely close to the exploitation-centred concept I have proposed in chapter three, and in practical terms they are almost indistinguishable. I have decided to focus on these two particular alternatives, therefore, partly because an empirical intervention into the debate is likely to produce relatively robust and interpretable results.[2]

In the first section of this chapter I will lay out the basic logic of my empirical strategy. This will be followed by a discussion of the practical task of operationalizing the variables to be used in this strategy. The final section of the chapter will examine the results of a statistical study using these operationalizations.

The Empirical Strategy

Definitions of specific classes can be regarded as a particular kind of proposition. All things being equal, all units (individuals and/or families, depending upon the specific issues under discussion) within a given class should be more like each other than like units in other classes *with respect to whatever it is that class is meant to explain*. The proviso 'with respect to whatever it is that class is meant to explain' is equivalent to saying that these kinds of definitional-propositions are always with respect to a given theoretical object. The disputes in question are not over how best to use *words*, although such issues may be important to avoid confusion in theoretical discussions. The debates are over how best to define a concept given that it designates a theoretical object that is subject to basic agreement. Class is not necessarily meant to explain dietary preferences, for example. There is therefore no reason to believe that individuals in the same class but in different ethnic groups will be more like each other with respect to such preferences than they will be like people who are in the same ethnic group but in different classes. On the other hand, class structure is meant to explain (along with other mechanisms) class conflict. A particular definition of the working class is thus a proposition about the lines of demarcation in the conflict producing process. This is *not* equivalent, it must be emphasized, to saying that all workers will act in identical ways, since the claim is not that class location is the *only* mechanism affecting class action. There may be ethnic or gender or other mechanisms that vary among workers and produce empirically heterogeneous outcomes in spite of a homogeneous class determinant. What is being claimed, however, is that all other things being equal, two people who fall within these lines of class demarcation will have a higher probability of behaving in a similar fashion within class conflicts than will two people falling on different sides of the line of demarcation. Accordingly, each contending definition of the same class is an implicit proposition about the homogeneity of effects generated by the structure which the definition attempts to specify.

If definitions are propositions about lines of demarcation for homogeneous effects, then this suggests that the appropriate strategy for adjudicating disputes over definitions of class is to focus on those cases where one definition places two positions on different sides of the line of demarcation whereas the rival definition

treats them as homogeneous. These are the cases where the differ
ences in definitions have different empirical implications.

These disputed cases can be identified by a simple cross
tabulation of the two definitions. This is illustrated in table 5.1 for
two contending definitions of the working class.

TABLE 5.1

**Categories in the adjudication of contending definitions of the
working class**

| | | *Definition A* | |
		Working class	'Middle-class' wage-earners
Definition B	Working class	[1] agreed-upon working class	[2] disputed category 1
	'Middle-class' wage-earners	[3] disputed category 2	[4] agreed-upon 'middle' class

Cell 1 in this table consists of positions which both definitions
define as working class. Cell 4, on the other hand, consists of
wage-labour positions which both definitions see as 'middle' class.
Cells 2 and 3 are the disputed categories. Definition A argues that
cell 3 should be much more like cell 1 than it is like cell 4, and
cell 2 should be much more like cell 4 than it is like cell 1, whereas
definition B argues that cell 3 should be basically similar to cell 4
and cell 2 should be basically similar to cell 1. The empirical
adjudication of these contending definitions of the working class
consists of seeing whether the disputed categories are closer to the
agreed-upon workers or to the agreed-upon 'middle' class in terms
of criteria on which both definitions agree the working class and
the 'middle' class should differ.

It should be noted that the logic of this strategy for adjudication
does not imply that the disputed category should be indistinguishable from the class in which a definition claims it belongs. Take the
problem of the identification of the working class with manual
labour. Even if one rejects the claim that this is an appropriate way
of defining the working class, one might still believe that for a
variety of reasons the manual–non-manual distinction constitutes

an internal division within the working class. This could imply, for example, that white-collar workers would be less ideologically pro-working class than manual workers and yet would still be within the working class. The hypotheses, therefore, are not that the disputed category is indistinguishable from either of the agreed-upon categories, but that it is significantly closer to one or the other.

In the specific comparisons we will be making in this chapter, the precise formulation of these hypotheses differs somewhat from the simple model in Table 5.1. There are two modifications. First, the exploitation-centred class concept includes a specific acknow-ledgement of certain kinds of 'marginal' class locations, particu-larly wage-earners with marginal credential assets and wage-earners with marginal organization assets. Such positions should not be simply amalgamated with either workers or non-workers in the adjudications, since this could conceivably have significant effects on the interpretations of results. It is more appropriate, therefore, formally to include such marginal workers in the adjudi-cation typology. This is illustrated in table 5.2. While the bulk of the adjudication analysis will focus on the corners of these tables,

TABLE 5.2

**Categories in the adjudication of exploition-centred
class concept with manual-labour and
unproductive-labour concepts**

Exploitation-centred definition	Rival definitions	
	Working class	'Middle-class'
Working class	[1] agreed-upon working class	[2] disputed category 1
Marginal working class	[3] ambiguous	[4] ambiguous
'Middle-class'	[5][a] disputed category 2	[6] agreed-upon 'middle-class'

[a]Cell [5] is empty in the comparison with Poulantzas's defini-tion of the working class using unproductive labour.

explicitly including the marginal categories will enable us to pursue a more nuanced analysis where necessary.

A second modification of the simple adjudication table in table 5.1, is that in the case of the comparisons with Poulantzas's definition of the working class, there are no cases in the lower-left-hand corner of the table (cell 5): there are no positions which Poulantzas would consider working class but which would be considered unambiguously outside of the working class by an exploitation-centred concept. The debate with Poulantzas's definition, therefore, is strictly over his allocation of certain positions which are working class by the framework elaborated in this book to the 'new petty bourgeoisie', especially unproductive wage earners.

It is important to emphasize that even if one definition is unambiguously shown to be inferior to another in this procedure, this does not definitively prove that it is 'incorrect'. It is always possible that some independent mechanism is at work which confounds the results. Let us suppose, for example, that women are predominantly subordinate clerical employees, and we were to use income as the 'dependent' variable in our adjudication. And further suppose, as is the case, that there is systematic wage-discrimination against women in general. In this case, the relationship between gender and the contending class criteria could have the effect of depressing the overall average income of cell 2 in table 5.2 and thus making it much closer to cell 1, even if among men or women *taken separately* the manual–mental distinction was a sharp one and cell 2 was much closer to cell 6. The defender of the manual-labour definition would then be able to show that the adjudication was confounded by the effects of gender-mechanisms. The verdict of the initial adjudication, which ignored the effects of gender mechanisms, would therefore be overturned in this subsequent analysis. Empirical differences must therefore be viewed strictly as a provisional basis for choosing between the contending definitions.[3]

These adjudication hypotheses will form the basis for the empirical analysis in this chapter. It is of course not a trivial problem to specify precisely what is meant either theoretically or empirically by 'more like' in these hypotheses. To do this involves both defining the *content* of the object of explanation (eg. consciousness, forms of collective action, income, etc.) and the appropriate *standard* for defining similarity. Once these tasks have been accomplished, however, the empirical test is straightforward. It is to this ask of transforming these general propositions into more concrete testable' hypotheses that we now turn.

Operationalizing the Adjudications

It is one thing to map out the logic of an empirical adjudication of contending definitions, and quite another to generate the necessary kinds of data and statistical procedures to carry out the exercise convincingly. The difficulty is that most existing sociological data which would be relevant to the task were gathered within a non-Marxist conceptual framework for quite different purposes. There are very few social surveys which contain either the necessary information to operationalize the exploitation-centred concept of class or to address the pertinent kinds of issues which make use of the Marxist concept of class consciousness.

It was for this reason that in 1978 I embarked on what has become a large comparative survey research project on class structure and class consciousness. This involved first developing a survey questionnaire which adequately measured a variety of alternative Marxist and non-Marxist class concepts along with a range of other issues, and then administering it to national samples of adults in a number of countries.[4] The data from the United States survey in this project will provide the basis for the empirical adjudication of the debates which we are considering.

We will first examine the 'dependent' variables in terms of which the comparisons of concepts will be assessed, before turning to the problems of specifying the various class structure categories in the two adjudications and the statistical procedures to be employed.[5] While the details of these operationalizations may seem rather tedious, they are nevertheless important, for the cogency of the final comparisons depends largely on the persuasiveness of the operational choices made in setting up the analysis. I will therefore go through each of these steps quite carefully. Readers who are impatient to see the punchline of the story could skip the rest of this section and turn directly to the statistical results which follow.

DEPENDENT VARIABLES FOR THE ADJUDICATION

In many ways the most delicate part of a conceptual adjudication lies in the specification of the 'dependent variables' in the analysis.

The adjudication proposed here only makes sense because the rival definitions are meant to explain at least some of the same things. It is therefore crucial that appropriate variables for making the comparisons are selected.

This task poses a rather substantial problem for the definitional adjudication at hand. In Marxist theory class structure is above all meant to explain a range of macro-social processes: class formation, class alliances, social conflict, historical trajectories of social change and so forth. Of course, Marxists frequently make claims about the consequences of class location for individuals (eg. in explanations of individual consciousness), but such claims are typically undertheorized and in any event are not the core of the theory within which the concept of class structure figures. A defender of Poulantzas's general stance towards class structure could therefore argue, with some justification, that the micro-level variables which I will investigate are at best of secondary importance within Marxist theory, and therefore cannot constitute a decisive basis for comparing the definitions.

Nevertheless, I will propose a number of individual-level variables to be used in the adjudication of the conceptual debates we have been discussing. I do this for two reasons. First, even though Marxist class analysis is, above all, a macro-theory of social relations and social change, that theory must be linked to a micro-theory of outcomes for individuals if it is to be complete. For class structure to explain social change it must have systematic effects on individual action. This does not prejudge the question of the extent to which the practices of individuals are explainable by class relations or by other determinants, but it is hard to imagine how class structure could explain class struggle and social change if individual behaviours were random with respect to class. This suggests that individual-level variables are appropriate criteria for comparing class concepts, even if they are not a sufficient basis for a definitive judgement of their relative merits.[6]

Second, to engage properly in an adjudication of class structure concepts using macro-historical data requires a very broad comparative analysis of the relationship between class structure on the one hand and class formation and class struggle on the other. The logic of the adjudication using macro-structural data is that one way of specifying the variations in class structures, both across time and cases, will better explain the variations in class formation and struggle than the rival specification. This is clearly a much more arduous empirical enterprise than the more micro-centred approach being used here. This is not to say that such a task is unimportant, but it is beyond my present research capabilities.

In the adjudication of contending class definitions, I will therefore focus primarily on dependent variables which are directly tied to individuals, in particular class-oriented attitudes and personal income. In what follows I will briefly justify the use of these specific variables and explain how they will be measured.

Attitudes: Justification

There are two critical objections which could be raised against the proposal to use attitudes as a criterion for adjudicating class definitions: first, that attitudes cannot be considered a valid indicator of class consciousness; and secondly, that even if attitudes perfectly reflected class consciousness, consciousness itself is only loosely related to class action, and this is the only appropriate criterion for assessing class concepts.

Attitude responses on a survey, however well designed the questionnaire, are at best loosely related to the Marxist concept of 'class consciousness'.[7] As critics of surveys have often pointed out, the opinions individuals express are heavily context-dependent, and the peculiar context of a questionnaire interview—an isolated individual talking to a representative of a scientific/elite institution—undoubtedly shapes the pattern of responses. It could well happen, for example, that workers will express much more conservative views in response to the questions posed in such interviews than they would in a conversation with their workmates.[8]

Nothing in the questions which we will use to construct attitude variables avoids these potential biases, and such biases might well influence the conclusions which we draw from the data. But it is important to remember that biases in data do not in and of themselves invalidate the use of such data to 'test' hypotheses, since biases may be neutral with respect to the expectations of a proposition or even make it more, rather than less, difficult to establish the plausibility of the hypothesis. In the case of our definitional adjudications, the critical empirical tests are always of the *differences* between various categories. Unless the biases differ across the class categories being compared in ways which influence the critical tests, then the adjudication comparisons can be perfectly sound even if the data is quite distorted. Thus, for example, we would indeed face problems if the biases in the responses operated in the opposite direction for proletarianized clerical employee than they did for manual workers. This could have the effect o making it appear that the two categories had similar class con sciousness (as measured by the attitude questions) when in fac their 'real' consciousness was quite different. In the absence o strong reasons for believing that such complex interactions of bia with class occur, I will assume that although there are certainl significant biases of various sorts in the responses to the attitud questions, these biases are random with respect to the comparison we are making.

A more serious objection to using attitudes as a criterion fo adjudicating contending class definitions is that class conscious ness, at least if this is understood as designating stable forms o consciously understood beliefs by individuals, is only very weakl linked to actual class behavior. Thus quite apart from the problen of using attitudes to measure class consciousness, they are no appropriate as adjudication criteria, since the contending specifi cations of class structure are meant to explain class practices struggles, and since consciousness is not a very important deter minant of actual behaviour. This is not to suggest that class actor are automatons, unconsciously playing out scripts in a drama; i implies merely that class action is much more heavily determinec by the concrete choices and pressures that people face in giver circumstances than by any stable or enduring patterns of con sciousness (beliefs, cognitive structures, values, etc.) which the bring to those choices. The only appropriate adjudication crite rion, therefore, would be the actual choices made, that is, the patterns of class behaviour.

My assumption in adopting attitudes as a criterion is thus tha they are not in fact 'epiphenomenal', that they have real conse quences for class action, and that they are, to some extent at least determined by class location. This implies that behind my use o attitudes is a causal argument about the relationship betweer forms of conscious subjectivity, class action and individual class location.

Class location is a basic determinant of the matrix of objective possibilities faced by individuals, the real alternatives people face in making decisions. At one level this concerns what Weber refer red to as the individual's 'life chances', the overall trajectory o possibilities individuals face over the life cycle. In a more mundane way it concerns the daily choices people face about what to do and how to do it.

The objective alternatives faced by individuals, however, are not directly transformed into actual choices or practices. Those objective alternatives must be perceived, the consequences (both material and normative) of different choices assessed, and a specific alternative chosen in light of such assessments. This process is partially the result of conscious, active mental evaluations and calculations; it is partially the result of what Giddens refers to as 'practical consciousness', the routinized ways people negotiate and understand their social world; and it is partially structured by largely unconscious psychological determinants. In any case, this subjectivity *mediates* the ways in which the objective conditions of class locations are translated into the active choices of class actions. While the objective social context of choice is clearly important in this explanation, I would argue that the subjective mediation of choices—the actual process of choosing—is an essential part of the process as well.

For our present purposes, the critical link in the argument is between class location and forms of stable, class-relevant subjectivity. It could be the case, for example, that although forms of consciousness mattered a great deal for explanations of class struggle, the mechanisms which determined such consciousness were not located within class relations as such (or at least, not located there in important ways). Schools, churches, the family, the media and so on, could all be much more significant determinants of forms of consciousness than location within the class structure. If this were the case, then class consciousness—let alone attitudes which only indirectly derive from such consciousness—would not be a very effective criterion for adjudicating debates over definitions of class structures.

I am assuming, therefore, that one's location within the structure of class relations is an important mechanism determining forms of consciousness. This assumption is based, at least in part, on the view that class locations objectively structure the interests of actors and that people are sufficiently rational to come to know those interests. There should, therefore, be at least a tendency for those aspects of consciousness which revolve around class interests to be structured by class location.

If one accepts this kind of reasoning, then class consciousness can be treated as an appropriate criterion in the adjudication of contending class definitions and responses to a survey questionnaire can be viewed as an appropriate indicator of class consciousness. Again, as I have said previously, this is not to claim that class is the sole determinant of consciousness, but simply that it gene ates sufficiently systematic effects that consciousness can be us as the basis for evaluating contending views of class.

Attitudes: Measurement

Most of the attitude questions used in this analysis are what a called 'Likert' items. Respondents are read a statement and the asked to indicate whether they strongly agree, somewhat agre somewhat disagree or strongly disagree with the statement. Th class structure survey contains a large number of such question ranging over many different topics. For purposes of the adjudica tion of contending class definitions I will restrict the analysis to th survey items which have the clearest class content, since thes should be the kinds of attitudes most systematically shaped by th individual's location within the class structure:

1. Corporations benefit owners at the expense of workers an consumers.

2. During a strike, management should be prohibited by la from hiring workers to take the place of strikers.

3. Striking workers are generally justified in physically prevent ing strike-breakers from entering the place of work.

4. Big corporations have far too much power in America society today.

5. One of the main reasons for poverty is that the economy based on private property and profits.

6. If given the chance, non-management employees at the plac where you work could run things effectively without bosses.

7. It is possible for a modern society to run effectively withou the profit motive.

An eighth item was the following:

8. Imagine that workers in a major industry are out on strik over working conditions and wages. Which of the following out comes would you like to see occur: (1). the workers win their mos important demands; (2). the workers win some of their demand and make some concessions; (3). the workers win only a few o their demands and make major concessions; (4). the workers g back to work without winning any of their demands.

:ach of these items was coded +1 if the respondent took the
vorking class position, −1 if they took the pro-capitalist class
»osition, and 0 if they said that they didn't know the answer or, in
he case of item 8, if they gave response category (2).[9] These eight
esponses were then added up, generating a scale ranging from −8
maximally pro-capitalist) to +8 (maximally pro-worker) that
neasures the net pro-worker or pro-capitalist orientation on this
et of questions: a negative value means that the respondent took
he pro-capitalist position more frequently than the pro-worker
»osition, a positive value indicates the opposite.[10]

In addition to using this constructed consciousness scale, we will
ılso examine the relationship between class structure and a fairly
onventional variable measuring class identification.[11] Respon-
lents were first asked the following question: 'Do you think of
/ourself as belonging to a particular social class?' If they
esponded 'yes', they were then asked in an open-ended fashion
which class is that?' If they said 'no' or 'don't know', they were
ısked a closed-category follow-up: 'Many people say that they
)elong to the working class, the middle class or the upper-middle
:lass. If you had to make a choice, which would you say you belong
:o?' We are thus able with this set of questions to distinguish
)eople with a strong class identification (those who answered yes
:o the initial question) and those with a weak class identification.[12]
Since we will be using this variable to adjudicate contending structural definitions of the working class, we will code it simply as a
working class identification variable'.

Income: Justification

In some ways income is a less satisfactory variable than attitudes
for adjudicating contending class definitions within a Marxist
framework, even given the problems of using attitudes and consciousness discussed above. While Marxist theory has systematic
things to say about the distribution of income between capital and
labour, in general the theory is much less elaborated in the analysis
of income inequality among wage-earners. Since the disputes in
question all concern definitional problems among categories of
wage-earners, income could therefore be considered a fairly weak
criterion for a definitional adjudication.

Nevertheless, I have chosen to adopt income as a secondary
criterion. All of the class definitions we will be exploring typically
characterize 'middle-class' wage-earners as a privileged social

category. Furthermore, since the adjudications being considered all involve comparisons with an exploitation-centred concept of class, and such a concept surely has systematic implications for income differences, it is appropriate to use income in the adjudications.

Income: Measurement

Respondents in the survey were asked what their total personal income before taxes was for the previous calendar year. This figure was meant to include income from all sources—wages and salaries, state transfers, interest on savings and investments, etc.

There are three sources of potential error in this variable which may conceivably influence our analysis. First, as in most surveys there is a relatively high rate of refusals by respondents to the income question, about 15 per cent. Second, the income data is for the previous year, rather than for the respondent's current job, while our class-assignments are based on data for the respondent's present position. Third, the fact that the variable includes non-wage income means that it is not strictly a measure of the income attached to positions, but of income which goes to individuals, whereas the adjudication logic directly concerns the positions themselves. In the use of the income variable in the adjudication of contending class definitions we must assume that these possible measurement errors are random with respect to the critical categories used in the analysis. If it should happen, for example, that there was much greater income mobility in one of the class categories used in the adjudication than in the others, with the result that the income for that category was biased downward, this could conceivably affect the conclusions we might draw. I do not think that these biases are in fact a problem, but they should be kept in mind.

OPERATIONALIZING THE CLASS STRUCTURE VARIABLES

The Exploitation-Centred Concept of Class Structure

The conceptual map of class relations adopted in this book is fairly complex. It is based on three principal dimensions of exploitation relations—exploitation based on control of capital, organization and credentials/skills—combined in various ways. The essential task of constructing a class typology consists in operationalizing each of these dimensions, and then combining them.

The strategy I have adopted is to classify the relation of each respondent to the relevant assets into three categories: (1) clearly an exploiter with respect to that asset; (2) clearly exploited with respect to that asset; and (3) ambiguous. The ambiguous category, in this context, is ambiguous for one of two reasons: either the respondent genuinely appears to occupy a marginal position within the relations of exploitation with respect to that asset, or we lack sufficiently precise data to clearly define the respondent's location. The ambiguous cases are thus a combination of 'intermediate' positions—positions which may be neither exploiters nor exploited with respect to the asset in question—and measurement error. Throughout most of the analysis, therefore, our attention will focus more on the polarized locations than the ambiguous ones.

The basic operational criteria used for each of the three dimensions of exploitation are presented in table 5.3. Without going into excessive detail, a few comments clarifying these operationalizations will be helpful.[13]

1. Assets in Means of Production. Differential ownership of assets in the means of production generates two principal classes in capitalism: workers, who by virtue of owning no means of production must sell their labour power on a labour market in order to work, and capitalists, who by virtue of owning substantial quantities of means of production are able to hire wage-earners to use those means of production and need not themselves work at all.[14] These two categories constitute the traditional polarized classes of the capitalist mode of production.

These polarized classes, however, do not exhaust the class positions generated by unequal distribution of capitalist assets. Three other sorts of class positions are also potentially important. First of all, there are people who own just enough means of production to reproduce themselves, but not enough to hire anyone else. This is the traditional 'petty bourgeoisie'. Secondly, other persons own some means of production, enough to provide for some of their subsistence but not enough to reproduce themselves, thus forcing them to also sell their labour power on a labour market. This is the classic 'semi-proletarianized wage-earner' of early capitalism (and the part-time peasants of many third-world countries today). And

TABLE 5.3
Criteria for operationalization of exploitation-asset concept of class structure

I. Assets in the means of production

	Self employed	Number of employees
1. Bourgeoisie	Yes	10 or more
2. Small employers	Yes	2–10
3. Petty bourgeoisie	Yes	0–1*
4. Wage-earner	No	

*Conceptually, the petty bourgeoisie should be restricted to owners of the means of production who have no employees. However, because of an unintended ambiguity in the questionnaire design, an unknown proportion of respondents who state that they have one employee really had none (i.e. they considered themselves an employee), and thus we have defined the petty bourgeoisie as having no more than one employee.

II. Assets in organization control

	Directly involved in making policy decisions for the organization	Supervisor with real authority over subordinates
1. Managers	Yes	Yes
2. Supervisors	No	Yes
3. Non-management	No	No

Note: The actual criteria used were somewhat more complex than indicated here, since a variety of other criteria were used to deal with certain kinds of problematic cases (eg. a respondent who claims to directly make policy decisions and yet does not have real authority over subordinates). See Appendix II, Table II.3 for details.

III. Assets in scarce skills/talent

	Occupation	Education credential	Job autonomy
1. Experts	Professionals Professors		
	Managers Technicians	B.A. or more* B.A. or more	
2. Marginal	School teachers Craftworkers		
	Managers Technicians	less than B.A. less than B.A.	
	Sales Clerical	B.A. or more B.A. or more	Autonomous Autonomous
3. Uncredentialled	Sales Clerical	less than B.A. *or* less than B.A. *or*	Non-autonomous Non-autonomous
	Manual non-crafts		

*In Sweden the criterion adopted here was a High School degree or more because of the differences in the timing of the expansion of university education in the two countries and the nature of the real training involved in a high school degree in Sweden.

inally there are people who own enough means of production to hire workers, but not enough that they really have the option of not working at all. This is the small employer—employer artisans, small farmers, shopkeepers, etc.—who work alongside their employees, frequently doing much the same kind of work as the people they hire.

In the data used in this study we cannot rigorously distinguish all of these categories. In particular, the only data available to distinguish small employers from proper capitalists is the number of employees of the respondent, and this is at best a weak indicator, since it does not really measure the amount of capital owned by the capitalist.[15] For present purposes, therefore, I will adopt a rather arbitrary convention, and define all employers employing ten or more people as fully-fledged capitalists, and employers employing between two and nine employees as small employers. The petty bourgeoisie is defined as any self-employed person employing no more than one employee. We will not, in the present data analysis, attempt to distinguish fully proletarianized wage-earners from semi-proletarianized workers, although on the basis of data about second jobs and jobs of other members of the household we will be able to introduce this distinction in subsequent work.

2. Assets in Organization. Organization assets consist in the effective control over the coordination and integration of the division of labour. Typically, such assets are particularly salient in defining the exploitation relations of management, although not all jobs which are formally labelled 'manager' involve control over organization assets. Some 'manager' jobs may simply be technical experts who provide advice to the effective controllers of organizational planning and coordination. In the terms of the exploitation-centred concept of class, such 'managers' might be credential-exploiters, but not organization-exploiters.

With respect to organization assets, we will distinguish three basic positions:

(1) *Managers*: positions which are directly involved in making policy decisions within the workplace and which have effective authority over subordinates.

(2) *Supervisors*: positions which have effective authority over subordinates, but are not involved in organizational decision-

making. These positions I shall treat as having marginal organization assets.

(3) *Non-management*: positions without any organization assets
within production.

3. Assets in Credentials. Assets in credentials are quite difficul
to operationalize in a nuanced way. On the face of it, it might seen
that simply using formal academic qualifications might be satisfactory. There are two basic problems with such a strategy: first
because of the rapid expansion of education over the past two
generations and the changing formal education requirements for
certain kinds of jobs, any formal credential variable would have to
involve cohort specific credentials and some provision for histori
cal devaluation of credentials over time. Second, a formal creden
tial only becomes the basis for an exploitation relation when it is
matched with a job that requires such credentials. A person with a
doctorate in English who drives a taxicab is not a credential
exploiter. What this implies is that in order to specify properly the
exploitation relations built upon credential assets we must include
information on the actual job a person holds and not simply on
that person's formal academic certificates.[16]

This immediately poses an additional problem: many job title
and occupational designations are extremely vague with respect to
the credentials they demand. This is not particularly a problem for
professional occupations, but it certainly is for the wide range of
'manager' jobs and even for 'sales' and 'clerical' jobs. Some sale
jobs require engineering degrees and are, in practical terms, more
like an engineering consultancy than a simple salesperson job
some manager jobs, on the other hand, require no particular cre
dentials at all. They might still constitute exploiters with respect to
organization assets, but not in relation to credentials or skills
Some jobs grouped as 'clerical' occupations involve high levels of
training and experience, others require very little.[17] Even the
detailed occupational titles do not always distinguish these circum
stances in a satisfactory way.

We will solve this complex of issues by using a combination of
occupational titles, formal credentials and job traits as a basis for
distinguishing people in jobs where certain credentials are man
datory—and thus positions involving credential asset exploita
tion—from those not in such jobs. As in the other assets, we will
also define an intermediate situation in which it is ambiguou

exactly what credential assets the individual actually controls. This yields the following three categories:

(1) *Experts*: This includes (a) all professionals; (b) technicians and managers (by occupational title, not by the criteria used to define the organizational assets specified above) with college degrees.

(2) *Skilled employees*: (a) school teachers and craftworkers; (b) managers and technicians with less than college degrees; (c)salespersons or clericals with college degrees *and* whose jobs have real autonomy.[18]

(3) *Non-skilled*: (a) clerical and salespersons not satisfying the credential *or* autonomy criterion for skilled employees; (b) noncraft manual occupations and service occupations.

Taking these three sets of exploitation-asset criteria together generates the overall map of class locations displayed in table 3.3 in chapter three.

Our focus in this chapter is not on this entire matrix of class locations, but on the definition of boundary criteria distinguishing the working class from the 'middle class'.[19] As mentioned earlier, this raises the question of how to treat these 'marginal' categories in the adjudications—particularly those cells in table 3.3 designated 'marginally credentialled workers' and 'uncredentialled supervisors'. The procedure I will adopt will be to include these two marginal categories as a distinct category in the analysis. If it turns out that for practical purposes these categories can be treated as basically similar to workers, then in subsequent analyses it could be justifiable to merge them with the more restrictively defined working class.

Manual Labour Definitions of the Working Class

Even though manual labour definitions of the working class are certainly the simplest, it is not trivial to define rigorously the appropriate criteria for distinguishing 'manual' from 'nonmanual' labour. The conventional approach is to equate this with the purely ideological distinction between 'blue-collar' and 'white-collar' occupations, as defined in popular discourse. But this has the effect of putting a variety of highly routinized clerical jobs—key-punch operators, typists in large semi-automated offices, etc.—which in real terms involve less 'mental labour' than many skilled artisanal jobs, into the 'middle class'. It is precisely because of this kind of ambiguity that many theorists are hesitant to adopt a simple mental–manual distinction as the basis for defining the working class.

In spite of these reservations, I will adopt the conventional blue-collar criterion for defining 'manual labour', and thus the working class. Since this definition is the least self-consciously theorized of the ones we are considering and does, in fact, rely most heavily on categories given in everyday discourse, this operationalization is, I believe, faithful to usage.

Productive Labour Definitions of the Working Class

Poulantzas's discussions of class are complex and not always consistent. It is thus not a simple task to provide a fair operational specification of his class concept. The purpose of the present exercise, however, makes this task a bit easier. The point is not so much one of faithfully settling a dispute between two theorists, but rather assessing the adequacy of two contending types of class definitions. In these terms Poulantzas's efforts represent a particular example of a more general intuition among Marxists, namely that the working class consists of productive, subordinated manual wage-earners. One finds this definition in Adam Przeworski's empirical work, in some of Göran Therborn's writings and elsewhere, even if the conceptual details are not identical to those found in Poulantzas.

The task of operationalizing Poulantzas's definition, therefore, revolves around specifying four core criteria: productive–unproductive labour; mental–manual labour; supervisory–non-supervisory labour; decision-maker–non-decision-maker.

1. Productive—Unproductive Labour. Productive labour is defined as labour which produces surplus-value; unproductive labour is labour which is paid out of surplus-value. There is a general agreement among Marxists (at least among those who accept the framework of the labour theory of value) that employees in the sphere of circulation (finance, retail, insurance, etc.) and most state employees are unproductive, while production workers in manufacturing, mining and agriculture are productive. There is much less agreement over a wide range of other positions: administrative positions within production, service workers of various sorts (eg. health workers), technical and scientific positions within manufacturing, and so on.

Poulantzas takes a rather extreme position on these issues. He argues that only agents engaged in the production of physical commodities are productive. Service workers, he insists, are always unproductive. Productive workers do, however, include technical workers involved in the design and planning of production (engineers, draftsmen, etc.). In contrast, many Marxists argue that anyone engaged in the production of commodities, physical or non-physical, is a productive worker. Marx seems to endorse this view in his description of entertainers and school teachers as productive when they work for capital.

As it turns out, none of the empirical results in the comparison of alternative definitions of the working class are significantly affected by the choice of the criteria for productive/unproductive labour. For the purposes of the analysis in this chapter, therefore, I will only report the results using the broader definition of productive labour as anyone engaged in the production of commodities.

Constructing this variable involves reclassifying census industry and occupation categories into productive–unproductive occupations and productive–unproductive industries.[20] To be classified a productive labourer one has to be *both* in a productive occupation and employed in a productive sector of the economy.

2. Mental—Manual Labour. This is more straightforward than the productive–unproductive labour distinction. Poulantzas formally defines 'mental labour' as positions which have real possession of the 'secret knowledge of production', by which he means the intellectual control over the production process. He explicitly asserts that manual labour is not equivalent to 'hand work' and mental labour to 'brain work'. Rather, the distinction revolves around cognitive control over the labour process.

If this criterion were applied, however, it would mean that many clerical jobs would become non-mental, and this contradicts the general intution held by many Marxists that clerical employees and other 'white-collar' occupations are not really proper 'manual' labourers. To avoid this possibility, Poulantzas makes a rather ad hoc argument that all clerical employees share the ideologically defined status of being 'mental labourers' regardless of their concrete situation, and by virtue of this ideological factor should be considered non-workers. In practice, therefore, Poulantzas adopts the simple criterion of the mental–manual ideological status of the occupational category, rather than the real control over conceptual dimensions of the specific job. This means that his distinction can be effectively operationalized using the conventional sociological distinction between white-collar and blue-collar occupations.

3. *Supervision*. Poulantzas's concept of supervision is centred on control and surveillance. It therefore excludes what could be called nominal supervisors—people who are conduits for information but have no capacities to impose sanctions on subordinates. What is needed, therefore, is a criterion which identifies individuals with real control over their subordinates. In practical terms, this is virtually identical to the category 'marginal organization assets' adopted in the operationalization of the exploitation-centred concept of class.

4. *Decision-making*. Poulantzas's discussion of decision-making is less clear-cut than his discussion of supervision as such. He argues that managers who are engaged in basic decisions concerning budgets and investments—basic profit and accumulation decisions—should actually be considered part of the bourgeoisie proper, rather than even the new petty bourgeoisie. However, he never explicitly discusses the broad range of production, organizational and marketing decisions that are the preoccupation of most managers for a majority of the time. My guess is that he would basically treat such positions as mental labourers and therefore part of the new petty bourgeoisie, regardless of whether or not they were also directly engaged in the tasks of supervision and surveillance.

Strictly speaking, therefore, if we were to literally follow Poulantzas's theoretical specifications, we would distinguish among managerial wage-labourers between those that were part of the bourgeoisie and those that were in the new petty bourgeoisie. However, many Marxists who adopt a Poulantzas-type approach would exclude all but the top executives of large corporations from the bourgeoisie proper. Since these alternative ways of treating managers could conceivably generate different patterns of results, I explored both ways of categorizing managers in the data analysis. It turns out that there were no substantive differences in the results. To simplify the exposition, therefore, I will present only the data in which all managers are considered new petty bourgeois.

Taking these four criteria together we can construct the

perationalization of Poulantzas's definition of the working class, s presented in table 5.4.

TABLE 5.4
Operationalization of Poulantzas's definition of working class

put variables				
nproductive bour	Mental labour	Sanction supervision	Decision making	Interpretation
o	No	No	No	Worker using Poulantzas's definition
es or	Yes or Yes		or Yes	New petty bourgeoisie

eformulation of Hypotheses

o far we have been quite vague in specifying what 'more like' leans in the formulation of the different predictions of the various efinitions of the working class. In order actually to perform statiscal tests on these hypotheses, we will have to formalize this otion.

To do this it is necessary first to note that in all of the definitions nder consideration, there is not simply an assertion that systemac differences exist between the working class and the middle class terms of income and class consciousness. All of these concepts lso imply claims about the directionality of the differences in uestion. Concretely, we can formulate two empirical hypotheses lat are common to all of the definitions under investigation (see lble 5.5, part I). The analysis of the disputed categories in the djudication of contending definitions, therefore, should be done ith respect to this common set of expectations about the nonisputed categories.

In each of the adjudications there will be several sets of pairs of ypotheses. In each pair, the expectations of each definition are pecified in Table 5.5. Our task, therefore, will always be one of omparing the relative support for a given hypothesis within each air of hypotheses, rather than simply 'testing' a hypothesis gainst the data'.[21] While this generates a rather lengthy list of rmal hypotheses to be tested, it will help to pur order into the mpirical investigation to formalize them in this way. Since the adjudications with Poulantzas's definition of the working class are somewhat simpler than with the manual labour definition (since in Poulantzas's definition there is only one category in dispute, while in the manual labour definition there are two) we will examine these first and then turn to the problem of the manual labour definition of the working class.

TABLE 5.5

Formal hypotheses for adjudication of contending definitions

I. *Common hypotheses*:

I.1. Agreed-upon 'middle' class wage earners (cell 6)[a] will have higher mean incomes than the agreed-upon working-class wage-earners (cell 1):
(cell 6) − (cell 1) > 0.

I.2. Agreed-upon 'middle' class wage earners will tend to be less pro-worker and more pro-capitalist than agreed-upon working-class wage-earners:
(cell 6) − (cell) > 0

II. *Adjudication of productive-labour defintion hypotheses*

II.1A. The difference in incomes between the disputed category (cell 2) and agreed-upon workers will be significantly *less* than between them and the agreed-upon 'middle' class:
| cell 1 − cell 2 | − | cell 2 − cell 6 | < 0

II.1B. The difference in incomes between the disputed category and agreed-upon workers will be significantly *more* than between them and the agreed-upon 'middle' class:
| cell 1 − cell 2 | − | cell 2 − cell 6 | > 0

II.2A. The difference in class attitudes between the disputed category and agreed-upon workers will significantly be *less* than between them and the agreed-upon 'middle' class:
| cell 1 − cell 2 | − | cell 2 − cell 6 | < 0

II.2B. The difference in class attitudes between the disputed category and agreed-upon workers will be significantly *more* than between them and the agreed-upon 'middle-class:
| cell 1 − cell 2 | − | cell 2 − cell 6 | > 0

III. *Adjudication of manual-labour definition hypotheses*

III.1A. The difference in income between disputed category 1 (cell 2) and the agreed-upon workers will be significantly *less* than between them and the agreed-upon 'middle' class;
| cell 1 − cell 2 | − | cell 2 − cell 6 | < 0

III.1B. The difference in incomes between disputed category 1 and the agreed-upon workers will be significantly *more* than between them and the agreed-upon 'middle' class:
| cell 1 − cell 2 | − | cell 2 − cell 6 | > 0

TABLE 5.5 (*continued*)

I.2A. The difference in incomes between disputed category 2 (cell 5) and the agreed-upon workers will be significantly *more* than between them and the agreed-upon 'middle' class:
| cell 1 − cell 5 | − | cell 5 − cell 6 | > 0

I.2B. The difference in incomes between disputed category 2 and the agreed-upon workers will be considerably *less* than between them and the agreed-upon 'middle' class:
| cell 1 − cell 5 | − | cell 5 − cell 6 | < 0

I.3A. The difference in class attitudes between disputed category 1 and the agreed-upon workers will be significantly *less* than between them and the agreed-upon 'middle' class:
|cell 1 − cell 2 | − | cell 2 − cell 6 | < 0

I.3B. The difference in class attitudes between disputed category 1 and the agreed-upon workers will be significantly *more* than between them and agreed-upon 'middle' class:
| cell 1 − cell 2 | − | cell 2 − cell 6 | > 0

I.4A. The difference in class attitudes between disputed category 2 and the agreed-upon workers will be considerably *more* than between them and the agreed-upon 'middle' class:
| cell 1 − cell 5 | − | cell 5 − cell 6 | > 0

I.4B. The difference in class attitudes between disputed category 2 and the agreed-upon workers will be considerably *less* than between them and the agreed-upon 'middle' class:
| cell 1 − cell 5 | − | cell 5 − cell 6 | < 0.

All reference to 'cells' in these hypotheses refer to the adjudication typology in Table 5.2.
In each of the pairs of formal hypotheses in table 5.5, the first hypothesis (designated *A*) represents the prediction from the exploitation-centred concept, while the second hypothesis (designated *B*), represents the prediction from the rival definition.

Note on Statistical Procedures

SAMPLE

The data for the United States was gathered in a national telephone survey conducted by the University of Michigan Survey Research Center in the summer of 1980. Respondents were sampled on the basis of a conventional two-stage systematic cluster sample of telephone numbers in the coterminus United States. The first stage consisted of sampling clusters of telephone numbers. In

the second stage telephone numbers within clusters were randoml
selected. Finally, within households, eligible respondents wei
selected at random.[22] The resulting sample consists of a total (
1499 adults over the age of sixteen working in the labour force, 9
unemployed in the labour force, and 170 housewives for a total (
1761 respondents. The response rate was about 78 per cent,
fairly typical rate for this kind of survey. Throughout this book w
will only analyse the working labour force sample.

The Swedish sample (not used in this chapter) consists of 114
adults between the ages of eighteen and sixty-five selected ra
domly from a national list of the population. Respondents wei
initially mailed a questionnaire, and then, if they did not send
back, were contacted by telephone.[23] The overall response ra
was about 76 per cent.

A word needs to be said about telephone interviews, sinc
people unfamiliar with survey research may be somewhat sceptic
about the validity of such interviews. Research which has con
pared telephone and personal interviews has shown that there a
no systematic differences in responses to questions using the tw
techniques.[24] There are, however, certain advantages and disa
vantages to each. One the one hand, personal interviews allow f
much more complicated questions, particularly questions th
require visual aids of various sorts. Telephone interviews tend t
restrict the questionnaire to fairly simple questions. On the oth
hand, personal interviews are vastly more expensive than tel
phone interviews, require much more clustering in the samp
strategy, and in certain respects (at least in the United States) m
generate a more biased sample, since many people will be willir
to talk to a stranger on the telephone who would not be willing t
let them into their house. In any event, for better or worse, th
data for the United States in this study come entirely from tel
phone interviews.

WEIGHTS

For reasons which are not entirely clear to us, the educ
tion-by-occupation distribution of respondents in the United Stat
sample is somewhat more biased towards higher status occup
tions and higher levels of education than one would expect from
survey of this type. Some of this is typical of telephone survey
since only around 95 per cent of individuals in the United Stat
live in dwellings with telephones and non-coverage is certainly n

qually distributed in socio-economic terms, but the over-
epresentation of high status respondents was greater in our survey
han in most others.[25] Since such biases could affect some of the
ross-national comparisons we will be doing in chapters six and
even, and since they might also have effects on the data analysis in
his chapter, I have applied a set of post-hoc weights to the data
which have the consequence of reproducing the 1980 census
ducation-by-occupation distributions in the data we will be using.
he weights are designed in such a way that the total N in the
ample is not affected by the weighting system. Throughout the
nalysis in this book we will use the weighted data.

TATISTICAL TESTS

hroughout this analysis I will rely on fairly simple statistical tests.
Ve will primarily be examining the differences in means between
roups, and therefore will use conventional '*t*-tests' to test the
tatistical significance of the differences observed. Since not all
eaders will be familiar with such tests, a brief word needs to be
nade about how they should be interpreted and how they are
alculated.

Let us suppose we record information from a sample of workers
nd supervisors, and on the basis of this information, we estimate
hat workers have a mean income of $13,000 and supervisors have
ne of $16,000. What we want to test is whether the difference in
hese observed incomes—$3,000—is 'significant'. Significance, in
his context, is a statement about how confident we are that the
bserved difference is really different from zero. It is always poss-
ble, after all, that two groups being compared could in reality have
dentical incomes, but that because of random variations in gather-
ng the data we might observe a difference. When we say that the
bserved difference is 'significant at the .01 level' what we mean is
hat based on certain statistical assumptions, our best guess is that
n only one out of a hundred surveys could this large a difference
e observed when the real difference was zero.

The technical procedure for performing this kind of test involves
alculating what is called a '*t* statistic'. To calculate this we have to
livide our estimate of the difference in means between the two
roups by what is called the 'standard error' of this difference. The
igger the standard error relative to the difference in the means,
he less likely we are to be very confident that the observed differ-

ence in means reflects a true difference. How is the standard err
itself measured? It is based on two pieces of information: first, th
sample size on which the observations have been made, and se
ond, what is called the 'standard deviations' of each of the mean
A 'standard deviation' is basically a measure of the dispersion c
values around the mean. If everyone in a sample had identic;
incomes, for example, the standard deviation would be zero
where incomes are quite dispersed, the standard deviation will b
large. The larger the sample size and/or the smaller the standar
deviations (relative to the differences in means) the smaller will b
the standard error.

In more technical terms, the t statistic used to test the signif
cance of differences in means between two groups is calculated a
follows:

$$t = \frac{(\text{Mean of group 1}) - (\text{Mean of group 2})}{\sqrt{\dfrac{(\text{Standard deviation of group 1})^2}{(\text{sample size in group 1})} + \dfrac{(\text{Standard deviation of group 2})^2}{(\text{sample size in group 2})}}}$$

The larger the value of this t statistic, the more confident we can k
that the observed differences between groups reflect true diffe
ences in the world rather than chance differences in our measur
ments. From the formula it is clear that there are two ways i
which our confidence in an observed difference between mea
can be high: first, if the standard deviations of each group a
small, and second, if the sample sizes are large for each grou
With a very large sample, even if the values within each group a
quite dispersed we may be quite confident that a relatively sma
difference in means is not just a random result of sampling.

T-tests can be used in what are called one-tailed and two-taile
tests. A two-tailed test is used when you simply want to see if
difference between two means exists, but you have no prior expe
tations about the direction of the difference. A one-tailed test, c
the other hand, is designed to test whether the mean of one grou
is greater (or smaller) than another group. In general we will u
one-tailed tests in our analyses since we have strong *a priori* expe
tations about the directionality of the differences in question.

Most of the hypotheses we are exploring are not simply abo
the differences in means between groups, but rather concern th
differences in differences between groups (the hypotheses under
and III in table 5.5). In such cases the use of the *t*-test become
somewhat more complicated. This is because the usual assumptic

f a *t*-test is that the groups being compared are independent of ach other. This assumption holds for the comparisons of the disuted category with workers and the disputed category with nonworkers in our adjudication of the definition of the working class, ut it does not hold for the comparison of the two differences, ince the disputed category appears in both of these. What this neans technically is that when we calculate the standard error for he difference in differences we have to include a term for the covariance' of the two differences. This is accomplished by the ollowing formula (in which s.e. means standard error):[26]

$$t = \frac{|\,(\text{Difference 1})\,| - |\,(\text{Difference 2})\,|}{\sqrt{(\text{s.e. of diff. 1})^2 + (\text{s.e. of diff. 2})^2 - 2(\text{Covariance of the differences})}}$$

ociologists are often prone to fetishize significance tests, paying nore attention to them than to the substantive meaning of statistial results. Significance tests are strictly measures of one's confience that the observed results are not random, but it is still the esults themselves that should be of theoretical interest. While I vill rely fairly heavily in places on the statistical tests to add peruasiveness to particular arguments the real burden of the discusion will be on the substantive results themselves and not on ignificance levels as such.

Empirical Results

ADJUDICATION OF THE PRODUCTIVE LABOUR DEFINITION OF THE WORKING CLASS

The basic results comparing Poulantzas's definition of the working lass and the exploitation-centred definition appear in tables 5.6, .7 and 5.8. We will begin by examining the two hypotheses held n common by both contending definitions of the working class and hen turn to the substantive adjudication using the empirical preictions of each definition.

Common Hypotheses

A precondition for the adjudication strategy to work is that the greed-upon workers and the agreed-upon 'middle' class differ in he expected ways on the dependent variables which are to be used

TABLE 5.6

Adjudication of productive-labour definition of the working class: incom

Entries in cells of Table:
 Means
 (Standard deviations)
Number of cases (weighted)

Exploitation-centred definition[a]	*Productive labour definition*		Row Totals
	Working class	'Middle' class	
Working class	[1] $13,027 (7952) 143	[2] $10,241 (6921) 340	$11,06. (7344) 483
Marginal working class	[3] $19,285 (8441) 55	[4] $13,822 (7757) 192	$15,03: ('217) 247
'Middle' class	[5] [Empty cell]	[6] $19,843 (12422) 335	$19,84. (12422 335
Column Totals	$14,760 (8543) 198	$14,744 (10476) 867	

[a]Working class = cell 12 in Table 3.3; Marginal working class = cells 9 and 1▶
'Middle class' = cells 4–8 and 10.

in the adjudications. It obviously makes no sense to adjudicate th
class location of disputed categories on the basis of a criterion tha
does not properly differentiate between the non-dispute
categories.[27]

The first two rows of table 5.8 indicate that the two principa
dependent variables which we are using—income and clas
attitudes—do in fact behave in the expected manner. Th
agreed-upon working class, on the average, earns $6815 less pe
year than the agreed-upon middle-class wage-earners, while thei
value on the working class attitude scale is 2.3 points higher (i.e
out of eight items combined in the scale, on average agreed-upo
workers take a pro-working class stance on just over 2 more item
than 'middle-class' wage-earners). The high 'significance level' fo
these results indicate that we can be quite confident that th

TABLE 5.7
**Adjudication of productive-labour definition of the working class:
class-attitude scale[a]**

Entries in cells of Table:
    Means
    (Standard Deviations)
    Number of cases (weighted)

Exploitation-centred Definitions[b]	Productive labour definition		Row Totals
	Working class	'Middle' class	
Working class	[1] 1.04 (3.18) 167	[2] 0.61 (3.39) 405	0.74 (3.33) 572
Marginal working class	[3] 1.02 (3.54) 62	[4] 0.36 (3.29) 211	0.51 (3.35) 271
'Middle' class	[5] [Empty cell]	[6] −1.27 (3.20) 218	−1.27 (3.20) 218
Column Totals	1.04 (3.27) 227	−0.15 (3.52) 994	

[a]Values on the class attitude scale go from +8 (maximally pro-working class) to −8 (maximally pro-capitalist class).
[b]Working class = cell 12 in Table 3.3; Marginal working class = cells 9 and 11; 'Middle class' = cells 4–8 and 10.

observed differences are not due to chance. If, therefore, one agrees on theoretical grounds that these are indeed appropriate criteria for adjudicating the contending definitions, then we can assume that there is at least a presumptive empirical case that our concrete measures are appropriate as well.

Income Adjudication

The results of the adjudication using the income variable provide no support for Poulantzas's definition of the working class, while they are quite consistent with the definition I have been advancing. If the disputed category should in reality be classified with the agreed-upon 'middle' class then we would expect that, like other

TABLE 5.8
Test of adjudication hypotheses: productive-labour versus exploitation definition

Hypotheses[a]	Empirical results	t	Significance level (one-tailed)	Conclusion
COMMON HYPOTHESES				
Income				
I.1 (6)[b] − (1) > 0	\$6815	7.2	.000	supported
Pro-working-class attitudes				
I.2 (6) − (1) < 0	−2.30	7.6	.000	supported
ADJUDICATION HYPOTHESES				
Income				
II.1A $\mid 1 - 2 \mid - \mid 2 - 6 \mid < 0$	−\$6815	7.0	.000	II.1A strongly
II.1B $\mid - 2 \mid - \mid 2 - \mid 6 > 0$				supported over II.1B
Pro-working-class attitudes				
II.2A $\mid 1 - \mid - \mid 2 - 6 \mid < 0$	−1.45	3.1	.001	II.2A strongly
II.2B $\mid 1 - 2 \mid - \mid 2 - 6 \mid > 0$				supported over II.2B

[a]The Hypothesis numbers correspond to the number in Table 5.5.
[b]The numbers in parentheses refer to the cells in Tables 5.6 and 5.7.

non-workers, their income should be higher than that of workers; on the other hand, if they are properly part of the working class, then we would expect their income to be lower than that of non-workers. As the data indicate, the average income for individuals in the disputed category is over \$9000 less than the average income for 'middle-class' wage earners. Furthermore, among those categories which would be classified as 'marginal working class' by the exploitation-centred definition (cells 3 and 4 of the table), those positions which Poulantzas would consider working class have an average income virtually indistinguisable from the agreed-upon non-workers, whereas those which Poulantzas would consider new petty bourgeoisie have incomes virtually identical to the agreed-upon workers. If one accepts income as an appropriate criterion in this adjudication, this strongly supports the exploitation-centred definition over the definition based on productive labour proposed by Poultantzas.

Class Attitudes Adjudication

The data on class attitudes also supports the exploitation-centred definition of the working class over Poulantzas's definition. On the working class attitude scale, the agreed-upon workers have an average value of just over +1, the agreed-upon 'middle-class' wage-earners have a value of about −1.3, and the disputed category +0.6. While this value of +0.6 is less than the value for agreed-upon workers, it is decidedly closer to the agreed-upon workers than to the agreed-upon 'middle' class.[28] Even cell 4 in table 5.7— marginal workers by the exploitation concept and new petty bourgeois according to Poulantzas—are closer to the agreed-upon workers than the agreed-upon 'middle' class. Again, if one is willing to accept class attitudes as a legitimate basis for adjudicating contending definitions of the working class, then these results support the exploitation-centred concept over the productive labour concept quite strongly.

One objection to the results in table 5.8 might be that they revolve around an aggregate scale. It is always possible that such scales can distort real differences. For example, it could be the case that the differences between categories are in the opposite direction for most of the items, but that one or two of the items are so strongly in a particular direction that they have a disproportionate effect on the relevant means on the scale. It is therefore important to look at the values for individual questions to be sure that this is not the case. This is done in table 5.9. The results in this table are quite striking. On the class-identification question and on every item included in the scale except item number eight, the mean values of the disputed category are closer to those of the agreed-upon workers than to those of the agreed-upon 'middle' class. While of course one might question the validity of these items as measures of class consciousness or the very relevance of class consciousness for an adjudication of class definitions, the observed differences in the aggregated measures cannot be explained by pecularities in the differences on the individual items.

The Effects of Gender and Union Membership

An obvious rejoinder to these results is that they are artifacts of some other determinant of income and attitudes which is correlated with the categories in the adjudication debate. Two candidates for generating such spurious results are gender and union membership. The disputed category in the comparison between Poulantzas's definition of the working class and the exploitation-

TABLE 5.9
Responses to individual items in attitude scale for adjudication of unproductive labour definitions

	Agreed-upon working class	Disputed category	Agreed-upon 'middle' class
1. Corporations benefit owners at expense of others[a]	0.21[b]	0.26	0.04
2. Employers should be prohibited from hiring scabs in a strike	0.35	0.12	−0.20
3. Strikers are justified in using force	−0.14	−0.27	−0.53
4. Big corporations have too much power today	0.59	0.58	0.51
5. A main reason for poverty is that the economy is based on private profits	0.22	0.18	−0.25
6. Non-management could run a place of work without bosses	−0.03	0.08	−0.33
7. A modern society can run effectively without the profit motive	−0.34	−0.37	−0.52
8. In a strike, it is generally desirable that the strikers win most of their demands[c]	0.17	0.04	0.01
9. Working Class self-identification (% who say that they are in the working class)	35.5	31.0	18.5

[a]For precise wording of items, see discussion in text.
[b]Entries are means on the individual items as entered into the class attitude scale. (+1 = pro-worker; −1 = pro-bourgeois; 0 = don't know)
[c]It should be noted in this item that between 65 per cent and 82 per cent of the respondents in the various adjudication categories advocated the class compromise position on this variable and thus received a value of 0 on the item.

centred concept I have proposed is made up primarily of lower-level white collar employees and state workers. These are the kinds of positions which would be considered unproductive and/or mental labour in Poultanzas's analysis of class relations (and thus part of the new petty bourgeoisie), but because they lack credential assets or organization assets would be considered workers in my analysis. Such positions are also, as we know, disproportionately female and much less unionized than the agreed-upon workers. 61 per cent of the agreed-upon workers and 68 per cent of the agreed-upon middle class are men, compared to only 30 per cent of the disputed category; 45 per cent of the agreed-upon workers are unionized compared to under 15 per cent of the disputed category and 11 per cent of the agreed upon middle class.[29] It could well be the case that the observed income differences and attitude differences are largely consequences of these factors, and are not class effects as such.

The data in table 5.10 indicate that results of the adjudication analyses cannot be attributed to the sex and union compositions of the various categories. The basic pattern observed in table 5.6 and 5.7 holds when we examine men and women taken separately, when we examine non-unionized employees separately, and when we examine unionized employees on the income variable. The one exception to the previous patterns is among unionized wage-earners for the adjudication involving class attitudes. Among these respondents, the disputed category scored significantly higher on pro-working class attitude scale than either the agreed-upon workers or the agreed-upon 'middle' class, while the two agreed-upon categories did not differ significantly.

How should this result be interpreted? The first thing to note is that union membership makes much less difference for attitudes among the agreed-upon workers than among the other categories under consideration: unionized and non-unionized agreed-upon workers differ by just 0.7 points on the pro-working class attitude scale, whereas within the disputed category and the agreed-upon 'middle-class' category, union membership increases the value on the scale by 2.7 and 2.9 points respectively.

This suggests several possible interpretations. One possibility is that there is some self-selection operating here: that among non-working class wage-earners it is precisely those who have particularly strong ideological dispositions against the bourgeoisie who are likely to become union members in the first place. Perhaps more plausibly, the results for 'middle-class' wage-earners suggest that when contradictory class locations become formed into unions—a typically working class form of organization—their consciousness begins to resemble that of workers to a much greater extent. This is precisely what the concept of contradictory loca-

TABLE 5.10

Adjudication comparisons for sex and union members categories taken separately: productive labour adjudications

	Agreed-upon working class	Disputed Category	Agreed-upon 'middle' class
SEX COMPARISONS			
Income			
Men	$15,103	$14,271	$22,870
Women	$9,742	$8,429	$13,551
Pro-Working-class attitudes			
Men	1.22	0.73	−1.43
Women	0.77	0.57	−0.92
Sample Size[a]			
Men	102	122	255
Women	65	283	123
% Men	61%	30%	67%
UNION MEMBERSHIP COMPARISONS			
Income			
Union members	$16,679	$13,596	$20,653
Non-union	$9,545	$9,567	$19,739
Pro-Working-class attitudes			
Union members	1.43	2.88	1.30
Non-union	0.73	0.22	−1.57
Sample size			
Union members	75	60	40
Non-union	92	345	338
%Unionized	45%	15%	11%

[a]All Ns are weighted.

tions is meant to suggest: such positions have an internally contradictory character, being simultaneously exploiters and exploited, and are therefore likely to have their attitudes more strongly affected by organizational and political mediations, such as unionization. What unionization indicates is that such positions have in fact been 'formed' into the working class, and once so formed, have a consciousness profile that is much more like that of workers. This is a theme we will explore much more thoroughly in chapter six. A final interpretation of these results is that it is the more proletarianized locations within the 'agreed-upon middle-class' category that become unionized, and that, therefore, the unionization variable is really just an indirect measure of the proletarian weight of the location. Only 10 per cent of the people in the agreed-upon 'middle-class' cell of the typology are unionized compared to 45 per cent of the agreed-upon workers, and it is entirely possible that this 10 per cent contains a disproportionate number of individuals who, save for measurement error, should have been placed in the working class to begin with. The same kind of argument could apply to the disputed category.

Regardless of which of these interpretations one adopts, in terms of the empirical task at hand, the results for union members in table 5.10 do not support Poulantzas's concept relative to the exploitation-centred concept. Indeed, the fact that among unionized employees the agreed-upon workers and agreed-upon 'middle' class do not differ significantly on the scale contradicts the common hypothesis I.1 of both definitions.

Taken together these results indicate that productive–unproductive labour is not a legitimate criterion for defining the boundary of the working class. At least, when class attitudes and income are used as criteria in the adjudication between Poulantzas's specification of the working class as productive, non-supervisory manual labour, and the rival definition of workers in terms of exploitation relations, the latter fares much better empirically.

A supporter of Poulantzas's general definition of the working class has one final line of defence. I have been treating unionization as an organizational mediation in the consciousness-producing process. But unionization can equally plausibly be regarded as a direct effect of class itself, and thus the rates of unionization for the different categories under discussion could be regarded as an appropriate adjudication criterion. If this stance is adopted, then the disputed category in our analysis looks much more like the agreed-upon non-workers (15 per cent and 10 per cent unionized respectively), whereas both are dramatically different from the agreed-upon workers (45 per cent unionized). Presumably other forms of economic class practices besides union membership—participation in strikes, trade union militancy, etc.—would probably follow a roughly similar pattern. The rates of unionization associated with the different categories in the adjudication analysis, therefore, lend support to Poulantzas's definition of workers over the one proposed in this book.

These results, of course, are not surprising. It is hardly necessary to go to the trouble of a careful statistical study to show that white-collar and/or unproductive employees are less unionized than manual, non-supervisory industrial workers. This fact, however, does demonstrate the difficulty in performing this kind of definitional adjudication, since the conlusions may hinge on the adjudication criteria adopted. The issue then becomes whether or not rates of unionization are an appropriate criterion for adjudicating contending definitions of the working class.

The assumption underlying the use of unionization as an adjudication criterion is that two people within the same class—for example, two workers—will have a higher probability of sharing the same unionization status than two people in different classes. The overall unionization figures are certainly consistent with this. It could be the case, however, that the reason the disputed category looks so much like the agreed-upon non-workers on levels of unionization is not because of the class determinants of unionization, but because of some other determinant of unionization which is associated strongly with the disputed category, for example, gender.

If we look at unionization rates for the three categories of the adjudication typology by sex, we see that among agreed-upon 'middle' class there is relatively little difference between men (12.5 per cent unionized) and women (7.5 per cent unionized). Similarly, among agreed-upon workers there is only a modest difference between men (46.0 per cent) and women (41.5 per cent) who are unionized. The big difference comes precisely in the disputed category, where 20.2 per cent of men are unionized compared to only 12.4 per cent among women. The result of this is that among women, the disputed category and the agreed-upon 'middle' class have similar rates of unionization, whereas among men the disputed category falls about half way between the agreed-upon workers and the agreed-upon 'middle' class. That is, among men the unionization criterion supports neither definition of the working class (the adjudication is indeterminate in its conclusions), whereas among women it is formally more consistent with Poulantzas's definition.

What can we make of all of this? The results suggest, I think, that variations in levels of unionization of particular categories of subordinate wage-earners are to a significant extent shaped by the strategies of unions and various kinds of structural obstacles to organizing certain categories of labour. There are a variety of reasons why unions, at least in the United States, have concen-

rated on manual labour in manufacturing, over white collar employees (the heart of the disputed category): sexism, both in the
unions themselves (preference for organizing men instead of
women) and in the employment situation (greater vulnerability of
female employees to various kinds of control by employers); the
fragmentation and dispersion of white-collar employees in offices;
legal constraints on organizing the state sector; and so on. Non-
manual subordinate employees could be fully in the working class,
and yet because of such factors, have dramatically different levels
of unionization. The fact that in some countries, such as Sweden,
the rate of unionization among white collar non-supervisory emp-
oyees is virtually the same as it is for manual workers supports the
view that variations in levels of unionization between non-
supervisory manual and non-manual wage-earners is more the
result of political and ideological determinants than of possible
differences in their class location.

If this interpretation of the unionization results is correct, then
the level of unionization is not a very satisfactory adjudication
criterion. Accordingly, while the unionization results do introduce
some ambiguity into the analysis, nevertheless the overall weight
of the empirical findings lends little support to definitions of the
working class built around the criterion of productive and unproductive labour.

ADJUDICATION OF MANUAL LABOUR DEFINITIONS

Let us now turn to the comparison of the definition of the working
class as blue-collar–manual wage-earners with the exploitation-
centred concept. While this definition is both conceptually and
operationally very simple, the adjudication is more complex than
in the case of Poulantzas's definition of the working class. In the
analysis of Poulantzas's definition there was only one disputed
category—positions which I claimed to be in the working class but
Poulantzas claimed to be new petty bourgeois. In the case of the
manual-labour definition there are two disputed categories: positions which I claim are working class but the rival definition claims
to be 'middle' class (mainly proletarianized white collar jobs) and
positions which I claim are 'middle' class but a simple manual
labour definition would regard as in the working class (mainly blue
collar wage-earners in supervisory and decision-making jobs). The
former I will refer to as disputed category 1 and the latter as
disputed category 2. Our task, then, as charted in table 5.5, is to

TABLE 5.11

Adjudication of manual labour definition of working class: income analysis

Entries in cells of table:
Means
(Standard Deviations)
Number of cases (weighted)

Exploitation-centred definition[a]	_Manual-labour definition_		Row Totals
	Working class	'Middle' class	
Working class	[1] Agreed-upon working class $10,733 (7523) 290	[2] Disputed category no. 1. $11,756 (7040) 209	$11,161 (7335) 499
Marginal working class	[3] $16,326 (8995) 138	[4] $13,350 (7098) 118	$14,953 (8293) 256
'Middle' class	[5] Disputed category no. 2. $16,434 (7791) 103	[6] Agreed-upon 'middle' class $21,238 (13,590) 243	$19,812 (12,347) 346
Column Totals	$13,287 (8446) 531	$16,134 (11,264) 570	

[a] Working class = cell 12 in Table 3.3; Marginal working class = cells 9 and 11; 'Middle class' = cells 4–8 and 10.

explore the range of hypotheses for both of these adjudications.

The basic results are presented in tables 5.11 and 5.12, and the statistical tests for the various adjudication hypotheses appear in table 5.13.

Common Hypotheses

As in the adjudication of the Poulantzas definition, the agreed-upon workers and agreed-upon 'middle' class in the adjudication of the manual-labour definition differ in the appropriate ways: the

TABLE 5.12
Adjudication of manual-labour definition of working class: class attitude scale[a]

Entries in cells of table:
Means
(Standard deviations)
Number of cases (weighted)

Exploitation-centred definition	Manual-labour definition		Row Totals
	Working class	'Middle' class	
Working class	Agreed-upon working class [1] 1.12 (3.17) 344	Disputed category no. 1. [2] 0.27 (3.42) 250	0.76 (3.30) 593
Marginal working class	[3] 1.44 (3.34) 154	[4] −0.50 (3.03) 130	0.55 (3.34) 284
Middle class	[5] Disputed category no. 2. −0.28 (3.13) 111	[6] Agreed-upon 'middle' class −1.62 (3.57) 280	−1.24 (3.19) 391
Column Totals	0.95 (3.26) 609	−0.68 (3.51) 660	

[a]Values on the class attitude scale go from +8 (maximally pro-working class) to −8 (maximally pro-capitalist class).
[b]Working class = Cell 12 in Table 3.3; Marginal working class = cells 9 and 11; 'Middle class = cells 4–8 and 10.

agreed upon 'middle' class earn on average over $10,000 more per year and score, on average, 2.73 points lower on the pro-working-class attitude scale.

Income Adjudication

The results for the income adjudication are essentially the same for disputed category 1 as they were in the adjudication of the

TABLE 5.13

Test of adjudication hypotheses: manual-labour versus exploitation definiti

Hypotheses[a]		Empirical results	t	Significance level (One-tailed)	Conclusion
COMMON HYPOTHESES					
Income					
1.1	$(6)^b - (1) > 0$	\$10,505	10.8	.000	supported
Pro-working-class attitudes					
I.2	$(6) - (1) < 0$	−2.73	10.0	.000	supported
ADJUDICATION HYPOTHESES					
Income					
III.1A	$\|1 - 2\| - \|2 - 6\| < 0$	−\$8459	5.3	.000	II.1A strongly
III.1B	$\|1 - 2\| - \|2 - 6\| > 0$				supported over
III.2A	$\|1 - 5\| - \|5 - 6\| > 0$	\$896	0.4	n.s.	Neither hypoth
III.2B	$\|1 - 5\| - \|5 - 6\| < 0$				supported
Pro-working-class attitudes					
III.3A	$\|1 - 2\| - \|2 - 6\| < 0$	−1.04	2.1	.020	II.2A strongly
III.3B	$\|1 - 2\| - \|2 - 6\| > 0$				supported over
III.4A	$\|1 - 5\| - \|5 - 6\| > 0$	0.06	0.1	n.s.	neither hypothe
III.4B	$\|1 - 5\| - \|5 - 6\| < 0$				supported

[a]The Hypothesis numbers correspond to the numbers in Table 5.6.
[b]The numbers in parentheses refer to the cells in Tables 5.10 and 5.11.

productive labour definition: this category is clearly much closer to the agreed-upon workers than to the agreed-upon non-workers The results for disputed category 2, however, are inconsisten with both definitions under scrutiny: the average income of thi category falls almost exactly half-way between the incomes of the agreed-upon workers and agreed-upon 'middle' class.

Attitude Adjudication

The attitude adjudication mirrors quite closely the income adjudi cation. There is substantial support for the hypothesis that dis puted category 1 is significantly closer to agreed-upon worker than agreed-upon 'middle' class (hypothesis III.3A), and no sup port for either of the two hypotheses concerning the second dis puted category. Again, the result falls almost exactly between the two agreed-upon categories. When we look at the item-by-item breakdown of the attitude scale in table 5.14 we see the same basi

TABLE 5.14
**Responses to individual items in attitude scale for adjudication of
manual-labour definitions**

	Agreed-upon working class	Disputed category 1	Disputed category 2	Agreed-upon 'middle' class
Corporations benefit ners at expense of ers[a]	0.26[b]	0.20	0.06	0.03
Employers should be hibited from hiring bs in a strike	0.31	0.04	−0.02	−0.26
Strikers are justified ising force	−0.17	−0.29	−0.31	−0.60
Big corporations have much power today	0.54	0.64	0.65	0.45
A main reason for erty is that the economy ased on private profits	0.25	0.13	0.01	−0.33
Non-management could place of work without sses	0.08	−0.01	−0.23	−0.38
A modern society can effectively without the fit motive	−0.30	−0.44	−0.49	−0.52
In a strike, it is erally desirable that strikers win most of ir demands[c]	0.15	0.02	0.05	−0.02
Working-class self-ntification (% who say t they are in the working ss)	36.7	25.9	29.5	14.8

or precise wording of items, see discusion in text.
ntries are means on the individual items as entered into the class attitude scale.
1 = pro-worker; −1 = pro-bourgeois; 0 = don't know).
should be noted in this item that between 65 per cent and 82 per cent of the
spondents in the various adjudication categories advocated the class compromise posi-
n on this variable and thus received a value of 0 on the item.

pattern. The first disputed category is clearly much more like th
agreed-upon workers than the agreed-upon non-workers on five c
the items, it is closer to the agreed-upon non-workers on only on
item (item number eight) and it falls fairly much in the middle o
three of the items. The second disputed category, on the othe
hand, is closer to the agreed-upon workers on two items, closer t
the agreed-upon non-workers on three items, and right in the mid
dle on four.

The Effects of Gender and Union Membership

Table 5.15 presents the results for the adjudication of the manual
labour definition looking at men and women, and union and non
union members separately. These results are rather complex i
certain respects. For the income adjudications, disputed categ
ory 1 is closer to the agreed-upon workers in each of these com
parisons, except for men, for whom this category is at the mid-poin
between agreed-upon workers and 'middle' class. For disputed
category 2, on the other hand, the results are quite inconsisten
across comparisons: for men and especially for women taken sepa
rately, this category is closer to the agreed-upon workers; fo
union members, this category is identical to the agreed-upon 'mid
dle' class; and for non-union members it falls in between the
agreed-upon categories.

For the class-attitude adjudication, the results are perhaps even
more indecisive. While among women, the pattern is pretty much
as expected (disputed category 1 closer to agreed-upon worker
and disputed category 2 closer to agreed-upon 'middle' class)
among men both of the disputed categories fall in the mid
dle, between the two agreed-upon categories. Among union
members, as in the evaluation of Poulantzas's definition of class
there is no clear pattern—while disputed category 1 has the high
est value on this variable, all of the other categories have roughly
the same values. Among non-unionized employees, on the other
hand, both of the disputed categories fall around the middle.

Overall Assessment of the Manual Labour Adjudication

What sense can we make of these seemingly inconsistent findings?
Two things should be noted: first, the difficulty mainly involves
disputed category 2. In general the results support the proposition that disputed category 1 is closer to the agreed-upon work-

TABLE 5.15
Adjudication comparisons for sex and union members categories taken separately: manual-labour adjudications

	Agreed-upon working class	Disputed category 1	Disputed category	Agreed-upon middle class
SEX COMPARISONS				
Income				
Men	$13,306	$19,413	$18,120	$25,453
Women	$7,718	$9,567	$7,813	$14,710
Pro-working-class attitudes				
Men	1.50	−0.83	−0.11	−2.15
Women	0.69	0.56	−1.23	−0.81
Sample size[a]				
Men	183	51	94	170
Women	161	199	17	110
%Men	53%	20%	85%	61%
UNION MEMBERSHIP COMPARISONS				
Income				
Union members	$16,043	$13,540	$20,807	$20,500
Non-union	$7,945	$11,394	$15,447	$21,301
Pro-working-class attitudes				
Union members	1.95	2.65	1.48	1.13
Non-union	0.75	−0.15	−0.65	−1.85
Sample size				
Union	106	37	19	21
Non-union	237	212	92	259
%Unionized	31%	15%	17%	8%

[a] All Ns are weighted

ers than the agreed-upon 'middle' class. Although there are some instances in which this disputed category falls close to the mid-point between the agreed-upon categories—for example the con-sciousness results for men—there is no instance in which it is closer to the agreed-upon 'middle' class. With respect to pro-letarianized white collar employees, therefore, the data offer no support to the claim that they are 'middle class' and considerable support to the claim that they are part of the working class. Sec-ond, with respect to disputed category 2 in nearly every case the results are completely indecisive. In terms of the problem of adjudicating *between* contending definitions, therefore, they sup-port none of the hypotheses we have been entertaining, and thus

do not allow us to distinguish between the two definitions unde
investigation.

My guess is that there are two principal explanations for th
results involving disputed category 2: first, problems with th
operational criteria adopted in constructing the exploitatior
centred class variables, and second, the issue of class biography.

It is, of course, easy to blame contradictory results o
problems of measurement and operationalization. The universalit
of measurement problems is one of the things about sociologic:
research which encourages researchers to talk themselves out c
difficulties. Nevertheless, I do think a reasonable case can be mad
that some of the anomalies we have observed are linked to mea:
urement issues. Some indication of this can be seen by looking :
the 'marginal working class' category, cells 3 and 4 in table 5.1.
The manual–non-manual demarcation within this category show
a sharp difference in scores on the attitude scale: white-collar mar
ginal workers (largely white-collar supervisors and semi
credentialled white collar employees) have a value of -0.50 on th
scale while manual marginal workers (largely craft workers an
manual supervisors) have a mean of 1.44. This seems to indicat
that many of the people in category three really belong in th
agreed-upon worker category, and perhaps some of the people i
category four belong in the agreed-upon 'middle' class.

Two measurement issues are implicated in these possible clas
sification problems. First, there is the problem of distinguishin
between supervision that is really part of the managemen
apparatus and thus partakes in at least marginal levels c
organization-exploitation, and supervision which is nominal, which
is mainly a transmission belt for orders from above. We have relie
on a series of questions about what supervisors can do to thei
subordinates in order to specify this marginal level of organizatior
asset exploitation, arguing that the ability to impose sanctions or
subordinates is the important line of differentiation. This may not
in fact, be a satisfactory way of specifying the problem (assuming
of course, that the basic conceptual status of organization asset
and exploitation is accepted). Some kind of minimal participatior
in co-ordinative decision-making may also be necessary. With :
more stringent criterion for organization asset exploitation, mos
of the blue collar supervisors that we have included in the 'margi
nal working class' category would no longer be treated as prope
supervisors at all and would thus be placed in the agreed-upor
worker category. This would also lead to a reclassification of :
large part of disputed category 2 into cells 1 and 3 of the table.

A second problem of operationalization concerns the treatment of craft labour as having marginal levels of skill/credential assets, thus placing them outside of the pure working class. If they were also supervisors, they would be placed in one of the unambiguous non-working-class categories. If craft labour had not been treated in this way, then most of the individuals currently in cell 3 would have been in cell 1, and many of the people in disputed category 2 would have been in cell 3. This again would have substantially affected the values of the dependent variables in these cells and potentially affected the conclusions reached from the adjudication analysis.

It is unlikely that the results displayed in these tables are entirely the artifacts of errors in judgement on the operationalization of concepts. They probably also reflect salient properties of the real mechanisms at work in the relationship between class structure and class consciousness. In particular, I suspect that at least some of the results are significantly affected by the problem of class biographies. Most of the incumbents of positions in disputed category 2—blue-collar employees in managerial and supervisory positions—have biographies that are tightly bound up with the agreed-upon working class category. In many instances they are in careers which begin in cell 1 of the typology and move gradually through cell 3 to cell 5, and their social ties through family and friends are likely to be closely linked to the working class. Similarly, many of the people in disputed category 2—proltearianized white-collar employees—are likely to have biographies tied to the agreed-upon 'middle-class' locations. Indeed, this may be why their ideological stance is significantly *less* pro-working class than the agreed-upon workers even though they are much closer to agreed-upon workers than agreed-upon 'middle' class.[30] Class conciousness does not emanate from the relational properties of the positions people fill at one point in time. Rather, it is formed through the accumulation of class experiences that constitute a person's biography. To the extent that such biographical trajectories vary across the cells of adjudication typology they can confound the adjudications themselves.

Conclusion

The exercises in this chapter have been designed to provide a systematic empirical intervention into debates over the concept of class structure. Two basic conclusions can be drawn from the investigation:

1) In the debate over Poulantzas's conceptualization of class structure, there is very little support for the view that productive labour is an appropriate criterion for distinguishing the working class from non-working-class wage-earners. Except for the rates of unionization of different categories in the adjudication, the disputed category was closer to the agreed-upon workers in every instance. At least as far as this specific adjudication is concerned, there is much more empirical support for the structural definition of the working class as uncredentialled non-managerial employees.

2) In the debate over the manual-labour definition of the working class, there is almost no support for treating this division as a class distinction. Proletarianized white collar workers are generally more like proletarianized manual workers (i.e. the agreed-upon workers in the analysis) than they are like non-proletarianized white-collar employees. It is less clear how non-proletarianized manual wage earners should be treated, but in any event the data do not support the thesis that they are part of the working class.

These debates will hardly be settled, needless to say, by the data and analyses we have explored. Defenders of the positions I have criticized have a variety of avenues open for reply. First, of course, they can reject the entire enterprise of the empirical adjudication of contending definitions, arguing that definitions are strictly conventions and that their adjudication is therefore strictly a matter of their logical coherence.

Second, the need for empirical adjudication can be accepted, but the micro-individual logic of the empirical investigations of this chapter can be viewed as inappropriate for adjudicating contending class concepts. If those concepts are meant to explain historical trajectories of struggle and change, then, it could be argued, the data explored in this chapter are radically unsuited to the present task. This is a serious criticism, and it cannot be dismissed out of hand. The rejoinder to such criticisms is that even if the concept of class structure is centrally preoccupied with such macro-historical and dynamic problems, there are, after all, real people in that class structure, real people who are systematically affected in various ways by virtue of being in one class rather than another. Unless one is prepared to argue that the effects of class on individuals are completely contingent—that is, that there is nothing systematic about those effects that are rooted in the class structure itself—then the results reported in this chapter have to be explained, and those explanations have to be consistent with the structural map of class relations employed in the theory.

Third, the general logic of the strategy adopted in this chapter can be accepted, but the specific empirical indicators and criteria can be viewed as faulty. On the one hand, it could be claimed, that the operationalizations of the contending class definitions are flawed and thus do not provide the basis for appropriate tests; or, alternatively, the selection or measurement of the dependent variables could be unsatisfactory, and thus the conclusions based on those variables are unjustified.

We have already encountered this problem of the selection of the adjudication criterion variable in the discussion of union membership in the debate over unproductive labour, and in our consideration of the problem of supervision and craft labour in the operationalization of the exploitation-centred concept of class. These kinds of criticisms are important, and it is always possible that alternative operationalizations and variables could produce quite different results. The burden of proof in such accusations, however, falls on the critics: they must show that alternative measures of either the contending class concepts or the adjudication criteria do in fact produce different results. Furthermore, if alternative measures do produce different conclusions, the fact of the differences must itself be structurally explained: what is it about the mechanisms at work in the world that produces different adjudication outcomes depending upon the specific measures employed?[31]

Finally, the results of the empirical analysis could be accepted, but the conclusions drawn from them could be regarded as unwarranted. None of the results we have discussed are so completely unambiguous in their theoretical implications that plausible alternative interpretations could not be produced. For example in the various adjudications we have explored, there is clear evidence in the data that the people in disputed category in cell 2 of table 5.11 are ideologically different from the agreed-upon workers, even though they are more like workers than they are like the agreed-upon 'middle' class. A defender of Poulantzas's position could respond that the explanation for their relative closeness to workers is because workers as a whole in the United States are generally affected by petty-bourgeois ideology and thus tend to be less sharply differentiated from non-workers in general. The disputed category, then, could be viewed as the part of the new petty bourgeoisie to which workers are most closely drawn. The historical context of the data could be taken as the basis for explaining how the results might be consistent with the class concept in question.

These kinds of alternative explanations suggest the need for historical and comparative research to deepen the conceptual adjudications we have explored. If the adjudication results were essentially the same in countries in which the working class is more class conscious, more mobilized and organized than in the United States, for example, it would undermine the kind of critique suggested above. If, on the other hand, the adjudications look very different in societies with different historical contexts, then this would suggest that the conclusions I have drawn need to be modified.

AMBIGUITIES AND ISSUES FOR FUTURE WORK

As I have stressed throughout this analysis, there is no possibility of the absolute validation of a concept; adjudications are always among actively contending concepts, rivals which attempt to capture the same theoretical objects. The conclusions established in this chapter are therefore of necessity provisional, both because the defenders of the concepts I have criticized may effectively respond in subsequent research and argument, and because new alternatives to the conceptualizations I have proposed may be produced in the future. One final issue to be discussed, therefore, is whether the adjudication analyses we have explored suggest any directions for such future conceptual elaboration. What are the anomalies in the data? What results point to the need for further conceptual work? These ambiguities and loose ends fall under two categories. First, the question of specifying the criteria for the working class, and second the choice between concepts of class based on trajectory and concepts based on position.

Specifying the Working Class

While I feel that in the debates over the definition of the working class, the empirical evidence is most supportive of the exploitation-centred concept, a number of results in the analysis suggest that some further refinement is needed. Above all, there is indication that the logic of the credential-exploitation criterion needs further work. This issue played a particularly important role in the ambiguities in the adjudication with the manual–nonmanual definition of class structure, especially around the treatment of craft labour as marginal credential exploiters.

At the heart of this problem of the status of skill/credential assets in the analysis of class structure is the lack of clear relational criteria linked to the ownership of credentials. The ownership of capital corresponds to a social relation between employers and employees; the ownership of labour-power assets in feudalism corresponds to the social relation between lords and serfs; the effective control of organization assets corresponds to the authority relations between managers and workers. There is no such relational correspondence to credential asset exploitation. This is one of the reasons why the precise allocation of people to class positions seems much more arbitrary with respect to this asset than others, and why there are particularly sharp problems in the treatment of craft labour. In order to reduce this arbitrariness in the operational use of the concept of credential asset exploitation in class analysis, additional theoretical clarification is needed.

Class Trajectories

All of the adjudications we have explored in this chapter have been between positional definitions of class structure, that is, definitions which revolve around essentially static characterizations of the locations of people within class relations. Yet, as the results in the adjudication of the manual-labour definition show, the existence of class trajectories may significantly influence the observed results.

Ultimately, I believe that a trajectory concept of class is preferable to a positional one. The concept of interests always implies some sort of time horizon on the part of the actors who hold those interests. The exploitation-centred interests which constitute the basis for defining classes, therefore, must be treated as having a temporal dimension to them. The class position of an exploited apprentice is different if that apprentice knows that he or she will become a master artisan than if this is a rare event, because the real interests linked to that exploitation will be different. Proletarianized white-collar jobs that are really pre-managerial jobs should therefore not be considered in the same location within class relations as proletarianized jobs which are not part of such career trajectories.

Such a trajectory notion of class structure implies that the class character of a given *position* must in a double sense be viewed in probabilistic terms. First, as I have already stressed in the discussion of class formation in chapter four, the relational properties of a position do not strictly determine class outcomes, but only the probabilistic tendencies for such outcomes. We can now add a second sense in which class is a probabilistic concept: the relational properties of a position determine only probabilistically the relational location of the incumbents over time. In some positions the probability is extremely high that incumbents will stay in positions with the same relational characteristics. Where deviations occur it is due to factors which are contingent relative to the effects of the positions themselves.[32] In other positions there is a high probability of movement with respect to relational properties. And in still other positions, the outcomes may be relatively indeterminate.[33]

The importance of such trajectories does not imply that a positional account of class structure is unimportant. Indeed, in order even to begin to specify the temporal dimension of class relations it is necessary to be able to characterize the destinations to which the probabilities will be linked. Unless managerial positions are understood to be structurally different from non-managerial positions in class terms, there would be no need to treat the movement into such positions as a problem of class trajectory. There is a sense, therefore, in which the kind of positional analysis conducted in this chapter is a logical pre-condition for the exploration of a trajectory approach to class. Nevertheless, a full account of 'class structure', where class structure is meant to designate the interest-generating process linked to exploitation, has to include some kind of recognition of these probabilistic trajectories.[34]

While the adjudication of contending definitions of concepts is a crucial aspect of scientific work, such adjudication is not the final product of scientific investigation. Concepts are not simply produced, formed and transformed; they are also *used*. Ultimately the point of worrying about the correctness of definitions is that on the one hand, we want to use the concepts in building general theories of social processes, and on the other, we need them in order to pursue concrete empirical investigations of various sorts.

Exploring such uses of the exploitation-centred concept of class is the basic objective of the rest of this book.

Notes

1. For convenience I will use the expression 'middle class' interchangeably with the expression 'non-working class wage-earners' throughout this chapter, even though the term is not necessarily employed by the theorists we will discuss. Poulantzas, for example, uses the term 'new petty bourgeoisie' to label non-working class wage-earners, and I have preferred the expression 'contradictory locations.'

2. I explored the possibility of also adjudicating empirically between my earlier conceptualization of contradictory locations and the present framework. The problem in doing this is that the two definitions of the working class overlap so much that an empirical comparison is difficult to pursue and is quite vulnerable to the details of the empirical operationalizations adopted. On the basis of the operationalizations employed in this chapter, 93.5 per cent of the individuals classified as working class in the exploitation concept are also categorized as working class in my earlier conceptualization; and 96 per cent of those classified as workers in my earlier approach were classified as either workers or marginal workers in the exploitation concept. The exploitation conceptualization, therefore, is less of a decisive empirical break with the previous approach than a retheorization of the criteria previously employed. For the record, in an exploratory analysis which examined the empirical differences in predictions between these two concepts, the results were quite equivocal on their relative merits. Because of the small numbers involved in the disputed categories and the sensitivity of the results to small changes in the operational criteria employed, I have no confidence that these results reflect real differences in the empirical power of the two conceptualizations.

3. The provisional character of the conclusions reached through this kind of empirical adjudication is clearly not something distinctive to the problem of definitional disputes. All empirical 'tests' of propositions are provisional because of the possibilities of the existence of counfounding mechanisms of the sort indicated above.

4. See chapter two, note 36.

5. I will see the term 'dependent variable' in the standard statistical sense throughout this discussion, even though the term usually implies a rather rigid distinction between 'causes' (independent variables) and 'effects' (dependent variables). This is at odds with the more 'dialectical' view of causation within Marxism within which reciprocal effects between structures and practices is of central concern.

6. In any event, Poulantzas and other theorists using his general approach to analysing class structures, together with theorists who adopt manual labour definitions, do not hesitate to use class in explanations of individual-level processes. Although Poulantzas avoids using the term 'class consciousness', he argues that the ideologies carried by agents are systematically shaped by their locations within the social relations of production. Even though this is not his central pre-occupation, there is the repeated suggestion that classes are consequential for individual subjec-

tivity and practices, and thus it is not 'unfair' to his explanatory objectives to pursue a comparison in these terms.

7. For a fuller substantive discussion of the problem of class consciousness, see chapter seven below.

8. Marxist critics of surveys typically make this kind of argument, on the ground that 'hegemonic' bourgeois ideology is likely to be more systematically expressed in atomized, authority-laden situations like interviews. It is not obvious, however, that the biases will work in this direction. It is not unthinkable that the pressures towards a bourgeois consensus could be greater within the collective context of working class associations, whereas individual workers might feel freer to express 'deviant' views in the anonymous and private setting of an interview. I suspect that the usual assumption is probably correct, but it needs to be verified, and to my knowledge it has not been.

9. Response (2) constitutes the pure 'class compromise' response, stating that neither workers nor capitalists should come out clearly ahead in a conflict. For this reason it was given a 0 in the scale.

10. This simple additive procedure assumes that all eight of the items should be given equal weighting in constructing the scale. There are, of course, fancier statistical strategies (eg. factor analysis) for assigning weights to variables within scales. I have opted for a more simple-minded approach in the present context so that the meaning of the scale's metric will be relatively transparent.

11. For much mainstream sociology, class identification *is* class consciousness. I am including it in the analysis here not so much because in and of itself it is such a salient dimension of consciousness within Marxist theory, but because it has been accorded so much attention in the sociological literature. For the best overview of the problem of class identification from a non-Marxist perspective, see Mary Jackman and Robert Jackman, *Class Awareness in the United States*, Berkeley 1983.

12. Jackman and Jackman *ibid*, argue that closed-category versions of class identification questions are superior to open-ended versions since the closed categories are essential to specifying the meaning of the term 'class' for respondents. The format we have adopted attempts to capture the virtues of each strategy, since respondents are initially allowed to say that they do not think of themselves as a member of any class, and only then are asked to state a class identification from a list of closed categories.

13. A more detailed discussion of the procedures for variable constructions used in these analyses can be found in appendix II.

14. The expression 'need not themselves work' is important conceptually in this specification. The point is that capitalists own sufficient capital that they are able to obtain at least the socially average standard of living without working at all—they are able to reproduce themselves and their families entirely on the labour of others. This does not imply that capitalists always refrain from work—that is, from engaging in socially productive labour—but simply that they need not work to obtain the socially average standard of living.

15. Depending upon the capital-intensity of production, a specific number of employees may indicate being a small employer—someone who has to work alongside the employees—or being a proper capitalist. It would have been desirable to obtain data on the division of labour within small businesses in order to see the extent to which a small employer indeed did engage in the productive work of the business, but we did not collect such information.

16. The use of occupational titles in specifying exploitation relations, and thus as criteria which enter into the specification of class locations, is a departure from my

earlier work in which I insisted that the concept of 'occupation' designated positions within the technical division of labour rather than the social division of labor. See especially, my paper, 'Class and Occupation', *Theory and Society,* vol. 9, no. 1, 1980. The conceptual shift is based on the claim that incumbency in a technically defined position implies, under conditions of 'private ownership of credentials', a specific kind of exploitation relation. It is still the case, of course, that occupational titles do not by themselves constitute specific 'classes', since credential exploitation is only one of several forms of exploitation relations in capitalist societies which are concretely combined in determining the class structure.

17. For example, in the official U.S. Census occupational codes, the person in charge of the admissions department of a hospital—the 'admissions officer'—is classified as a 'receptionist' in the three-digit occupation codes, a rubric that also includes people who greet clients in an office. We had one admissions officer in our sample (which is why this example came to our attention) who was a registered nurse with twenty-five years of experience in the hospital in question and for whom her position as 'receptionist' represented a substantial promotion. Initially we thought that her classification as a receptionist was a coding error, but when we investigated the matter further, we discovered that this is indeed the way the Dictionary of Occupational Titles classifies her job.

18. The 'autonomy' criterion is being used in this case not because autonomy as such is considered an exploitation-asset, but because it is considered an indicator that a sales and clerical job held by a person with a high academic credential is really a semi-professional credentialled position.

19. The entire structure is the object of investigation in subsequent chapters.

20. The precise coding for this variable is found in appendix II. It should be noted that it is not always unambiguous whether a particular occupational title is or is not involved in the production of commodities. A computer specialist, for example, may be involved in the financial affairs of a company or production itself (or both). I therefore initially coded occupations into three categories: productive, ambiguous, unproductive. This made it possible to construct operational variables for productive labour which are more or less restrictive. As it turned out, none of the statistical results depended at all on whether we used a restrictive or unrestrictive classification of occupations, and thus throughout this chapter I will rely on the more restrictive definition of unproductive labor (i.e. the ambiguous occupations will be considered productive).

21. This is in accord with the general methodological stance enunciated earlier that empirical adjudications are always between rival concepts or propositions, not directly between a proposition and the 'real world' as such.

22. A full description of this design can be found in Robert M. Groves, 'An Empirical Comparison of Two Telephone Sample Designs', *Journal of Marketing Research,* 15, 1979, pp. 622–31.

23. Of the Swedish respondents, 60 per cent responded to the initial mailed questionnaire, 27 per cent responded to a second mailed questionnaire after having been reminded via telephone, and 13 per cent were interviewed by telephone.

24. See Robert M. Groves and Robert L. Kahn, *Surveys by Telephone*, Orlando, Florida 1979.

25. My best guess is that much of this bias is due to refusals to participate in the survey. Among people who initially refused to participate, but after follow-up telephone calls agreed to participate (30 per cent of the initial refusers, or 9 per cent of the final sample), the education and occupation distributions are much closer to the Census figures. Assuming the 'converted refusers' are likely to have

demographic characteristics intermediate between initial participators and uncon
verted refusers, this suggests that among the people who refused to participate in
the survey there was a lower proportion of high status individuals than among
participants. I do not know why less educated people in lower status occupation
were more likely to refuse to participate in this particular survey than in othe
telephone surveys fielded by the Survey Research Center.

26. Technically, the easiest way to obtain an estimate of the terms in this equa
tion is to analyse the differences involved using dummy variable regression equa
tions. If W is a dummy variable for the agreed-upon workers and M is a dummy
variable for the agreed-upon 'middle' class (with the appropriate disputed category
being the 'left out' category in the regression), then all we need to do is estimate the
following regression equation:

$$Y = a + B_1(W + M) + B_2(W - M)$$

It can be shown from a simple rearrangement of terms that (a) if the disputed
category falls *in between* the two agreed upon categories, then the coefficient B_1 is
equal to twice the difference between the differences and (b) if the disputed categ
ory is not between the agreed-upon categories, than the coefficient B_2 is equal to
twice the difference between the differences. (The reason for the shift in which
coefficient tests the hypothesis is that we are interested in the differences between
the absolute values of the original differences, and depending upon whether or no
the disputed category falls in between the agreed upon categories, only on of B_1 or
B_2 is the appropriate coefficient for testing this). The standard errors of these
regression coefficients thus enable us to calculate the *t*-statistic above. I am grateful
to Robert Hauser and Charles Halaby for showing me the simple way of perform
ing these tests.

27. A failure of a given variable to differentiate between the working class and
the agreed-upon non-workers could be due to several things: the operational vari
able could be a bad measure of the theoretical variable; the theoretical expectation
that the agreed-upon categories should differ with respect to this theoretical vari
able could be incorrect; or the claim that the agreed-upon categories are in fac
distinct classes could be false.

28. The *t*-statistic for the difference between workers and the disputed category
is 1.44 which has a probability of .075 on a one-tailed test, while the *t*-statistic for
the difference in the differences is 3.1, which has a probability of less than .001.

29. It is worth noting that the debate over the two definitions of the working
class being considered here is particularly consequential for the evaluation of the
class location of women. In Poulantzas's definition, only about 15 per cent of all
women in the labor force are in the working class; in the exploitation-centred
concept, the figure is over 60 per cent.

30. The fact that the distance between the agreed-upon workers and disputed
category 1 is so much greater for men than for women (see table 5.15) supports
this interpretation, since in various ways proletarianized white-collar women are
less likely to be embedded in class trajectories that link them to the agreed-upon
'middle' class category.

31. Even if one rejects the survey methodology as a valid technique for obtain
ing information on class consciousness, it is still necessary to explain why the survey
results turn out the way they do in an analysis of this sort. If survey results are
literally 'meaningless', as some critics have implied, then there should not be sys
tematic strong differences between the structural categories employed in an adjudi

cation analysis. At a minimum an alternative explanation of these results is needed, an explanation which demonstrates the falsity of the conclusions drawn from the data.

32. This implies being able to distinguish between mobility which is engendered by the nature of the positions themselves—e.g. they are embedded in career ladders—from mobility which is due to the operation of factors extrinsic to the positions. A war may generate considerable mobility, and thus affect the post-facto probabilities of individuals in working-class positions staying in the working class, but this is not due to structural properties of working-class positions per se. While theoretically one can make this distinction between endogenous and exogenous sources of mobility, in practice it is often empirically impossible to sort them out.

33. There is another complication which I will not explore here: the probabilities themselves may change over time as social structures change.

34. For an important exploration of this problem from a broadly Marxist orientation, see Daniel Bertaux, *Destins personnels et structure de classe*, Paris 1977; for a non-Marxist discussion of many of the same issues, see A. Stewart, K. Prandy and R. M. Blackburn, *Social Stratification and Occupation*, London 1980.

6

Class Structure in Contemporary Capitalism

A Comparison of Sweden and The United States

In this chapter we will explore a range of empirical problems concerning the class structure of advanced capitalist societies using the exploitation-centred conceptualization of class relations. Although we will test formal hypotheses in a number of places, most of the chapter will be largely descriptive in character. There have been very few systematic empirical studies of class structure from a Marxist perspective, and none using the exploitation-centred concept of class elaborated in this book. It is therefore of some importance to improve our descriptive maps of the class structure, since the concept figures in so many different kinds of problems Marxists study. This will be our basic goal here.

The data analysis will revolve around systematic comparison between the United States and Sweden. Within the family of highly developed capitalist countries, Sweden and the United States represent an important contrast. On the one hand they are in many ways rather similar economically: they have roughly the same level of technological development, very similar average standards of living, very little state ownership of industrial production. On the other hand, politically they are in many ways polar opposites. According to one estimate, as a result of state policies Sweden has the lowest level of real income inequality (after taxes and after transfer payments) of any developed capitalist country, while the United States has one of the highest.[1] If we take the ratio of the real income at the ninety-fifth percentile to the real income at the fifth percentile, this figure was only about 3:1 for Sweden in the early 1970s, whereas in the United States it was 13:1.[2] Sweden has a higher proportion of its civilian labour force directly employed by the state than any other advanced capitalist nation, well over forty per cent, while the United States has perhaps the lowest, under twenty per cent. Politically, Sweden has had the highest level of governance by social democratic parties of any capitalist country; the United States, the lowest. We therefore have two countries with roughly similar economic bases but sharply different political 'superstructures'. From a Marxist point of view, this is fertile terrain on which to explore the problem of class structure and its consequences.

In chapter seven we will focus mainly on the consequences of class structure for class consciousness. In this chapter the focus of attention will be on the class structure itself. The investigation will begin with an examination of the basic distribution of the labour force into classes. Attention will be paid to the relationship between this class distribution and sex, race, industrial sector, size of employing organization and the state. The following section will then attempt to explain the observed differences in class structure by decomposing these differences in various ways. The next section will shift the focus from individuals as units of analysis to families. The basic question will be how families are distributed in the class structure, with particular attention to the problem of class-heterogeneity within families. Finally, the chapter will conclude with an examination of the relationship between class structure and income inequality in Sweden and the United States. Since the concept of class used throughout this analysis is rooted in the concept of exploitation, there should be a direct relationship between our matrix of class locations and income.

Class Distributions

Before looking at the data, a brief word on operationalization is needed. In general, the criteria we will employ in operationalizating concepts of the class structure are identical in the two countries we are studying. The one exception involves the specification of 'credential assets'. Because of the nationally-specific meanings of given academic qualifications and the historical evolution of the relationship between different kinds of credentials and the labour market, it does not make theoretical sense to adopt mechanically the same formal academic degrees in the specification of this exploitation-generating asset. On the other hand, there are considerable risks in undermining the strict comparability of the data if different credentials are adopted as criteria for different countries. Ideally one would like some direct measure of the skill-scarcity of labour power itself, but I do not have a clear idea how this could be measured, and there is certainly nothing in the data which can plausibly be used to measure this.[3]

In order to balance these various concerns, it seemed advisable to shift the operational criteria for credential assets for Sweden. Instead of using a college degree as the salient criterion for differentiating different levels of credential assets for those occupations for which this is necessary (see table 5.3.III in the previous chapter), a high-school degree is adopted as the criterion. While Sweden may be in the process of becoming more like the United States in this regard, until recently a high-school degree was a much more substantial and important certification in Sweden than in the United States. A much smaller proportion of people went on to the University, and a university degree was not considered necessary for a range of highly skilled positions.[4]

One final prefatory comment on the exposition of the results. Ploughing through masses of detailed statistical tables can often be a tedious and cumbersome affair. The problem is compounded in the present case because the complexity of the class typology being used—twelve categories in all—and the logical structure of the typology—a matrix—can make the tabular presentation of result rather unwieldy. I have therefore adopted the following strategy: complete data tables for the various substantive topics in this chapter appear in appendix III. In the body of the chapter I will collapse and simplify the class typology in various ways, tailoring the tables to the descriptive generalizations I wish to emphasize in the text.

OVERALL CLASS DISTRIBUTIONS

Let us now turn to the data analysis. Table 6.1 presents the distribution of people in the labour force into classes in Sweden and the United States. In broad contours the two class structures are very similar. In spite of their vast differences in levels of social inequality and patterns of class formation, the basic distribution of people in the class structure does not vary dramatically between these two countries. In both countries the working class is by far the largest class numerically, around 40 per cent of the labour force. If we add the contradictory locations with marginal control over organization or skill assets, this increases to about 60 per cent in each country. In both countries the bourgeoisie and petty

TABLE 6.1

istribution of the labour force in the class matrix using the exploitation-centred
concept of class[a]

Assets in the means of production

Owners	Non-owners [wage labourers]			

Bourgeoisie
 	
J.S.   1.8%
Sweden   0.7%
	4 Expert
	  managers
	
	U.S. 3.9%
	Sweden 4.4%
		7 Semi-cre-
		  dentialed
		  managers
		U.S. 6.2%
		Sweden 4.0%
			10 Uncre-
			  dentialed
			  managers
			U.S. 2.3%
			Sweden 2.5%
				+

2 Small
  employers
 	
J.S.   6.0%
Sweden   4.8%
	5 Expert
	  supervisors
	
	U.S. 3.7%
	Sweden 3.8%
		8 Semi-cre-
		  dentialled
		  supervisors
		U.S. 6.8%
		Sweden 3.2%
			11 Uncre-
			  dentialled
			  supervisor
			U.S. 6.9%
			Sweden 3.1%
				>0 *Organ-
				ization
				assets*

3 Petty
  bourgeoisie
 	
J.S.   6.9%
Sweden   5.4%
	6 Expert
	  non-managers
	
	U.S. 3.4%
	Sweden 6.8%
		9 Semi-cre-
		  dentialled
		  workers
		U.S. 12.2%
		Sweden 17.8%
			12 Proletarians
			
			U.S. 39.9%
			Sweden 43.5%
				−

+   >0   −

Skill/credential assets

nited States: N = 1487
veden: N = 1179

istribution are of people working in the labour force, thus excluding unemployed,
usewives, pensioners, etc.
or operationalizations of the criteria for assets in this table, see Table 5.3.

bourgeoisie constitute a very small proportion of the labour force:
around 5 to 7 per cent are pure petty bourgeois and another 5 to 6
per cent small employers in both countries, and less than 2 per cent
fully-fledged capitalists.

While the basic outlines of the class structure are similar in the
two societies, there are some differences that deserve attention.
First, although approximately the same proportion of the labour
force in the two countries—11 to 12 per cent—occupy proper

managerial positions (positions involving organization-policy decision-making), there are significantly more supervisors (non-decision-makers with sanctioning authority) in the United States than in Sweden: 17.4 per cent compared to 10.1 per cent. This contrast is particularly striking for people without substantial credential assets. Non-expert supervisors constitute 13.7 per cent of the US labour force but only 6.3 per cent of the Swedish labour force. I will offer some interpretations of this difference in the level of supervision in the two countries in the next section of this chapter where we try to explain the differences in the two class structures. For the moment the thing to note is that work in the United States appears to be significantly more supervised than in Sweden.

A second point of contrast between the two countries is the working class. While the working class is the largest class in both countries, it is somewhat larger in Sweden. If we combine pure proletarians with semi-credentialled workers (cells 9 and 12 in the typology), the Swedish working class is about nine percentage points larger than the American (61.3 compared to 52.1). Most of this difference, as we shall see later, is attributable to the higher levels of supervision in the United States.

Third, if we look only at people with high levels of credential/skill assets—experts of various sorts—a considerably higher proportion in Sweden are completely outside of the managerial apparatus: 45 per cent of Swedish experts have no organizational assets, compared to only 31 per cent of experts in the United States. The reason for this is not that there are fewer expert managers or expert supervisors in Sweden. To the contrary, in Sweden there are slightly more people in such positions than in the United States. Rather, the reason is that there are more non-managerial experts—about twice the frequency of the United States.

Finally, while in both the United States and Sweden the vast majority of the labour force are wage-labourers, there are slightly more self-employed in the United States: 14.7 per cent compared to 10.9 per cent of the labour force in Sweden.[5] If we add to this those wage-labourers who have at some time in the past been self-employed—13.8 per cent of the labour force in the US and 6.7 per cent in Sweden—the proportion of the labour force with strong petty-bourgeois experiences is considerably larger in the United States than in Sweden: 28.5 per cent compared to 17.6 per cent. While becoming a capitalist remains largely a fantasy for most people in both societies, there are more people who have at least tried being self-employed in the United States, and this may have important ideological ramifications.

CLASS AND SEX

As one would expect, the class distribution among men and women differs sharply in both Sweden and the United States (see table 6.2). In both countries women in the labour force are disproportionately in the working class, while men are disproportionately in exploiting class positions, particularly the capitalist class and managerial positions. The result is that in both countries women constitute a clear majority of the working class: just over 60 per cent of all workers are women. Even if we add the marginally-credentialled employee category—which includes a fair number of highly skilled craft positions largely filled by men—to the 'pure' working class, it is still the case that a majority of work-

TABLE 6.2

Distribution of classes within sex categories, United States and Sweden[a]

| lass categories[b] | Distribution of sexes within classes | | | | Distribution of classes within sexes | | | |
| | United States | | Sweden | | United States | | Sweden | |
	Men	Women	Men	Women	Men	Women	Men	Women
Employers	69.7	30.3	83.1	16.9	10.1	5.2	8.2	2.1
Petty bourgeois	50.3	49.7	75.7	24.3	6.4	7.5	7.3	3.0
Managers	67.6	32.4	77.5	22.5	15.5	8.6	15.2	5.5
Supervisors	60.9	39.1	63.9	36.1	18.8	14.2	11.5	7.4
otal managers nd supervisors	63.7	36.3	71.0	29.0	34.3	22.8	26.7	12.9
Expert non-manager	47.7	52.3	56.1	43.9	3.0	3.9	6.8	6.8
Skilled workers	73.6	26.4	63.4	36.6	16.6	7.1	20.2	14.8
Workers	39.5	60.5	39.8	60.2	29.0	52.8	30.9	59.6
otal workers and killed workers	47.5	52.5	46.6	53.4	45.6	59.9	51.1	64.4
Overall total	54.3	45.7	56.0	44.0				

For complete data, see Table III.1 in the data appendix (Appendix III).
The categories are collapsed from the full class typology in Table 6.1 in the following manner: employers = 1,2; petty bourgeois = 3; managers = 4,7,10; supervisors = , 8, 11; expert non-managers = 6; skilled workers = 9; workers = 12.

ers are women in both countries. The image which is still present in many Marxist accounts that the working class consists primarily of male factory workers simply does not hold true any longer (if one adopts the concept of class proposed here).

Looking at the distributions the other way around—the class distribution within sexes—approximately one third of all men in both Sweden and the United States are clear exploiters (managers, experts and employers), compared to only about one fifth of women. Over half of all women in the labour force are in the working class, compared to only about 30 per cent of men.

The one thing that was not anticipated in the results in table 6.2 is that the degree of sexual difference in class distributions is greater in Sweden than in the United States. In virtually every position of exploitation privilege, women are more under-represented in the Swedish class structure than in the American. In Sweden, the percentage of men who are employers is 3.9 times greater than the percentage of women who are employers, whereas in the United States the figure is only 1.9 times greater; and the percentage of men who are either expert-managers or semi-credentialled managers is 4.8 times greater than the percentage of women in these positions in Sweden, whereas in the United States the over-representation of men is only 2.8 times. Following most of the popular prejudices about 'enlightened' Swedish social democracy, I had expected there to be less sex-bias in the class distribution in Sweden, but this is clearly not the case, at least not according to this data.

While it is beyond the scope of the present analysis to investigate in depth the actual process by which men and women are differentially sorted into classes, we can get a first glimpse at the process by looking at the class distributions for men and women within age groups. As table 6.3 indicates, in the United States the proportion of women who are working class does not vary substantially in different age groups between age twenty-one and sixty-five. Among men, on the other hand, there is a clear age pattern: the proportion in the working class declines until middle age and then rises slightly among older men. The age distributions among managers differ even more sharply between men and women in the United States: an increasing proportion of men are managers as we move from early stages in careers to mid-career, whereas for women there is a monotonic decline in the proportion in managerial positions as we move from the 21 to 25-year-old group to the 56 to 65-year-old group. In Sweden the contrast between men and women is not quite so clear-cut as in the United States, but a basically similar pattern exists: men appear to have a much sharper age profile for managerial positions than do women, rising from 7.8 per cent in the 21 to 25-year-old group to 19 per cent in the 36 to 45-year-old group, compared to virtually no change for women, about 5 per cent in both groups.

These various age–class profiles within sex categories suggest that men have much greater probabilities of promotional mobility from working-class positions into managerial positions than women do, particularly during the early and middle stages of careers. Of course, the patterns in table 6.3 are a complex result of the intersection of career patterns, transformations in the class

TABLE 6.3
Class distribution within age-sex categories[a]

I. United States

% of men and women who are:

	Workers		Managers	
	Men	*Women*	*Men*	*Women*
Under 21	36.7	69.0	8.8	2.7
21–25	35.3	51.5	12.9	12.7
26–35	21.4	48.5	17.4	10.5
36–45	23.9	51.0	20.4	8.5
46–55	30.5	53.6	16.1	6.1
56–65	36.5	59.1	10.0	5.9
Over 65	41.8	47.9	12.3	11.0

II. Sweden

% of men and women who are:

	Workers		Managers	
	Men	*Women*	*Men*	*Women*
Under 21	61.1	73.1	2.8	3.8
21–25	40.3	75.0	7.8	5.4
26–35	27.3	45.7	17.0	7.1
36–45	25.2	54.3	19.2	4.7
46–55	27.0	66.4	18.3	4.7
56–65	31.5	68.8	12.0	3.8

[a]For complete data, see Table III.2 in Appendix III.

structure and changes in rates of labour-force participation. For example, how should the curvilinear relationship between age and the proportion of men in managerial positions be interpreted? It is unlikely that this is the result of demotions of managers at the end of their careers. Rather, one would suspect, that this reflects the intersection of two causal processes: first, the career-trajectory process in which promotions into managerial positions occur in the first half of men's careers, so that by the latter part of one's career it becomes relatively rarer to be promoted from non-management to managerial positions; and second, a historical cohort dynamic, in which the probabilities of becoming a manager have increased over time (as the relative number of managerial positions has expanded). The first tendency would mean that the proportion of men in managerial positions would increase with age (although at a decreasing rate beyond mid-career); the second tendency would mean that the proportion of men in managerial positions would decrease with age. The combination of these two tendencies produces the curvilinear relationship in table 6.3. Given this kind of complexity, it is not a simple statistical task to demonstrate conclusively that the differential outcomes for men and women observed in this table are primarily the result of gender discrimination in promotions. Nevertheless, as a provisional conclusion, it is a plausible hypothesis that this is a substantial contributor to the gender differences in class distributions.

CLASS AND RACE

Because of the racial homogeneity of Swedish society, it is not possible with the data at hand to explore the issue of class and race in Sweden. Table 6.4, therefore, only presents the data for the United States. The pattern of racial differences in class distributions is, if anything, more pronounced than the pattern for sexual differences. 59 per cent of blacks are in the working class, compared to only 37 per cent of whites; at the other extreme, about 16 per cent of whites are employers or petty bourgeois compared to less than 3 per cent of blacks. These racial contrasts become even more marked when we break them down by sex: Nearly 70 per cent of black women in the labour force are in the working class, compared to only 27 per cent of white men, with white women and black men falling between the two at about 50 per cent.

TABLE 6.4
Distribution of race and class in the United States[a]

| | Distribution of classes within race and sex categories | | | | | |
| | Whites | | | Blacks | | |
Class categories[b]	Men	Women	Total	Men	Women	Total
1. Employers	11.1	5.7	8.7	0.0	1.4	0.7
2. Petty bourgeois	6.4	8.9	7.5	3.7	0.0	2.0
3. Managers	17.0	9.5	13.6	8.0	6.3	7.4
4. Supervisors	18.3	15.0	16.8	15.1	11.6	13.4
Total managers and supervisors	35.3	24.5	30.4	23.1	17.9	20.8
5. Expert non-manager	3.0	4.4	3.6	4.0	2.6	3.4
6. Skilled workers	16.7	6.9	12.4	21.4	9.7	15.4
7. Workers	27.4	49.7	37.3	47.8	68.5	59.1
Total workers and skilled workers	44.1	56.6	49.7	69.2	78.2	74.5
Weighted N	648	517	1165	71	78	149

[a]For complete data, see Table III.3 in Appendix III.
[b]The categories are collapsed from the full class typology in Table 6.1 in the following manner: employers = 1,2; petty bourgeois = 3; managers = 4,7,10; supervisors = 5,8,11; expert non-managers = 6; skilled workers = 9; workers = 12.

Taken together with the gender results, we can draw two strong conclusions from these data. First, white males are clearly in a highly priviliged position in class terms. About one white man in six is either a capitalist or an expert manager, that is, in class locations which are either part of the dominant class or closely tied to the dominant class. If we add to this other managers and experts, over a third of all white men in the labour force are in solidly exploiting class positions.

Secondly, the working class in contemporary American capitalism is constituted substantially by women and minorities. As already noted, 60.5 per cent of the working class in the United States are women. If we add black men to this, the figure approaches two-thirds. Any political strategy for the mobilization of the working class has to take this demographic structure into consideration.

CLASS AND ECONOMIC SECTOR[6]

Historically, Marxists have tended to identify the working class with industrial production. As we have seen, this identification has been canonized in certain definitions of the working class, such as Poulantzas's, which effectively restricts the working class to industrial (i.e. productive) labour.

The conceptualization of class structure proposed in this book does not link the working class to industrial production by definition. Yet it remains the case that in both Sweden and the United States, industrial production, or what I term (following the usage adopted by Joachim Singelmann) the transformative sector, remains the core of the working class: in Sweden nearly 42 per cent and in the United States 41 per cent of all workers are employed in the transformative sector (see table 6.5).[7] If skilled workers are added to this to constitute an extended working class, the figure increases to 45 per cent in Sweden (although it remains essentially the same in the US). This, it should be noted, is not a dramatically disproportionate representation of industrial production among workers, since 36 per cent of the US labour force and 40 per cent of the Swedish labour force are in the transformative sector. Still, it remains the case that industrial production constitutes the core of the working class.

The situation is quite different for experts, whether they be managers, supervisors or non-managerial employees. These class locations are highly concentrated in social and political services in both the United States and Sweden. Whereas only 22 per cent of the entire labour forces is in this sector in the United States, and 36 per cent in Sweden, 42 per cent of all experts in the United States and 59 per cent in Sweden work in this sector. As we will see below, the core of this service sector employment is in the state.

CLASS STRUCTURE AND THE STATE[8]

On the face of it, it is a simple matter to study the statistical relationship between state employment and the class structure, since with a few exceptions it is fairly unambiguous whether or not a given person works for the state. On closer examination, however, the problem is more complex, since many firms in the private sector may be closely linked to the state without actually being legally part of the state itself. This is certainly the case, for example, for military contractors. Should a worker employed in a military weapons factory be treated as located within the state sector or the private sector? In certain respects at least, employees in such firms may have interests more like those of direct state employees than other private-sector workers. For example, as in the case of fully-fledged state employees, people in state-dependent firms have direct interests in the expansion of state budgets.

To map out properly the relationship between the state and class structure, therefore, we would ideally like to distinguish among private sector firms on the basis of their financial links to the state. Needless to say, it is not an easy empirical task to get reliable information on such ties. The best we have been able to do is to ask the private sector respondents on the survey to give an estimate for the firm for which they work of the percentage of the firm's business that is done with the state. These estimates are unlikely to be very accurate, but they may give us some very rough idea of these indirect links to the state.

Table 6.6 presents the distribution of 'state-linked employment' within various locations in the class structure. The table indicates an interesting pattern of differences and similarities between Sweden and the United States. Most striking, perhaps, are the dramatically different levels of direct state employment in the two countries: 17.5 per cent (20.6 per cent of wage-earners) in the US sample and 41.6 per cent (46.6 per cent of wage-earners) in the Swedish sample are state employees. This difference occurs throughout the class structure, but it is particularly noticable among experts (63 per cent are state employees in Sweden compared to 29.5 per cent in the United States). On the other hand, it appears that a higher proportion of Americans work in private sector firms with at least minimal ties to the state. Again, the case of experts appears to be the most striking: 39 per cent of experts are in such firms in the US compared to only 17 per cent in Sweden.

The result of these two patterns is that in both countries, experts are the category in the class structure with the closest links, direct or indirect, with the state: only 31 per cent in the US and less than 20 per cent in Sweden report that they are in private sector firms that do no business at all with the state. In contrast, in both Sweden and the United States, workers are the category of wage-earners with the least employment ties to the state: 56 per cent of US workers and 45 per cent of Swedish workers. Also, as would be expected, in both countries the class locations that are most iso-

TABLE 6.5

Distribution of economic sectors within classes, United States and Sweden[a]

Percentages sum horizontally

Economic sector

Classes[b]	EXTRACTIVE	TRANSFOR-MATIVE	DISTRIBUTIVE SERVICES	BUSINESS SERVICES	PERSONAL SERVICES	SOCIAL AND POLITICAL SERVICES
I. United States						
1. Employers	17.1	26.0	21.2	10.1	20.2	5.3
2. Petty bourgeoisie	11.5	22.5	13.0	15.7	26.4	10.9
Total self-employed	14.5	24.4	17.4	12.7	23.1	7.9
3. Manager experts	1.4	27.9	10.6	12.1	2.7	40.9
4. Other experts	1.6	28.4	5.9	11.6	3.5	49.1
Total experts	1.5	28.2	7.6	11.8	3.2	47.7
5. Non-expert managers and supervisors	3.2	35.7	13.5	11.2	9.5	26.8
6. Skilled workers	3.1	43.1	6.9	3.5	6.7	36.7
7. Workers	2.5	40.8	13.0	9.8	11.5	23.4
Total of workers and skilled workers	2.7	41.3	11.6	8.3	10.4	25.7
Labour force total	4.5	36.1	12.4	10.0	11.3	25.7

TABLE 6.5 *(continued)*

II. Sweden

1. Employers	17.5	39.4	22.4	6.3	6.4	8.0
2. Petty bourgeoisie	36.1	37.3	8.7	5.0	11.4	1.6
Total self-employed	26.7	38.4	15.6	5.6	8.9	4.8
3. Manager experts	0.0	33.0	3.9	11.7	4.1	47.4
4. Other experts	0.8	25.9	2.6	3.4	2.6	64.8
Total experts	0.6	28.0	3.0	5.8	3.0	59.7
5. Non-expert managers and supervisors	6.0	35.9	10.2	3.4	11.6	33.0
6. Skilled workers	0.0	51.3	1.5	2.9	5.3	38.9
7. Workers	3.6	41.9	11.7	1.5	5.6	35.7
Total of workers and skilled workers	2.6	44.6	8.7	1.9	5.6	36.6
Labour force total	5.3	40.3	8.8	3.1	6.3	36.2

[a]For data of class distributions within economic sectors, see Table III.4 in Appendix III.
[b]The categories are collapsed from the full class typology in Table 6.1 in the following manner: employers = 1,2; petty bourgeois = 3; expert managers = 4; other experts = 5,6; non-expert managers and supervisors = 7,8,10,11; skilled workers = 9; workers = 12.

206

TABLE 6.6
Class structure and the state in Sweden and the United States[a]

Distribution of state-linked[b] employment within classes

Class categories[c]	UNITED STATES				SWEDEN			
	In private firms, extent of business done with state:			State employee	In private firms, extent of business done with state:			State employee
	None	Minimal	Some		None	Minimal	Some	
1. Self-employed	88.9	7.8	3.3	0.0	93.7	3.9	2.4	0.0
2. Experts	31.2	30.3	9.1	29.5	19.7	13.2	4.0	63.2
3. Non-expert managers and supervisors	51.6	21.1	7.0	20.0	38.5	16.6	2.7	42.2
4. Skilled workers	37.4	22.2	7.9	32.6	38.0	14.2	1.0	46.9
5. Workers	56.3	20.7	6.8	16.2	45.3	11.8	0.8	42.0
Total	55.0	20.7	6.8	17.5	44.5	12.2	1.7	41.6
Total for wage-earners only	49.1	22.9	7.4	20.6	38.6	13.7	1.6	46.5

[a]For complete data, see Table III.5, Appendix III.

[b]Respondents who were not state employees were asked to give rough estimates of the proportion of the total business of their firm that was done with the state. In this table, minimal = 1–9%, some = over 10%. (Only 2.4% of respondents in the United States and 0.8% in Sweden reported that their firms did more than half of its business with the state).

[c]The categories are collapsed from the full class typology in Table 6.1 in the following manner: self-employed = 1,2,3; experts = 4,5,6; non-expert managers and supervisors = 7,8,10,11; skilled workers = 9, workers = 12.

ated from the state are the petty bourgeoisie and small empoyers—around 90 per cent of such individuals in both countries do no business at all with the state.

These data on the state and class structure indicate the importance of the state for various categories of 'contradictory class locations'. As I have argued in an earlier study (using my previous conceptualization of class), much of the expansion of what are usually thought of as 'middle-class' positions can be directly attributed to the growth of state employment.[9] Between 1960 and 1970 virtually all of the growth of 'semi-autonomous employee' positions in the United States occurred within the state or in those private sectors (such as hospitals) which are heavily state-dependent. In the rest of the economy there was actually an overall decline of such locations during the period. Managerial locations, while less dependent upon state expansion than semi-autonomous locations, nevertheless also increased considerably due to the expansion of the state.

Politically, the fact that workers and other uncredentialled employees are under-represented in state employment and in state-linked employment is probably one of the reasons that there tends to be a certain amount of anti-statist sentiment in the working class, particularly in the United States. The absence of economic ties to the state also probably contributes to the anti-statism in the petty bourgeoisie. Of course, workers may still receive material benefits from state redistributive and social service policies, but their livelihoods are less likely to be directly bound up with state expansion, and this creates a context for anti-state sentiments to develop.

One other observation about the class-by-state distributions should be mentioned: although in the society at large there are somewhat more capitalists and petty bourgeois in the United States than in Sweden, when the analysis is restricted to the private sector itself, there are, if anything, slightly more self-employed in Sweden than in the United States (18.5 per cent compared to 17.8 per cent). It is as if the market sector at a given level of technical development generates a certain level of self-employment opportunities. Although the total social space for such self-employment is smaller in Sweden because of the very large amount of state employment, this does not seem to dampen the impulse for self-employment in the private sector itself.

208

CLASS AND SIZE OF EMPLOYER

Marxists have generally characterized the present era as the era c 'monopoly capitalism'. To be sure, there is no doubt that th growth and power of the multinationals is a decisive feature c advanced capitalist societies. It shapes the political possibilities o workers and the economic manoeuverability of states in pervasiv ways.

Nevertheless, it is a mistake to conclude from this that mos workers are employed directly within such giant capitalist enter prises. Table 6.7 indicates the distributions of class and size o employer.[10] Only 14.8 per cent of the working class and 17.5 pe cent of skilled workers in the United States, and about 10 per cen of each of these in Sweden, work in gigantic corporations, corpora tions employing above ten thousand employees. If we exclud state employment from the calculations, these figures rise to 18 and 25 per cent of private employment in the United States, anc 18 and 22 per cent in Sweden, but are still far from a majority o workers.[11] Indeed, a larger proportion of the working class in bot countries works for firms with less than fifty employees than firm employing over ten thousand people: 22 per cent of US worker and 17 per cent of Swedish workers work in such small firms (or 2(per cent and 32 per cent respectively of private-sector workers) This may be the era of monopoly capital, but this does not impl that monopoly corporations directly organize most wage-labour i these societies.

The data in table 6.7 point to a second set of interesting find ings. In both Sweden and the United States, medium-sized com panies—those ranging in size from 500 to 10,000 employees—are the most proletarianized: 52 per cent of the positions in such cor porations in both countries are in the working class. The gian corporations in this respect look rather more like the state, with under 40 per cent of their employees in working-class positions ir the US and around 45 per cent in Sweden.

In one respect, for which I can offer no interpretation, the US and Swedish data are quite different. In the United States, the large corporation has by far the highest proportion of supervisors in its labour force: 27.6 per cent. When combined with the nearly 13 per cent managers, this brings the total employment in the managerial apparatus in these corporations to over 40 per cent in the US. This is considerably larger than in either the state (just under 33 per cent) or the middle size corporation (36 per cent). In

TABLE 6.7
Class distributions by size of firm[a]

	Size of employing firm				
s categories[b]	<50	50–500	501–10000	>10,000	State[d]
United States					
Employers	23.5/96.0[c]	2.1/4.0	0.0/0.0	0.0/0.0	0.0/0.0
Petty bourgeoisie	22.2/100	0.0/0.0	0.0/0.0	0.0/0.0	0.0/0.0
Managers	10.0/25.6	14.5/17.4	13.2/21.0	13.0/14.7	14.8/21.4
Supervisors	10.6/19.4	15.9/13.6	22.7/25.8	27.6/22.4	18.1/18.8
Expert non-managers	0.5/4.8	4.0/17.3	3.8/21.7	4.2/16.9	7.6/39.4
Skilled workers	7.1/18.2	15.5/18.6	7.9/12.6	15.4/17.5	22.7/33.1
Workers	26.0/21.8	48.0/18.8	52.3/27.2	39.8/14.8	36.8/17.5
Overall total	32.3	15.1	20.0	14.3	18.3
Sweden					
Employers	21.2/93.0	3.3/7.0	0.0/0.0	0.0/0.0	0.0/0.0
Petty bourgeoisie	22.4/100	0.0/0.0	0.0/0.0	0.0/0.0	0.0/0.0
Managers	5.7/11.5	13.5/13.0	13.2/15.5	17.4/14.7	11.1/43.7
Supervisors	4.1/8.9	9.3/9.8	10.4/13.4	6.8/6.2	14.3/61.8
Expert non-managers	2.1/6.6	3.4/5.2	6.3/11.6	8.7/11.5	10.3/63.8
Skilled workers	9.4/11.8	23.2/13.9	18.3/13.4	21.3/11.2	20.1/49.3
Workers	33.3/17.3	47.3/11.8	51.7/15.7	45.8/10.0	44.0/45.0
Overall total	22.4	10.7	13.1	9.4	44.0

r complete data, see Table III.6, Appendix III.
e categories are collapsed from the full class typology in Table 6.1 in the following
nner: employers = 1,2; petty bourgeois = 3; managers = 4,7,10; supervisors =
,11; expert non-managers = 6; skilled workers = 9; workers = 12.
e figures to the left of the stroke in each pair are the percentage of people in the
n-size category who are in a given class (i.e. column %); the figures to the right of
stroke are the percentage of people in a given class who are in that firm size
. row %).
he percentages for state employment differ slightly from Table 6.6 because of missing
a on the firm-size variable.

Sweden the pattern is quite different: the proportion of supervisors is quite low in the largest corporations, even by Swedish
standards—under 7 per cent of their labour forces—and overall
the size of bureaucratic apparatuses does not vary very much
across organization size (23.7 per cent in medium sized corporations, 24.2 per cent in large corporations and 25.5 per cent in the
state).

SUMMARY

We have explored a diverse set of findings in this section. Four general observations are worth keeping in mind. First, in spite of the various differences, a number of important characteristics of the class structures of these two countries are relatively similar: the working class is the largest class; the working class and those contradictory locations that are marginal exploiters constitute a substantial majority of the labour forces of both countries; the petty bourgeoisie and capitalist class are quite small; and credential exploiters in particular, and contradictory locations more generally, are particularly tied to the state in both countries.

Second, women are disproportionately proletarianized in both countries, although slightly more so in Sweden than in the United States. The result is that women constitute a majority of the working class.

Third, in the United States work is more heavily supervised than in Sweden: there are considerably more supervisors in the class structure, particularly in large corporations.

Fourth, Sweden has a higher proportion of non-managerial experts than does the United States. The possession of credentials and the control over organization assets seem to be less intimately linked in Sweden than in the US.

Explaining Differences in Class Structures[12]

In the previous section our focus was on describing the similarities and differences in the Swedish and American class structures. In this section we will pursue a strategy for understanding at least some of the structural causes for these differences. In particular, we will explore two principal hypotheses: first, that the differences in class structures are the result of differences in the mix of economic activities in the two countries (i.e. differences in the labour-force distributions across economic sectors); and second, that they are the result of the differences in the size of the state in the two societies.

The first of these hypotheses corresponds to the view that variations in class structures are largely to be explained by technolocal factors of various sorts. If we assume that within given types of economic activity technologies are quite similar in the United States and Sweden, then the principal way in which technological factors could explain the differences in class distributions would be via the different mixes of economic acitivities in the two countries. For example, the manufacturing sector is somewhat larger in Sweden than in the United States, and this is precisely the sector in which there is the highest proportion of workers. This could help to explain why there are somewhat fewer workers in the United States than in Sweden.

The second hypothesis corresponds to the claim that the state constitutes the essential basis for a non-capitalist mode of production. If this is a satisfactory formulation, then all other things being equal, the relative size of the state should have a considerable impact on overall class distributions. At the very minimum it should help to account for differences in size of the capitalist class and the traditional petty bourgeoisie.

In order to explore these hypotheses we will have to elaborate a statistical strategy for structurally decomposing differences in class structures. This will be followed by an examination of the extent to which the observed differences in class distributions in the two countries can be attributed to differences in sectoral distributions, the size of the state, or the structural link between authority and credentials.

A STRATEGY FOR DECOMPOSING DIFFERENCES IN CLASS STRUCTURE

The basic statistical strategy we will adopt in this analysis is based on the 'shift-share' technique commonly used in economics and demography.[13] The purpose of this technique is to decompose the *differences* in class distributions between the two countries into a number of different structural components. In the case of the hypothesis about the effects of sectoral distributions, for example, we would be interested in two primary components, one indicating how much of the total difference in class distributions between the two countries is attributable to differences in the class distributions *within* economic sectors, and a second indicating how much is attributable to the differences in the distribution of the labour force *across* economic sectors. (A third component, referred to as an 'interaction term', which indicates how much of the difference between countries cannot be uniquely attributed to either of the other components will also be calculated).

The technique for decomposing the total differences between the two countries into these components involves playing a kind of counterfactual game. In the case of the hypothesis involving sec toral distributions, we begin by asking the question, what woul the overall US class structure look like if the United States had (a the US distribution of classes *within* economic sectors but (b) th Swedish distribution of employment *across* sectors (or what i technically referred to as the *marginal* distribution of economi sectors, or more succinctly, the sectoral marginal)? This would te us how much the US class structure would change if its industria structure changed to match that of Sweden, while its class structur within economic sectors remained constant. This counterfactual esti mate provides the basis for calculating the part of the total differ ence between the two countries attributable to differences in sec toral distributions. We will call this component of the total differ ence the 'Swedish economic sector distribution effect on the U class structure' (or the Swedish sector effect for short).

Once this counterfactual distribution has been estimated, we as a second question: what would the overall US class distributio look like if the United States had (a) the Swedish distribution o classes *within* economic sectors, but (b) the US distribution o employment *across* sectors? This tells us how much the US clas structure would change if its sectoral distribution remaine unchanged, but the class distributions within sectors matched tha of Sweden. This counterfactual enables us to calculate what will b referred to as the 'Swedish within-sector class distribution effec on the US class structure' (or more succinctly simply the Swedis class effect).

Finally, after calculating these two components of the total dif ference between countries, we can compute what is termed a 'interaction' effect. Mathematically, the interaction effect is a residual term: it is the difference between the total difference i the class distributions for the two countries, and the sum of the tw components discussed above. It reflects that part of the total dif ference that cannot be uniquely assigned either to differences i sectoral distributions or to differences in class distributions withi sectors. It implies that there is a correlation in the way the tw countries differ in both their sectoral distributions and the clas structures within sectors.[14]

We have expressed these three components in terms of the counterfactual effects of Swedish distributions on the US class structure. We could, alternatively, have expressed the decomposi tion as effects of the US distributions on the Swedish class struc ture. When the interaction term is zero, we would get identical nswers in either decomposition; where the interaction terms are rge, however, the decomposition will look different from the antage point of each country.[15] In the tables which follow we will ive both sets of decompositions. As it turns out, the interaction rms are quite small in nearly every case, so the conclusions are argely unaffected by the specific decomposition which is chosen.

Using this basic strategy we will examine three different decompositions: (1) by economic sector, (2) by state employment, and 3) a more complex decomposition involving the linkages between redentials and authority.

One final preliminary methodological point. Because of the omplexity of the data analysis in these decompositions, both the xposition and interpretation of the results quickly become inwieldy if the number of categories involved becomes too large. 'or this reason it is necessary to collapse some of the distinctions nade in the full class typology. Table 6.8 indicates how this will be lone and the class distributions for Sweden and the United States ssociated with the collapsed class typology.

TABLE 6.8

Class structure typology and distribution for decomposition of differences

Categories to be used in decomposition	Categories from original class typology (Table 6.1)	United States	Sweden	Difference to be explained
1. Workers	12	39.9	43.5	−3.6
2. Uncredentialled managers and supervisors	10,11	9.2	5.6	+3.6
3. Credentialled employees	6,9	15.6	24.6	−9.0
4. Credentialled supervisors	5,8	10.5	7.0	+3.5
5. Credentialled managers	4,7	10.1	8.4	+1.7
6. Self-employed.	1,2,3	14.7	10.9	+3.8

DECOMPOSITION BY ECONOMIC SECTOR

Although in terms of the range of economic sector distributions across all countries in the world, the United States and Sweden have rather similar economic structures, there are nevertheless striking differences between them. As table 6.5 indicated, the United States has a much larger proportion of total employment in what could be termed the traditional capitalist-market services

(distributive services, business services and personal services)—
33.7 per cent compared to 18.2 per cent for Sweden—
whereas Sweden has a correspondingly larger proportion of
total employment in social and political services—36.2 per cent
compared to 25.7 per cent in the US. Thus, while the total 'tertiary
sector' in the two countries is of roughly similar size in the two
countries—59.5 per cent in the US compared to 54.2 per cent in

TABLE 6.9

Decomposition of differences in class structure by economic sector

A. *Estimates of counterfactual distributions*

Classes[a]	(1) US	(2) Sweden	(3) US sector marginal + Swedish class distribution within sectors	(4) Swedish sector marginal + US class distribution within sectors
	Distributions			
1. Workers	39.9	43.4	42.3	39.3
2. Uncredentialled supervisors and managers	9.0	5.6	6.2	8.4
3. Non-management experts	15.4	24.7	23.5	17.7
4. Credentialled supervisors	10.6	7.0	5.9	11.2
5. Credentialled managers	10.1	8.4	9.5	10.6
6. Self-employed	15.1	10.8	12.6	12.9

B. *US decomposition*[b]

	(5) Total difference (1)–(2)	(6) Class effect (1)–(3)	(7) Sector effect (1)–(4)	(8) Interaction effect (5)–(6)–(7)
1. Workers	−3.5	−2.4	+0.6	−1.7
2. Uncredentialled supervisors and managers	+3.4	+2.8	+0.6	+0.0
3. Non-management experts	−9.3	−8.1	−2.3	+1.1
4. Credentialled supervisors	+3.6	+4.7	−0.6	−0.5
5. Credentialled managers	+1.7	+0.6	−0.4	+1.5
6. Self-employed	+4.3	+2.5	+2.2	−0.4

TABLE 6.9 (*continued*)

C. *Swedish decomposition*[b]

	(9) Total difference (2)−(1)	(10) Class effect (2)−(4)	(11) Sector effect (2)−(3)	(12) Interaction effect (9)−(10)−(11)
1. Workers	+3.5	+4.1	+1.1	−1.7
2. Uncredentialled supervisors and managers	−3.4	−2.8	−0.6	+0.0
3. Non-management experts	+9.3	+7.0	+1.2	+1.1
4. Credentialled supervisors	−3.6	−4.2	+1.1	−0.5
5. Credentialled managers	−1.7	−2.1	−1.1	+1.5
6. Self-employed	−4.3	−2.1	−1.8	−0.4

[a]See Table 6.8 for operationalizations of these class categories.
[b]In the 'US decomposition' all imputed class distributions are subtracted from the actual US class distributions; in the 'Swedish decomposition' they are subtracted from the actual Swedish distributions. If the interaction effect term is zero, then these two decompositions will be the same magnitudes, but with different signs.

Sweden—the detailed activities which contribute to these totals are quite different. It might be expected, therefore, that these differences in sectoral distributions might contribute to the overall differences in class structures.

Table 6.9 indicates that this is not in fact the case. This table should be read as follows: column 3 indicates what the class distribution would be in a society with the United States marginal sectoral distribution but the Swedish distribution of classes within economic sectors; column 4 tells us the complementary counterfactual in which the Swedish sector marginal is combined with the US class distributions within sectors. Columns 5 and 9 are the gross differences between the two class distributions (the signs are opposite because in column 5 the Swedish figures are substracted from the US figures whereas in column 9 the US figures are subtracted from the Swedish ones). All of the other columns are calculated by subtracting in different ways columns 3 and 4 from the original distributions for each country. Columns 6 to 8 give the decompositions in terms of imputing Swedish distributions on the US class structure; columns 10 to 12 give decompositions in terms of imputing the US distributions on the Swedish class structure.

If much of the differences in class structures in these two countries could be attributed to the differences in economic sector distributions, then the sector effect in columns 7 and 11 in table 6.9 would be large relative to the class effect in columns 6 and 10. This is not the case. Except for the self-employed, where the sector effect is between 40 and 50 per cent of the total difference between the countries (depending upon which decomposition one examines), the sector effect is quite small relative to the class effect. And in some instances it actually works in the opposite direction. For example, in the case of credentialled supervisors, if the United States had the Swedish sector marginals the differences in the proportion of such supervisors in their class structures would actually increase, not decrease. The higher proportion of supervisors in the United States therefore cannot be attributed at all to the differences between its sectoral distribution and that of Sweden.

DECOMPOSITION BY STATE EMPLOYMENT

One of the most striking differences between the United States and Sweden is state employment. Given that the internal organization of state activities is not subjected directly to market pressures as in private-capitalist employment, it might be expected that the internal distribution of exploitation-assets, and the accompanying class relations, would be quite different in the state from the private sector, and that as a result this could account for a good part of the difference between the two countries.

Table 6.10 indicates that the state effect—the part of the total difference attributable to differences in the marginal distributions of state employment in the two countries—is substantial for only two class categories: non-management experts and the self-employed. For non-management experts, about 50 per cent of the total difference in proportions in the US decomposition and 25 per cent in the Swedish decomposition can be attributed to state employment (the reason the Swedish figure is smaller is because of the relatively large and positive interaction term). In contrast the class effect accounts for about 70 per cent of the total in the US and 50 per cent in Sweden. For the self-employed, on the other hand, the direct effect of the state is overwhelming: in the private sector Sweden actually has a slightly higher proportion of self-employed, and thus the class effect would actually increase the differences in self-employment between the two countries. We cannot tell from this analysis exactly why the state has this tremendous effect on overall self-employment—whether it is primarily because certain activities (eg. medicine) cease to be organized privately and thus the number of economic opportunities for self-employment declines, or whether the tax system that accompanies such a large state makes small businesses more precarious, or whether it is simply that the state provides so many employment opportunities that the incentives for being self-employed decline. Whatever the cause, the state is implicated heavily in explaining the smaller Swedish petty bourgeoisie and employer-class categories.

DECOMPOSITION BY THE AUTHORITY-CREDENTIAL ASSOCIATION

Let us summarize the findings so far. There are two basic conclusions we can draw from these decomposition exercises. First, while there are some exceptions, in general the most important determinants of the overall differences between the US and Swedish class structures are the differences in distributions of classes within economic sectors rather than the differences in the distributions of employment across sectors. Second, where there are exceptions to this, the state is usually involved. Most notably, the size of state employment seems to have a decisive impact on differences in self-employment and at least some impact on non-managerial experts.

To demonstrate that the overall differences in class structures between Sweden and the United States are largely accounted for by the class effects in the structural decompositions is only the first step. What we now need to do is to describe the structural basis of the class effects themselves.

As I have conceptualized the class structure, the empirical distribution of people into particular cells in the class typology depends structurally on two sources of variation: first, the patterns of distribution of specific exploitation-assets; and second, the degree of interdependence among these assets. Take, for example, the category of expert managers. This category consists of those wage-earner positions which are simultaneously organization asset and credential asset exploiters. Its size in the class structure therefore depends upon: the distribution of organization assets, the distribution of credential assets and the association between these two. Two societies could have the same marginal distributions of each asset taken separately, and yet very different proportions of their labour force in expert-manager locations if they differed in the degree of association between the two assets.

What we want to find out, then, is the extent to which some of the differences between Sweden and the United States can be

TABLE 6.10
Decomposition of differences in class structure by state employment

A. *Estimates of counterfactual distributions*

Classes[a]	(1) US	(2) Sweden	(3) US State employment marginal + Swedish class distribution within sectors	(4) Swedish state marginal + US class distribution within sectors
	distributions[b]			
1. Workers	39.9	43.5	43.3	39.0
2. Uncredentialled supervisors and managers	9.2	5.6	5.9	8.2
3. Non-management experts	15.7	24.6	22.2	20.0
4. Credentialled supervisors	10.5	7.0	5.3	11.3
5. Credentialled managers	10.0	8.4	8.1	11.2
6. Self-employed	14.7	10.9	15.4	10.5

B. *US decomposition[c]*

	(5) Total difference (1)–(2)	(6) Class effect (1)–(3)	(7) State effect (1)–(4)	(8) Interaction effect (5)–(6)–(7)
1. Workers	−3.6	−3.4	+0.9	−1.0
2. Uncredentialled supervisors and managers	+3.6	+3.4	+1.0	−0.8
3. Non-management experts	−8.9	−6.5	−4.3	+1.9
4. Credentialled supervisors	+3.5	+5.2	−0.8	−0.9
5. Credentialled managers	+1.6	+1.9	−1.2	+0.9
6. Self-employed	+3.8	−0.7	+4.3	+0.2

TABLE 6.10 (*continued*)

C. *Swedish decomposition*[c]

	(9) Total difference (2)–(1)	(10) Class effect (2)–(4)	(11) State effect (2)–(3)	(12) Interaction effect (9)–(10)–(11)
1. Workers	+3.6	+4.5	+0.2	−1.0
2. Uncredentialled supervisors and managers	−3.6	−2.6	−0.3	−0.7
3. Non-management experts	+8.9	+4.7	+2.4	+1.8
4. Credentialled supervisors	−3.5	−4.3	+1.7	−0.9
5. Credentialled managers	−1.6	−2.8	+0.3	+0.9
6. Self-employed	−3.8	+0.5	−4.5	−0.2

[a]See Table 6.8 for operationalizations of these class categories.
[b]The slight descrepencies in the figures for the actual distributions in this Table and Table 6.9 are due to differences in missing data.
[c]In the 'US decomposition' all imputed class distributions are subtracted from the actual US class distributions; in the 'Swedish decomposition' they are subtracted from the actual Swedish distributions. If the interaction effect term is zero, then these two decompositions will be the same magnitudes, but with different signs.

attributed to the differences in the marginal distributions of the basic assets or to the association between assets. To accomplish this we will conduct a set of structural decompositions, analogous to those we have already done, on the dimensions of the class typology itself. In order to simplify the analysis, we will collapse the basic class typology even further and restrict the analysis to wage-earners. We will therefore focus on four categories: credentialled management (cells 4, 5, 7, 8 from table 6.1); credentialled non-management (cells 6, 9 in table 6.1); non-credentialled management (cells 10, 11); and workers (cell 12). These four categories can be arranged in a simple two-by-two table, with one dimension being the dichotomy credentialled–non-credentialled and the other management–non-management.

The strategy of the analysis is to decompose this two-by-two table by playing the same kind of counterfactual game we did for the decompositions by sector and state employment. First we will ask: what would the US class structure look like if the US had the

Swedish authority-marginal distribution but the US distribution o
credentials within authority categories? Then we ask: what woul
the US class structure look like if we had the Swedish marginal
credential distribution, but the US distribution of authority withi
credential categories? The first of these provides the basis fo
calculating what can be called the Swedish authority margins effec
on the US class structure (or the Swedish authority margins effec
for short), the second, the Swedish credential margins effect on the
US distribution.[16] As in the earlier decompositions, a residua
'interaction' term is defined as that part of the total difference i
class distributions for the two countries that cannot be uniquel
attributed to either the authority margins or the credential mar
gins. It reflects the differences between the two countries in the
ways in which authority and credentials are linked together. These
three components can also be calculated by imputing the effects o
the US marginal distributions on the Swedish class structure. As i
our earlier analyses, both sets of decompositions will be presented.

The results of this relatively complex set of decomposition:
appear in table 6.11. Several conclusions can be drawn from these
results.

TABLE 6.11

**Decomposition of class distributions in terms of authority and credentia
marginals, wage earners only**

A. *Estimates of counterfactual distributions*

Classes[a]	Distributions of classes in		United States distributions with Swedish:		Swedish distributions with United States:	
	US (1)	Sweden (2)	Authority marginals (3)	Credential marginals (4)	Authority marginals (5)	Crede margi (6)
1. Credentialled management	24.1	17.2	16.2	25.4	25.6	16.3
2. Credentialled non-management	18.4	27.6	21.5	19.4	23.5	26.2
3. Non-credentialled management	10.8	6.3	7.3	10.4	9.3	6.7
4. Workers	46.8	48.8	55.0	44.7	41.6	50.9

TABLE 6.11 (*continued*)

B. *United States decomposition*

Classes	(7) Total diff. (1-2)	(8) Auth. margin (1-3)	(9) Cred. margin (1-4)	(10) Inter- action (7-8-9)
1. Credentialled management	6.9	7.9	-1.3	0.3
2. Credentialled non-management	-9.2	-3.1	-1.0	-5.1
3. Non-credentialled management	4.5	3.5	0.4	0.6
4. Workers	-2.0	-8.2	2.1	4.1

C. *Swedish decomposition*

Classes	(11) Total diff. (2-1)	(12) Auth. margin (2-5)	(13) Cred. margin (2-6)	(14) Inter- action (11-12-13)
1. Credentialled management	-6.9	-8.4	0.9	0.6
2. Credentialled non-management	9.2	4.1	1.4	3.7
3. Non-credentialled management	-4.5	-3.0	-0.4	-1.1
4. Workers	2.0	7.2	-2.1	3.1

[a]These class categories are collapsed from Table 6.1 as follows: credentialled/ management = 4,5,7,8; credentialled non-management + 6,9; non-credentialled management = 10,11; workers = 12.

First, the credential margins effect (columns 9 and 13) are relatively small, and if anything in some cases would serve to *increase* the differences between the countries. Very little of the observed difference between the two class structures can be accounted for by differences in the marginal distributions of credential assets in the two countries.[17]

Second, in contrast to the credential marginals, the authority marginals have a substantial effect on the class structures. The higher proportion of managers and supervisors (either credential led or uncredentialled) is largely accounted for by the higher proportion of the labour force in positions of authority in the US compared to Sweden.

Third, the effect of differences between the two countries in the association of authority and credentials (the interaction term) is also particularly important in certain cases. For credentialled non-management—experts of all sorts that have no organization assets—much of the difference between the United States and Sweden can be attributed to the differences in the association between credentials and authority. People in the United States with organization assets have a higher probability of also having credential assets than in Sweden, and this difference in the association between assets accounts for between 40 and 55 percent of the total differences in the proportion of credentialled non-management in the two countries.

The interaction term is also important for the working class in the two countries. As columns 10 and 14 in table 6.11 indicate, the difference in the association of credentials and authority between the two countries actually acts as a countervailing force to the effects of the authority marginals on the relative size of the working class.

GENERAL INTERPRETATIONS[18]

In the initial decompositions of the overall differences in class structure by economic sector and state employment, we concluded first, that in general the class effects were greater than the sector effects, and second, when the distribution of employment across sectors did matter, the role of the state was generally implicated. This was followed by a decomposition of the class effects themselves, and here the basic conclusion is that the differences in the authority distributions in the two societies and the linkage between authority and credentials accounts for most of the differences in the distributions of contradictory class locations in the two societies.

The most general interpretation of these results is that the differences between the class structures of Sweden and the United States largely revolve around political determinants. While it is possible that the general employment distribution across sectors and the distribution of credential assets might explain the differences between countries with a lower level of capitalist development on the one hand, and both Sweden and the United States on the other, the differences between these two advanced capitalist countries are largely accounted for by the effects of the state and the effects of the more political aspects of production relations (authority) on class distributions.

How can these political determinants of class structures themselves be explained? There is an extensive literature on the growth of the welfare state which attempts to explain why it is that countries like Sweden have such a large welfare-state sector. While there is not a consensus in such research, the explanations seem to suggest that the relatively more rapid expansion of state employment in Sweden compared to a country like the United States is to be explained both by specific constraints on accumulation faced by a small country in the world capitalist system and by the forms of political struggle adopted by workers and capitalists within those constraints.[19]

As far as I know, there is no research which addresses the question of why the organization of authority within production differs so drastically between the United States and Sweden. One way of getting a grasp of this problem is to examine the authority distributions within specific occupations. These data are presented in table 6.12. For high status occupations—professionals, technicians, teachers, managers—there is only a modestly higher proportion of people with authority in the United States compared to Sweden. Except in the case of labourers, the difference between the two countries is much greater for those occupations which are usually thought of as part of the 'working class'—clericals, crafts, operatives and service workers. Among these occupations, by far the biggest difference between the United States and Sweden is among craft workers: in the US 39.2 per cent occupy supervisory positions compared to only 8.7 per cent in Sweden.

What these results seem to indicate is that the critical difference between Sweden and the United States is the extent to which the supervisory aspect of managerial functions has been delegated to positions which would otherwise be part of the working class. In particular, highly skilled working class positions—craft occupations—tend to be assigned supervisory authority over other workers in the United States much more frequently than in Sweden.

While it is impossible to provide a rigorous explanation of these differences without looking at historical data on both structural transformations within production and political strategies of work-

TABLE 6.12
Distribution of supervisory authority within occupational categories

| Occupation | % of employees with supervisory authority | | Ratio US:Sweden |
	United States	Sweden	
1. Professionals	54.9	51.2	1.1 :1
2. Teachers	23.2	15.6	1.5 :1
3. Technicians	58.3	40.2	1.45:1
4. Managers	85.1	79.5	1.1 :1
5. Clerks	25.9	13.1	2.0 :1
6. Sales	15.6	21.8	0.7 :1
7. Foremen	93.2	75.5	1.2 :1
8. Crafts	39.2	8.7	4.5 :1
9. Operatives	18.6	8.9	2.1 :1
10. Labourers	15.8	16.7	0.95:1
11. Skilled services	51.9	17.5	3.0 :1
12. Unskilled services	23.3	5.9	3.9 :1

ers and capitalists in both countries, I can offer some general speculations on the mechanisms at work. The labour movement in Sweden is both more powerful and more centralized than in the United States. This has two important consequences. First, the union movement in Sweden has been able to eliminate restrictions on its ability to organize wage-earners much more successfully than in the United States. In particular, managerial employees in the United States are generally excluded by law from the union bargaining unit. This means that it is in the interests of American capitalists to integrate into the lower levels of management at least some jobs which fall within key categories of wage-earners categories which otherwise would remain working class.[20] The extension of supervisory functions to segments of the working class may be one facet of the general efforts by capital to weaken the union movement in the United States.

Second, the greater centralization of the labour movement in Sweden means that unions themselves may be able to perform certain control functions over workers which otherwise would have to be handled directly by supervisors within production. There may be fewer supervisory employees in Sweden than in the United States at least in part because the differences in the labour movements and the problems of labour discipline in the two coun tries make it less necessary for Swedish capitalists to devote so many positions to social-control activities.

Class and Family

So far I have proceeded as if individuals were isolated entities filling slots in the class structure. Individuals, however, live in families, and the process of class formation—the transformation of classes from structures of positions into collective actors—confronts this fact powerfully. In general in capitalist societies, even given the patriarchal character of internal relations within families, the family is the unit of primary consumption. The interests which are determined by class exploitation, therefore, will vary depending upon how they intersect the class compositions of families. In particular, it would be expected that where one spouse was an exploiter and the other exploited—for example, a male expert manager married to a clerical worker—the probability of the worker becoming a participant in the collective struggles of the working class is considerably reduced. If we look at the problem more structurally, it would be expected that class formation will be facilitated to the extent that families are class-homogeneous and retarded to the extent that they are heterogeneous.[21]

Before examining the data for Sweden and the United States on the class composition of households, a word needs to be said about the operationalizations we will use in this part of the analysis. While data necessary for the construction of a class typology were gathered on spouse's jobs, the questions asked were much more limited than for the respondents in our sample. In particular, we did not think it feasible to ask questions concerning the autonomy on the job of the spouse, the specific role in decision-making at the place of work or the kinds of powers he or she might have as a supervisor. We also failed to ask about spouse's education, although clearly we should have. The result is that we cannot replicate precisely the class typology used in the analysis of respondents for their spouses. Instead we will use the somewhat simpler typology laid out in table 6.13. For symmetry in this part of the analysis we will adopt the same criteria for the respondents. This has the effect of increasing the proportion of workers in the sample from 39.9 to 45.0 per cent in the United States and from 43.5 to 54.5 per cent in Sweden. Virtually all of this expansion comes from a reallocation of craftworkers from the semi-

TABLE 6.13
Criteria used for operationalizing spouse's class

Operational criteria	Class typology[a]						
	(0)	(1)	(2)	(3)	(4)	(5)	(6)
1. Spouse has a paying job or works without pay in a business	No	Yes	Yes	Yes	Yes	Yes	Yes
2. Self employed		Yes	Yes	No	No	No	No
3. Has employees		Yes	No	No	No	No	No
4. Occupies a management or supervisor position				Yes	Yes	No	No
5. Occupation is professional technical or managerial				Yes	No	Yes	No

[a](0) = no spouse or spouse not in labour force
(1) = employer
(2) = petty bourgeois
(3) = expert manager-supervisor
(4) = uncredentialled manager-supervisor
(5) = non-managerial expert
(6) = worker

credentialled employee category (category 11 in Table 6.1) to the working class. Since these craft workers are in many respects so similar to workers anyway, this does not seem a serious problem.

Table 6.14 presents the class composition of households in Sweden and the United States in which at least one adult is in the labour force. Households in which all adult members are retired unemployed, students or in other ways are not in the labour force are excluded. The table should be read in the following manner the left-hand column indicates the proportion of all households with a single person in the labour force (i.e. single person households plus married households with only one spouse working in the labour force). The diagonal cells in the rest of the table are the class-homogeneous households. The figures below the diagonal are the various combinations of classes within class heterogeneous families. Table 6.15 then converts the figures in this table into proportions of households that are class homogeneous in specific classes.

In about 10 per cent of all labour-force households in the United States both husband and wife are in the working class. An additional 29 per cent contain one working class single person or mar

TABLE 6.14
Class composition of households

s in cells are % of the total sample that fall into households with particular class
ositions.[a]

	0. No spouse or spouse not in the labour force	1. Employer	2. Petty Bourg.	3. Cred. Manager	4. Uncred. Manager	5. Non-mgr Expert	6. Worker
ted States							
ıployer	3.9	1.0					
tty urg.	3.2	1.6	1.4				
ed. ınager	9.5	0.8	0.9	1.4			
ıcred. ınager	9.0	0.6	0.5	1.8	1.1		
›n-mgr. pert	4.7	0.4	0.6	2.3	1.0	1.1	
›rker	29.2	1.5	1.7	4.8	4.7	1.6	9.7
eden							
nployer	1.7	0.6					
tty urg.	1.9	1.3	1.0				
ed. ınager	3.4	0.3	0.6	1.6			
ıcred. ınager	3.6	0.6	0.6	1.1	0.6		
›n-mgr. pert	5.1	0.1	0.7	4.6	0.8	2.4	
›rker	23.9	1.9	2.1	5.4	7.7	6.0	20.0

Table 6.13 for operationalization of class categories.

ried person in a family in which the spouse is not in the labour
force. This means that approximately 39 per cent of households in
the United States are homogeneously working class. Even though
the proportionate size of the working class is somewhat larger in
Sweden, the corresponding figure for homogenous working-class
households is quite close to the American figure: just under 44 per

TABLE 6.15
Class homogeneity and heterogeneity of households

	(1) Households with at least one member in a given class as a % of all households	(2) Households with members only in one class as a % of all households	(3) % households one member in class that are class homogene (3) = (2) ÷ (1
I. The United States			
A. All households			
1. Employers	9.9	4.9	53.3
2. Petty bourgeois	9.8	4.6	46.9
All self employed	18.1	11.1	61.3
3. Cred. management	21.6	10.9	50.4
4. Uncred. manag.	18.8	10.1	53.7
5. Cred. non-manag.	11.8	5.8	49.2
All contradictory locations	47.0	32.0	68.1
6. Workers	52.9	38.9	73.5
B. Households with both people in labour force			
1. Employers	15.1	2.7	17.8
2. Petty bourgeois	17.0	3.4	20.0
All self employed	27.8	10.4	37.4
3. Cred. management.	29.9	3.7	12.3
4. Uncred. manag.	24.6	2.7	11.0
5. Cred. non-manag.	16.5	2.7	16.4
All contradictory locations	58.7	21.5	36.6
6. Workers	58.4	23.2	39.7
II. Sweden			
A. All households			
1. Employers	6.5	2.3	35.4
2. Petty bourgeois	8.4	2.9	34.5
All self employed	13.4	6.5	48.5
3. Cred. management	16.8	5.0	29.8
4. Uncred. manag.	15.4	4.7	30.5
5. Cred. non-manag.	19.8	7.5	·37.9
All contradictory locations	45.5	23.7	52.1
6. Workers	67.0	43.9	65.5

TABLE 6.15 (*continued*)

Households with both people in labour force			
Employers	7.9	1.1	13.9
Petty bourgeois	10.4	1.7	16.3
ll self employed	16.2	4.9	30.2
Cred. management	22.3	2.7	12.1
Uncred. manag.	18.7	1.1	5.8
Cred. non-manag.	24.5	4.0	16.3
ll contradictory cations	54.9	18.5	33.7
Workers	72.1	33.4	46.3

cent. Stated in somewhat different terms, 53 per cent of all labour-force households in the United States have at least one spouse or a single adult in the working class. Of these about 74 per cent are class homogeneous. In Sweden, two thirds of all households have at least one worker, and of these 66 per cent are class homogeneous.

Looking at the other end of the class structure, 18 per cent of the households in the United States have at least one self-employed person, and of these households 61 per cent are class homogeneous (if we are willing to consider an employer-petty bourgeois combination as homogeneous). The comparable figure in Sweden is 49 per cent.

What about contradictory locations? Taken separately, the three types of contradictory locations in table 6.12—credentialled managers, uncredentialled managers and non-managerial experts—all live in families that are much less class homogeneous than is the case for either the working class or the bourgeoisie. In the United States approximately 50 per cent of each of these class locations are in homogeneous families, while in Sweden the figure is closer to 30 per cent. If we consider these classes a block—the usual 'middle class' of popular discourse—then the class homogeneity of households rises to 68 per cent in the United States and 52 per cent in Sweden.[22]

What general conclusions can be drawn from these data? First of all, in both countries a substantial majority of workers live in households that contain only workers. The number in mixed class households involving workers is not trivial—about one in four in the United States and one in three in Sweden—but still most workers live in unambiguously working-class families.

Second, the differences in class homogeneity across classes is greater in Sweden than in the United States. In the United States, when the various contradictory locations are grouped together, their level of internal homogeneity in families is quite close to that of workers—68 compared to 74 per cent; in Sweden the difference is 52 compared to 66 per cent. This contrast is even sharper if we look only at those households which have both spouses in the labour force: in Sweden 46 per cent of the workers who are in households with two earners are in class-homogeneous families compared to 34 per cent of 'middle class' employees in two earner families and 30 per cent of self-employed in such families. In the United States, in contrast, there is virtually no difference across classes in such two earner families: 40 per cent of the workers are in class homogeneous families, 37 per cent of the 'middle' class and 37 per cent of self-employed.

The critical source of this variation between the two countries is in the number of households that contain one 'middle-class' spouse and one working-class spouse: in Sweden, of the households with at least one person in a contradictory class location, 42 per cent also contain a worker; in the United States the figure is only 24 per cent. A similar contrast exists for the self-employed: 30 per cent of households with one self-employed person in Sweden also have a worker in them; in the United States the figure is only 18 per cent.

These contrasts suggest the following general characterization of the differences in the two countries: while the working classes in the two countries do not differ very much in the extent to which their families are firmly part of the working class, the American 'middle class' family is structurally more isolated from the working class than in Sweden.

So far in this discussion of family composition we have not distinguished between husbands and wives. Table 6.16 presents the data for the relationship between the husband's class position and the wife's for families in which both spouses are in the labour force. Perhaps the most striking feature of this table is that a higher proportion of working-class husbands in two-earner families live in homogeneous working-class families than do working class wives: 65 compared to 53 per cent in the United States, and 79 compared to 57 per cent in Sweden. Even if we include single working-class women in the figures, it is still the case that women are more likely to live in class-heterogeneous families than

TABLE 6.16

Family class composition by sex for families with both spouses in the labour force only

ntries in cell are % of the total sample of respondents with working spouses.[a]

Wife's class[b]

usband's ass	1. Employer	2. Petty bourg.	3. Cred. manager	4. Uncred. manager	5. Non-mgr. expert	6. Worker	Total
United States							
Employer	2.5	3.6	1.3	1.3	1.1	2.5	12.3
Petty bourg	0.5	3.4	0.7	0.5	0.9	2.2	8.3
Cred. manager	0.9	1.6	3.4	2.3	5.1	9.4	22.7
Uncred. manager	0.2	0.7	1.1	1.8	1.8	5.6	11.1
Non-mgr. expert	0.0	0.9	0.7	1.3	3.1	2.5	8.5
Worker	1.1	1.6	2.5	6.1	2.0	24.9	38.3
otals	5.2	11.9	9.7	13.4	13.9	47.1	
Sweden							
Employer	1.1	1.6	0.3	0.8	0.2	3.2	7.2
Petty bourg.	0.6	1.8	0.5	0.3	1.0	3.1	7.2
Cred. manager	0.0	0.3	2.6	0.8	5.8	7.6	17.0
Uncred. manager	0.2	0.6	1.0	1.1	1.3	10.5	14.6
Non-mgr. expert	0.0	0.0	2.1	0.2	3.5	5.0	10.8
Worker	0.2	0.6	1.9	2.6	3.9	33.9	43.1
otals	2.3	5.1	8.4	5.9	15.6	59.1	

= 554

The entries in the cells are calculated by adding together the responses of the male spondents for their own class with the responses of the female respondents for their usbands' class, and adding together the responses of the female respondents for their wn class with the responses of the male respondents for their wives' class. The estimates erefore are an average of the figures we would have got by looking separately at the bles for male respondents or female respondents.

ee Table 6.13 for operationalization of class categories.

men: 76 per cent of all working-class men are in homogeneous families compared to 69 per cent of working class women in the US, and 83 compared to 61 per cent in Sweden. Stated somewhat differently, working-class women have a higher probability than working-class men of living in families in which some of the income comes from exploitation. While I will not explore this issue here, this could help to explain, in some instances at least, the differences in the class actions of working class men and women.

Class Structure and Income

HYPOTHESES

The conceptualization of class elaborated in this book is built around the concept of exploitation. While the relationship between the theoretical concept of exploitation and empirical data on personal income is not a simple one, nevertheless, personal income should be systematically linked to exploitation relations. As a result, if the conceptualization being proposed is to be a compelling one, then there should be a strong relationship between class location and expected income. More precisely, we can frame the following hypotheses:

Hypothesis 1. Income should be polarized between the working class and the bourgeoisie.

Hypothesis 2. Average income among wage earners should increase monotonically as you move along each of the dimensions of exploitation from the working class to expert managers.

Hypothesis 3 The pattern for unearned income should also be monotonically increasing along each of the dimensions of the class-structure matrix.

These hypotheses could be made considerably more complex by including the operation of a range of other variables besides class structure. It would be of interest, for example, to investigate the interactions between class structure and industrial sector or size of firm in predicting income, and it would certainly be of considerable importance to examine the relationship between these class determinants of income and such things as sex and race. For present purposes, however, I will restrict the analysis to the direct the relationship between class structure and income, since clarifying this relationship is a necessary precondition to making more nuanced analyses.

VARIABLES

Personal Annual Income. The question on personal income was asked in the form of a series of categorical questions about income, since this tends to reduce the amount of missing data in respones. As a result, income was initially coded as an eleven-point scale, in which 1 represents an annual income less than $5,000 and 11 represents yearly income over $75,000, and in which the income brackets gradually increase in size as we move from the lower to the higher end of the scale. The values of these intervals in the Swedish data were constructed on the basis of the actual dollar exchange rate at the time the surveys were conducted.

Actual dollar amounts were calculated by assigning the midpoint for each of the closed categories and by extrapolating a value for the open-ended category based on the assumption that the upper tail of the income distribution has a Pareto distribution.[23] The annual-income variable is pre-tax total personal income and thus includes both wage earnings and other sources of income.

Unearned Income. Respondents were asked whether or not they had any income from investments other than bank savings or the sale of personal houses. If they answered 'yes', they were then asked to indicate about what proportion of their total *family* income came from that source. We asked this question in terms of family income since in so many cases it would be difficult to assign such income to any single individual in a family. While such percentage estimates will have a fair amount of error in them, it was our hope that it would give us a reasonable order of magnitude estimate and that there would be less missing data than if we directly asked for an amount.

There are two measurement problems with this variable. First, there were a significant number of respondents, particularly in their late teens and early twenties, who still lived with their parents and who as a result reported such unearned income for the 'family income' of their parents' household. In the US data we had a complete listing of all household members, and thus it was possible to identify such respondents and exclude them from this particular part of the analysis. This was not possible in the Swedish data.[24] Thus, in the analysis of unearned income, we will only use the US sample. Second, some self-employed respondents excluded income from investments in their own business from the report of 'investment income', others included such investments. The result is that the values on this variable do not have a consistent meaning among self-employed respondents. As a result we will only examine the unearned income variable for wage-earners.

EMPIRICAL RESULTS

Table 6.17 presents the data for mean personal income by class for the United States and Sweden. Table 6.18 presents the figures for unearned income for the United States. In general, the data in these tables are strongly consistent with the theoretical rationale for the exploitation-based conceptualization of class structure.

In the United States, income is strongly polarized between the proletarian cell in the typology and the bourgeoisie: the former earn, on average, just over $11,000 a year, the latter over $52,000. In Sweden, the results are not quite as striking: the bourgeoisie in the sample has essentially identical income to expert managers. Two things need to be said about this: first, there are only eight respondents in the bourgeoisie category in the Swedish sample, and they are certainly relatively small capitalists. Secondly, because of the very heavy taxation on personal income in Sweden, business people take a substantial part of their income in the form of business expenses and other forms of consumption 'in kind' rather than as salary. It is impossible to measure such non-monetary elements in personal income with the data we have available, but the figure in table 6.17 is certainly an underestimate. Hypothesis 1 is thus strongly supported in the United States, and at least provisionally supported in Sweden.

The results for hypothesis 2 are less equivocal. In both the United States and Sweden incomes increase in a largely monotonic manner in every dimension of the table as we move from the proletarian corner in the class structure matrix to the expert-manager corner. The only exceptions are that categories 10 and 11 (uncredentialled managers and uncredentialled supervisors) are essentially identical and categories 6 and 9 (credentialled and marginally-credentialled non-managerial employees) are essentially identical in both the United States and Sweden. Given the conceptual status of the 'intermediate' categories of 'uncredentialled supervisors' (category 11) and 'marginally-credentialled

TABLE 6.17

Mean annual individual incomes by class location in Sweden and the United States

Assets in the means of production

Owners	Non-owners [wage labourers]			
1 Bourgeoisie US: $52,621 SW: $28,333	4 Expert manager US: $28,665 SW: $29,952	7 Semi-cred. manager US: $20,701 SW: $20,820	10 Uncred. manager US: $12,276 SW: $15,475	+
2 Small employers US: $24,828 SW: $17,237	5 Expert supervisors US: $23,057 SW: $18,859	8 Semi-cred. supervisors US: $18,023 SW: $19,711	11 Uncred. supervisors US: $13,045 SW: $15,411	>0 *Organization assets*
3 Petty bourgeoisie US: $14,496 SW: $13,503	6 Expert non-manager US: $15,251 SW: $14,890	9 Semi-cred. workers US: $16,034 SW: $14,879	12 Proletarian US: $11,161 SW: $11,876	−
	+	>0	−	

Skill assets

United States: N = 1282
Sweden: N = 1049

Entries in cells are the means for gross annual individual income from all sources before taxes. The Swedish incomes were converted to dollars at the 1980 exchange rate.

workers' (category 9), these results are not inconsistent with the theoretical model.

What is particularly striking in the pattern in table 6.17 is the interaction between the two dimensions of exploitation relations among wage-earners. The increase in average income is relatively modest as you move along either organization assets or credential assets taken separately (i.e. as you move along the bottom of the table and the right hand column). Where the sharp increase in incomes occurs is when you combine these two exploitation mechanisms (i.e. moving along the top of the table and the left hand column among wage earers). Hypothesis 2 is thus strongly supported.

TABLE 6.18

Unearned income by class location among wage earners in the United State

4 Expert manager $1646[a]	7 Semi-cred. manager $856	10 Uncred. manager $763	+
5 Expert supervisors $942	8 Semi-cred. supervisors $272	11 Uncred. supervisors $368	>0 *Organization assets*
6 Expert non-manager $686	9 Semi-cred. workers $206	12 Proletarian $393	–
+	>0	–	

Skill assets

[a]Entries in cells are the means for family income (not individual income) from investme other than bank savings (stocks, bonds, etc.) and from rent or sale of property (exclud sale of personal houses).

[b]Notes:
1. Respondents living with parents have been excluded from this table, since the conce of 'family income' has a different meaning for such individuals.
2. Comparable data is not available for Sweden.
3. Figures for self-employed categories have been excluded from the table since so self-employed respondents in the survey included income from their own businesses 'income from investments whereas other respondents restricted their estima of investment income to outside investments, thus excluding earnings from their o business.

Hypothesis 3 concerns the relationship between unearned income and class location. Income from investments among wage earners depends upon savings, which in turn are closely tied to the amount of 'discretionary' income available to an individual, i.e. income above the necessary expenses for daily 'reproduction'. Such discretionary income should be closely linked to exploitation, and thus it would be expected that income from investments should follow the predicted monotonic pattern across the dimensions of the class matrix.

The results in table 6.18 support this hypothesis. Although proletarians and uncredentialled supervisors (cells 12 and 11) have more unearned income than marginally-credentialled workers and supervisors (cells 9 and 8), the overall pattern in this table still basically conforms to the expectations. Expert managers have over four times the unearned income of workers, and twice the unearned income of non-managerial experts and uncredentialled managers.

Overall, then, each of the three hypotheses concerning the relationship between class structure and income is broadly supported by the data we have examined: income inequality is polarized between the bourgeoisie and the working class, incomes vary nonmonotonically along the dimensions of exploitation taken separately and together, and unearned income varies in much the same pattern as wage income. These results add considerably to the credibility of the exploitation-centred concept of class.

In this chapter we have been mainly concerned with empirically mapping out the structural contours of the exploitation-centred concept of class. The Marxist concept of class, however, in whatever incarnation, is not meant to be used simply in the description and analysis of the structural properties of society. It is also, fundamentally, meant to provide a way of understanding class formation and class struggle. In the next chapter we will explore one aspect of this broader agenda in the investigation of the relationship between class structure and class consciousness.

Notes

1. See Peter Wiles, *The Distribution of Income East and West*, Amsterdam 1974.

2. This statistic in effect measures the inequality between the tails of the distribution and is thus quite sensitive to extremes of poverty and wealth in societies in which the majority of people are relatively well off.

3. Once again, as I have remarked several times, this difficulty in rigorously specifying the criteria for credential/skill assets reflects the theoretical underdevelopment of the concept itself.

4. In order to see if these operational decisions had substantial empirical consequences, I constructed parallel class variables in which the educational credential criterion was dropped entirely from the specification of credential assets, and we

relied strictly on the occupation and autonomy criteria as indicated in table 5.3. While this did affect modestly the distributions of individuals into classes within countries, it did not in any way affect the pattern of differences between countries (i.e. there was no national bias in the changes in distributions).

5. This figure of 14.7 per cent for the United States is considerably larger than the figure reported in the 1980 US decennial census, where less than 10 per cent are classified as self-employed. There are several possible reasons for this. First of all, the census is a self-administered questionnaire. In the section of the survey where employment status is introduced, self-employment is the last option in a list that begins 'do you work for a wage or salary?'. Many self-employed individuals who are paid on an hourly basis for their services probably tick this first option. The survey used in this book was administered by interviewers with specific instructions about the meaning of self-employment, and all response options were read and explained before the respondent answered. Second, for tax reasons it may be the case that more people hesitate to identify themselves as self-employed to an official government agency than to an academic research institute. This is confirmed by the fact that academic research institute estimates of self-employment are usually above government estimates. At any rate, there is little reason in this instance to believe that the official government figures are more accurate than the ones we are employing.

6. The definitions of the sectors discussed in this section can be found in Appendix II.

7. See Joachim Singelmann, *From Agriculture to Services*, Beverly Hills 1977.

8. I will, for the purposes of this analysis, treat control over the relevant kind of asset as the critical determinant of class location, regardless of the specific institutional site for that control: an owner of capital remains a capitalist even if he or she is engaged in long-term defence contracts with the state and is clearly part of the 'state-sector' of production; an owner of credentials remains an 'expert' even if he or she moves back and forth between the state agencies and private corporations; and, perhaps most problematically, a controller of organization assets is a manager, whether those assets be embedded in public bureaucracies or private enterprises. I will therefore not treat the distinction between state and private workers, state and private experts and state and private managers, as a distinction between classes rooted in different modes of production.

9. See Erik Olin Wright and Joachim Singelmann, 'Proletarianization in the American Class Structure', in *Marxist Inquiries*, edited by Michael Burawoy and Theda Skocpol, *Supplement* to the *American Journal of Sociology*, vol 88, 1982.

10. These figures are based on self-reports by respondents of the number of employees in the total organization for which they work. Respondents were first asked if their employer had multiple branches, plants, companies, etc. If they said yes, they were then asked to think of the entire firm and then give a rough estimate of employment size. If they said no they were probed further, and then asked for the number of employees in the firm. There are, undoubtedly, considerable errors in these reports. In some cases employees may even be unaware that their business is owned by some conglomerate multinational, and they certainly will not have a very precise idea of the world-wide employment of such conglomerates. My assumption, however, is that as rough estimates, the numbers will not be innacurate by orders-of-magnitude. Few people who work for firms employing more than ten thousand employees will give figures of several hundred, for example. The firm size data for the self-employed is simply the number of people they employ.

11. It is noteworthy that once the state is excluded from the analysis, very similar proportions of workers work for very large corporations in Sweden and the

United States even though the population of Sweden is so much smaller than the US.

12. The analysis presented here is a revision of an earlier paper, using the previous conceptualization of contradictory class location, written by myself and Göran Ahrne, 'Classes in the United States and Sweden: a Comparison', *Acta Sociologica*, Vol. 26, no. 3–4, 1983, pp. 211–235.

13. The approach used here is modified from the one adopted by H. Browning and J. Singelmann, *The Emergence of a Service Society*, Springfield 1975, and used in Erik Olin Wright and Joachim Singelmann, 'Proletarianization . . .'. Those studies drew on the techniques developed by G. Palmer and A. Miller, *Industrial and Occupational Trends in Employment*, Philadelphia 1949, and E. Kitagawa, 'Components of a difference between two rates', *Journal of the American Statistical Association*, vol. 50, pp. 1168–1174, 1955. The strategy is described in detail in Wright and Singelmann, op. cit., pp. 202–205.

14. For example, let us suppose that the US and Sweden had the same proportion of workers in every sector except social services, in which Sweden had more workers than the United States, and let us suppose that there were also proportionately many more people altogether in social services in Sweden than in the United States. The fact that these two differences—the within and between sector differences—co-varied would produce a large interaction effect.

15. Technically, the reason for this is as follows: when we compute counterfactual step 1 above, we *subtract* the results from the US class structure figures to see how much difference the differences in sectoral distributions make for the overall difference in the class structure of the two countries. To calculate the sectoral distribution effect on the Swedish class structure, on the other hand, we subtract counterfactual step 2 (not step 1) from the Swedish class structure figures. These numbers will be the same, but with opposite signs, when the interaction terms are zero.

16. The Authority margins effect is calculated as follows: Construct a four-fold authority-by-credential table for the US data in which the cells of the table are the percentage of people in a given authority category who have and do not have credentials. If you multiply the figure in each cell of this table by the corresponding figure from the Swedish marginal authority distribution, you will have the counterfactual estimate of the class distribution for the US if the US had the Swedish authority marginals. The decomposition is accomplished by subtracting the proportions in this counterfactual table from the actual US data (subtracting column 3 from column 1 in table 6.11). The credential margins effect is calculated in a parallel manner.

17. This conclusion, it must be remembered, is potentially vulnerable to the measurement problems involved with credential assets discussed earlier.

18. These interpretations were jointly formulated with Göran Ahrne in the original research on these issues published in 1983.

19. The relevant literature includes, among other things, Gosta Esping-Anderson, *Politics Against Markets: The Social-Democratic Road to Power*, Princeton 1985; J. Cameron, 'The Expansion of the Public Economy', *American Political Science Review*, vol. 72, 1978; John Stephens, *The Transition to Socialism*, London 1979; Ian Gough, *The Political Economy of the Welfare State*, London 1979; Michael Shalev, 'The Social Democratic Model and Beyond: two generations of comparative research on the welfare state', *Comparative Social Research*, vol. 6, 1984.

20. See, Institute for Labor Education and Research, *What's Wrong with the US Economy?*, Boston 1982, p. 315.

21. This may not be a universal principle. Under certain circumstances, having family connections outside of the working class—such as to subsistence farmers for example—may provide workers with increased capacities for struggle, since their survival may depend less on their wage-labour jobs. In general, therefore, we might expect the following: class heterogeneity of families may reduce the interests workers might have in militant struggle but increase their capacities for struggle.

22. How homogeneous a family is obviously depends upon how narrowly or broadly one defines the lines of demarcation. If the categories are defined in extremely broad terms—all wage-earners for example—then the vast majority of families would be homogeneous; if the distinctions were drawn very finely, very few would be.

23. For details of how this extrapolation is done, see Erik Olin Wright, *Class Structure and Income Inequality*, PhD Dissertation, Berkeley 1976, pp. 162–164.

24. The household composition information was gathered in the US survey since in the US sampling procedure this was necessary in order to pick at random a respondent from the household. In Sweden this was unnecessary since the sample was drawn from a list of individuals rather than a list of telephone numbers.

7

Class Structure and Class Consciousness in Contemporary Capitalist Society

The problem of 'class consciousness' has frequently been at the heart of Marxist theoretical and political debates. Indeed, in the recent renaissance of Marxist scholarship, one of the central lines of cleavage has been precisely over whether consciousness is a legitimate concept at all. 'Structuralist' writers in the tradition of Louis Althusser have argued that consciousness is an epistemologically suspect category and of dubious explanatory relevance, whereas Marxists identified with the 'humanist marxist' tradition have placed consciousness at the centre of their analysis.

One of the hallmarks of these Marxist debates over consciousness is their tendency to be preoccupied with philosophical and methodological issues. The idiom of the discussion revolves around questions of whether or not human beings are the 'authors' of their own acts, whether intentions have explanatory power, whether the distinction between 'subjects' and 'objects' is an admissable one, and so on. The result is that, with relatively rare exceptions, the systematic discussion of class consciousness in the Marxist tradition has not focused on empirical problems of its explanation and consequences.

The central purpose of this chapter is to examine the empirical relation between class structure and an attitudinal measure of class consciousness. In the following section I will briefly discuss the concept of class consciousness as I will use it. This will be followed by a discussion of the causal logic of the relationship between class structure and class consciousness that will form the basis for the hypotheses we will explore empirically. In particular, I will explain why I think the micro-relationship between class structure and class consciousness can only be understood properly when it is investigated in a macro-comparative framework. The next section of the chapter will discuss briefly the problems of operationalizing consciousness. Once all of these preliminaries are completed, we will turn to a statistical investigation of class structure and class consciousness in the United States and Sweden.

What is Class Consciousness?

There are two quite different usages of the expression 'class consciousness' in the Marxist tradition. For some theorists it is seen as a counterfactual or imputed characteristic of classes as collective entities, whereas for others it is understood as a concrete attribute of human individuals as members of classes.

The first of these usages is closely associated with the Hegelian strands of Marxist theory and is probably best represented in the work of Georg Lukács. Lukács defines class consciousness in the following manner:

> Now class consciousness consists in fact of the appropriate and rational reactions "imputed" to a particular typical position in the process of production. This consciousness is, therefore, neither the sum nor the average of what is thought or felt by the single individuals who make up the class. And yet the historically significant actions of the class as a whole are determined in the last resort by this consciousness and not by the thought of the individual—and these actions can be understood only by reference to this consciousness.[1]

Lukács defines class consciousness counterfactually: it is what people, as occupants of a particular location within the production process, would feel and believe if they were rational. Up to this point the concept is very close to a Weberian ideal-typical construct, and could be regarded simply as a potentially useful heuristic device for studying class societies.[2] It is the next step in the argument that is most problematic and which has lead to such sharp criticism of Lukács's position. Lukács argues that while class consciousness as 'imputed consciousness' does not correspond to the actual consciousness of individuals, nevertheless, this imputed consciousness is causally efficacious. In particular, the 'historically significant actions of the class as a whole are determined in the last resort by this consciousness'. What is counterfactual and imputed with respect to *individuals* is therefore treated as a *real mechanism* causally operating with respect to classes as a whole.

Such a claim, of course, could be just a short-hand way of talking about historical tendencies for the individuals involved to become ational in the counterfactually specified manner. This imputed consciousness, therefore, could be regarded as causally efficacious or the 'action of the class as a whole' in so far as it tends to become causally efficacious for the class actions of the individuals within that class. 'Imputed consciousness' could therefore be an elliptic and rather awkward way of theorizing this emergent tendency at the individual level.

Lukács clearly rejects this interpretation. He seems to insist that his counterfactual state actually exists in some way at the supra-individual level and is causally effective even when individuals do not think in the counterfactually rational way. Class consciousness as a causally efficacious mechanism, therefore, is an attribute of classes as such, not of the individuals who make up that class. While there will in fact be tendencies for individual workers to develop individual embodiments of this generic class consciousness, what matters for understanding historical trajectories is this consciousness of the class *per se*. It is this insistence on the causal power of supra-individual consciousness that makes Lukács's work vulnerable to the critique that it is fundamentally committed to an objective teleology of history.[3]

The second general usage of the expression 'class consciousness' identifies it as a particular aspect of the concrete subjectivity of human individuals. When it figures in macro-social explanations it does so by virtue of the ways it helps to explain individual choices and actions. In this usage, when the term is applied to collectivities or organizations, it either refers to the patterned distribution of individual consciousness within the relevant aggregate, or it is a way of characterizing central tendencies. But such supra-individual entities, and in particular 'classes', do not have consciousness in the literal sense, since they are not the kind of entities which have minds, which think, weigh alternatives, have preferences, etc.

In practice, when Marxist historians and sociologists employ the term 'class consciousness', they frequently amalgamate these two senses of the concept. On the one hand, one often encounters expressions like 'the proletariat lacked the necessary consciousness to do X' or 'the bourgeoisie in this period was particularly class conscious'. Such expressions seem to suggest that consciousness is attached to classes as such. On the other hand, consciousness is also treated as an explanation of individual actions and choices. In this case, the counterfactual use of the term 'class consciousness' to designate true understandings of class interests is employed strictly as a heuristic device to facilitate the assessment of the actual consciousness of individuals, not as a designation of some supra-individual mechanism operating independently of individual subjectivity at the level of classes.

I will use the concept of class consciousness in this discussion strictly in the second general sense. It is at best awkward, and more frequently theoretically misleading, to employ the concept as a way of characterizing real mechanisms operating at supra-individual levels. This is not to imply, of course, that supra-individual social mechanisms are unimportant, but simply that they should not be conceptualized with the category 'consciousness'. It is also not to imply that the actual distribution of individual consciousness in a society is not of social significance and causal importance. It may well be; but a distribution of consciousness is not 'consciousness'.[4]

Understood in this way, to study 'consciousness' is to study a particular aspect of the mental life of individuals, namely, those elements of a person's subjectivity which are *discursively accessible to the individual's own awareness*. Consciousness is thus counterposed to 'unconsciousness'—the discursively inaccessible aspects of mental life. The elements of consciousness—beliefs, ideas, observations, information, theories, preferences—may not continually be in people's awareness, but they are accessible to that awareness.

This conceptualization of consciousness is closely bound up with the problem of *will* and *intentionality*. To say that something is subjectively accessible is to say that by an act of will the person can make themselves aware of it. When people make choices over alternative courses of action, the resulting action is, at least in part, to be explained by the particular conscious elements that entered into the intentions of the actor making the choice. While the problem of consciousness is not reducible to the problem of intentionality, from the point of view of social theory the most important way in which consciousness figures in social explanations is in the way it is implicated in the intentions and resulting choices of actors.

This is not to suggest, of course, that *subjectivity* only has effects through intentional choices; a wide range of psychological mechanisms may directly influence behaviour without passing through conscious intentions. Nor does the specification of consciousness in terms of intentionality and choice imply that in every social situation the most important determinants of outcomes operate through consciousness. It may well be that the crucial determinants are to be found in the processes which determine the ange of possible course of action open to actors, rather than in the ctual conscious processes implicated in the choice among those lternatives. What is being claimed is that in order to understand ully the real mechanisms that link social structures to social prac- ices, the subjective basis of the intentional choices made by the ctors who live within those structures and engage in those prac- ices must be investigated, and this implies studying conscious- ess.[5]

The way in which I will use the term 'consciousness' is closely inked to the problem of ideology, particularly as that concept has een elaborated in the work of Göran Therborn. Therborn defines deology in the following way:

> Ideology is the medium through which . . . consciosness and meaning-
> fulness is formed . . . Thus the conception of ideology employed here
> deliberately includes both everyday notions and "experience" and
> elaborate intellectual doctrines, both the "consciousness" of social
> actors and the institutionalized thought-systems and discourses of a
> given society. But to study these as ideology means to look at them from
> a particular perspective: not as bodies of thought or structures of dis-
> course per se, but as manifestations of a particular being-in-the-world of
> conscious actors, human subjects. In other words, to conceive of a text
> or an utterance as ideology is to focus on the way it operates in the
> formation and transformation of human subjectivity.[6]

would modify Therborn's formulation in one respect only: ideol- gy concerns the process of the formation of human *consciousness*, ot the totality of human subjectivity.[7] *Culture*, in these terms, as listinct from ideology, could be viewed as social practices, or erhaps more precisely, that dimension of social practice, which hapes the non-conscious aspects of subjectivity: character struc- ure, personality, habits, affective styles, etc. Thus, for example, deology produces beliefs in both the desirability of competition as way of life and the inevitability of aggressive competitiveness as a node of human interaction; culture, on the other hand, produces he competitive personalities capable of acting on those beliefs in n effective manner.[8] It may well be the case that culture is consid- rably more important than ideology: beliefs in competitiveness nay be reproducible in a society only so long as they conform to ppropriate personality structures. This would correspond to the laim that the conscious dimensions of human subjectivity matter nuch less than the unconscious ones in explaining social practices. Nevertheless, our preoccupation in this chapter will be on con- ciousness and for that reason, indirectly, on ideology. This implies that intentional action involving the conscious weighing of alterna tives is an important property of social practice, and that its rela tionship to class is an important problem of social analysis.

Given this definition of 'consciousness', 'class' consciousness ca be viewed as those aspects of consciousness with a distinctive clas content to them. 'Content' can mean one of two things. First, it ca refer to a logical derivation of aspects of consciousness from a analysis of class. Competitive-market relations are a distinctiv structural feature of capitalism; the belief in the desirability o competition, therefore, could be viewed as having a class characte to it because of its correspondence to this practice, regardless c the effects of this belief on the choices and practices of individuals Alternatively, the class content of consciousness can refer t those aspects of consciousness which are implicated in intentions choices and practices which have 'class pertinent effects' in th world, effects on how individuals operate within a given structur of class relations and effects on those relations themselves. This i the usage that will be emphasized in the present discussion. If clas structure is understood as a terrain of social relations that deter mine objective material interests of actors, and class struggle i understood as the forms of social practices which attempt to real ize those interests, then class consciousness can be understood a the subjective processes that shape intentional choices with respec to those interests and struggles.

A potential terminological confusion needs to be clarified at thi point. It is common in Marxist discussions to distinguish worker who 'have' class consciousness from those that do not. 'Class con sciousness', in these terms, constitutes a particular type of class pertinent consciousness, namely a class-pertinent consciousness i which individuals have a relatively 'true' and 'consistent' under standing of their class interests. I am using the term class con sciousness in a more general way to designate all forms o class-pertinent consciosness regardless of its faithfulness to rea interests. Where I want to indicate specifically the presence of particular type of class consciosness, therefore, it will be necessar to employ suitable adjectives: pro-working class consciosness, anti capitalist class consciousness, revolutionary working-class con sciousness, and so forth. When I use the unmodified expressio 'class consciousness' it will always refer to the general domain o consciousness with a class content.

This way of understanding class consciousness suggests that th concept can be decomposed into several elements. Wheneve people make conscious choices, three dimensions of subjectivity are implicated:

1. *Perceptions of Alternatives*. To choose is to select among a set of perceived alternative courses of action. One important element of consciousness, therefore, is the subjective perception of what possibilities exist. 'Class consciousness', in these terms, involves the ways in which the perceptions of alternatives have a class content and are thus consequential for class actions.

2. *Theories of Consequences*. Perceptions of alternative possibilities are insufficient by themselves to make choices; people must also have some understanding of the expected consequences of a given choice of action. This implies that choices involve theories. These may be 'practical' theories rather than abstractly formalized theories, they may have the character of 'rules of thumb' rather than being explanatory principles. Class consciousness, in these terms, revolves around the ways in which the theories people hold shape the choices they make around class practices.

3. *Preferences*. Knowing a person's perceived alternatives and their theories of the consequences of each alternative is still not enough to explain a particular conscious choice; in addition, of course, it is necessary to know their preferences, that is, their evaluation of the desirability of those consequences. 'Desirability', in this context, can mean desirable in terms of the material benefits to the person, but there is no necessary restriction of preferences to selfish or egotistical evaluations. Class consciousness, in these terms, revolves around the subjective specification of class interests.

These three dimensions of subjectivity—perceived alternatives, theories and preferences—have been the object of classical Marxist discussions of consciousness and ideology, although generally under different names from those given here. The problem of *legitimation* revolves around the value preferences of actors. The problem of *mystification* is, above all, a problem of the theories actors hold about the causes and consequences of particular practices and social relations. And the problem of *hegemony* revolves around the way social possibilities are structured so as to restrict the perception of the possible options to those that are compatible with dominant class interests.

The definition of class consciousness which I have proposed makes it possible to specify the sense in which consciousness can be 'false': actors may make choices under false information, with distorted perceptions of alternative possibilities and with incorrect theories of the effects of their choices. In these ways it is fairly clear what the 'falsity' of consciousness means, although it may not be so easy to establish what 'true' consciousness actually is in these cases. But what about the third element, 'preferences'? Can we say that an actor holds 'false' preferences? When Marxists talk about 'objective interests' they are, in effect, saying that there are cases when choices can be made in which the actor has correct information and correct theories, but distorted subjective understanding of their *interests*, that is of the preferences they attach to different possible courses of action.

The problem of specifying true interests (undistorted preferences) is a difficult and contentious one, and it would take us far away from the central objectives of this chapter to explore it thoroughly. A few brief comments, however, may help to clarify the position I will adopt.[9]

There are two basic senses in which we can say that a person has a distorted understanding of their true interests. The first, and simplest, is when what a person 'really wants' is blocked psychologically through some kind of mechanism. The preferences that are subjectively accessible—that are part of the individual's 'consciousness'—are therefore different from the preferences the individual would consciously hold in the absence of this block. The block in question is a real mechanism, obstructing awareness of preferences/wants that actually exist in the person's subjectivity. If we understand the operation of such psychological obstructions then we can say something about the character of the resulting distortions.

The second way in which we can talk about distorted preferences does not imply that the undistorted preferences are actually present in the individual's subjectivity, only buried deep in the unconscious waiting to be uncovered. The second sense allows for the possibility that the distortion-mechanism operates at the level of the very formation of preferences in the first place. The obstruction, in a sense, is biographically historical; and the counterfactual is, therefore, a claim about what preferences the individual would have developed in the absence of such distortion-mechanisms during

ing the process of preference formation. The usual form of such an argument is to say that 'true' interests are the interests actors would hold if their subjectivities were formed under conditions of maximum possible autonomy and self-direction.

There are advantages and disadvantages with each of these approaches. The first has the advantage of being much more tractable and potentially open to empirical investigation. It is limited, however, in its ability to contend with the deepest kinds of effects cultural practices may have on the subjectivities of actors. The second alternative, however, suffers from an almost inevitable speculative quality that may have a crucial critical function but which renders the concept very problematic within scientific explanations. I will therefore adopt the first sense of distortions of interests, acknowledging the way in which it narrows the field of vision of the problems that can be addressed.

With this narrow notion of distortion as subjective obstructions to understanding interests which one actually holds, we can begin to talk about the 'true' interests attached to a person by virtue of their incumbency in a class location, and the corresponding distortions of those interests. My argument will be based on an assertion about a certain kind of preference, which I believe people in general hold even if they are not consciously aware of it, namely an interest in expanding their capacity to make choices and act upon them. This preference may be blocked, but 'deep down inside' people in general have a desire for freedom and autonomy.[10] Insofar as the actual capacity that individuals have to make choices and act upon them—their real freedom—is shaped systematically by their position within the class structure, they have objective class interests based on this real interest in freedom.[11] To the extent that the conscious preferences of people lead them to make choices which reduce that capacity or block its expansion, then, I would say, they are acting against their 'true' or 'objective' class interests.

With this understanding of class consciousness, one can begin to develop fairly complex typologies of qualitatively distinct forms of class consciousness. These will have their basis in the ways in which perceptions, theories and preferences held by individuals advance or impede the pursuit of class interests. It is possible, for example, to distinguish between 'hegemonic', 'reformist', 'oppositional' and 'revolutionary' working class consciousness in terms of particular combinations of perceptions, theories and preferences.

This is essentially what the more sophisticated typologies of class consciousness developed in recent years have tried to do.[12]

In the present study I will not attempt to elaborate a nuanced typology of forms of class consciousness. The data that we will employ could be stretched to operationalize such typologies, but my general feeling is that the limitations of survey research methodology make it preferable to adopt relatively simple and transparent variables. Certainly in the initial explorations of the problem, it will be desirable to adopt a fairly straightforward approach. The measures of class consciousness which we will use therefore, are designed to discover, in a general way, the extent to which individuals have attitudes that are consistent with working class or capitalist class interests.

Causal Logic

If class consciousness is understood in terms of the class content of perceptions, theories and preferences that shape intentional choices, then the explanatory problem in the analysis of class consciousness is to elaborate the processes by which such class content is determined and the effects it has on the patterns of class formation and class conflict. The classical Marxist theory of commodity fetishism is precisely such a theory: it is an account of how the perceptions and theories of actors are imbued with a particular class content by virtue of the operation of commodity relations. The immediate lived experience of producers in a commodity-producing society, the story goes, represents the social relations between people as relations between things (commodities), and this in turn generates the mental structures characterized as 'fetishized consciousness'. Such consciousness in turn, it is argued, plays an important role in conveying a sense of the permanence and naturalness of capitalism, thus impeding revolutionary projects for the transformation of capitalist society.

The causal model of consciousness formation which underlies the empirical investigations in this chapter is deliberately simple. Its purpose is to try to capture the most pervasive and systematic determinations at work, rather than to map the full range of complexities that may enter into the consciousness formation process of individuals. The model is based on two general premisses:

Premiss 1. The material interests rooted in exploitation relations and thus linked to the class structure are real; they exist independently of the concrete subjectivities and personal characteristics of the incumbents of class locations. If this premiss is accepted, then two general expectations follow: first, given certain minimum assumptions about human rationality, all things being equal there will be at least a weak tendency for individuals to develop forms of consciousness consistent with their objective class interests. 'Tendency', of course, does not imply that all incumbents of a given location in the class structure will have the same consciousness, but simply that the probability of them having forms of consciousness consistent with the objective interests attached to that class location is higher than for incumbents of other class locations. The perceptions of those interests may be partial and incomplete, but the tendency will be for such distorted perceptions of interests to take the form of deviations from a full understanding of interests rather than completely imaginary ones. Second, while the personal attributes of individuals may affect the strength of the association between class structure and class consciousness, the linkage between class and consciousness will not be an artifact of personal attributes of incumbents; it is based in the objective properties of the class structure itself.

On the basis of these expectations, we can formulate two empirically 'testable' hypotheses:

Hypothesis 1. The class content of consciousness will vary monotonically with class location along the dimensions of the class-exploitation matrix in table 6.1.

Hypothesis 2. The relationship between location in the class structure and the class content of consciousness will not disappear when various personal attributes of incumbents in class locations (social origins, age, sex, etc.) are controlled for statistically.

Premiss 2. While consciousness-formation is a process that occurs within individuals, the process itself is heavily conditioned by social structural and historical factors. The class experiences that shape consciousness are always organized socially; they are never simply the result of an unmediated encounter of an atomized individual with an 'event'. This can be viewed both as an epistemological and a sociological claim. Epistemologically, it is equivalent to a rejection of pure empiricism where knowledge is generated from the accumulation of pure sense-data. 'Facts' are never neutrally perceived; there is always some cognitive mediation through already existing mental (theoretical) categories. Sociologically,

252

this is an argument about the social construction of the ideological categories in terms of which people interpret their world. For example, whether a person experiences unemployment as personal failure or as social injustice depends upon such things as the strategies of political parties and trade unions, the policies of the state, the curriculum in schools, and so forth. The event itself does not dictate a unique subjective experience, and thus does not generate a unique pattern of consciousness-formation.

This social mediation of the consciousness-formation process suggests the following empirical hypothesis:

Hypothesis 3. Where political parties and trade unions adopt strategies that emphasize class-interpretations of the world, the pattern of class consciousness variations hypothesized in Hypothesis 1 will be more polarized and more systematic.

This hypothesis can be schematically represented in the simple interactive causal model illustrated in Figure 7.1. This will be the core model for the comparative empirical investigation of class structure and class consciousness in Sweden and the United States.

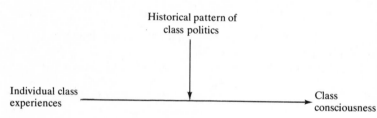

FIGURE 7.1
Model of class structure and class location

Operationalizations

Class Consciousness

Class consciousness, as we noted in chapter five, is notoriously hard to measure. The concept is meant to denote subjective properties which impinge on conscious choosing activity with a class content. The question then arises whether or not the subjective states which the concept taps are really only 'activated' under conditions of meaningful choice situations. In the case of class consciousness this would above all imply that they would be activated in situations of class struggle. There is no necessary reason to assume that these subjective states will be the same when respondents are engaged in other kinds of conscious choosing (such as occurs in an interview). The interview setting is itself, after all, a social relation, and this may influence the responses of respondents, either out of deference, or hostility or through some other reaction. Furthermore, it is always possible that there is not simply a slippage between the way people respond to the artificial choices in a survey and the real choices of social practices, but that there is a systematic inversion of responses. As a result, it has been argued that there is little value in even attempting to measure class consciousness through survey instruments.[13]

These problems are serious ones, and potentially undermine the value of questionnaire studies of class consciousness. My assumption, however, is that the cognitive processes of people have some stability across the artificial setting of an interview and the real life setting of class struggle, and that in spite of the possible distortions of structured inverviews, social surveys can potentially measure these stable elements. While the ability of a survey to predict for any given individual the way they would behave in a 'real life setting' may be very limited, surveys may be able to provide a broad image of how class structure is linked to likely class behaviours.

The survey used in this research contains a wide variety of attitude items, ranging from questions dealing directly with political issues, to normative issues on equal opportunity for women, to explanations for various kinds of social problems. Many of these items can be interpreted as indicators of class consciousness, but for most of them the specific class-content of the items is indirect and presupposes fairly strong theoretical assumptions.[14] For the purposes of this initial investigation, therefore, it seemed advisable to focus on those items with the most direct class implications, and to aggregate these questions into a fairly simple, transparent class consciousness scale.

The measure of class consciousness we will adopt is basically the same as the attitude scale used in the adjudication of contending definitions of the working class in chapter five. The only difference is that two of the items used in the construction of that scale were not asked on the Swedish survey, and therefore the scale is based on only six, rather than eight, survey questions (and thus has a range of values from −6 to +6). The excluded questions from those used in chapter five are:

3. Striking workers are generally justified in physically preventing strikebreakers from entering the place of work.
5. One of the main reasons for poverty is that the economy is based on private property and profits.

The first of these was left off the Swedish survey because the forming of picket-lines and physically preventing scabs from entering a workplace is largely absent from contemporary working class practices in Sweden. Since the practice was absent from the strategic repertoire of Swedish workers, it was difficult to convey meaningfully the degree of coercion embedded in the word 'physically' in this statement. The question on causes of poverty was excluded because it was felt that since poverty was not generally considered a salient social problem in Sweden, the question would make little sense.

In addition to this constructed consciousness scale, we will also examine the relationship between class structure and the conventional variable measuring class identification discussed in chapter five. In terms of the earlier theoretical discussion of class consciousness, 'class identification' in a sense combines all three dimensions of consciousness—the perceptual, theoretical and normative. To identify with a particular class is to perceive the world in certain categories, probably to hold some theories about the causes and consequences of class membership, and to hold at least some evaluative sense of interests tied to that class. It is because class identification seems to link these various aspects in such a compact way that it has generally been the favourite variable of sociologists engaged in the empirical investigation of class attitudes.

Working Class Trajectory

This is a constructed variable combining information on the respondent's class origins and prior job history.[15] The highest value of 6 is assigned to people with working-class origins who have never been self-employed or held a supervisory job; the lowest value of 1 is given to people who come from a non-working-class background and have been self-employed. It should be noted that respondents who are currently self-employed *cannot* have the highest value on this variable since they have had the experience of self-employment.[16]

Working Class Networks

This variable combines information about the class character of the individual's social networks, present family, and secondary jobs. The highest value of 9 is for people whose three best friends are all working class, whose spouse (if they are married) is working class and who do not have a non-working-class second job. The lowest value of 1 is for people whose three best friends are all non-workers, whose spouse is a non-worker and whose second job (if they have one) is non-working class.

A Note on Statistical Procedures

INTERPRETING REGRESSION EQUATIONS

A good deal of the data analysis which will be presented in this chapter revolves around the use of multiple regression analysis. For readers unfamiliar with statistics, a brief word about how to interpret such equations might be helpful.

A regression equation basically answers the following kind of question: if we were to compare two people who differed by, say, one unit of education, by how much would we expect their income (or some other outcome) to differ? The amount of that income difference is the 'raw coefficient' (also called the 'B' coefficient) for the education variable in a regression equation in which education is used to predict income.

There are basically two sorts of regression equations that are typically employed in data analysis. First there are 'simple regressions' in which one 'independent variable' is used to predict a dependent variable. In the example above this was education being used to predict income. Second, there are 'multiple regression equations' or 'multi-variate regressions'. Let us suppose that we wanted to ask a more complex question than the one posed above: if we were to compare two people who differed by one unit of education but who had the same age, sex, and social origin, by how much would we expect their income to differ? In this multi-variate equation, education, sex, age and origin are all treated as independent variables which simultaneously predict income. The coefficients for each of these variables tell us how much we expect people to differ on the 'dependent variable' (income in this case) for one unit difference in the independent variable, controlling for the other independent variables in the equation.

A regression equation always contains a set of coefficients for each of the independent variables and a 'constant' term. The constant term tells you what value on the dependent variable one would expect to observe if the values on the predictor variables were all equal to zero.

If the mean value on each of the independent variables are multiplied by the raw coefficients for that variable, and all of these products are added together with the constant term, the resulting figure is always exactly the mean value on the dependent variable.

In the equations we will be examining, there are two sorts of variables that will be used as 'independent' variables or predictors. One kind of variable has a continuous metric of some sort. Age and income are examples. A second sort of variable is a dichotomy. Sex is an example. In regression equations, dichotomies are generally referred to as 'dummy variables', variables which can have a value of either 0 or 1. The coefficient of a dummy variable for sex would tell us, for example, how much the average income of men and women differ (controlling for whatever other variables are in the equation); the mean value for a dummy variable is simply the proportion of the respondents in category 1 of the dichotomy.

Dummy variables will be particularly important in our analysis because the class typology is basically a typology of qualitatively distinct positions. Such a typology is represented in a regression equation by a series of dummy variables. If there are twelve categories in the typology, then eleven dummy variables are needed to fully represent the cells in the typology.[17]

The coefficients of variables in regressions are generally presented in two forms. The first is the 'raw' coefficient. This tells you how much the dependent variable is expected to change for a unit change in the predictor variable, where those 'units' are the natural metrics of the variables: dollars, years of education, values on an attitude scale, etc. The second is what is called a 'standardized' coefficient, or a 'β' coefficient. In many instances the raw units of the variables in question are not particularly meaningful or interesting. For example, if we want to know whether education or age makes more of a difference for income, it is not very interesting to know whether a year of education matters more than a year of age. What we would like to do is convert these two variables into some kind of 'standardized' scale which would make them comparable. This is what the standardized coefficients accomplish. Essentially, they convert all of the variables in the equation into standard-deviation units, units that are defined relative to the actual distributions of each variable. This makes it possible to compare coefficients within an equation in a reasonable manner.

There are two properties of any coefficients that are of statistical interest. One is the magnitude of the coefficient (in either raw form or standardized form); the other is its significance level. The significance level tells us how confident we are that the coefficient is really different from zero. (There is no necessary reason why zero should be the standard for evaluating significance levels, but in most situations there is no other value that has any strong theoretical status). A significance level of .001 means that on the basis of certain statistical assumptions, it would be expected that in only one out of a thousand samples would we expect a coefficient of this size if the coefficient were really indistinguishable from zero. As in the statistical tests of differences in means in the adjudication analysis in chapter five, it is important not to become preoccupied with significance levels. A variable which has a higher level of statistical significance is not thereby a more 'important' causal factor; it just means that we have more confidence that it has whatever importance it has.

One final statistical element of a regression equation is termed the 'explained variance' in the equation, usually designated R^2. This number in effect tells you what proportion of the variability in the dependent variable is accounted for by all of the independent variables in the equation. An R^2 of .25 indicates that one quarter of the variance has been accounted for by the variables in the equation, three-quarters has not. The unexplained variance is a combination of variance that could potentially be accounted for if additional variables were included in the equation, and variance which is essentially due to random factors (measurement error, strictly idiosyncratic determinants of the dependent variable, etc.). There is no way of knowing, of course, what part of the unexplained variance is 'explainable' statistically—i.e. what part is genuinely random and what part is systematic—and this makes it difficult to know whether a given R^2 is high or low, reflecting a success or a failure in an equation. For this reason, in general, all that really matters (with respect to the assessment of R^2) is its relative magnitude compared to rival equations. In general in regression equations predicting attitude scales, an R^2 of even. 15 is quite respectable.

ANALYSING ADJUSTED MEANS

In part of the analysis which follows we will be analysing the adjusted means for the class-consciousness scale for specific classes (see tables 7.4 and 7.6). Since this is not a conventional way of displaying regression results, some commentary is necessary.

Our hypotheses are framed in terms of expected differences in ideology across the various dimensions of the class structure matrix. These expectations are most effectively displayed in the form of expected values in the cells of the table. For the direct relationship between class structure and consciousness—hypothesis 1 — this is simply the mean for the consciousness scale for each cell in the typology.

In order to examine the effects of personal attributes on the relationship between class structure and class consciousness—hypothesis 2—we need to calculate 'adjusted means' for this typology. That is, we need to calculate the expected values in the cells controlling for whatever variables are being included as personal attributes which might affect the process of consciousness formation. If indeed all of the differences between cells in the simple analysis were results of these attributes, then these adjusted means would all be the same.

These adjusted means are calculated as follows: a regression equation is calculated containing all of the class typology dummy variables (eleven in all) together with whatever variables are being treated as personal attributes. The *relative* differences in these adjusted means are directly given by the unstandardized (raw) coefficients of the class dummy variables in this multiple regression equation. How are the *absolute* values calculated? It will be recalled from the discussion of interpreting regression equations that if we multiply the coefficient of each independent variable by the mean value for that independent variable and then add them together with the constant term we get the overall sample mean for the dependent variable. To calculate the adjusted means for the *cells* in the table (rather than the overall sample mean) we multiply each of the coefficients of the *control* variables (personal attributes in this case) by their mean values and add these products together with the constant term. This sum constitutes an adjustment which is then added to the coefficients of each of the class-typology dummy variables, giving the adjusted means for the typology. The entries in the tables using such adjusted means should be interpreted as the expected value on the consciousness scale for people in the cell, controlling for the relevant independent variables, evaluated at the socially average levels of sex, age, and so on, within that country.

Empirical Results

The data analysis will involve three steps:

(1) *Examining the direct relationship between class structure and class consciousness in the United States and Sweden.* This will be done by comparing the mean values on the consciousness scale for the various cells in the class typology for the United States and Sweden. Particular attention will be paid to the differences in the overall pattern of these means in the two countries.

(2) *Examining the extent to which the patterns observed in the analysis of the direct relationship between class structure and class consciousness are significantly modified when various control variables are added.* This will enable us to examine three inter-related issues: (a) whether or not the observed relation between class location and class consciousness could be a spurious effect of certain personal attributes of the incumbents of these positions; (b) the extent to which the effects of class structure on class consciousness operate largely through certain 'intervening variables' such as union membership, income, unemployment history, etc., or are direct consequences of class location as such; and (c) whether the different overall patterns between the United States and Sweden are largely the result of the link between class and these intervening variables or are directly tied to the way class structure influences consciousness.

(3) *Examining the differences between the United States and Sweden in the overall structure of the consciousness-formation process.* The above analyses are mainly concerned with the effects of class structure as such on consciousness in the two countries. In this final part of the investigation we will examine the differences between the two countries in the effects of various other variables on

consciousness. The methodological assumption will be that the pattern of coefficients in a multiple regression equation predicting consciousness can be viewed as tapping a particular society's macro-structural process of consciousness formation. Comparing the patterning of such coefficients across countries, therefore, gives us an empirical handle on the differences in that process.

1. DIRECT RELATIONSHIP OF CLASS STRUCTURE TO CLASS CONSCIOUSNESS

Table 7.1 presents the mean values on the class consciousness scale by class location in the United States and Sweden. Table 7.2 presents the proportion of respondents in each class who say that they are in the working class on the class identification question and who take the pro-working class position on each of the indi-

TABLE 7.1
Class consciousness by location in the class structure

I. United States

Assets in the means of production

Owners	Non-owners [wage labourers]			
1 Bourgeoisie −1.31[a]	4 Expert managers −1.46	7 Semi-cred. managers −0.34	10 Uncred. managers −0.29	+
2 Small employers −0.87	5 Expert supervisors −0.78	8 Semi-cred. supervisors −0.24	11 Uncred. supervisors +0.54	>0 *Orgizat asse*
3 Petty bourgeoisie −0.09	6 Expert non-managers −0.09	9 Semi-cred. workers +0.78	12 Proletarians +0.78	−
	+	>0	−	

Skill/credential assets

vidual items that go into the class attitude scale.[18] Several generalizations can be drawn from these results:

(1) *The Overall Pattern of Variations.* In table 7.1 the overall *pattern* of variations in means (not the absolute value of the means, but the patterning of the means) is quite similiar in the United States and Sweden. In both countries the table is basically polarized between the capitalist class and the working class (in neither country is there a statistically significant difference between proletarians and the marginal categories adjacent to the working class).[19] In both countries the values on the scale become decreasingly pro-working class and eventually pro-capitalist class as one moves from the proletarian corner of the table to the expert-manager corner of the table. As in the analysis of income varia-

TABLE 7.1 (*continued*)

I. Sweden

Assets in the means of production

Owners	Non-owners [wage labourers]			
1 Bourgeoisie −2.00	4 Expert managers −0.70	7 Semi-cred. managers +1.03	10 Uncred. managers +1.81	+
2 Small employers −0.98	5 Expert supervisors +0.07	8 Semi-cred. supervisors +0.74	11 Uncred. supervisors +1.98	>0 *Organization assets*
3 Petty bourgeoisie +0.46	6 Expert non-manager +1.29	9 Semi-cred. workers +2.81	12 Proletarian +2.60	−
	+	>0	−	
	Skill/credential assets			

[a]Entries in the table are means on the working class consciousness scale. The values on the scale range from +6 (pro-working class on every item) to −6 (pro-capitalist class on every item).

TABLE 7.2
Working Class identification and responses to individual items by class location

I. United States	%who take the working class position on:						
	Working class I.D.	Individual items in consciousness scale[a]					
Class location		(1)	(2)	(3)	(4)	(5)	(6)
1. Proletarians (12)[b]	32	56	27	49	55	75	19
2. Semi-credentialled workers (9)	28	61	28	48	58	82	14
3. Uncredentialled supervisors (11)	31	56	24	56	44	87	16
4. Expert employees (6)	15	58	26	36	36	80	13
5. Semi-credentialled supervisors (8)	32	50	27	35	42	77	11
6. Uncredentialled managers (10)	28	55	15	28	46	76	13
7. Expert supervisors (5)	9	57	22	26	34	69	5
8. Semi-credentialled managers (7)	16	52	19	33	45	80	7
9. Expert managers (4)	8	33	24	27	22	60	9
10. Petty bourgeoisie (3)	31	49	35	30	43	79	7
11. Small employers (2)	29	50	17	31	24	66	8
12. Bourgeoisie (1)	9	28	27	23	25	65	0
II. Sweden							
1. Proletarians (12)	57	70	48	51	81	81	58
2. Semi-credentialled workers (9)	51	72	52	59	82	82	63
3. Uncredentialled supervisors (11)	61	59	52	55	81	77	39
4. Expert employees (6)	21	62	39	44	71	64	32
5. Semi-credentialled supervisors (8)	40	57	27	35	78	68	30
6. Uncredentialled managers (10)	39	64	40	46	82	82	47
7. Expert supervisors (5)	19	36	26	19	84	67	20
8. Semi-credentialled managers (7)	36	68	47	35	77	66	30
9. Expert managers (4)	14	37	35	22	65	47	14
10. Petty bourgeoisie (3)	43	38	31	40	65	60	22
11. Small employers (2)	31	31	20	34	50	54	15
12. Bourgeoisie (1)	25	13	13	25	25	50	13

tions by class in chapter six, the means on the attitude scale change in a largely monotonic manner along every dimension of the table. And in both countries, the means become increasingly pro-capitalist as you move from the petty bourgeoisie to the capitalist class proper among the self-employed.

A basically similar pattern of results occurs for the working class identification responses in table 7.2. In Sweden, 57 per cent of proletarians and between 50 and 60 per cent of the respondents in the marginal locations close to the working class say that they are in the working class, compared to 39 per cent of uncredentialled managers, 21 per cent of non-managerial experts, 14 per cent of expert managers and 25 per cent of capitalists. In the United States around 30 per cent of the respondents in the working class and marginal working-class locations identify with the working class. This figure does not decline significantly for uncredentialled managers (28 per cent), but drops to 15 per cent for non-managerial experts and less than 10 per cent for expert managers and capitalists. These various results are thus quite supportive of hypothesis 1.

(2) *The Degree of Polarization.* The degree of polarization in the two countries is very different. In the United States the difference between the capitalist class and the working class is just over 2 points on the scale; in Sweden the difference is 4.6 points. (The difference between these differences is statistically significant at the .05 level).

The difference in degrees of polarization is particularly dramatic in the questionnaire item concerning the outcome of strikes (item

---

[a]The items are as follows:
(1) Corporations benefit owners at the expense of workers and consumers;
(2) It is possible for a modern society to run effectively without the profit motive;
(3) If given the chance, the non-management employees at the place where you work could run things effectively without bosses;
(4) During a strike, management should be prohibited by law from hiring workers to take the place of strikers;
(5) Big corporations have far too much power in American [Swedish] society today;
(6) Imagine that workers in a major industry are out on strike over working conditions and wages. Which of the following outcomes would you like to see occur: (a) the workers win their most important demands; (b) the workers win some of their demands and make major concessions; (c) the workers win only a few of their demands and make major concessions; (d) the workers go back to work without winning any of their demands. (% who give response a).
[b]The numbers in parentheses correspond to the cells in Table 7.1.

6 in table 7.2). In the United States, while more workers than expert managers and capitalists take the pro-working class position, the overwhelming majority of respondents in every class location opt for the class compromise response, namely that in a strike the workers should win some of their demands and make some concessions. In Sweden, on the other hand, about 60 per cent of proletarians and semi-credentialled employees (i.e. mainly skilled workers) say that they feel the workers should win most of their demands, compared to less than 15 per cent of the expert managers and capitalists. While the class hegemony of the bourgeoisie in the United States has not been able to obliterate tendencies towards ideological polarization in the American class structure, that polarization is very muted compared to Sweden, at least as measured by these class-pertinent attitudes.

These data indicate that there is basically an international consensus within the capitalist class on class-based attitudes, whereas no such consensus exists in the working class: Swedish and American workers on average differ on this scale by nearly as much as American workers and capitalists. These results are consistent with hypothesis 3, that the degree of polarization will depend in part on the extent to which political parties and unions adopt strategies which help to crystallize workers' experiences in class terms.

(3) *Class Alliances.* The patterns of class alliances—the ways in which the terrain of class structure becomes transformed into class formations—suggested by the patterns of consciousness in table 7.1 varies considerably in the two countries. In Sweden the only wage-earner category with an average pro-capitalist position is expert managers; in the United States, pro-capitalist positions penetrate much further into the wage-earner population. In the United States, only the three cells in the lower right hand corner of the table can be considered part of a working class coalition; in Sweden the coalition extends to all uncredentialled wage-earners and all non-management wage earners, and, at least in a weak sense, includes semi-credentialled managers and semi-credentialled supervisors as well. Turning these results into proportions of the labour force based on the distributions in table 6.1, in the United States approximately 30 per cent of the labour force are in class locations that can be considered part of a bourgeois coalition, compared to only about 10 per cent in Sweden. On the other hand, in Sweden between 70 and 80 per cent of

the labour force are in class locations that are ideologically part of a working class coalition, compared to only about 58 per cent in the United States.[20] To say this, of course, is *not* equivalent to saying that 58 per cent of the individuals in the labour force in the United States and 70–80 per cent in Sweden are in the working class coalition, since there are individual workers who are ideologically part of the bourgeois coalition and individual managers (and even capitalists) who are ideologically part of the working class coalition. But it does mean that the working class coalition in the United States is not only less polarized ideologically from the bourgeoisie than in Sweden, but also that it has a much smaller class base.

2. MULTIVARIATE ANALYSIS OF ADJUSTED MEANS

Two kinds of questions can be raised about the results in tables 7.1 and 7.2. First, it is important to know whether or not the results can be reinterpreted as consequences of various attributes of the incumbents of class locations that are not themselves direct consequences of class as such. For example, different classes have different mixes of sexes and ages, and it could be that the consciousness maps in these tables are really age and gender maps, only incidentally linked to class structure. Second, it is important to know the extent to which these results are *direct* consequences of incumbency in class locations *per se* or whether they operate through intervening mechanisms. Class locations, for example, determine (in part) income and union membership, and it is possible that the gross class structure–class consciousness relationship mapped out in tables 7.1 and 7.2 is generated largely through such intervening mechanisms. The second of these problems does not challenge the hypothesis that class structure shapes class consciousness, but simply indicates some of the mechanisms through which these effects are generated. The first problem, however, calls into question the claim that class structure as such is a central determinant.

(1) *Is the relationship between class structure and class consciousness spurious?* Table 7.3 presents the results observed in table 7.1 separately for men and women in Sweden and the United States. Table 7.4 presents the results for the adjusted mean values on the working class consciousness scale of different locations in the class structure typology, controlling for three personal attri-

butes that potentially might call into question the results in table 7.1—age, sex and class biography.[21]

Table 7.3 indicates that for both the United States and Sweden the basic patterns observed in table 7.1 can be observed among men and women taken separately. This is especially the case for men, where the pattern of polarization and monotonicity holds very strongly in both countries.

There are, nevertheless, some differences between men and women that are worth noting. In general the degree of class polarization among men is considerably greater than among women. Male proletarians and expert managers differ by 2.8 points in the United States and 3.6 points in Sweden, whereas their women

TABLE 7.3
Class attitudes by class locations within sex categories, United States and Sweden

I. United States

Assets in the means of production

Owners   Non-owners [wage labourers]

1 Bourgeoisie M −1.45 (22)[a] W −0.75 (6)	4 Expert managers M −1.84 (43) W −0.32 (14)	7 Semi-cred. managers M −0.33 (71) W −0.29 (21)	10 Uncred. managers M +0.55 (11) W −0.65 (24)	+
2 Small employers M −1.18 (60) W −0.27 (30)	5 Expert supervisors M −1.02 (39) W −0.21 (16)	8 Semi-cred. supervisors M −0.21 (76) W −0.32 (25)	11 Uncred. supervisors M +0.77 (42) W +0.38 (60)	>0 Organization assets
3 Petty bourgeoisie M −0.18 (51) W +0.01 (51)	6 Expert non-manager M −0.83 (24) W +0.58 (27)	9 Semi-cred. workers M +0.81 (134) W +0.70 (48)	12 Proletarian M +0.97 (234) W +0.66 (359)	−

+   >0   −

Skill/credential assets

Men (M): N = 807
Women (W): N = 680

TABLE 7.3 (*continued*)

II. Sweden

Assets in the means of production

Owners | Non-owners [wage labourers]

1 Bourgeoisie
 	
M −2.00 (8)
W +0.20 (0)
	4 Expert
	  managers
	
	M −0.89 (45)
	W +0.62 (7)
		7 Semi-cred.
		  managers
		
		M +1.05 (40)
		W +0.92 (8)
			10 Uncred.
			  managers
			
			M +1.40 (15)
			W +2.23 (14)
				+

2 Small
  employers
 	
M −1.24 (46)
W +0.10 (11)
	5 Expert
	  supervisors
	
	M −0.95 (19)
	W +0.83 (25)
		8 Semi-cred.
		  supervisors
		
		M +0.62 (29)
		W +1.13 (9)
			11 Uncred.
			  supervisors
			
			M +2.21 (28)
			W +1.25 (9)
				>0 Organ-
				ization
				assets

3 Petty
  bourgeoisie
 	
M +0.38 (48)
W +0.71 (15)
	6 Expert
	  non-manager
	
	M +1.24 (45)
	W +1.34 (35)
		9 Semi-cred.
		  workers
		
		M +3.24 (133)
		W +2.08 (77)
			12 Proletarian
			
			M +2.70 (204)
			W +2.53 (309)
				−

+   >0   −

Skill/credential assets

Men (M): N = 660
Women (W): N = 519

Numbers in parentheses are weighted Ns.

counterparts differ by only 1 point in the United States and 1.9 points in Sweden. Most of this lower degree of polarization comes from the fact that women expert managers are considerably less pro-capitalist than men expert managers, probably reflecting their concentration in lower levels of management.

In one other respect the table differs between men and women: the uncredentialled manager cell does not 'behave' properly for women: in Sweden this cell is nearly as pro-working class as the proletarian cell and certainly does not follow the prescribed monotonic pattern; among American women, on the other hand, it is the least pro-working class of all the wage-earner categories. I cannot offer any explanations for these specific results. In any event, it is certainly not the case that the overall class structure patterns in table 7.1 are artifacts of the sex compositions of classes.

When we expand the possible sources of spuriousness to include age and class trajectory and calculate the adjusted means in table 7.4 we again see that there is no evidence that the observed relations in table 7.1 are artifacts of the personal attributes of the incumbents in class locations. While classes certainly do vary considerably on these variables, they are not the source of variations across classes in class consciousness.

(2) *Intervening mechanisms in the consciousness formation process.* Table 7.5 examines the patterns in table 7.1 separately for union members and non-union members in each country. Table 7.6 then examines the adjusted means, adding to the con-

TABLE 7.4

Adjusted mean class consciousness by class location controlling for personal attributes

I. United States

Assets in the means of production

Owners | Non-owners [wage labourers]

1 Bourgeoisie	4 Expert managers	7 Semi-cred. managers	10 Uncred. managers	
−1.11[a]	−1.45	−0.36	−0.29	+
2 Small employers	5 Expert supervisors	8 Semi-cred. supervisors	11 Uncred. supervisors	>0 Organization assets
−0.80	−0.81	−0.28	+0.50	
3 Petty bourgeoisie	6 Expert non-manager	9 Semi-cred. workers	12 Proletarians	−
+0.05	−0.20	+0.70	+0.80	

+ | >0 | −

Skill/credential assets

TABLE 7.4 (*continued*)

Sweden

Assets in the means of production

Owners   Non-owners [wage labourers]

Bourgeoisie	4 Expert managers	7 Semi-cred. managers	10 Uncred. managers		
−1.46	−0.58	+1.15	+1.90	+	
Small employers	5 Expert supervisors	8 Semi-cred. supervisors	11 Uncred. supervisors		*Organ-*
−0.39	+0.24	+0.78	+2.05	>0	*ization assets*
Petty bourgeoisie	6 Expert non-manager	9 Semi-cred. workers	12 Proletarians		
+1.05	+1.23	+2.69	+2.40	−	

+   >0   −

Skill/credential assets

ntries in cells are adjusted mean values on the working class consciousness scale, culated from a multiple regression equation containing the class dummy variables, e, sex and class trajectory. See Table 7.7 equation (2).

trols in table 7.4 a number of intervening variables: personal income, unearned income, home ownership, unemployment experience, working-class networks and union membership.[22]

Union membership is likely to be among the most important intervening factors in the consciousness formation process. It is certainly closely tied to class location, particularly in the United States where the legal system prohibits certain class locations among wage-earners from becoming unionized—management positions are generally not allowed to be in unions—and one would expect that unions ought to have at least some impact on class attitudes. In these terms, the results in table 7.5 are quite interesting. First of all, they clearly indicate the mediating role of unions: in every cell, union members have emphatically more pro-working-class attitudes than non-union members in both the United States and Sweden. But equally interesting is the fact that at least in Sweden, the same basic pattern of polarization and monotonicity is observed among union and non-union members alike. (In the United States there are so few union members in the non-working-class corners of the table that it is hard to draw any inferences). This indicates that class structure shapes consciousness not simply via the effects of class structure on class formation (as measured by union membership), but also because of a direct impact of class location on the incumbents of positions.

When we calculate the adjusted means controlling for all of the mediating variables, there is, as would be expected, a substantial change from the values of the unadjusted means in table 7.1, in general reducing the differences across cells in the typology.[2]

TABLE 7.5
Class attitudes by class location for union and non-union members, United States and Sweden

I. United States

Assets in the means of production

Non-owners [wage labourers]

4 Expert managers U^a −0.53 (3)^b N −1.52 (55)	7 Semi-cred. managers U +1.31 (13) N −0.59 (78)	10 Uncred. managers U −0.16 (3) N −0.31 (31)	+
5 Expert supervisors U +2.14 (1) N −0.85 (53)	8 Semi-cred. supervisors U +2.19 (16) N −0.68 (85)	11 Uncred. supervisors U +1.87 (16) N 0.29 (86)	>0 Organ-ization assets
6 Expert non-managers U +1.06 (4) N −0.18 (47)	9 Semi-cred. workers U +1.17 (58) N +0.60 (124)	12 Proletarians U +1.68 (144) N +0.50 (450)	−

+	>0	−

Skill/credential assets

TABLE 7.5 (*continued*)

Sweden

Assets in the means of production

Non-owners [wage labourers]

4 Expert managers	7 Semi-cred. managers	10 Uncred. managers	
U +0.04 (36)	U +1.55 (41)	U +2.90 (21)	+
N −2.47 (15)	N −2.00 (7)	N −0.83 (9)	
5 Expert supervisors	8 Semi-cred. supervisors	11 Uncred. supervisors	*Organ-*
U +0.17 (39)	U +0.93 (35)	U +2.51 (29)	>0 *ization*
N −0.71 (5)	N −1.35 (3)	N +0.12 (8)	*assets*
6 Expert non-manager	9 Semi-cred. workers	12 Proletarian	
U +1.47 (64)	U +3.06 (182)	U +2.99 (395)	−
N +0.55 (16)	N +1.20 (28)	N +1.29 (118)	

+	>0	−

Skill/credential assets

= Unionized; N = Non-unionized.
umbers in parentheses are weighted Ns.

However, it is still the case in both the United States and Sweden that, with a few deviations, the basic monotonic relationship between class and consciousness is retained.

Several principal differences between table 7.6 and table 7.1 are worth noting: first, when the various controls are included in table 7.6, the adjusted mean consciousness for expert managers in Sweden is no longer pro-capitalist. What this means is that the aggregate pro-capitalist stance of Swedish expert managers is generated by the link between their class location and their incomes, union membership and other intervening processes. This is not the case in the United States. In fact, in the United States expert managers are more pro-capitalist relative to the bourgeoisie in table 7.6 than they were in table 7.1. My interpretation of these results is that in Sweden the labour movement has been able to

unionize significant segments of management and as a result ha
driven a wedge into this class location, generating a fairly shar
line of demarcation between upper level managers and the bulk o
managerial employees. Most of this change in the adjusted mean
of the expert-manager cell can be attributed to the operation of the
union variable. As table 7.4 indicates, the overall pro-capitalis
stance of expert managers in Sweden comes from the very pro
capitalist position—more pro-capitalist in fact than their American
counterparts—of non-unionized expert managers in Sweden. Thi
division between unionized and non-unionized expert manager
undoubtedly corresponds to a division between top managemen
and other managers. What we are observing here is that the union
movement is able to pull lower and middle levels of managemen
into at least a passive coalition with workers. In part because

TABLE 7.6

**Adjusted mean class consciousness by class location controlling for mediati
variables**

I. *United States*

Assets in the means of production

Owners   Non-owners [wage labourers]

Owners	Non-owners [wage labourers]			
1 Bourgeoisie −0.20[a]	4 Expert managers −0.87	7 Semi-cred. managers −0.08	10 Uncred. managers −0.33	+
2 Small employers −0.50	5 Expert supervisors −0.30	8 Semi-cred. supervisors −0.20	11 Uncred. supervisors +0.42	>0 *Org izat asse*
3 Petty bourgeoisie −0.01	6 Expert non-managers +0.07	9 Semi-cred. workers +0.55	12 Proletarians +0.53	−
	+	>0	−	

Skill/credential assets

TABLE 7.6 (*continued*)

Sweden

Assets in the means of production

Owners	Non-owners [wage labourers]			
Bourgeoisie −0.85	4 Expert managers +0.53	7 Semi-cred. managers +1.34	10 Uncred. managers +1.85	+
Small employers −0.04	5 Expert supervisors +0.41	8 Semi-cred. supervisors +0.60	11 Uncred. supervisors +2.03	>0 *Organ- ization assets*
Petty bourgeoisie +0.61	6 Expert non-managers +1.32	9 Semi-cred. workers +2.40	12 Proletarians +2.04	−
	+	>0	−	

Skill/credential assets

ntries in cells are adjusted mean values on the working class consciousness scale,
lculated from a multiple regression equation containing the class dummy variables, age,
x, working class trajectory, working class networks, ever unemployed dummy, personal
:ome, unearned income dummy, home ownership dummy, and union member dummy.
e Table 7.7, equation (3).

of legal obstacles to unionizing managers, and in part because
of the general weakness of the American labour movement, this
has not happened in the United States, and as a result the rank-
and-file of management is firmly integrated with the bourgeoisie
ideologically.

A second point of contrast between table 7.1 and table 7.6, is
that the difference in the degree of polarization among wage earners between the United States and Sweden is no long as striking
as in the original table. In table 7.1 expert managers and proletarians differed by 3.3 points in Sweden and by 2.24 in the
United States; in table 7.6 the respective differences are 1.51 and
1.40 (not statistically significant). Most of this reduction in the

difference between countries in degrees of polarization between classes can be attributed to the inclusion of unionization as an intervening variable. This supports the interpretation suggested in hypothesis 2 that the degree of polarization is mediated by organizational and political factors.

A third, and related point, is that the difference between non-unionized workers in Sweden and in the United States is somewhat less than between unionized workers. This suggests that it is not simply the fact of unionization that acts as a mediating process in consciousness-formation, but the strength and social weight of the labour movement.

Finally, in one important respect, the patterns in table 7.6 differ from those in table 7.1: for the United States, the bourgeoisie itself is now less pro-capitalist then nearly any of the wage-earner categories that are pro-capitalist. My expectation had been that the ideological stance of capitalists would be more directly tied to their class position than would be the case for wage-earners, and thus their adjusted means would be less affected by the inclusion of intervening variables in the equation. This is indeed the case in Sweden, but not in the United States. I do not have an explanation for this result. The intervening variables which most affected the regression coefficients for the bourgeoisie dummy variable were the income variables, particularly the 'unearned income' dummy variable. Since this variable is so closely tied to their class location, it may be inappropriate to consider it an intervening variable at all in their case.[24]

3. ANALYSIS OF THE OVERALL CONSCIOUSNESS DETERMINATION PROCESS

So far we have looked exclusively at the relationship between class structure and consciousness. In this final analysis we will examine the relationship between the other independent variables used to generate tables 7.4 and 7.6 and consciousness. The results are presented in table 7.7.

There are a number of striking properties of these equations. First, class and class biography variables (working-class trajectory, unemployment experience and working-class networks) consistently have bigger effects in Sweden than in the United States. The class dummy variables alone explain 13 per cent of the variance in the Swedish equation but only 6 per cent in the US equation. When the various class experience variables are added

TABLE 7.7

Class structure, class biography and class consciousness in Sweden and the United States: multiple regression analysis

Dependent variable = working class consciousness scale

	Equation (1)	
	United States B (β)	Sweden B (β)
Class dummy variables		
(proletariat: left out category)		
Bourgeoisie	−2.09 (−0.11)***	−4.54 (−0.12)***
Small employer	−1.66 (−0.15)***	−3.52 (−0.23)***
Petty bourgeoisie	−0.87 (−0.08)**	−2.08 (−0.15)***
Expert manager	−2.25 (−0.17)***	−3.23 (−0.21)***
Expert supervisor	−1.56 (−0.11)***	−2.47 (−0.15)***
Expert non-manager	−0.88 (−0.06)*	−1.25 (−0.10)***
Semi-credentialled manager	−1.10 (−0.10)***	−1.51 (−0.09)***
Semi-credentialled supervisor	−1.02 (−0.10)***	−1.80 (−0.10)***
Semi-credentialled worker	−0.00 (−0.00)	0.27 (0.03)
Uncredentialled manager	−1.08 (−0.06)*	−0.73 (−0.04)
Uncredentialled supervisor	−0.24 (−0.02)	−0.56 (−0.03)
Constant	0.79	2.54
Adjusted R^2	0.06	0.13
	1491	1191

	Equation (2)	
	United States B (β)	Sweden B (β)
Class dummy variables		
Bourgeoisie	−1.92 (−0.10)***	−3.85 (−0.10)***
Small employer	−1.61 (−0.15)***	−2.79 (−0.19)***
Petty bourgeoisie	−0.75 (−0.07)*	−1.34 (−0.09)**
Expert managers	−2.26 (−0.17)***	−2.98 (−0.19)***
Expert supervisors	−1.62 (−0.12)***	−2.15 (−0.13)***
Expert workers	−1.00 (−0.07)**	−1.16 (−0.09)**
Semi-credentialled managers	−1.17 (−0.11)***	−1.25 (−0.08)**
Semi-credentialled supervisors	−1.08 (−0.10)***	−1.62 (−0.09)**
Semi-credentialled workers	−0.10 (−0.01)	0.30 (0.04)
Uncredentialled managers	−1.09 (−0.06)*	−0.49 (−0.02)
Uncredentialled supervisors	−0.30 (−0.03)	−0.35 (−0.02)
Demographic variables		
Sex	−0.04 (−0.01)	0.21 (0.03)
Age	−0.03 (−0.17)***	0.003 (0.01)
Class biography		
Working class trajectory	−0.01 (−0.01)	0.25 (0.14)***
Constant	2.07	1.18
Adjusted R^2	0.09	0.14
	1463	1188

TABLE 7.7 (continued)

	United States B (β)	Sweden B (β)	Significance level of difference between US and Swedish coefficients in eq. (1) t
		Equation (3)	
Class dummy variables			
1. Bourgeoisie	−0.50 (−0.03)	−1.52 (−0.04)	
2. Small employers	−0.80 (−0.07)*	−0.71 (−0.05)	
3. Petty bourgeoisie	−0.31 (−0.03)	−0.06 (−0.00)	
4. Expert managers	−1.40 (−0.10)***	−1.51 (−0.10)**	
5. Expert supervisors	−0.83 (−0.06)*	−1.63 (−0.10)**	
6. Expert workers	−0.46 (−0.03)	−0.71 (−0.06)*	<1[a]
7. Semi-credentialled managers	−0.61 (−0.06)*	−0.70 (−0.04)	
8. Semi-credentialled supervisors	−0.73 (−0.07)*	−1.45 (−0.08)**	
9. Semi-credentialled workers	0.02 (0.00	0.36 (0.04)	
10. Uncredentialled managers	−0.86 (−0.05)	−0.19 (−0.01)	
11. Uncredentialled supervisors	−0.12 (−0.01)	−0.01 (−0.00)	
Demographic variables			
12. Sex	−0.10 (−0.02)	0.04 (0.01)	<1
13. Age	−0.02 (0.12)***	0.007 (0.03)	3.07
Class biography			
14. Working class trajectory	−0.06 (−0.03)	0.18 (0.10)**	2.76
15. Working class networks	0.04 (0.04)	0.11 (0.10)***	1.71
16. Ever unemployed (dummy)	0.44 (0.08)**	0.93 (0.12)***	1.87
Class consequences			
17. Personal income ($1000s)	−0.20 (−0.10)**	−0.43 (−0.11)**	1.44
18. Unearned income (dummy)	−0.55 (−0.09)***	−0.85 (−0.07)*	<1
19. Home owner (dummy)	−0.35 (−0.07)*	−0.48 (−0.07)**	<1
20. Union member (dummy)	1.33 (0.19)***	1.88 (0.26)***	1.80
Constant	1.60	−0.14	
Adjusted R^2	0.15	0.23	
N	1243	1003	

Significance levels (two-tailed): *** <0.001; ** <0.01; * <0.05
[a]For the class dummy variables, the significance level is based on a test of the difference between the entire set of class dummy variable coefficients in Sweden and the United States. 'ns' means not significant.

to this equation (variables 14 to 16), the R^2 increases only to 8 per cent in the United States, but 17 per cent in Sweden. The magnitudes and significance levels of the regression coefficients for the class dummy variables in equations 1 and 2 in table 7.7 and the class experience variables in equation 3 are also consistently greater in Sweden. In particular, except for unemployment experience, the class experience variables are at best marginally significant in the United States equations but are quite significant in the Swedish equations. (On these coefficients, the difference between the US and Swedish equations are generally statistically significant). Clearly, class position and class biography are more salient determinants of consciousness in Sweden than in the United States.

Second, in both Sweden and the United States, all of the class-consequences variables have significant effects on consciousness. As in the case of the class dummy variables and the class experience variables, the magnitudes of the raw regression coefficients are greater in Sweden than in the United States for these variables, but the differences are not statistically significant except for the union membership variable. Immediate class experience, measured both by current location and biography, thus appears to be a more salient determinant of consciousness in Sweden than in the United States, whereas the consequences of class—income, home-ownership, etc.—appear to be equally salient in both countries.

Third, in neither the United States nor in Sweden does gender, net of the other variables in the equation have any effect at all on class consciousness, as a measured in this study. On the other hand, the effects of age differ dramatically between the two countries: in equation 3, age is the second best predictor of the consciousness scale in the US, while in Sweden it has no predictive power whatsoever.[25] There are several possible explanations for this. Age could constitute a *life-cycle* variable, and it is possible that because of the way labour markets and social security are organized in the two countries there are more antagonisms along age lines in the US than in Sweden. More plausibly, age is a *cohort* variable. The relative historical continuity in Sweden in class politics from the 1930s to the 1980s could explain the absence of any strong cohort effects on class consciousness, whereas in the United States the relative discontinuity represented both by the pre-war and post-war eras, and later, by the experiences of the 1960s could explain the much stronger age effects.

Finally, even though we have observed dramatic differences between Sweden and the United States, if we pool the two samples into a single equation (not shown) in which country appears as a dummy variable, nationality is by no means the best predictor of consciousness. In this pooled equation, working-class consciousness depends more upon whether or not one is a worker or a union member than whether or not one is a Swede or and American.

Conclusions

The results in this chapter can be summarized in three overarching conclusions. First, the data are systematically consistent with the proposed reconceptualization of class in terms of relations of exploitation. Class attitudes are polarized in the ways predicted by the exploitation-centred concept, and in general they vary across the dimensions of the class typology matrix in the expected monotonic manner.

Second, the data support the thesis that the underlying structure of class relations shapes the overall pattern of class consciousness. As we noted in chapter six, Sweden and the United States are in many respects polar cases among advanced capitalist countries in terms of class formation, state expansion, income inequality, welfare state programmes and so on. Yet, in spite of these dramatic differences, the basic pattern linking class structure to class consciousness is very similar in the two countries: they are both polarized along the three dimensions of exploitation, and the values on the consciousness scale basically vary monotonically as one moves along these dimensions.

Finally, while the overall patterning of consciousness is structurally determined by class relations, the level of working-class consciousness in a given society and the nature of the class coalitions that are built upon those class relations are shaped by the organizational and political practices that characterize the history of class struggle. For all of their reformism and their efforts at building a stable class compromise in Swedish society, the Swedish Social Democratic Party and the associated Swedish labour movement have adopted strategies which reinforce certain aspects of working class consciousness rather than absorbing it into a solid bourgeois ideological hegemony.

These strategies have affected each of the three elements of class consciousness discussed earlier: perceptions of alternatives, theories of consequences and preferences (or understandings of interests). To a much greater extent than in the United States, the liscourse of politics in Sweden often explicitly involves 'class'. The very name given in the mass media to the Conservative parties in Sweden—the 'bourgeois parties'—reflects this salience accorded class in defining the terrain of politics. But more important than the use of words, the Social Democratic Party has been an arena in which issues of power and property have been debated and become part of the agenda of politics in Sweden. The effect of these debates has been to emphasize the existence of alternatives to the existing distributions of power and property. Proposals such as the Meidner plan—a programme currently under consideration to gradually erode private-capitalist ownership of the principal means of production through the use of union controlled investment funds—illustrate this well. The Meidner plan has been widely debated as a proposal to transform power relations in the society as a whole. Even though the more radical versions of the proposal have not received wide support, the very fact of the debate itself opens up the terrain of alternatives.

The strategies of parties and unions in Sweden have also had the effect of shaping the real and perceived interests of various categories of wage-earners. State-welfare policies pursued by the Social Democratic Party have generally had a relatively universal character to them, distributing benefits of different sorts to most categories of wage earners, thus reducing the tendency for wage earners in contradictory exploiting class locations to see their interests as polarized with those in exploited positions. Above all, perhaps, the effectiveness of the Swedish labour movement in massively unionizing white-collar employees and even substantial segments of managerial employees, has heightened the degree of perceived community of interests among wage earners in different class positions. This does not imply that the objective basis of conflicts of interests among wage earners in different classes has disappeared, but simply that their common interests as capitalistically exploited wage-earners have assumed greater weight relative to their differential interests with respect to organization and credential exploitation.

In contrast to the Swedish case, political parties and unions in the United States have engaged in practices which, wittingly or unwittingly, have undermined working-class consciousness. The Democratic Party has systematically displaced political discourse from a language of class. While there are exceptions of course, the general tendency has been to organize social conflicts in non-class ways and to emphasize the extremely limited range of alternatives for dealing with problems of power and property. State welfare policies have tended to heighten rather than reduce class-base divisions among wage earners. And the ineffectiveness of the labour movement to unionize even a majority of manual industria workers, let alone white collar employees, has meant that the per ceived divisions of exploitation-based interests among wage earners have tended to be large relative to their common interest vis-à-vis capital. As a result, as the rhetoric of the 1984 Presiden tial campaign demonstrated, the labour movement is regarded as 'special interest' group in the United States, rather than a repre sentative of the general economic interests of wage-earners.

The net result of these differences in the political strategies an ideologies of parties and unions in the two countries is that clas has considerably greater ideological salience in Sweden than in th United States: class location and class experiences have a bigge impact on class consciousness; classes are more polarized ideologi cally; and the working class coalition built upon that more polar ized ideological terrain is much bigger.

Notes

1. Georg Lukács, *History and Class Consciousness*, Cambridge, Mass. 197 (original edition), 1922, p. 51.

2. Lukács himself, in a footnote (ibid. n. 11, p. 81), suggests that there is relationship between his argument and Max Weber's ideal types, but he fails t elaborate the connection.

3. An 'objective teleology of history' implies that there exists some objective given end-state of history or 'goal' of history, distinct from the goals and objective of human individuals, which determines the actual trajectory of historical develop ment.

4. There is one sense in which one could legitimately refer to class 'consciou ness' as a property of a collectivity, namely when consciousness is used to describ the practices themselves and not simply the forms of subjectivity that shape th intentional choices implicated in those practices. Since the actual practices involv the use of organizational resources and various other kinds of collective capacitie when the term 'consciousness' is extended to cover the practices as such, then it i no longer strictly an attribute of individuals. I prefer to limit the expression cor sciousness to the subjective dimensions of the problem and use the term 'capacitie to describe the collectively organized resources used in struggles, and the ter 'practices' to describe the individual and collective activities that result from th linkage of individual consciousness and collective capacities.

5. The abstract conceptualization of consciousness and class consciousnes adopted in this chapter is rooted in a view of human action that is sometime referred to as 'rational choice' or 'strategic action' theory. For an important elab oration of this theoretical tradition and its relation to Marxism, which has bee

nfluential in the formulations adopted here, see Jon Elster, 'Marxism, Functional-ism and Game Theory', *Theory and Society*, vol. 11, no. 4, July 1982, pp. 453–485; and *Making Sense of Marx*, Cambridge 1985.

6. Göran Therborn, *The Power of Ideology and the Ideology of Power*, London 1980, p. 2.

7. The term 'subjectivity' has a rather vague theoretical status. It is not clear whether it refers only to the conscious dimensions of the psyche—i.e. those aspects of the psyche that make people 'subjects'—or whether it is basically used to designate all facets of the psyche. Given Therborn's emphasis on consciousness in his discussion of ideology, I suspect that he is using the term subjectivity in the narrower sense.

8. Ideology and culture are not two distinct kinds of events in the world. In the actual practices of social actors they are continually intertwined. The distinction being made is between the kinds of effects produced by given practices. Ideological effects are effects centred on consciousness and cognition; cultural effects are effects centred on nonconscious aspects of subjectivity.

9. For useful related discussions of the problem of 'objective interests', see Raymond Geuss, *The Idea of Critical Theory: Habermas and the Frankfurt School*, Cambridge 1981, pp. 45–551; Issac Balbus, 'The Concept of Interest in Pluralist and Marxist Analysis', *Politics & Society*, February, 1971; Ted Benton, 'Objective Interests and the Sociology of Power', *Sociology*, vol. 15, no. 2, May, 1981, pp. 161–84; Steven Lukes, *Power: a Radical View*, London, 1974; William Connolly, 'On Interests in Politics', *Politics & Society*, vol. 2, no. 4, 1972, pp. 459–77; Jon Elster, *Sour Grapes*, Cambridge 1983.

10. Freedom is not simply the absence of restraint, but the capacity to act. For a systematic discussion of this concept which bears on the present discussion, see Andrew Levine, *Arguing for Socialism*, London 1984, pp. 20–49.

11. Simple material interests in income and consumption are one instance of this general interest in freedom: being exploited is a restriction on freedom, since it reduces one's capacity to act in that material resources are crucial constituents of that capacity. In these terms, as Levine brilliantly shows, equality is not really a value distinct from freedom, since inequalities are an important impediment to freedom itself.

12. See in particular the conceptual typologies of class consciousness proposed by D. W. Livingstone, *Class and Class Consciousness in Advanced Capitalism*, Toronto 1984, (unpublished manuscript); Michael Mann, *Consciousness and Action among the Western Working Class*, London 1973; Bertell Ollmann, 'Toward Class Consciousness in the Working Class', *Politics & Society*, Fall 1972, pp. 1–24; Therborn, *op. cit.*

13. See, for example, Gordon Marshall, 'Some Remarks on the Study of Working Class Consciousness', *Politics & Society*, vol. 12, no. 3, 1983, pp. 263–302.

14. For example, Marxists often argue that the distinction between explaining social problems in individualist terms ('the poor are poor because they are lazy') instead of social structural terms ('the poor are poor because of the way capitalism generates inequalities') is an aspect of class consciousness. While I accept this claim, it does require a fairly strong commitment to the Marxist theory of mystification.

15. See appendix II, table II.7 for a detailed presentation of the logic for constructing this typology.

16. We should have asked all respondents including currently self-employed, whether or not they had been self-employed in the past. This would have enabled

us to have built this variable strictly as an historical experience variable uncontami nated by the respondent's current situation. Unfortunately, the prior-self-employ ment questions were only asked of people currently not self-employed.

17. Only eleven dummy variables are needed, since the twelfth category corres ponds to a value of zero on all of the others. In the simple case of a dichotomy— which is a typology with two cells—only one dummy variable is needed, for exam ple men = 0 and women = 1. It would be redundant to have a complimentar variable with the values reversed.

18. In this table we have combined people who spontaneously say that they ar in the working class in the open-ended version of the question with those who sa that they are in the working class in the closed-ended follow-up.

19. In the United States, expert managers are slightly more pro-capitalist tha the bourgeoisie itself, but the difference between them is not statistically signifi cant. It should be remembered in this context that most respondents in what I ar calling the 'bourgeoisie' are still fairly modest capitalists. 83 per cent of thes capitalists employ less than fifty employees. Only 8 per cent of expert managers, o the other hand, work for businesses with less than fifty employees. It is to b expected that if we had data on a sample of large capitalists, the results would b somewhat different.

20. These estimates are based on the following aggregations from table 7.1 Swedish bourgeois coalition = cells 1, 2, 4; US bourgeois coalition = cells 1, 2, 4, 5 7, 8, 10; Swedish working class coalition = cells 6, 9, 10, 11, 12 (low estimate) an also 7,8 (high estimate); US working class coalition = cells 9, 11, 12. Note that i neither country is the petty bourgeoisie—category 3—part of either coalition.

21. For an explanation of the procedures used to calculate the adjusted mean and their interpretation, see the discussion of statistical procedures on p. 25 above.

22. In calculating the adjusted means in table 7.6, we depart from the procedur discussed earlier in one respect: for the union-membership dummy variable it doe not make sense to 'adjust' the means of capitalists by the socially average contribu tion of this variable to consciousness, since none of them can be union members The counterfactual question implicit in the procedure used to adjust the mea values—what would be the expected consciousness of capitalists if the sociall average proportion of them were union members—does not make sense. I have therefore evaluated the union membership dummy variable at zero (i.e. the appropriate value for capitalists) when calculating the adjusted means for owners o the means of production.

23. If the intervening variables included in the regression in fact measured all of the mechanisms which translated class location into class consciousness, then the adjusted means would all be identical.

24. There is a further ambiguity with this variable, referred to in the note to table 6.18, since some self-employed respondents regarded all of their income as income from investments, whereas others treated the question as referring only to investments other than in their own businesses. Only about 55 per cent of the US capitalists in the sample stated that they had any investment income.

25. The US age coefficient is statistically significantly larger than the Swedish coefficient at the .002 confidence level.

Conclusion

This book began by arguing that contemporary Marxist class analysis has been attempting to bridge the gap between the abstract, polarized structural map of classes and the concrete conjunctural analysis of class formation and class struggle. In this study our main preoccupation has been to approach this problem by systematically rethinking the structural categories themselves in a way suitable for incorporation into middle-level theories and empirical research. While we have explored many diverse problems, three overarching conclusions seem particularly important: the first concerns the viability of the proposed reconceptualization of class structure; the second involves the salient features of contemporary capitalist class structures using this reconceptualization; and the third is about the role of politics in class analysis.

The Exploitation Centred Concept of Class

My earlier work on class structure suffered, I have argued, from the tendency to displace the concept of exploitation from the centre of class analysis. This weakened the sense in which class relations were intrinsically relations of objectively opposed interests, and posed a series of specific conceptual difficulties.

These difficulties, combined with my empirical research on class structure and my encounter with the theoretical work of John Roemer, have precipitated the reconceptualization of class relations in terms of the multidimensional view of exploitation elaborated in chapter three. Classes in capitalist society, I now argue, should be seen as rooted in the complex intersection of three forms of exploitation: exploitation based on the ownership of capital assets, the control of organization assets and the possession of skill or credential assets. While I have some reservations about the class character of the third of these categories, this reconceptualization nevertheless resolved many of the difficulties I had encountered with my previous approach to class structure.

The empirical investigations we have explored add considerable credibility to this reconceptualization. First, in chapter five when we formally compared the exploitation-centred concept to two rivals—the manual-labour definition of the working class and the productive-labour definition—the exploitation-centred concept fared considerably better. While the results were not without some ambiguities and are thus subject to alternative interpretations, in general where the alternative definitions disagreed about the class of particular positions, the data supported their class placement according to the logic and criteria of the exploitation-based concept.

Second, when we examined the relationship between class structure and income inequality in chapter six, the results were almost exactly as predicted by the exploitation-centred concept. This was a complex prediction, since it involved specifying the way income would vary across the three dimensions of the class structure matrix. The patterns followed these expectations very closely: income increased essentially monotonically as we moved along all of the dimensions of exploitation taken singly or together.

Finally, in chapter seven, the investigation of the relationship between class structure and class consciousness has added further to the credibility of the reconceptualization. The patterns of variation of consciousness across positions in the class structure matrix conform closely to the theoretical expectations. The results seem to be relatively robust and, at least on the basis of the variables we have considered, do not appear to be artifacts of certain possible sources of spuriousness. Furthermore, the same basic pattern is observed in two countries which are dramatically different in their general political complexion.

Taken together, these diverse empirical results lend considerable support to the new conceptualization of class structure. Empirical results of this sort, however, can never provide definitive judgements. Alternative explanations of the observed patterns are always available and the conclusions I have drawn are inevitably open to both theoretical and methodological question. But until a more compelling rival conception of class enters the fray of theoretical and empirical adjudication, there are compelling reasons to adopt some variant of the approach proposed here.

The Class Structure of Contemporary Capitalism

Using this new conceptualization of class structure, we have systematically explored the contours of the American and Swedish class structures. Leaving aside all of the details of that analysis, there are two broad generalizations that we can make.

First, in both countries, in spite of the technical and social changes of contemporary capitalism, the working class remains by far the largest class in the labour force. Even if we adopt a narrow specification of the working class, which excludes various holders of 'marginal' exploitation assets, around forty per cent of the labour force is in this class. If these marginal categories are added—and there are good reasons to do so, particularly in the case of the 'semi-credentialled employee' category—then the working class becomes a clear majority in both countries.

Second, and equally important, while the working class is the largest class, a substantial proportion of the labour force occupies exploitative locations within the class structure. Even if, again, we exclude all possessors of marginal exploitation assets from this designation, somewhere around one quarter of the labour force in Sweden and the United States are exploiters. Looked at in terms of families rather than individuals, an even higher proportion of families have at least one person in an exploiting class within them, probably around forty per cent of all households. This is not to say that such individuals and families are *net* exploiters. The central argument in the reconceptualization of the 'middle class' is that such positions are *simultaneously* exploiters and exploited. This is precisely what defines the complexity of their class interests and puts them into what I have called 'contradictory locations within exploitation relations'. My guess is that most of these individuals and families are still more capitalistically exploited than they are exploiters through other mechanisms. Nevertheless, this does not obliterate the fact that they are exploiters and that, as a result, they have material interests which are fundamentally different from those of workers.

Class Structure and Politics

Class structure is of pervasive importance in contemporary social life. The control over society's productive assets determines the fundamental material interests of actors and heavily shapes the capacities of both individuals and collectivities to pursue their interests. The fact that a substantial portion of the population may be relatively comfortable materially does not negate the fact that their capacities and interests remain bound up with property relations and the associated processes of exploitation.

Nevertheless, in spite of this importance, the effects of class structure are mediated by politics. Class relations may define the terrain upon which interests are formed and collective capacities forged, but the outcome of that process of class formation cannot be 'read off' the class structure itself.

In the empirical investigations we have discussed, political factors have entered in two central ways. First of all, in the structural comparisons of classes in Sweden and the United States, the differences in their class structures seem largely attributable to political processes. The size of the state itself has a significant impact on the class distributions of the two countries, contributing to the greater number of non-managerial experts in Sweden than in the United States, and explaining almost entirely the smaller number of small employers and petty bourgeois in Sweden. More subtly, political dynamics are probably implicated in the much higher levels of supervision of the American than of the Swedish workforce, and of the much closer association between expertise and authority in the United States than in Sweden. While the broadest contours of the two countries' class structures are shaped by the level of economic development and the fundamentally capitalist character of both societies, the variations in their class structures are certainly significantly affected by political processes.

The second crucial way that politics have entered our empirical investigation is in the process of consciousness formation, and by extension, class formation. Although the same basic linkage between class structure and class consciousness exists in both countries, the ideological consequences of this link are contingent on their political and historical differences. The higher degree of polarization in Sweden and the much broader ideological basis for a working class coalition are the results of this political mediation of the consciousness-formation process.

Political Implications

The preoccupation throughout this book has been on conceptual problems in the analysis of classes, and the theoretical and empirical implications of a proposed solution to those problems. Except

in passing, relatively little attention has been given to the impli
tions of the analysis for socialist politics. Three such implications
seem particularly important: the centrality of radical democracy in
the political agenda for socialism; the necessity of conceiving the
process of class formation in contemporary capitalism as a problem of class alliances; and the importance of creating the political
mediations which will make such alliances possible. Let us briefly
look at each of these in turn.

So long as Marxists believed that socialism was the only possible
future to capitalism, to be militantly anti-capitalist was equivalent
to being pro-socialist. Destroying capitalism was both necessary
and sufficient for creating the conditions for socialism. Once capitalism is viewed as having multiple futures, once it is admitted that
post-capitalist societies are possible with new forms of class structures, new mechanisms of exploitation and domination, then this
simple equation of anti-capitalism with socialism breaks down. It
then becomes necessary to think through rigorously what it means
to struggle positively for socialism rather than simply against
capitalism.

The reconceptualization of class proposed in this book suggests
that the heart of the positive struggle for socialism is radical democracy. Socialism, as it has been defined in this book, is a society
within which control over capital assets and organizational assets
are no longer significant sources of exploitation. For this to occur,
private ownership of capital assets and hierarchical-authoritarian
control over organization assets must be eliminated. Taken
together, this implies that socialism *means* radical democratic control over the physical and organizational resources used in production.

This is, of course, not a novel conclusion. The increasing awareness of the importance of democracy has been one of the hallmarks of recent political debates on the left.[1] Indeed, it would not
be going too far to say that, at least in the American context, the
problem of democracy has tended to displace the problem of
socialism from the centre stage of leftist political discourse. Instead
of displacing socialism by democracy as the core political agenda
of the left, the arguments in this book suggest that the struggle for
socialism and the struggle for democracy are two sides of a single
process. Without a redistribution of organization assets through a
democratization of the process of control and co-ordination of
production, organization-asset exploitation would continue and
upon that exploitation a new structure of class relations would be

built. Democracy is not simply a question of how the political institutions of the state are organized; it also bears directly on how class relations themselves are constituted.

If the importance of radical democracy as an objective of struggle is one of the basic political implications of this study, the problematic character of the process of class formation needed to accomplish that goal is another. If it were true that the class structure of contemporary capitalism was basically polarized between a massive working class and the bourgeoisie, then the problem of class formation would be much simpler than it is. Basically the task would be one of forging collective organizations of individuals all of whom share the same fundamental class interests. But, as I have argued, the class structures of 'actually existing capitalism' are not simple polarized structures. A substantial proportion of the population, at least in the advanced capitalist countries, occupy contradictory locations within exploitation relations, locations in which they are simultaneously exploited and exploiters. It is difficult to imagine a scenario in which socialism would become a real possibility in these societies without the co-operation of a significant segment of the people in such contradictory locations. Yet, at least in terms of their material interests, the incumbents of these contradictory locations are either directly threatened by socialism, or at least have relatively ambiguous material interests in a socialist transformation.

This poses a deep dilemma for socialists: socialism is achievable only with the co-operation of segments of the population for whom socialism does not pose clear material advantages.[2] How can this dilemma be dealt with? There are basically two kinds of approaches that are implicit in socialist arguments. The first is to basically deny the problem. Socialism, it is argued, will so radically eliminate the massive waste in capitalism (excessive military spending, advertising, conspicuous corporate consumption, etc.) that the vast majority of the population will be better off in a socialist society. In terms of the analysis in this book, real productivity of useful consumption would expand so much that many people in contradictory locations within exploitation relations would actually be better off, and only a very few would be worse off, if capitalist and organization exploitation were eliminated. In effect, this argument implies that most of the labour-time liberated by the reduction of capitalist waste could be redirected towards useful material consumption, thus significantly raising the average standard of living. This would mean that even if consumption levels were substantially equalized in a socialist society this might not imply a reduction of the standards of living of most people in contradictory locations.

This kind of argument often meets with a fair amount of scepticism. A radically democratic socialism will have to devote a great deal of 'socially necessary labour-time' to democratic participation in order for the democratic institutions of production to function effectively. Much of the reduction of waste from capitalism, therefore, will be needed simply to make time available for democratic participation, rather than to produce for personal consumption. Furthermore, it would be reasonable to expect in a socialist society that quite different kinds of efficiency criteria would be instituted in production. For example, under democratic conditions workers may opt for a slower pace of work which could reduce total social productivity. It is therefore very difficult to know in advance what will happen to overall social productivity in a socialist society, and thus what will be the fate of the material interests of people in contradictory locations in capitalism.

The second solution to the general dilemma faced by socialists in trying to gain the collaboration of people in contradictory locations is to emphasize a range of interests other than individual consumption. Arguments for socialism in terms of the quality of life, the expansion of real freedom, the reduction of violence and so on, provide a basis for building class coalitions for socialist objectives.[3] Such goals do not eliminate the contradictory material interests which members of such a coalition would bring to a socialist struggle, but they have the potential of neutralizing their effects.

The process of class formation through which a viable, cohesive socialist coalition is forged is not simply a question of socialists figuring out what kinds of goals will have the greatest appeal to contradictory locations within exploitation relations. As our empirical investigations have emphasized, the entire process of class formation is heavily mediated by politics and ideology. This, then, is the third general political implication of the analysis: in order to create the conditions under which a democratic-socialist class coalition is possible, these mediations themselves have to be transformed.

This is not a new idea in Marxism. Lenin's classic call for 'smashing' the capitalist state was based on the view that this state apparatus was organized in such a way that it prevented the working class from becoming the 'ruling class'. Only by destroying this apparatus and replacing it by a qualitatively distinct kind o apparatus would socialism be possible.[4]

Even if we reject Lenin's rather monolithic view of the struc ture of the capitalist state and see greater possibilities for politica action within its apparatuses, the basic intuition behind Lenin' thesis remains sound. The political and ideological context withi which struggles for socialism occur significantly shapes the poten tial for different kinds of class formations. This means that it i important for socialists to identify those features of capitalist polit ical and ideological institutions which play particularly importan roles in defining this 'terrain of struggle' and thus most pervasivel curtail or enhance the long-term possibilities of creating radicall democratic socialist coalitions. To take just a few examples: th differences in labour law between the United States and Swede explain, in part, why the levels of unionization are so dramaticall different in the two countries, and this in turn has significant impli cations for the class coalitions between workers and contradictor locations. The differences in electoral institutions between coun tries can make it extremely difficult for radical parties to gain an political presence (as in the United Stgates) or relatively easier (as ir West Germany). The extent to which social welfare programme are primarily organized around means-tests, in which recipient are sharply distinguished from non-recipients, or as universa programs, in which everyone receives benefits (but differen people pay different amounts of taxes) may have a large impact on the level of support for such programmes in particular, and the broader political coalitions that are formed around such support.

In each of these cases, political reforms have the potential to enlarge the social space for socialist struggles. This is the core o what was called 'nonreformist reforms' in the 1970s: reforms within the existing society which transform the conditions of sub sequent struggle and potentially expand the very horizon of histor ical possibilities.

Class structures may determine the limits of possible class for mations and class struggles, but within those limits a wide range of different kinds of struggle can occur. Such struggles may largely reproduce the existing class structure, or may set the stage for new forms of post-capitalist exploitation, or open the possibilities for socialism. Whether or not the left will be able to forge the condi tions in capitalism which make democratic socialism possible depends, in part, on its ability to identify the kinds of institutional reforms of existing society that enhance the potential for class formations engaged in struggle for such a future.

Notes

1. Two important and lucid examples of discussions of the problem of democracy and socialism are Joshua Cohen and Joel Rogers, *On Democracy*, London 1983, and Samuel Bowles, David Gordon and Thomas Weiskopf, *Beyond the Wasteland*, Garden City, New York 1984.

2. The problem of the 'transition costs' of any feasible process through which capitalism would be transformed into socialism (discussed briefly in chapter four) makes this dilemma even deeper. If the transition costs are high and prolonged, then even the material interests of workers who would clearly benefit from socialism might still be insufficient to motivate them to struggle for socialism.

3. Adam Przeworski has argued that the shift towards such 'cultural' goals is also important as a way of mitigating the effects of transition costs on support for socialism. See Adam Przeworski, 'Material Interests, Class Compromise and the Transition to Socialism', *Politics & Society*, vol. 10, no. 2, 1981. Claus Offe and Helmut Weisenthal have made a similar argument, emphasizing the ways in which treating the full range of human needs as the object of struggle can change the trade-offs people experience in deciding whether or not to support a given struggle. See their 'Two Logics of Collective Action', *Political Power and Social Theory*, vol. I, edited by Maurice Zeitlin, Greenwich 1979.

4. For a discussion of Lenin's views that is pertinent to the present analysis, see my *Class, Crisis and the State*, chapters four and five.

Appendix I

Practical Strategies for Transforming Concepts

The process of concept formation is always simultaneously a process of concept transformation. There are always conceptual raw materials which go into the production of any new concept. The task of this appendix is to lay out some of the ways in which such a transformation of existing concepts occurs. To do this we will first look briefly at the circumstances within which an impulse for launching the attempt at producing new concepts is likely to occur. This will be followed by a discussion of different forms of concept transformation, different practical ways in which conceptual raw materials are worked on to produce new concepts. This discussion is not meant to be a comprehensive methodological analysis of alternative approaches to producing and transforming concepts, but rather an exposition of a variety of practical strategies that I have found useful in different contexts.

Occasions for Concept Formation

Many, perhaps most, theoretical innovations hinge on the introduction of new concepts or the reconstruction of old ones. Three circumstances typically stimulate such changes: encounters with empirical problems, discoveries of conceptual inconsistencies and dealing with the ramifications of earlier conceptual transformations.

The most common motivation for producing new concepts is undoubtedly dissatisfaction with the ability of existing concepts to deal with empirical problems. The accumulation of empirical cases that do not comfortably fit the existing conceptual map of society suggests that the map is not properly drawn, that new concepts are needed. Two such examples have been discussed in this book: the emergence of locations within the social relations of production of capitalist societies which do not easily fit into either the capitalist class or the working class, and the emergence of post-capitalist societies which do not easily fit into the capitalism–socialism dichotomy. The first of these provided the stimulus for the introduction of the concept 'contradictory locations within class relations', the second for the concept 'state mode of production'. In both cases the pre-existing concepts within Marxist theory seemed unable to deal effectively with these structural changes.[1]

Now, it may turn out that these apparent counterexamples to the existing conceptual framework can, on closer inspection, be accommodated. What is needed may be simply a clarification of existing definitions or a drawing out of their more subtle implications rather than a substantive transformation of those definitions. This possibility is acutely posed in the debate over the class character of 'actually existing socialism' (the USSR, Eastern Europe, China, Cuba, etc.). Instead of treating these cases as inconsistent with the capitalism–socialism conceptual dichotomy, they can, for example, be regarded as socialist societies whose concrete institutional forms have been influenced by the continuing existence of powerful capitalist societies. This implies a specific causal argument about the effects of capitalism on socialist institutions, but it leaves intact a particular definition of socialism as public ownership of the means of production.

A second stimulus for the transformation of concepts comes from the discovery of theoretical inconsistencies within the array of existing concepts. Theories are not just collections of concepts which are linked through various kinds of propositions. The concepts themselves are interdependent in various ways. In particular, some concepts can be viewed as sub-species of more general concepts. It may turn out, then, that the criteria which define the general concept may be incompatible with the specification of a particular sub-category within it.

A good example of this problem is posed in the recent debates over the concept of the 'Asiatic mode of production', particularly as elaborated in the controversial book by Barry Hindess and Paul Q. Hirst, *Precapitalist Modes of Production*.[2] Their essential argument is that the concept of an Asiatic mode of production is illegitimate because it cannot be properly subsumed under the general concept of mode of production. The general concept specifies that to count as a mode of production there must be a specific form of correspondence between the relations and forces of production. Such a correspondence, they argue, can be established for the capitalist and the feudal modes of production, but not for the hypothesized Asiatic mode of production:

No concept of a mode of production can be derived from the tax/rent couple, no articulated combination of relations/forces of production can be deduced, and no systematic conditions of existence for the mode of appropriation of the surplus product, tax/rent, can be constituted.[3]

The societies identified with that concept, therefore, should be seen as peculiar varieties of communal production, or perhaps in some cases feudal production. I do not want to enter the debate on the cogency of their critique of the concept of the Asiatic mode of production. The important point in the present context is that the critique, and the associated process of concept formation, centred around inconsistencies among different concepts rather than specific empirical problems.

The third context within which an extended process of concept formation is likely to occur is in attempting to deal with the ramifications of earlier transformations of concepts. It is unlikely that a significant transformation of an important concept in a theoretical framework will have no implications for the definitions of other concepts. Tampering with concepts tends to produce sequences of concept transformations, as attempts at theoretical reintegration occur. At times, such tampering may appear to open a Pandora's box as such ramifications are pursued and more and more associated concepts are modified or abandoned. Hindess and Hirst's initial questioning of the concept of Asiatic mode of production led them ultimately to abandon the concept of mode of production altogether. In other situations what might initially appear as a conceptual modification with drastic implications may have fairly narrow effects on other concepts within the theory as a whole. This is the case, I believe, with the important challenges to the core concepts in the labour theory of value. Although clearly of great importance for the whole family of concepts directly employing value categories, it does not appear that the general Marxist concepts of class, exploitation, capitalism, class struggle, etc., require substantial respecification in light of these critiques of the concept of labour values.[4]

Forms of Concept Formation

Once the need is recognized, a variety of strategies can be employed for transforming concepts. In practice, of course, the process may be quite haphazard and unsystematic, and without much self consciousness. Four general strategies, however, seem to underlie many successful productions of new concepts: drawing new lines of demarcation; respecifying existing lines of demarcation; re-aggregating categories under more general criteria; and decoding the conceptual dimensionality of a descriptive taxonomy.[5]

New Demarcations. One of the basic ways in which an existing concept may prove unsatisfactory is that it incorrectly subsumes quite heterogeneous cases under a single heading. The task of concept formation, then, is to specify a new line of demarcation within the conceptual field.

A good example of this is the problem of post-capitalist societies. Traditionally most Marxists have argued that socialism, as the transitional form of production to communism (or the 'lower stage' of communism), was the only possible form of post-capitalist society. The simple capitalism–socialism dichotomy was seen as an adequate conceptual map of real possibilities. Under such a conceptual framework, societies such as the Soviet Union were necessarily treated as either a variety of socialism or a variety of capitalism (i.e. state-capitalist society). As I argued in chapter three, an alternative is to introduce a new line of demarcation: the distinction between the socialist mode of production, the capitalist mode of production and what might be called the 'state mode of production'. What was previously subsumed under either capitalism or socialism is then treated as a distinct mode of production in its own right.

A similar operation occurs in the transformation of the concept of the working class as wage-labourers into a variety of alternative concepts. Poulantzas's concept of the new petty bourgeoisie, for example, represents a new line of demarcation within the category 'wage labour'. He argues that mental labourers and unproductive labourers, although they are wage-earners, are in an entirely different class from manual, productive wage-earners. What was previously a single conceptual category is thus split into two.

Respecifications of Lines of Demarcation. It may happen that the problem with a concept is not that it needs to be split into a number of distinct concepts, but that the criteria which define its boundaries need modification. There may be redundant criteria, insufficient criteria or simply incorrect criteria.

This kind of dispute over concepts has played an important role in the long-standing debate over the proper definition of capital-ism within discussions of the transition from feudalism to capitalism.[6] There is no dispute among theorists over the descriptions of the end points of the process: mature industrial capitalism is seen as a system of production with wage-labour and private ownership of the means of production; classical feudalism is seen as agricultural production within which surplus is appropriated through extra-economic coercion. The disagreement centres on the appropriate criteria for specifying the onset of capitalism, and thus for defining the theoretically pertinent minimum conditions for capitalism to be capitalism: is it sufficient to have economic activity oriented towards profit maximization and accumulation on a market for an economic system to be capitalist, or is it also necessary that there be a free market in labour power—i.e. that exploitation operates through the hiring of free wage labour?

In a similar manner, my debate with Poulantzas over the definition of the working class can be interpreted as a dispute over the appropriate lines of demarcation of the concept.[7] Poulantzas considered all unproductive wage labourers to be non-workers; I argued that the productive–unproductive labour distinction was an inappropriate criterion for specifying the boundary of the working class. Poulantzas also considered the mental–manual labour distinction to be a criterion for the boundary of the working class. Here my disagreement with him was slightly different. This distinction does derive from a structural feature of production relations which is appropriate for defining the working class, I argued, but the formulation in terms of mental labour was incorrect. It is not by virtue of being a manual labourer *per se* that a wage labourer is outside of the working class, but by virtue of having pervasive control over one's own labour process, or what I called 'semi-autonomy'. While it is true that such autonomy is characteristic of much mental labour, Poulantzas mis-specified the precise nature of the class criterion. My transformation of Poulantzas's concept of the working class in this instance was to respecify this line of demarcation in terms of real relations of autonomy and control.

Reaggregating Categories. A third way of transforming concepts is to subsume them in a new way under a more encompassing concept, a concept which identifies a more fundamental boundary criterion for the concepts aggregated within it. Whereas the first strategy discussed above involved splitting a single concept on the grounds of its internal heterogeneity, in this case distinct concepts are reaggregated on the grounds of their essential homogeneity.

An example of such conceptual aggregation is the elaboration and refinement of the concept of the 'capitalist state' in recent Marxist theory. A range of concrete forms of the state can be found in capitalist societies: liberal bourgeois democracies, fascist dictatorships, military juntas, social-democratic welfare states, and so on. The central thesis of defenders of the concept of the 'capitalist state' such as Poulantzas and Therborn is that all of these diverse forms of the state can be subsumed under the more general concept of the capitalist state.[8] This concept does not, of course, imply that there are no theoretically significant differences among these diverse sub-types of the capitalist state, but simply that there are certain deep structural properties which they all hold in common and which justify identifying them all with a single encompassing concept. This aggregation process has the effect of transforming the concepts of each of the specific forms of the state being aggregated, for they are no longer defined solely in terms of formal political institutional characteristics, but in terms of their class character as well. Of course, it goes without saying that this claim may be incorrect. Each of these types of the state may be simply 'states in capitalist society' rather than sub-types of the 'capitalist state'. They may have no distinctive or common class character. The debate over the concept of the capitalist state is thus a debate over the legitimacy of this particular conceptual aggregation as a process of concept formation.[9]

Decoding the Dimensionality of Taxonomies. The final general strategy of concept formation is perhaps the most complex. It involves transforming the taxonomies used descriptively in social theories into conceptual typologies. A taxonomy is a list of categories which are differentiated on the basis of immediately apparent empirical criteria; a typology, on the other hand, is a theoretically constructed set of categories differentiated on the basis of theoretically specified dimensions.[10] Sometimes it may happen that a theory may develop an intuitive typology without recognizing the underlying dimensionality of the categories. In such cases, concept formation consists of making explicit the implicit, undertheorized logic of the typology already in use.

Let me give an example of this strategy from work on the theory of the state. One of the problems facing anyone doing research on the state is how to classify state policies. One approach is simply to take as given the spending categories defined bureaucratically within state budgets. This would constitute a descriptive taxonomy of state spending, with items broken down by state agency and programmes in various ways.

Such a list of state budgetary items is obviously unsatisfactory from a theoretical point of view. The task of concept formation, then, is to transform this list into a conceptually structured typology. One such typology reorganizes state policies along two dimensions:[11]

(1) Whether the intervention is primarily at the level of *circulation* or *production*;

(2) Whether the intervention is *commodified* or *decommodified*.

Circulation interventions involve the allocation and redistribution of resources that have already been produced. Most welfare spending would fall under this category. Production level interventions, on the other hand, involve the state directly in decisions to produce certain use-values, rather than simply allocating existing resources. Military spending is a classical example of a production-level intervention. The distinction between commodified and decommodified interventions concerns the extent to which the intervention works through the market, reinforcing the commodified character of social production, or, on the contrary, operates outside of the market, potentially even acting against the logic of market relations. A national health service in which the state directly organizes the provision of health care is a relatively decommodified intervention; national health insurance, on the other hand, is a relatively commodified form.

Taking these two dimensions together produces the four-fold typology of state interventions in table I.1:

TABLE I.1
Typology of state interventions in capitalist society

		Forms of state intervention	
		Commodified	Decommodified
Level of state intervention	Circulation	(1)	(2)
	Production	(3)	(4)

To take an example of the differences between these types, state interventions to deal with the problem of malnutrition among poor familes could potentially fall into any of these cells. Food stamps would be a paradigmatic commodified-circulation intervention (cell 1): it simply redistributes a targeted income to certain groups to be spent on the open market for the acquisition of food. Free distribution of surplus food to the poor would be a decommodified-circulation intervention (cell 2). Government subsidies to farmers to encourage them to produce certain food products for poor people which otherwise might not be profitable would be a commodified production intervention (cell 3), and state run farms to produce food for the poor would be a decommodified production intervention (cell 4).

The theoretical rationale behind this typology was that as interventions moved from the upper left-hand cell of the typology to the lower right-hand cell, they became potentially more and more contradictory to capitalism itself. The typology of state interventions, therefore, was designed to provide a conceptual map of the potential for unreproductive consequences of state interventions.

In addition to providing conceptual order to empirical taxonomies, this kind of dimensionalizing of a conceptual field is useful for clarifying the precise differences between contending concepts within a theoretical debate. Clarifying the dimensionality of the differences in concepts is often a critical step in understanding the real stakes in a debate and pointing the directions for resolution.

For example, within sociology there is a vast array of differing concepts all of which go under the name of 'class'. And there are probably nearly as many different ways of typologizing these differences. To indicate just a few of the possibilities, various theorists have distinguished class concepts as being: continuous or discontinuous (Landecker); dichotomous or gradational (Ossowski); unidimensional or multidimensional (Lipset); market-based or production-based (Crompton and Gubbay); realist or nominalist (Lenski).[12]

I have argued that if our objective is understanding the specificity of the Marxian concept of class, two dimensions on which class concepts vary are particularly important: (1) whether or not the concept of class involves *appropriation relations*, and (2) whether or not it involves *domination relations*.[13] Appropriation relations are social relations between people within which economic

TABLE I.2
Typology of alternative conceptualizations of class

| | | Domination relations | |
		Central to the concept of class	Marginal or absent in the concept of class
Appropriation relations	Central	Marxist definitions	Market definitions: Weber
	Marginal	Authority definitions: Dahrendorf, Lenski	Status-gradational definitions: Parsons

resources (principally means of production, products and income) are distributed. In capitalist societies the central form of appropriation relations is markets of various sorts, although non-market forms of appropriation relations also exist (e.g. taxation). Domination relations are social relations within which the activities of one group of people are controlled by another. Taking these two dimensions together gives us the four different ways of conceptualizing class represented in table 1.2.

In terms of this typology, the distinctiveness of the Marxist definition of class is that class relations are defined simultaneously by relations of domination and appropriation (with appropriation relations—i.e. exploitation—being primary). As in the Weberian analysis of classes in capitalist society, this means that market relations play an important part in specifying class structures. Marx, like Weber, stressed that workers are dispossessed of the means of production and must sell their labour power to employers on the market in order to obtain their means of subsistence (in the form of wages). But unlike Weber, the Marxist concept of the working class also specifies that workers are subordinated to capital within the production process itself. They are systematically related to the capitalist class not only via the exchange relation in the market, but via the domination relation within production.

Classes are thus neither simply categories defined by the social relations which distribute economic resources, nor by the relations through which one group dominates another; they are defined by those appropriation relations which are simultaneously domination relations. Domination without appropriation or appropriation without domination do not constitute class relations.[14]

Within all of these strategies of concept formation—new demarcations, respecifications of demarcations, reaggregations and decoding dimensions—there is a great deal of trial and error. There are many false starts, many attempts at reformulating concepts which end up confusing matters more than clarifying them. When successful, however, the process of concept formation opens up new insights and possibilities within theories, enhances the explanatory capacity of the theory and points towards new research agendas.

Notes

1. Social changes can precipitate processes of concept formation for two reasons: first, such changes may simply require new concepts without bringing into question any existing concepts; or second, such changes may indicate that the original framework is itself inadequate and that existing concepts must be transformed. The two examples mentioned above are of the second variety.

2. *Pre-capitalist Modes of Production*, London 1979. Hindess and Hirst have subsequently repudiated some of the positions advanced in this book. Instead of simply arguing that the concept of the Asiatic mode of production is illegitimate, they now argue that the concept of mode of production itself should be abandoned and replaced with a simpler concept of relations of production.

3. Ibid., p. 200.

4. For various positions on the implications of the debate over the labour theory of value, see Steedman, *et al.* eds., *The Value Controversy*, London 1981. My own position has shifted considerably in the course of the debate. Initially, in 'The Value Controversy and Social Research' (reprinted in *The Value Controversy*), I felt that the stakes were fairly high in the debate, since a rejection of the concept of labour values would undermine the concept of capitalist exploitation, which would in turn undermine the Marxian account of class relations in capitalism. My later position, elaborated in 'Reconsiderations' (a reply to criticisms of my original essay and also published in *The Value Controversy*) was that it was possible to sustain the conceptual core of the Marxian theory of exploitation and class without the formal apparatus of the labour theory of value.

5. These four strategies are not meant to be exhaustive by any means. There is also no implication that they all have the same logical status. Specifying the dimensionality of a concept, for example, will often involve more basic issues of the essential meaning of a concept than changes involving reaggregation of categories under more general rubrics. This list, therefore, is mainly intended to be suggestive of the kinds of strategies which can be pragmatically used in the process of concept formation. It does not aim to provide a comprehensive and philosophically ordered discussion of alternative strategies.

6. Examples of the major participants in this debate include, Immanuel Wallerstein, *The Modern World System*, New York 1974; Robert Brenner, 'The Origins of Capitalist Development: a Critique of Neo-Smithian Marxism', *New Left Review*, 104, July–August, 1977, pp. 25–93; Paul Sweezy, 'The Debate on the Transition: a Critique', in Rodney Hilton, ed, *The Transition from Feudalism to Capitalism*,

London 1976; Maurice Dobb, *Studies in the Development of Capitalism*, Cambridge 1963.

7. See chapter two of *Class, Crisis and the State*, London 1978, for an account of this debate.

8. This thesis has a long pedigree in the Marxist tradition. What the more recent conceptual elaboration has done is given it much more precision and rigour. See in particular Nicos Poulantzas, *Political Power and Social Class*, London 1973, and Göran Therborn, *What Does the Ruling Class Do When It Rules?*, London 1978.

9. Theda Skocpol has probably been the most articulate critic of the thesis that the diverse forms of the state that exist in capitalist societies can be meaningfully subsumed under some general concept of the 'capitalist state'. See, for example, 'Political Responses to Capitalist Crisis: Neo-Marxist Theories of the State and the Case of the New Deal', *Politics & Society*, vol. 10, no. 2, 1980; 'Bringing the State Back In: False Leads and Promising Starts in Current Theories and Research', in *Bringing the State Back In*, edited by Peter Evans, Theda Skocpol and Dietrich Rueschemeyer, Cambridge 1985.

10. This is not to suggest that the descriptive distinctions in a taxonomy are based on 'pure' data in an empiricist sense. The point is that the distinctions are undertheorized, often based on pragmatic 'commonsense' criteria.

11. A version of this typology was initially proposed in 'Modes of Class Struggle and the Capitalist State', by Gösta Esping-Anderson, Roger Friedland, and Erik Olin Wright, *Kapitalistate*, no. 4, 1976.

12. See W. S. Landecker, 'Class Boundaries', *American Sociological Review*, vol. 25, 1960, pp. 868–877; Stanislaus Ossowski, *Class Structure in the Social Consciousness*, London 1963; Seymour Martin Lipset, 'Social Stratification: Social Class', *International Encyclopedia of the Social Sciences*, D. L. Sills (ed), vol. 15, pp. 296–316; Rosemary Crompton and John Gubbay, *Economy and Society*, New York 1978; Gerhard Lenski, *Power and Privilege: A Theory of Social Stratification*, New York 1966.

13. See Erik Olin Wright, 'The Status of the Political in the Concept of Class Structure', *Politics and Society*, vol. 11, no. 3, 1982.

14. An example of the former is the relationship between prison guards and prisoners; an example of the latter is the relationship between children (who appropriate resources from parents) and parents. Except in special cases, neither of these would constitute a class relation.

Appendix II
Variable Constructions

In many ways the pivotal step in a research enterprise such as the one reported in this book is the construction of the operational variables used in the analysis. While variable construction is often treated simply as a pragmatic problem, and typically a boring one at that, it is frequently the case that the contours of the empirical results one observes are highly sensitive to the operational choices embedded in such constructions. This sensitivity applies both to the problem of question-design, which determines the 'raw variables' available in a particular set of data, and to the problem of data-aggregation, which determines the specific variables actually employed in the substantive analysis.

In this appendix I will lay out in considerable detail the ways in which the key variables used in the empirical analyses were constructed. This will both enable others to replicate the results presented in the book if they so desire, and will also make the operational choices as open to criticism as possible.

1 Basic Class Typology

The process of moving from the 'raw' variables on a survey questionnaire to a complex constructed variable as in the class typology used throughout this book involves many intermediate steps. The overall map of this aggregation process is presented in table II.1 The questionnaire items which constitute the basis for these aggregations are presented in table II.2. I will discuss each of the clusters of variables in this aggregation process in turn, giving both the rationale for the procedures adopted and their technical details.

1.1 ORGANIZATION ASSETS

The most complex problem of aggregation in the construction of this class typology concerned organization assets. As table II.1 indicates, this variable was built on three clusters of questionnaire items: items dealing with participation in decision-making, items dealing with authority and an item dealing with position within the

TABLE II.1
Overall steps in construction of class typology

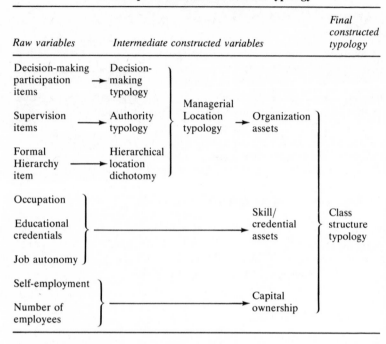

TABLE II.2
Raw variables that are inputs to constructing the class typology

Raw variables (Question numbers from US survey)	Content
1. Employment Status	
Self-employment (Question A7)	'Are you employed by *someone else*, are you *self-employed*, or do you *work without pay* in a family business or firm?'
Hidden self-employment (Question A8)	If respondents said that they work for someone else, and they indicate this is for a profit-making business, they were asked: 'Are you an owner or part owner of this firm? If they said 'Yes' they were asked a series of questions to determine if they were real owners/partners or just had nominal stock in the firm.

TABLE II.2 (*continued*)

Raw variables (Question numbers from US survey)	Content
Number of employees (Questions A9, A17, A24).	Self-employed respondents and respondents who worked without pay in a family firm were asked 'About how many people are employed in this business on a permanent basis?'

2. Decision-making

Decision-making filter (Question D1)	'The next question concerns policy-making at your workplace; that is, making decisions about such things as the products or services delivered, the total number of people employed, budgets, and so forth. Do *you* participate in making these kinds of decisions, or even provide advice about them?' [Response categories: YES, NO]
Decision-making items (Questions D2–D3)	Individuals who responded 'YES' to the general decision-making participation filter question, were then asked the following:

'Think of your specific place of work. If the organization for which you work has more than one branch, plant or store, think of the specific location where you work. I will ask you about decisions which might affect your workplace. For each, tell me if you are personally involved in this decision, including providing advice on it.'

Respondents were then asked about the following specific types of decisions:
(a) decisions to increase or decrease the total number of people employed in the place where you work.
(b) policy decisions to significantly change the products, programs or service delivered by the organization.
(c) decisions to change the policy concerning the routine pace of work or the amount of work performed in your workplace as a whole or some major part of it.
(d) policy decisions to significantly change the basic methods or procedures of work used in a major part of the workplace.
(e) decisions concerning the budget at the place where you work.
(f) [if YES to budget decisions] decisions concerning the overall size of the budget.

Raw variables (Question numbers from US survey)	Content
	(g) general policy decisions about the distribution of funds within the overall budget.
	(h) any other kinds of decisions important for the workplace as a whole [if YES, these are listed].
	For those types of decision in which the respondent indicated participation, they were then asked to indicate in which of the following ways they usually participated in making the decision:
	(1) make the decision on your own authority;
	(2) participate as a voting member of a group which makes the decision;
	(3) make the decision subject to approval;
	(4) provide advice to the person who actually makes the decision.

3. Supervision

Supervisor filter (Question C1)	'As an official part of your main job, do you supervise the work of other employees or tell other employees what work to do.' [Response categories: YES, NO]
Number of subordinates (Question C2)	Respondents who said that they were supervisors, were then asked how many people they directly supervised.
Subordinates' supervisory status Question C2b)	Supervisors were then asked if any of their subordinates had subordinates under them.
Subordinates' job (Question C2a)	If the supervisory respondent stated that they had only one subordinate, they were asked what that subordinate's main activities were. The purpose of this was to be able to identify people who supervised a single clerical employee.
Task authority items (Question C3)	Supervisors were asked to indicate whether or not they were directly responsible for any of the following:
	(a) deciding the specific tasks or work assignments performed by your subordinates.
	(b) deciding what procedures, tools, or materials your subordinates use in doing their work.
	(c) deciding how fast your subordinates work, how long they work or how much work they have to get done.
	[Response categories for each of these: YES, NO].
Sanctioning authority items (Questions C4–C6)	Supervisors were asked if they had any influence over a number of possible sanctions that could be imposed on subordinates. If they said they did have any influence on

TABLE II.2 *(continued)* *Appendix II* 307

Raw variables (Question numbers from US survey)	Content
	a given sanction, they were then asked whether they or someone higher up in the organization had the greatest influence. The sanctions were:

(a) granting a pay raise or promotion to a subordinate.
(b) preventing a subordinate from getting a pay raise or promotion because of poor work or misbehaviour.
(c) firing or temporarily suspending a subordinate.
(d) issuing a formal warning to a subordinate.

4. Formal hierarchical position

Formal position in managerial hierarchy (Question D4)	All wage earners, whether or not they indicated that they participated in policy decision-making or were supervisors, were asked the following: 'Which of the following best describes the position which you hold within your business or organization? Would it be a managerial position, a supervisory position, or a non-management position? Respondents who indicated that it was a 'managerial position' were then asked: 'Would that be a top, upper, middle or lower managerial position?'

5. Autonomy

Autonomy filter (Question B1)	All wage-earners were asked the following: 'Is yours a job in which you *are required* to design important aspects of your own work and to put your ideas into practice. *Or* is yours a job in which you are *not required* to design important aspects of your work or to put your ideas into practice, except perhaps in minor details?'
Degree of autonomy (Question B2)	Respodents who stated that they were required to design their own work, were then asked 'Could you give me an example of how you design your work and put your ideas into practice?' and a verbatim response was recorded. These responses were then coded into the following categories:

1 = high autonomy
2 = probably high autonomy
3 = intermediate autonomy
4 = probably intermediate autonomy
5 = low autonomy
6 = no autonomy (i.e. a negative resonse on the initial filter question, B1)

[Definitions of these categories are given in Table II.4]

formal managerial hierarchy. Table II.3 indicates the details of how these clusters were constructed and aggregated.

Decision-making. In constructing the decision-making scale, several strategic choices had to be made: should we differentiate among the *kinds* of policy decisions a person might make? For example, participation in budgetary decisions or decisions about what to produce could be seen as more central to the problem of organization assets than participation in decisions about the pace of work. Should we differentiate individuals on the basis of the *number* of different kinds of decisions in which they participate? Should the *form* of participation enter into the construction of the variable? Making a decision on one's own authority could be viewed as involving 'more' control over organization assets than participating in a decision as a voting member of a group. In the present analysis, I opted for the solution that was conceptually the simplest to these issues: all of the policy decisions in the list in table II.2 were considered equal; no distinction was made on the basis of how many kinds of decisions an individual participated in; the only distinction in forms of participation was between people who only provide advice and people who are directly involved in making the decision itself. The result is the three-category decision-making participation typology in table II.3: decision-makers, advisors, non-decision-makers. While in future work it would certainly be useful to add refinements into this simple aggregation, it seemed desirable to begin the analysis with a less complex set of distinctions.

Authority. The authority questions posed many of the same problems as the decision-making questions. In particular, there were three interconnected issues which had to be resolved. First, we asked supervisors a series of questions about the kinds of sanctions they could impose on subordinates. In constructing the authority variable, therefore, we had to decide whether to differentiate supervisors on the basis of the *number* of different kinds of sanctions they could impose, the specific *form* of the sanctions available to them, the relationship between their ability to impose sanctions and their superiors' ability so to do. Second, we asked supervisors about the kinds of tasks of their subordinates for which they were responsible. Should we distinguish individuals on the basis of the number and kinds of tasks for which they had supervisory responsibilites? Finally, in combining 'sanctioning authority' and 'task authority', do we want to distinguish individuals who are

TABLE II.3
Variable constructions for organization assets

1. Decision-making

Input variables		*Constructed variable*
Decision-making filter	*Individual decision-making items*	*Decision-making participation typology*
NO	x[a]	1. Non-decision-maker
YES	Provides advice on decision but directly participates in none	2. Advisor
YES	Participates directly in making any one of the decision making items	3. Decision-maker

2. Authority

Input variables				*Constructed variable*
Supervision filter	*Has only one clerical subordinate who does not have any subordinates*	*Task authority items*	*Sanction authority items*	*Authority typology*
NO	x[a]	x	x	1. Non-supervisor
YES	YES	x	x	1. Non-supervisor
YES	NO	NO	NO	2. Nominal supervisor
YES	NO	YES	NO	3. Task supervisor
YES	NO	x	YES	4. Sanction supervisor

TABLE II.3 (*continued*)

3. Managerial location typology

Input variables			*Constructed variable*
Decision-making typology	*Authority typology*	*Manager or supervisor in formal organization hierarchy*	*Managerial location typology*
3	3 or 4	YES	1. Manager on all criteria
3	3 or 4	NO	2. Manager not in formal hierarch
3	1 or 2	YES	3. Non-supervisory manager
3	1 or 2	NO	4. Non-supervisory decision-mak not in formal hierarchy
2	3 or 4	YES	5. Advisor-manager on all criteria
2	3 or 4	NO	6. Advisor not in hierarchy
2	1 or 2	YES	7. Non-supervisory advisor
2	1 or 2	NO	8. Non-supervisory advisor not in formal hierarchy
1	4	YES	9. Sanctioning supervisor
1	3	YES	10. Task supervisor
1	2	YES	11. Nominal supervisor in hierarchy
1	4	NO	12. Sanctioning supervisor not in formal hierarchy
1	3	NO	13. Task supervisor not in hierarchy
1	1	YES	14. No subordinates but in hierarchy
1	1 or 2	NO	15. Non-supervisor/non-manager on all criteria

4. Organization assets

Managerial location typology	*Organization asset typology*
1–3, 5–7	1. Manager
9–12	2. Supervisor
4, 8, 13–15	3. Non-management

[a]x = criterion inapplicable

nvolved in both of these kinds of authority from individuals nvolved in only one or the other?

As in the case of the decision-making variables, I opted for fairly imple solutions to these issues. For sanctioning authority, the only listinction made is between supervisors who can impose at least one kind of sanction and those who cannot impose any. If a super-visor can only issue formal warnings, this is not considered as being able to impose a real sanction. No distinction was made between supervisors who say that their superiors have more influence than they do on such sanctions and supervisors who say that they have the greatest influence. For task authority, no distinctions were made on the basis of the number and kind of tasks. In the aggrega-tion of the two kinds of authority, no distinction was made be-tween individuals with both kinds of authority and those who reported only sanctioning authority. In effect I was assuming that all people with sanctioning authority would have some kind of task responsibilities, even if our survey questionnaire failed to measure them. Respondents with task authority but no sanctioning author-ity, however, were distinguished from those with sanctioning authority. The result of these combinations is the four-category authority typology indicated in table II.3: sanctioning supervisors, task supervisors, nominal supervisors and non-supervisors.[1]

There is one additional wrinkle in the construction of the authority variable. There are work settings in which certain indi-viduals receive 'orders' from many other employees without really being supervised by them. A typical example is a typist in a typing pool who may receive things to type from many people but be supervised by a clerical supervisor of the pool itself. In such situa-tions we do *not* want the people who give the typing to the typist to say that they are supervisors. In effect, we wanted to eliminate from the supervisor category individuals who had only one subor-dinate who was a clerical employee without any subordinates him-self or herself. There were twenty-four such individuals in the US sample.

Formal Hierarchy. Initially we included the formal hierarchy ques-tion in the survey as a kind of methodological check on the decision-making and supervision questions. The plan was not to use it directly in building the class typology, but rather as a way of testing the validity of the other questions. In the end, however, it seemed appropriate to use this variable as an additional 'indicator' of the respondents' location within the managerial structure. For purposes of the construction of the class typology, this question was collapsed into a dichotomy: manager-supervisors versus non-management.

Managerial-Location Typology. From a strictly *a priori* conceptual point of view, the three constructed variables that served as inputs to this typology—decision-making, authority and hierarchy—should be ordered as a kind of 'Guttman Scale'. That is: everyone who is a decision-maker should have authority and be in the hierarchy; everyone who has authority, but is not a decision-maker should also be in the hierarchy; and the only people in the hierarchy who are not decision-makers and who do not have authority should be nominal supervisors. The formal hierarchy variable, then, should in principle be redundant, and there should be perfect consistency between the decision-making and authority variables.

As anyone with experience in survey data analysis would have guessed, the data were not so neat. There were respondents who appeared to be centrally involved in many kinds of decision-making who said that they did not have any authority over subordinates, and some who even said that they occupied non-management positions in the formal hierarchy; there were people who said that they were upper managers in the formal hierarchy but who were involved in no policy decisions; there were people who could impose severe sanctions on subordinates who claimed not to occupy a position in the managerial-supervisory hierarchy; and so on. To be sure, the large majority of respondents had consistent responses as expected, but many inconsistencies occurred in the data.

Such inconsistencies are the results of two kinds of problems. First there are 'measurement problems' of various sorts: people misunderstand the questions, interviewers write down the wrong response, the question is badly worded so that it misses some important alternative, etc. Secondly, there are in fact real situations in the world that do not fit into the conceptual categories embedded in the survey. In some work settings, for example, there may have developed the kind of collaboration of managers and workers such that workers legitimately respond that they are directly involved in certain kinds of decision-making without having authority or being in the hierarchy. This could be the kind of informal co-operation that is sometimes found in small shops and factories, or the more formal 'co-determination' that is being experimented with in certain corporations.

It is an important, and often very productive, empirical task to explore in some depth these 'inconsistent' combinations of criteria with an eye to distinguishing the measurement problems from the substantive complexities. In the present analysis, however, I have not engaged in such a task. I have thus used the formal hierarchy variable as a way of 'correcting' anomalies in the combination of the decision-making and authority variables. For example, a respondent who says that they participated directly in policy decisions (a decision-maker on the decision-making variable), but who was a nominal supervisor or non-supervisor on the authority variable, would still be classified as a manager if they were in the managerial-supervisory hierarchy on the formal hierarchy variable.

Organization Assets. The final task was to collapse the managerial-location typology into a simple trichotomy to be used in the class structure matrix. Where should the lines of demarcation be drawn in this collapsed variable? Should task supervisors who are not in the formal hierarchy be considered 'supervisors'? Should decision-makers who are not in the hierarchy and who do not have subordinates be considered managers? Where should advisor-managers be placed? These decisions, it must be emphasized again, are not inconsequential—the pattern of results are potentially affected by them.

My solution to these issues was to aggregate the categories in the managerial-location typology in such a way that I would have considerable confidence that both the manager location and the non-management location were internally homogeneous. The intermediate category—supervisors—is thus a combination of respondents who appear to genuinely have control over marginal levels of organization assets, and respondents for whom there are likely to be problems of measurement error. The allocation decisions are indicated in table II.3.

1.2 SKILL/CREDENTIAL ASSETS

The aggregation problem was less complex for skill assets than for organization assets, although as we discussed in chapter four, the conceptual problems are perhaps more difficult. In principle, skill/credential assets should be measured by the incumbency in jobs which require scarce skills, particularly credentialled skills.[2] In practice, at least with the data which we used in this project, the level of detail in occupational descriptions and coding was insufficient to unambiguously define the credentialled character of jobs. As a result I have deployed two other criteria in combination with occupational titles to define skill assets: formal educational credentials and, more problematically, job autonomy. In both cases these criteria are invoked when the occupational categories are too broad or diffuse to give us a satisfactory basis for judging the skill/credential assets involved. The particular way in which these additional criteria are combined with occupational titles is presented in table 5.3.

The coding of occupational title and educational credentials are entirely conventional and straightforward and do not require any specific commentary here. Some discussion of the coding of 'autonomy', however, is necessary.

Job Autonomy. The rationale for using job autonomy as a criterion for *skill* assets is that for those occupational titles, such as sales or clerical jobs, which are particularly diffuse in the real skill content of the job, the degree of conceptual autonomy in the job is likely to be a good indicator of the skill assets attached to the job. The argument is not that autonomy as such is an asset, but that it may be a good indirect indicator of such assets in what would otherwise be an ambiguous situation. It should be noted that in the present analysis, the autonomy criterion is used only to distinguish marginal skill assets from fully uncredentialled positions; it is not a criterion for defining expert positions at all.

The basic strategy for operationalizing job autonomy is as follows. All wage-earning respondents were first asked the general filter question about conceptual autonomy within work indicated in table II.2.[3] This filter question enabled us to identify those respondents who *claimed* to have conceptual autonomy within work. Our assumption—which is certainly open to question—was that everyone who indeed really had such autonomy would also subjectively think they had it, but that some people who lacked conceptual autonomy would claim to have it as well. We assumed, in other words, that we faced a problem of 'false positives', but not 'false negatives'.[4] The task, then, was to eliminate these false positives, these 'inflated' assessments of conceptual autonomy.

This task of eliminating exaggerated claims to autonomy was accomplished by asking respondents to give an example of how they designed their own work and put their ideas into practice on the job. We then coded these examples on a scale indicating the degree of conceptual autonomy they suggested.[5] The coding of examples into this scale involved two steps: first, we made the best guess we could of the 'level' of conceptual autonomy involved in the example—high, medium or low (to be defined below). Then we indicated how confident we were in that guess. The confidence code was not meant to be an intermediate code between two levels (although in practice it sometimes functioned in that way), but rather an indication of how adequate we felt the information to be in making our judgement. For the purposes of the present analysis, all respondents who scored medium or high levels of autonomy regardless of the level of confidence in the coding were considered incumbents of autonomous jobs.

Given this coding strategy, the problem was to develop a set of coding rules for distinguishing high, medium and low autonomy that were sufficiently clear and comprehensive that we could attain acceptably high reliability in the coding of the examples. Table II.4 indicates the essential definitions we developed for these levels of autonomy. In addition, coders were given more detailed instructions about how these general definitions applied to specific occupational settings.[6]

Once we elaborated these detailed coding instructions, we had three people code all of the examples: two coders who had some theoretical knowledge of the objectives of the coding and one who was 'naive'. As it turned out, the naive coder agreed with the sophisticated coders as frequently as they agreed with each other. In terms of overall reliability, there was an average complete agreement between pairs of coders in 80.1 per cent of the examples, a discrepancy of only 1 point in 18.4 per cent of the cases and a discrepancy of two or more points in a further 1.5 per cent. In 91.1 per cent of the cases there was either complete agreement or only disagreement on the degree of certainty in the code (rather than the 'level' of autonomy). Where disagreements occurred, the final codes adopted were the result of a consensus among the coders after a case-by-case discussion of the disagreements.

There are many objections that can be raised against this autonomy variable. However, in the present context I do not think that these are likely to undermine the usefulness of the variable, given that it enters the construction of the skill-asset variable in such a narrow way. The autonomy variable effects the skill—asset allocations only for those sales and clerical employees with at least a college education in the United States and a high-school education in Sweden.

1.3 CAPITAL ASSETS

In a more complex analysis than the one pursued in this book it would be desirable to distinguish between people who were

TABLE II.4

Definitions of autonomy coding categories

Autonomy code for respondent's examples of autonomy	Interpretation
1 High	Design/plan significant aspects of the *final product or service*, not just procedures used in one's own work.
	OR
	Problem-solving with non-routine solutions is a central aspect of the work, not just an occasional event.
2 Probably high	Same as 1, only less certain about the coding.
3 Medium	Design/plan most of the procedures used in one's work, but only have influence on very limited aspects of the final product or service.
	OR
	Problem-solving is a regular aspect of work, but generally of a routinized character *or* not a central activity in one' work.
4 Probably medium	Same as 3, only less certain about the coding.
5 Low	Design or plan *at most* a limited aspect of procedures with virtually no influence over aspects of the final product or service.
	OR
	Problem-solving is at most an occasional/marginal aspect of work.
6 None	Very marginal involvement with designing procedures. Most work activities highly routinized with rare problem-solving.

capitalist exploiters (i.e. exploiters on the basis of sheer ownership of capital) and individuals who occupied capitalist class location (i.e. were employers within the capital–labour relation). This would imply, for example, looking at the capital ownership of managerial wage-earners as well as including pure rentier capitalists in the analysis.

In the present investigation we have ignored these added complexities. Exploitation based on capital assets is therefore directly linked to the capital–labour social relation. The central criteria for the analysis are therefore: self-employment and number of employees. These criteria are used to distinguish among four categories: wage-labourers, petty bourgeois (self-employed with no more than one employee), small employers (two to nine employees), and capitalists (ten or more employees). The dividing line between capitalists and small employers is obviously an arbitrary one, and in any event the capitalists in the sample are themselves generally quite small capitalists.

There is one final nuance in the construction of this dimension of the class structure matrix. There are individuals who are wage earners in a formal sense, but who nevertheless are genuine owners of the business in which they work, either as partners or, sometimes, even as sole owners. Through incorporation a capitalist can become an employee of his or her own business. Such people should be considered self-employed in terms of the theoretical categories of this study, and we therefore asked a series of questions specifically designed to identify such positions. In the US survey this resulted in a re-classification of twelve individuals (about one per cent of the wage-earners in the sample).

2 Poulantzas's Class Typology

Poulantzas's class typology is built around the intersection of three basic criteria: productive–unproductive labour, manual–mental labour, and supervision. Of these, the most problematic is the first. Particularly in terms of occupations, there are many cases where it is quite ambiguous whether or not a particular position should be considered productive or unproductive in Poulantzas's terms. In classifying occupations in terms of the productive–unproductive-labour distinction in table II.5, therefore, I have explicitly introduced an 'ambiguously productive category. In constructing an unproductive labour variable for operationalizing Poulantzas's concept of class the ambiguous category has been combined with the productive occupations. In the actual data analysis I experimented with a variety of operational choices, and none of the results are substantively affected.

3 Industrial Sector Classification System

Table II.6 indicates the basic classification system used in the analyses involving industrial sectors. The central novelty of this

TABLE II.5

Productive and unproductive labour categories used in constructing Poulantzas's definition of the working Class

Productive occupants	Architects, engineers (except sales engineers), foresters and conservationists, engineering and science technicians, tool programmers, designers, editors and reporters, craftsmen, operatives, transport equipment operators, labourers (except gardeners), farmers and farm labourers, cooks.
Ambiguous occupations	Computer specialists, mathematical specialists, life and physical scientists, veterinarians, pilots, air traffic controllers, physicians, unspecified technicians, unspecified research workers, ship pilots, foremen, farm foremen, dishwashers, food counter and fountain workers.
Unproductive occupations	Accountants, sales engineers, farm management advisors, home management advisors, lawyers and judges, personnel and labour relations workers, physicians, dentists and related practitioners, nurses and therapists, religious workers, social scientists, social workers, teachers, embalmers, radio operators, vocational counsellors, writers, artists and entertainers, managers and administrators, sales workers, clerical and kindred workers, armed forces, parking attendants, taxicab drivers and chauffeurs, garbage collectors, unpaid family workers, cleaning service workers, waiters, health service workers, personal service workers, protective service workers, private household workers.
Productive economic sector	Agriculture, mining, construction, manufacturing, transportation of goods (i.e. all transportation except taxis and buses), utilities (if private sector).
Unproductive economic sector	State employment, transportation of people, wholesale and retail sales, finance, business services, personal services, entertainment and recreation, public administration.

Unproductive labour = Unproductive occupation *or* unproductive sector
Productive labour   = Productive *or* ambiguous occupation *and* productive sector

classification system, based on the work of Joachim Singelmann, is that it differentiates the amorphous 'service sector' of most analyses into several distinct sectors based on their functional role in the economic system.[7]

TABLE II.6
Industrial classification categories

Industrial sector	Detailed industries included in the sector
1. Extractive	Agriculture, mining, fishing.
2. Transformative	Construction, food processing, textiles, metal, machinery, chemical, miscellaneous manufacturing, utilities.
3. Distributive services	Transportation, communication, wholesale, retail.
4. Business services	Banking, insurance, real estate, engineering, accounting, miscellaneous business services.
5. Personal services	Domestic services, hotels, eating and drinking, repair, laundry, barber and beauty shops, entertainment, miscellaneous personal services.
6. Social and political services	Legal services, medical services, hospitals, education, welfare, non-profit, postal services, government, miscellaneous social services.

4 Class Biography Variables

Table II.7 presents the basic variable constructions for the class biography variables used in the analysis of class consciousness in chapter seven. The basic task of these variable constructions was to create one variable tapping salient feature of the individual's current class context other than their actual class location, and another variable tapping feautre of their class trajectories.

The working class networks variable is composed of two elements. The first is a measure of the working-class density of the respondent's social networks, based on data concerning the class location of friends and spouse (if the respondent had a spouse in the labour force); the second is defined by the class location of the respondent's second job, if any—about 15 per cent of the US sample have second jobs. These two variables are combined as indicated in the matrix in table II.7.4. In this constructed variable, the social network variable has considerably more weight than the second job variable, on the assumption that social ties are likely to reflect a

TABLE II.7
Construction of class biography variables

1. Class variable for: Friends[a], spouse, parent[b], second job[c]

Input variables   *Constructed variable*

Occupation		Management or supervisor position		Self-employed	Class
Professional, technical, managerial	*or*	YES	*or*	YES	Non-working class
Other occupations	*and*	NO	*and*	NO	Working class

[a]Respondents were asked a series of questions about the jobs of the three friends or relatives they felt personally closest to. If a friend/relative was not currently working, the question was asked about their prior job. If this friend had never worked, but was married, the question was asked about their spouse.

[b]The question about parent's job was asked for the person who the respondent said 'provided most of the financial support in your family while you were growing up.' Usually this was the father. The job information was not pegged to a particular age, but to the main occupation of the parent during the period while the respondent was growing up.

[c]For the respondent's second job, the question about occupying a management or supervisor position was not asked and thus does not enter into the construction of the second job class variable.

2. Social network links to the working class

Class of friends = 0 if none are workers, 1 if one is a worker, 2 if two are workers 3 if all three are workers

Class of spouse = 1 if spouse is a worker, 0 for all other cases (spouse is not a worker, spouse does not work or does not have a spouse)

$$\% \text{ working class links} = \frac{[\text{Class of friends} + \text{class of spouse}]}{\text{Number of possible links}}$$

Working class links scale:

    0 if % links = 0
    1 if % links = 1–49%
    2 if % links = 50%
    3 if % links = 51–99%
    4 if % links = 100%

TABLE II.7 (*continued*)

3. Prior working class job history

Input variables		Constructed variable
Ever self-employed?[a]	Ever a supervisor?[b]	Working class past jobs
NO	NO	1. Always a worker
NO	YES	2. Supervisor in the past
YES	NO or YES	3. Self-employed in the past

[a]People who are *currently* self-employed were not asked whether they had been self-employed in any prior job (because of an error in questionnaire design). I have therefore assumed that the answer is 'YES' for currently self-employed respondents.
[b]People who are *currently* supervisors or who are currently self-employed were not asked whether they had held a supervisory position on a prior job (because of an error in questionnaire design). I have therefore assumed that the answer is 'YES' for respondents who are currently classified as supervisors.

4. Working class networks

Entries in the cells of the matrix are values of the constructed variable, working class networks

Working class links scale

		4	3	2	1	0
	Working class job	10	9	7	5	3
Class of second job	No second job	10	8	6	4	2
	Non-working class job	8	7	5	3	1

TABLE II.7 (*continued*)

5. Working class trajectory

> Entries in the cells of the matrix are values of the constructed variable, working class trajectory

Working class past jobs

		Always a worker	Have been a supervisor	Have been self-employed
Class origin	Working class	6	4	2
	Not working class	5	3	1

more pervasive and long term property of a person's class context than a second job.

The working-class-trajectory variable is also composed of two elements: one indicating the respondent's class origins, the other indicating whether or not the respondent has ever been self-employed or a supervisor. There was an error in the questionnaire design which affects this second dimension of the variable. Ideally we would have liked to know for every respondent, regardless of their present class location, whether or not they had been self-employed or a supervisor on some past job. This would have enabled us rigorously to distinguish the effects of one's present location from past trajectory. Unfortunately, we only asked employees the past self-employment question, and non-supervisory employees the past supervision question. I do not think that this seriously compromises the usefulness of the working class trajectory variable, but it does make it a less rigorous measure than one would have liked.

Notes

1. 'Nominal supervisors' are, in principle, invididuals who are channels of communication from above but who have no real authority over subordinates, i.e. they

cannot either impose sanctions on them or order them to do anything. In the questionnaire, however, there will be a certain amount of measurement error in the distinction between nominal supervisors and task supervisors, since we did not ask supervisors a completely comprehensive list of tasks.

2. Since a skill–credential only becomes the basis for exploitation when it is productively deployed, the sheer possession of a credential is insufficient to define the location of a person within the relations of exploitation. A Ph.D. in chemistry working on an assembly line is not a credential exploiter.

3. Self-employed respondents were not asked this question on the United States and Swedish surveys. It would have been useful to have asked this question of everyone, but we did not. In some of the subsequent national surveys the autonomy questions were asked of all respondents.

4. The Canadian survey asked a series of follow-up questions to people who said that they did not have conceptual autonomy on the filter question in order to check for false negatives. When these data are analysed we will be able to see how inaccurate our assumption was.

5. Where the information in the example was too thin for coding we looked at the general job descriptions provided by respondents in response to the survey question about their occupation. In many cases it was possible to use this information to code autonomy when the autonomy examples were too vague or unclear.

6. In some cases the examples were simply too vague to provide us with sufficient information to make the required distinctions. This was particularly the case for school teachers and policemen. While this may certainly be open to criticism, in these two cases we relied on our general knowledge of the occupational conditions of such jobs and assigned all the respondents in that occupation who claimed to have conceptual autonomy 'high' autonomy scores. The full details of these coding instructions can be found in the public use codebook for the *Comparative Study of Class Structure and Class Consciousness*.

7. See Joachim Singelman, *From Agriculture to Services*, Beverley Hills 1978.

Appendix III

Full Data for Selected Tables

TABLE III.1

Distribution of classes within sex categories, United States and Sweden

Class categories	Distribution of sexes within classes				Distribution of classes within sexes			
	United States		Sweden		United States		Sweden	
	Men	Women	Men	Women	Men	Women	Men	Women
1. Capitalists	79.3	20.7	100.0	0.0	2.7	0.8	1.2	0.0
2. Small employers	66.7	33.3	80.7	19.3	7.4	4.4	7.0	2.1
3. Petty bourgeois	50.3	49.7	75.7	24.3	6.4	7.5	7.3	3.0
4. Expert manager	75.0	25.0	87.4	12.6	5.4	2.1	6.8	1.3
5. Expert supervisor	70.3	29.7	42.9	57.1	4.8	2.4	2.9	4.9
6. Expert non-manager	47.7	52.3	56.1	43.9	3.0	3.9	6.8	6.8
7. Semi-credentialled manager	77.4	22.6	84.2	15.8	8.8	3.0	6.1	1.4
8. Semi-credentialled supervisor	75.6	24.4	76.7	23.3	9.5	3.6	4.4	1.7
9. Semi-credentialled worker	73.6	26.4	63.4	36.5	16.6	7.1	20.2	14.8
10. Uncredentialled manager	31.0	69.0	51.2	48.8	1.3	3.5	30.9	59.6
11. Uncredentialled supervisor	41.4	58.6	76.1	23.9	5.2	8.8	4.2	1.7
12. Proletarian	39.5	60.5	39.8	60.2	29.0	52.8	30.9	59.6
Totals	54.3	45.7	56.0	44.0				
Weighted N	807	680	660	519				

Class distribution within age-sex categories

1. United States

Age categories

		<21	21–25	26–35	36–45	46–55	56–65	>65
1. Capitalists	Men	0.0	0.0	1.5	3.3	4.4	3.2	13.5
	Women	1.6	1.1	0.4	2.0	0.0	0.0	1.4
2. Small employers	Men	4.8	4.8	6.3	8.5	9.2	9.7	9.6
	Women	0.0	2.1	5.2	7.7	4.1	3.6	3.5
3. Petty bourgeois	Men	0.0	4.6	8.5	3.8	5.0	13.8	8.8
	Women	4.5	3.2	5.5	6.1	8.2	8.7	24.5
4. Expert manager	Men	0.0	4.1	6.3	6.6	5.6	6.0	5.0
	Women	0.0	2.3	3.6	1.5	2.4	2.1	0.0
5. Expert supervisor	Men	1.4	3.4	5.9	7.9	4.1	2.8	1.8
	Women	2.2	1.1	2.7	4.3	3.4	0.6	0.0
6. Expert non-manager	Men	3.1	4.9	4.5	2.6	0.6	1.5	1.8
	Women	5.8	4.0	3.5	4.3	4.0	3.7	2.8
7. Semi-credentialled manager	Men	7.2	5.5	10.0	13.1	10.0	4.0	3.2
	Women	2.7	3.9	3.6	3.7	1.0	3.9	1.4
8. Semi-credentialled supervisor	Men	7.1	12.5	8.1	11.6	11.5	6.5	1.5
	Women	0.0	4.8	5.5	3.5	2.9	1.7	3.4
9. Semi-credentialled worker	Men	29.6	14.3	20.7	14.8	15.0	8.5	9.1
	Women	0.0	12.8	9.6	5.7	4.2	6.3	5.5
10. Uncredentialled manager	Men	1.5	3.4	1.1	0.7	0.5	0.0	4.1
	Women	0.0	6.5	3.3	3.3	2.7	0.0	9.7
11. Uncredentialled supervisor	Men	8.6	7.1	5.7	3.1	3.6	7.6	0.0
	Women	14.3	6.8	8.6	6.9	13.5	10.3	0.0
12. Proletarian	Men	36.7	35.3	21.4	23.9	30.5	36.5	41.8
	Women	69.0	51.5	48.5	51.0	53.6	59.1	47.9
Weighted N	Men	58	123	224	151	135	82	34
	Women	45	95	164	128	116	81	51

TABLE III.2 (continued)

II. Sweden

		<21	21–25	26–35	36–45	46–55	56–65
1. Capitalists	Men	0.0	0.0	1.1	0.7	3.2	1.1
	Women	0.0	0.0	0.0	0.0	0.0	0.0
2. Small employers	Men	2.8	3.9	5.1	11.9	6.3	7.6
	Women	0.0	0.0	0.8	5.6	1.9	2.0
3. Petty bourgeois	Men	2.8	3.9	4.0	7.3	11.9	12.0
	Women	0.0	3.6	1.6	3.7	2.9	5.9
4. Expert manager	Men	0.0	0.0	8.5	8.6	9.5	5.4
	Women	0.0	0.0	1.6	1.9	1.0	0.0
5. Expert supervisor	Men	0.0	3.9	2.3	2.6	6.3	0.0
	Women	0.0	1.8	11.0	3.7	3.9	0.0
6. Expert non-manager	Men	0.0	11.7	10.2	6.0	3.2	5.4
	Women	11.5	3.6	10.2	2.8	4.8	11.8
7. Semi-credentialled manager	Men	0.0	5.2	6.8	8.6	5.6	4.3
	Women	0.0	1.8	3.2	0.0	0.9	1.8
8. Semi-credentialled supervisor	Men	2.8	1.3	6.3	4.0	4.8	4.3
	Women	0.0	0.0	0.8	1.9	3.9	2.0
9. Semi-credentialled worker	Men	27.8	20.8	23.9	19.9	17.5	14.1
	Women	11.5	10.7	21.2	21.4	8.7	3.9
10. Uncredentialled manager	Men	2.8	2.6	1.7	2.0	3.2	3.9
	Women	3.8	3.6	2.4	2.8	2.9	2.2
11. Uncredentialled supervisor	Men	0.0	6.5	2.8	3.3	1.6	12.0
	Women	0.0	0.0	1.6	1.9	2.9	2.0
12. Proletarian	Men	61.1	40.3	27.3	25.2	27.0	31.5
	Women	73.1	75.0	45.7	54.3	66.4	68.8
Weighted N	Men	36	77	176	151	126	92
	Women	29	62	140	118	114	56

TABLE III.3

Class distributions within race-sex categories, United States

	Race-sex categories						
	White men	White women	White total	Black men	Black women	Black total
1. Capitalists	2.9	0.8	2.0	0.0	0.0	0.0
2. Small employers	8.2	4.9	6.7	0.0	1.4	0.7
3. Petty bourgeois	6.4	8.9	7.5	3.7	0.0	1.7
4. Expert manager	5.7	2.0	4.0	1.4	0.0	0.7
5. Expert supervisor	4.4	2.4	3.5	2.4	2.9	2.7
6. Expert non-manager	3.0	4.4	3.6	4.0	2.6	3.2
7. Semi-credentialled manager	9.8	4.0	7.2	5.5	0.0	2.6
8. Semi-credentialled supervisor	9.2	3.8	6.8	8.2	1.8	4.8
9. Semi-credentialled worker	16.7	6.9	12.3	21.4	9.7	15.3
10. Uncredentialled manager	1.5	3.5	2.4	1.0	6.3	3.8
11. Uncredentialled supervisor	4.7	8.7	6.5	4.5	6.9	5.8
12. Proletarian	27.4	49.7	37.3	47.8	68.5	58.7
Weighted N	648	517	1165	71	78	149

TABLE III.4

Distribution of class within economic sectors, United States and Sweden

Classes	Economic sector[a]					
	Extractive	Transformative	Distributive services	Business services	Personal services	Social and political services
I. United States						
1. Capitalists	3.3	1.3	5.1	1.2	3.8	0.3
2. Small employers	27.9	4.6	8.7	7.0	10.7	1.4
3. Petty bourgeois	17.9	4.3	7.3	10.9	16.2	3.0
4. Expert manager	1.2	3.0	3.3	4.7	0.9	6.8
5. Expert supervisor	2.5	3.0	1.9	6.0	1.5	5.9
6. Expert non-manager	0.0	2.6	1.5	2.2	0.7	7.6
7. Semi-credentialled manager	0.0	6.9	7.8	5.9	3.8	6.8
8. Semi-credentialled supervisor	10.0	7.5	6.7	6.5	1.4	8.0
9. Semi-credentialled worker	8.3	14.3	6.7	4.2	7.1	17.1
10. Uncredentialled manager	3.7	0.6	1.3	2.2	6.7	3.0
11. Uncredentialled supervisor	2.3	6.8	8.3	10.1	6.7	5.3
12. Proletarian	22.8	45.1	41.5	39.0	40.4	34.8

TABLE III.4 (*continued*)

	Economic sector[a]					
	Extractive	*Transformative*	*Distributive services*	*Business services*	*Personal services*	*Social and political services*
II. Sweden						
1. Capitalists	0.0	1.5	1.0	1.2	3.8	0.3
2. Small employers	18.0	5.3	13.9	11.1	5.5	1.2
3. Petty bourgeois	36.2	4.9	5.2	8.6	9.6	0.2
4. Expert manager	0.0	3.6	1.9	16.7	2.8	5.8
5. Expert supervisor	0.0	2.1	0.0	0.0	0.0	8.1
6. Expert non-manager	1.6	4.7	3.1	11.7	4.3	11.0
7. Semi-credentialled manager	0.0	4.0	0.0	11.1	6.8	4.6
8. Semi-credentialled supervisor	0.0	3.8	1.0	3.1	2.7	3.7
9. Semi-credentialled worker	0.0	22.8	3.0	16.9	15.2	19.3
10. Uncredentialled manager	3.4	1.1	7.1	0.0	10.1	1.7
11. Uncredentialled supervisor	11.3	2.6	6.9	0.0	4.1	1.8
12. Proletarian	29.6	45.1	57.9	20.8	38.8	42.8

TABLE III.5
Class structure and the state in Sweden and the United States

| | Distribution of state-linked employment within classes | | | | | Distribution of classes within the state and private sectors | |
| | In private sector firms, estimate of percentage of business done with state | | | | State employees | Private | State |
	None	<10%	10–49%	>50%			
I. United States							
1–2. Employers	86.4	8.5	4.2	0.9	0.0	9.5	0.0
3. Petty bourgeois	91.9	6.9	0.6	0.6	0.0	8.3	0.0
4. Expert manager	25.5	30.5	7.5	4.9	31.7	3.3	7.0
5. Expert supervisor	36.1	38.0	0.9	6.6	18.4	3.6	3.9
6. Expert non-manager	32.3	21.7	3.1	4.1	38.7	2.6	7.6
7. Semi-credentialled manager	47.2	22.7	5.2	4.9	20.0	6.0	7.0
8. Semi-credentialled supervisor	45.7	25.0	3.5	1.6	24.3	6.2	9.4
9. Semi-credentialled worker	37.4	22.2	6.1	1.8	32.6	10.0	22.7
10. Uncredentialled manager	66.1	18.8	1.7	7.8	5.5	2.7	0.7
11. Uncredentialled supervisor	56.4	24.9	4.6	1.9	12.3	7.3	4.8
12. Proletarian	56.3	20.7	4.7	2.1	16.2	40.6	36.8
Totals	55.0	20.7	4.3	2.4	17.5		

[a] Percentages sum horizontally
[b] Percentages sum vertically

TABLE III 5 (*continued*)

	Distribution of state-linked employment within classes					Distribution of classes within the state and private sectors	
	In private sector firms, estimate of percentage of business done with state				*State employees*	*Private*	*State*
	None	*<10%*	*10–49%*	*>50%*			
II. Sweden							
1–2. Employers	90.6	6.3	1.5	1.5	0.0	9.4	0.0
3. Petty bourgeois	96.8	1.6	0.0	1.6	0.0	9.1	0.0
4. Expert manager	27.2	19.4	5.8	0.0	47.6	3.9	5.0
5. Expert supervisor	11.5	2.3	4.5	0.0	81.7	1.2	7.4
6. Expert non-manager	19.3	15.2	0.0	2.5	63.0	4.3	10.3
7. Semi-credentialled manager	25.5	27.4	4.2	0.0	42.9	3.9	4.2
8. Semi-credentialled supervisor	29.6	15.9	2.6	2.9	48.9	2.8	3.8
9. Semi-credentialled worker	38.0	14.2	0.5	0.5	46.9	16.2	20.1
10. Uncredentialled manager	61.1	6.8	0.0	0.0	32.1	2.9	1.9
11. Uncredentialled supervisor	46.5	11.1	0.0	0.0	42.4	3.1	3.2
12. Proletarian	45.3	11.8	0.2	0.6	42.0	43.2	44.0
Totals	44.5	12.2	0.9	0.8	41.6		

Bibliography

Aaronowitz, Stanley, *The Crisis of Historical Materialism*, New York, 1981.

Abraham, David, *The Collapse of the Weimar Republic*, Princeton, Princeton University Press, 1981.

Ahrne, Göran and Erik Olin Wright, 'Classes in the United States and Sweden: a comparison', *Acta Sociologica*, 26:3/4, 1983.

Albert, Michael and Robin Hahnel, *Marxism and Socialist Theory*, Boston, South End Press, 1981.

Althusser, Louis and Etienne Balibar, *Reading Capital*, London, New Left Books, 1970.

Aminzade, Ron, *Class, Politics and Early Industrial Capitalism*, Binghampton, S.U.N.Y. Press, 1981.

Anderson, Perry, *Lineages of the Absolutist State*, London, New Left Books, 1974.

Bailey, Anne, M. and Josep R. Llobera, *The Asiatic Mode of Production: Science and Politics*, London, Routledge & Kegan Paul, 1981.

Balbus, Issac, 'The Concept of Interest in Pluralist and Marxist Analysis', *Politics & Society*, February, 1971.

Balibar, Etienne, 'Basic Concepts of Historical Materialism', in Louis Althusser and Etienne Balibar, *Reading Capital*, London, New Left Books, 1970.

Becker, James, F., 'Class Structure and Conflict in the Managerial Phase, parts 1 and 2' *Science & Society*, vol. 37: 3 and 4, 1973 and 1974.

Benton, Ted, 'Objective Interests and the Sociology of Power', *Sociology*, vol. 15, No. 2, May, 1981.

Bertaux, Dabiel, *Destins personnels et structure de class*, Paris, Presses Universitaire de France, 1977.

Bowles, Sam, David Gordon and Thomas Weiskopf, *Beyond the Wasteland*, New York, Anchor, 1984.

Braverman, Harry, *Labor and Monopoly Capitalism*, New York, Monthly Review Press, 1974.

Brenner, Johanna and Maria Ramas, 'Rethinking Women's Oppression', *New Left Review*, Number 144, March–April, 1984.

Brenner, Robert, 'The Origins of Capitalist Development: a Critique of

Neo-Smithian Marxism', *New Left Review*, Number 104, July–August, 1977, pp. 25–93.

Browning, H. and J. Singelmann, *The Emergence of a Service Society*, National Technical Information Service, Springfield, Mo. 1975.

Burawoy, Michael, *Manufacturing Consent*, Chicago, University of Chicago Press, 1979.

Burawoy, Michael, *The Politics of Production*, London, New Left Books, 1985.

Cameron, J., 'The Expansion of the Public Economy', *American Political Science Review*, 1978, vol. 72.

Carchedi, G., *The Economic Identification of Social Classes*, London, Routledge & Kegan Paul, 1977.

Cohen, G. A., *Karl Marx's Theory of History: A defense*, Princeton, Princeton University Press, 1978.

Cohen, G. A., 'The Labor Theory of Value and the Concept of Exploitation', *Philosophy and Public Affairs*, 8, 1979.

Cohen, G. A., 'Reply to Elster', *Theory and Society*, vol. 11:3, July 1982.

Cohen, Jean, *Class and Civil Society*, Amherst, University of Massachusetts Press, 1982.

Cohen, Joshua and Joel Rogers, *On Democracy*, New York, Penguin Books, 1983.

Collins, R., *The Credential Society*: A Historical Sociology of Education and Stratification, Orlando, Florida, Academic Press, 1979.

Connolly, William, 'On Interests in Politics', *Politics & Society*, 2:4, 1972, pp. 459–77.

Crompton, Rosemary and John Gubbay, *Economy and Class Structure*, New York, St. Martin's Press, 1978.

Dahrendorf, Ralph, *Class and Class Conflict in Industrial Society*, Palo Alto, Stanford University Press, 1959.

Dobb, Maurice, *Studies in the Development of Capitalism*, Cambridge and New York, Cambridge University Press, 1963.

Edwards, Richard, *Contested Terrain*, New York, Basic Books, 1979.

Ehrenreich, Barbara and John Ehrenreich, 'The Professional-Managerial Class', *Radical America*, 11:2, 1971.

Elster, Jon, 'Marxism, Functionalism and Game Theory', *Theory and Society*, vol. 11:453–482, July 1982.

Elster, Jon, *Sour Grapes*, Cambridge, Cambridge University Press, 1983.

Elster, Jon, *Making Sense of Marx*, Cambridge, Cambridge University Press, 1985.

Esping-Anderson, Gösta, Roger Friedland and Erik Olin Wright, 'Modes of Class Struggle and the Capitalist State', *Kapitalistate*, Number 4, 1976.

Esping-Anderson, Gösta, *Politics Against Markets*, Princeton, Princeton University Press, 1985.

Freedman, Francesca, 'The Internal Structure of the Proletariat: a Marxist Analysis', *Socialist Revolution*, No. 26, 1975.

Geuss, Raymond, *The Idea of Critical Theory: Habermas and the Frankfurt School*, Cambridge, Cambridge University Press, 1981.

Giddens, Anthony, *The Class Structure of the Advanced Societies*, New York, Harper and Row, 1973.

Giddens, Anthony, 'Postcript' to *The Class Structure of the Advanced Societies*, second edition, New York, Harper and Row, 1979.

Giddens, Anthony, *A Contemporary Critique of Historical Materialism*, Berkeley, University of California Press, 1982.

Gough, Ian, *The Political Economy of the Welfare State*, London, 1979.

Gouldner, Alvin, *The Future of Intellectuals and the Rise of the New Class*, New York, The Seabury Press, 1979.

Groves, Robert, M. and Robert L. Kahn, *Surveys by Telephone*, Orlando, Academic Press, 1979.

Groves, Robert, M., 'An Empirical Comparison of two telephone sample designs', *Journal of Marketing Research*, 15, 1979, pp. 622–31.

Hartman, Heidi, 'The Family as the Locus of Gender, Class, and Political Struggle: the Example of Housework', *Signs*, vol. 6, no. 3, 1981.

Hindess, Barry and Paul Q. Hirst, *Pre-Capitalist Modes of Production*, London, Routledge & Kegan Paul, 1975.

Holloway, John and Sol Picciotto (eds), *State and Capital*, Austin, University of Texas Press, 1978.

Holmwood, J. M. and A. Stewart, 'The role of contradiction in Modern Theories of Social Stratification', *Sociology*, No. 17, May, 1983.

Institute for Labor Education and Research, *What's Wrong with the U.S. Economy?*, Boston, South End Press, 1982.

Jackman, Mary and Robert Jackman, *Class Awareness in the United States*, Berkeley, University of California Press, 1983.

Kitagawa, E., 'Components of a difference between two rates', *Journal of the American Statistical Association*, vol. 50, 1955, 1168–1174.

Konrad, George and Ivan Szelenyi, *Intellectuals on the Road to Class Power*, New York, Harcourt, Brace, Janovitch and World, 1979.

Landecker, W. S., 'Class Boundaries', *American Sociological Review*, vol. 25, 1960, pp. 868–877.

Lenski, Gerhard, *Power and Privilege: a theory of social stratification*, New York, McGraw-Hill, 1966.

Levine, Andrew and Erik Olin Wright, 'Rationality and Class Struggle'. *New Left Review*, Number 123, 1980, pp. 47–68.

Levine, Andrew, *Arguing for Socialism*, London, Routledge & Kegan Paul, 1984.

Lipset, Seymour, M., *Political Man*, Garden City, N.J., Anchor Books, 1963.

Lipset, Seymour, M., 'Social Stratification: Social Class', *International Encyclopedia of the Social Sciences*, D. L. Sills (ed), New York, Crowell, Collier and MacMillan, 1968, vol. 15: 296–316.

Livingstone, David, L., *Class and Class Consciousness in Advanced Capitalism*, unpublished manuscript, Ontario Institute for Studies in Education, Toronto, 1985.

Loren, Charles, *Classes in the United States*, Davis, California, Cardinal Publishers, 1977.

Lukács, Georg, *History and Class Consciousness*, Cambridge, Mass., M.I.T. Press, 1971, original edition, 1922.

Lukes, Steven, *Power: a radical view*, London, McMillan, 1974.

Mann, Michael, *Consciousness and Action among the Western Working Class*, London, McMillan, 1973.

Marshall, Gordon, 'Some remarks on the study of working class consciousness', *Politics & Society*, 12:3, 1983.

Marx, Karl, *Capital*, vol. III, New York, International Publishers, 1967.

Nicolaus, Martin, 'Proletariat and Middle Class in Marx', *Studies on the Left*, No. 7, 1967.

Noble, David, 'Social Choice in Machine Design', *Politics and Society*, 8:3–4, 1978.

Nozick, Robert, *Anarchy, State and Utopia*, New York, Basic Books, 1974.

Offe, Claus, 'Structural Problems of the Capitalist State: class rule and the political system', in C. von Beyme (ed), *German Political Studies*, vol. I, Russel Sage, 1974.

Offe, Claus and Helmut Wiesenthal, 'Two Logics of Collective Action', in Maurice Zeitlin (ed), *Political Power and Social Theory*, vol. I, Greenwhich, Connecticut, JAI Press, 1980.

Ollmann, Bertell, 'Toward Class Consciousness in the Working Class', *Politics & Society*, Fall, 1972.

Ossowski, Stanislaus, *Class Structure in the Social Consciousness*, London, Routledge & Kegan Paul, 1963.

Palmer, G. and A. Miller, *Industrial and Occupational Trends in Employment*, University of Pennsylvania, Wharton School, Industrial Research Department, Philadelphia, 1949.

Parkin, Frank, *Marxism and Class Theory: a bourgeois critique*, New York, Columbia University Press, 1979.

Politics & Society, Special Issue on John Roemer's Theory of Class and Exploitation, vol. 11:3, 1982.

Poulantzas, Nicos, *Political Power and Social Classes*, London, New Left Books, 1973.

Poulantzas, Nicos, *Classes in Contemporary Capitalism*, London, New Left Books, 1975.

Przeworski, Adam, 'From Proletariat into Class: the process of class formation from Karl Kautsky's *The Class Struggle* to Recent Debates', *Politics & Society*, 7:4, 1977.

Przeworski, Adam, 'The Material Bases of Consent: Economics and Politics in a Hegemonic System', in Maurice Zeitlin (ed), *Political Power and Social Theory*, vol. I, JAI Press, 1979.

Przeworski, Adam, 'Material interests, class compromise and the Transition to Socialism'. *Politics & Society*, 10:2, 1980.

Przeworski, Adam, 'Social Democracy as an Historical Phenomenon', *New Left Review*, Number 122, 1980.

Rawls, John, *A Theory of Justice*, Cambridge, Mass., Harvard University Press, 1971.

Roemer, John, *A General Theory of Exploitation and Class*, Cambridge, Mass., Harvard University Press, 1982.

Roemer, John, 'Should Marxists be Interested in Exploitation?', University of California, Davis, Department of Economics, Working Paper Number 221, 1983.

Shalev, Michael, 'The Social Democratic Model and Beyond: two generations of comparative research on the welfare state'. *Comparative Social Research*, vol. 6, 1984.

Shanin, Theodor, *The Late Marx and the Russian Road*, New York, Monthly Review Press, 1984.

Singelmann, Joachim, *From Agriculture to Services*, Beverly Hills, Sage Publications, 1977.

Siriani, Carmen, *Workers Control and Socialist Democracy*, London, New Left Books/Verso, 1982.

Skocpol, Theda, *States and Social Revolutions*, New York, Cambridge University Press, 1979.

Skocpol, Theda, 'Political Response to Capitalist Crisis: neo-Marxist Theories of the State and the Case of the New Deal', *Politics & Society*, 10:2, 1980.

Skocpol, Theda, 'Bringing the State Back In: False Leads and Promising Starts in Current Theories and Research', in Peter Evans, Theda Skocpol and Dietrich Rueschemeyer (eds), *Bringing the State Back In*, New York, Cambridge University Press, 1985.

Steedman, Ian, *Marx After Sraffa*, London, New Left Books/Verso, 1977.

Steedman, Ian *et al.*, *The Value Controversy*, London: New Left Books, 1981.

Stephens, John, *The Transition to Socialism*, London, McMillan, 1979.

Stewart, A., K. Prandy and R. M. Blackburn, *Social Stratification and Occupation*, London, MacMillan, 1980.

Sweezy, Paul, 'The Debate on the Transition: a critique', in Rodney Hilton (ed), *The Transition from Feudalism to Capitalism*, London, New Left Books, 1976.

Szelenyi, Ivan and Robert Manchin, 'Social Policy and State Socialism', in G. Esping-Anderson, L. Rainwater and M. Rein (eds), *Stagnation and Renewal in Social Policy*, White Plains, N.Y. Sharpe Publishers, 1985.

Szelenyi, Ivan and William Martin, *New Class Theories and Beyond*, unpublished manuscript, Department of Sociology, University of Wisconsin, Madison, 1985.

Therborn, Goran, *What Does the Ruling Class Do When it Rules?*, London, New Left Books, 1978.

Therborn, Goran, *The Power of Ideology and the Ideology of Power*, London, New Left Books, 1982.

Therborn, Goran, 'The Prospects of Labor and the Transformation of Advanced Capitalism', *New Left Review*, Number 145, 1984.

Thompson, E. P., *The Making of the English Working Class*, Harmondsworth, Penguin, 1968.

Walker, Pat, *Between Capital and Labor*, Boston, South End Press, 1979.

Wallerstein, Immanuel, *The Modern World System*, New York, Academic Press, 1974.

Wiles, Peter, *The Distribution of Income East and West*, Amsterdam, North Holland, 1974.

Wolpe, Harold (ed), *The Articulation of Modes of Production*, London, Routledge & Kegan Paul, 1980.

Wright, Erik Olin, 'Class Boundaries in Advanced Capitalist Societies', *New Left Review*, Number 98, 1976.

Wright, Erik Olin, *Class Structure and Income Inequality*, PhD dissertation, Department of Sociology, Berkeley, University of California, 1976.

Wright, Erik Olin, *Class, Crisis and the State*, London, New Left Books, 1978.

Wright, Erik Olin, 'The Value Controversy and Social Research', *New Left Review*, Number 116, 1979, reprinted in Ian Steedman *et al.* (eds), *The Value Controversy*, London, New Left Books, 1981.

Wright, Erik Olin, *Class Structure and Income Determination*, New York, Academic Press, 1979.

Wright, Erik Olin, 'Varieties of Marxist Conceptions of Class Structure', *Politics & Society*, 9:3, 1980.

Wright, Erik Olin, 'Class and Occupation', *Theory and Society*, 9:1, 1980.

Wright, Erik Olin, 'Reconsiderations' in Ian Steedman *et al.* (eds), *The Value Controversy*, London, New Left Books, 1981.

Wright, Erik Olin, 'The Status of the Political in the Concept of Class Structure', *Politics & Society*, 11:3, 1982.

Wright, Erik Olin, 'Capitalism's Futures', *Socialist Review*, no. 68, 1983.

Wright, Erik Olin, 'Gidden's Critique of Marxism', *New Left Review*, Number 139, 1983.

Wright, Erik Olin, 'The Fall and Rise of the Petty Bourgeoisie', unpublished manuscript, Class Structure and Class Consciousness Project Working Paper, Madison, Wisconsin, 1985.

Wright, Erik Olin, *The Comparative Study of Class Structure and Class Consciousness: Public Use Codebook*, Anne Arbor, Michigan, Inter-University Consortium for Political and Social Research, 1985.

Wright, Erik Olin and Luca Perrone, 'Marxist Class Categories and Income Inequality', *American Sociological Review*, 42:1, February, 1977.

Wright, Erik Olin and Joachim Singelmann, 'Proletarianization in the American Class Structure', in *Marxist Inquiries*, edited by Michael Burawoy and Theda Skocpol, *Supplement* to the *American Journal of Sociology*, vol. 88, 1982.

Index

Name Index